CONTEMPORAR

The GED Math Problem Solver

REASONING SKILLS TO PASS THE TEST

MYRNA MANLY

Project Editor
Caren Van Slyke

Fieldtesters and Consultants
Jackson County Adult Education Staff
Ripley, West Virginia

Joan Gross
Adult Learning Center
Iowa Western Community College
Council Bluffs, Iowa

CB
CONTEMPORARY
BOOKS
Two Prudential Plaza
Chicago, Illinois 60601-6790
(312) 540-4500

Library of Congress Cataloging-in-Publication Data

Manly, Myrna.
    The GED math problem solver : reasoning skills to pass the test /
Myrna Manly.
        p.   cm.
    ISBN 0-8092-4050-5 (paper)
    1. Mathematics—Examinations, questions, etc.   2. General
educational development tests.   I. Title.
QA43.M26   1992
510'.76—dc20

91-35286
CIP

Published by Contemporary Books, Inc.
Two Prudential Plaza, Chicago, Illinois 60601-6790
Manufactured in the United States of America
International Standard Book Number: 0-8092-4050-5

Published simultaneously in Canada by
Fitzhenry & Whiteside
195 Allstate Parkway
Markham, Ontario L3R 4T8
Canada

Editorial Director	*Production Editor*
Caren Van Slyke	Jean Farley Brown
Editorial	*Cover Design*
Kathy Osmus	Georgene Sainati
Ellen Frechette	
Erica Pochis	*Illustrator*
Lisa Black	Cliff Hayes
Lisa Dillman	
Holly Graskewitz	*Art & Production*
Eunice Hoshizaki	Carolyn Hopp
Robin O'Connor	
Karen Schenkenfelder	*Typography*
	Graystone Companies, Inc.
Editorial Production Manager	Waterbury, CT
Norma Underwood	

Front cover computer-generated graphics by Klug Präzis

Contents

To the Teacher

The GED Math Problem Solver has been developed to prepare your students for both the GED Math Test and the mathematics they will encounter in their lives. This text has been designed to promote number sense, mental flexibility, and problem-solving skills.

To accomplish these goals, *The GED Math Problem Solver* has been designed to

- build genuine understanding instead of rote memorization
- allow students to discover mathematical relationships and apply them to a variety of settings
- encourage students to use a range of math tools—including paper and pencil, mental math, and calculators

In keeping with the demands of the actual GED Test, this text

- **focuses on problem solving rather than computation**

  To actually focus on problem solving, the GED Math Test mainly uses "nice numbers" that are easy to work with computationally or by estimating.

- **develops estimation skills**

  Once students "see" how to solve a problem, they can solve many GED test items by estimating the answers.

- **introduces algebra and geometry from the beginning**

  Since 50 percent of the test involves algebra and geometry, students will learn to utilize these skills from the beginning of their study.

- **familiarizes students with special GED formats**

  In some of the problems on the test, examinees are not asked to find an answer but rather to recognize how a problem is set up or whether there is enough information to solve a problem.

The GED Math Problem Solver has been designed to facilitate progress toward the actual test. It is organized into 28 lessons that could be covered within a 16-week course of study. Frequent skill-maintenance and checkup sections help students to retain and apply their knowledge. A full-length GED Practice Test will enable students to determine whether they are ready to take the actual test. Finally, a detailed answer key at the end of the book is an invaluable resource.

This student text is only one part of *The GED Math Problem Solver* program. A unique resource, *The GED Math Problem Solver Teacher's Guide* has lesson-by-lesson information and guidelines as well as dozens of classroom activities. This teacher's guide fosters the types of group interactions and critical-thinking activities needed to develop genuine mathematical understanding.

GED Test Preview

To the student:

Congratulations! You are taking the first step toward successfully completing the GED Math Test. So that you will know what to expect from the test and from this book, let's begin with some sample questions like those that are actually on the test. By studying these carefully, you will see the kinds of math skills that are important to pass the test. Then, by evaluating your own abilities, you can plan your path toward your goal.

● What Is the GED Math Test Like? . . . .

The GED Math Test consists of 56 multiple-choice questions. You will be given 90 minutes to finish the test. The items are mostly "word problems" that ask you to <u>apply</u> or use mathematics to find a solution. Most of the situations described in the problems will be the kind that could occur in your everyday experiences.

No Tricks

First of all, you should know that the GED Math Test is fair. It contains no "trick" questions. If you know the math, you will pass the test. Even people who think that all word problems are tricky will get enough practice in this book to succeed on the test.

Computation Is Not the Skill Being Tested.

> **Example 1:**
> Matt bought a bottle of soda for $1.20 and a bag of oranges for $1.50. How much change should he expect from a $5.00 bill?
>
> (1) $7.70 (4) $2.70
> (2) $3.80 (5) $2.30
> (3) $3.50

To get the correct answer, you add the two purchases ($1.20 + $1.50) to get $2.70, then subtract that sum from $5.00 to get choice **(5)** $2.30.

The GED Math Test is a test to see whether you know <u>how</u> to do problems. It is not a test of complicated computations. Notice two things about Example 1.

● First, the numbers are "nice"—easy to compute.

● Second, the answer choices that are given correspond to common mistakes in thinking. For example:

  ● If you had added all the numbers, you would have chosen **(1)**.
  ● If you had just subtracted the $1.20, **(2)** would have been your choice.
  ● If you had subtracted only $1.50 from $5.00, you would have chosen **(3)**.
  ● If you added and missed the second step, your answer would have been **(4)**.

None of the answer choices correspond to a mistake in computation—adding or subtracting incorrectly. All of the problems on the GED Math Test are structured in this manner: the incorrect answers reflect common mistakes in <u>understanding</u> or <u>solving</u> problems.

As you read the problem in Example 2, keep these two points in mind:

1) The numbers are easy to work with.
2) The incorrect answer choices are based on common errors in thinking.

Example 2:

Paul needs 2 new tires. At Tire Town, they are priced at $51.99 apiece, while at Terrific Tire, they would cost $45.99 for each tire. Disregarding tax, how much would Paul save by buying 2 tires at Terrific Tire?

(1) $3.00
(2) $6.00
(3) $12.00

(4) $24.00
(5) Not enough information is given.

When you subtract the prices, the difference is $6.00. Since Paul is buying two tires, you double $6.00 to find the correct response, which is choice **(3)** $12.00.

- If you had stopped after subtracting, you would choose **(2)** as the answer.

- If you had divided that answer by 2, the result would be choice **(1)**.

- If you had assumed that 4 tires would be purchased, you would choose **(4)**.

Again, the answer choices fit in with mistakes that you may have made in <u>how</u> to do the problem.

Many students would not need to pick up paper and pencil to solve Example 2; they would do it "in their head." On the GED Test, you will be able to use **estimation** to choose the correct answer for many problems. Additionally, the ability to do **mental arithmetic** is valuable in everyday situations. This book will help you to develop both the mental math and estimation strategies you need to pass the test and in your daily life.

Set-Up Problems

Next is an example of a "set-up" problem, one that does not ask for the answer, but only how to get it. A significant number of problems on the GED Math Test (25 percent) require you to set up the solution rather than to <u>find</u> the final answer.

Example 3:

The sticker on Jackie's new car gives the EPA mileage figure for highway driving as 28 mpg. On a recent trip, she filled her tank when the odometer read 5235.8 miles and filled it again when it was almost empty at 5498.3 miles. It took 9.3 gallons to fill the tank. Which expression below will determine the number of miles per gallon she got on this trip?

(1) $\dfrac{5498.3}{9.3}$

(2) $5498.3 - 5235.8$

(3) 9.3×28

(4) $\dfrac{5498.3 - 5235.8}{9.3}$

(5) $\dfrac{5498.3 - 5235.8}{28}$

The correct answer, choice **(4)**, shows the proper combination of steps: First, you subtract the odometer readings to determine the number of miles driven. Then, to find the miles per gallon, you divide by the number of gallons used. If you do not recognize this way of setting up a problem, don't worry. You'll get a lot of this kind of practice throughout this book.

Extra Information

In Example 3, notice that two of the incorrect responses, choices **(3)** and **(5)**, use the 28 mpg figure. This information is <u>not required</u> to solve the problem. **Extra information** has been included in many problems so that you must select only the numbers needed to solve the problem. This may seem like a trick to you, however in daily life, you often have a lot of information. An important part of your thinking is to choose only the information you need.

Notice that the numbers involved in Example 3 seem quite complicated. If you would have had to find the answer, it would not have come out even. The GED Math Test will not require such complex computations. If you had to do such a problem in real life, you would most likely use a calculator.

Using Calculators and Estimation Skills

This book will encourage you to use your calculator when the situation requires it. Although the GED Math Test currently does not allow calculators, there are two good reasons to use them as you work through this book. First, calculator use is important for day-to-day living in today's world, and you need to know how to use one intelligently. Second, using a calculator while you use this book will actually <u>help</u> you learn the mathematics and thinking skills necessary to pass the test.

Estimation is one of the skills that will be helpful on the test and is necessary for intelligent calculator use. The following example shows how estimating can be the key to a quick solution.

Example 4:

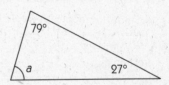

In the triangle above, one angle measures 79° and another measures 27°. What is the degree measure of the third angle, angle *a*?

(1) 11°
(2) 74°
(3) 90°

(4) 254°
(5) Not enough information is given.

For this problem, you need to know that all the angles in a triangle add to 180°. (You will learn this and other important geometry concepts in this book.) If you rounded 79° + 27° to 80° + 30°, you would get 110°. 180° − 110° = 70°. Among the answer choices, the only one that is close is choice **(2)** 74°. The correct answer will <u>often</u> be obvious if you first estimate.

In the practice tests authorized by the GED Testing Service, 75 percent of the problems can be solved without finding a precise computed answer. Some of these are the set-up type described earlier, and the others can be solved mentally and by estimating. This statistic reinforces the recommendations of this book that you should spend your time learning and understanding the processes of mathematics, not how to complete complicated computations. Throughout this book, you will be encouraged to use your common sense in solving problems.

Algebra and Geometry

The study of algebra can help you to understand arithmetic while it introduces you to more abstract thinking skills. Problems using algebraic skills make up 30 percent of the GED Math Test. This will not seem as difficult as it first appears after you see some sample problems.

Example 5:

It is 244 miles from Indianapolis to St. Louis on the interstate highway. Which expression below indicates the time it would take a truck traveling at x mph to travel this distance?

(1) $244x$

(2) $244 + x$

(3) $\dfrac{244}{x}$

(4) $\dfrac{x}{244}$

(5) $244 - x$

To find the time it would take to travel a certain distance, you must divide the distance by the rate of travel. In this case, the rate of travel is x mph, so the correct response is to divide 244 by x, choice **(3)**.

Although this is called an algebra problem, solving it does not require a formal course in algebra. To find the answer to this problem, you need a good understanding of the relationship between distance, rate, and time. You must also learn to feel comfortable using the letter x in place of an **unknown number**. You will be asked to use letters in place of numbers often in this book. In fact, algebra will be part of the first lesson and every lesson that follows. In this way, you will learn enough algebra to pass the test without the anxiety usually associated with algebra.

Another type of problem that is considered to be algebra involves the use of percents.

Example 6:

Bob and Carmen bought a home for $50,000 five years ago. This year, its value is appraised at $65,000. What percent of increase does this represent?

(1) 15%

(2) 30%

(3) 50%

(4) 65%

(5) Not enough information is given.

To find the percent of increase in Example 6, you can divide the amount of increase ($65,000 − 50,000 = $15,000) by the original price ($50,000), which gives the answer 0.3 or 30%. This problem could also have been solved by setting up the following proportion and solving it for x:

$$\frac{15,000}{50,000} = \frac{x}{100}$$

You may see why this percent problem is considered to be an algebra problem. Many problems that occur in our daily lives can be solved using **proportions**. Since the GED Math Test contains problems that are relevant to our lives, many problems on the test also can be solved using this technique. A major part of this book will be devoted to the mastery of the understanding of rates and the techniques of **ratio and proportion**.

The following example comes from the field of geometry.

Example 7:

In making a scale drawing of a race car whose actual length was 54 inches, Joseph decided to make the length of his drawing 9 inches. To maintain the proper proportions, how long should he draw the door whose actual length is 24 inches?

(1) 2.7 inches
(2) 4 inches
(3) 6 inches
(4) 8 inches
(5) Not enough information is given.

The correct answer, choice **(2)** 4 inches, can be found by solving this proportion:

$\frac{9}{54} = \frac{x}{24}$ OR By looking from bottom to top of each ratio,

$54x = 24 \times 9$ $\qquad 54 \div 6 = 9$, so, $24 \div 6 = 4$

$x = \frac{24 \times 9^{1}}{_{6}54}$

$x = \frac{24}{6} = 4$ inches

This is an example of the geometric concept of similar figures, which says that corresponding sides of similar figures are in proportion. This concept is taught in a geometry class but is also often part of general math classes because it is so useful. You will learn this and other useful geometry concepts throughout this book.

Not Enough Information Is Given

You may have noticed that response **(5)** in many of the previous examples states, "Not enough information is given." Many problems on the GED Math Test will feature this as choice **(5)**. It will be the correct response for a small number of problems on the actual test.

The next two problems refer to the following graph.

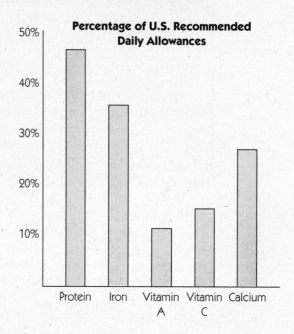

Percentage of U.S. Recommended Daily Allowances

A fast-food establishment released the above information about the nutritional value of one of its sandwiches.

Example 8:	**Example 9:**
After a person has eaten one of these sandwiches, how many more grams of iron should that person eat to meet the recommended requirements for the day?	Which of the following is a good estimate of the percentage of the recommended amount of Vitamin C provided by this sandwich?
(1) 15	(1) 5%
(2) 35	(2) 10%
(3) 45	(3) 15%
(4) 65	(4) 25%
(5) Not enough information is given.	(5) Not enough information is given.

In Example 8, if you chose **(2)** 35 or **(4)** 65, you made a common mistake. From the graph, you could determine that a person had consumed 35% and still needed to eat 65% of the recommended number of grams of iron. However the graph gives you <u>percents</u>, and the question asks about <u>grams</u>. Therefore, not enough information is given for you to answer the question about <u>grams</u>. In a case like this, you should select choice **(5)** Not enough information is given.

You could easily solve Example 9, however, by finding the bar labeled Vitamin C. By estimating its length as between 10% and 20% on the side of the graph, you could choose **(3)** 15%.

Reading graphs and interpreting their information are skills required of informed citizens in today's world. Because of this, graphs will be a part of the mathematics test, and they will also be included in the GED Social Studies and Science Tests.

Summary

If you were able to answer <u>all</u> the sample questions easily and did not need to be told why the answers were correct, you <u>may</u> be ready to take the GED Math Test. Ask your teacher to allow you to try the official practice test that is published by the GED Testing Service. The official practice test will give you a reliable prediction of your success on the actual GED Test.

However, if you think you should review some concepts and learn more about what to expect on the test, you should work through this book, starting with Lesson 1. The checkpoints at the end of each subject area will give you an idea of how well you are proceeding toward your goal—the GED Test. You will find this book to be different from a traditional math textbook. It concentrates only on the topics most likely to be on the GED Test, allowing you to make the best use of your time.

Good luck.

• LESSON 1 • "Seeing" Addition and Subtraction

• 1. Picture the Situation . . . .

Think about these problems. Don't try to find the answers—yet.

Example A:
Roberta has 5 children, and her sister Ronnie has 3. When their families get together, how many children are there in all?

Example B:
Maggie bought two packages of Halloween candy. One contains 14 miniature candy bars, and the other contains 12. How many individual treats did she buy?

Both of these situations involve **combining** objects. These problems require you to **add.**

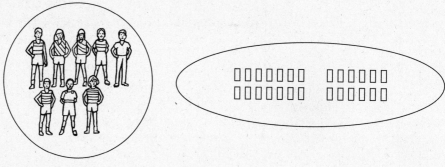

Example A   Example B

Notice how the next situation also involves combining amounts. This time, two distances are **joined** together.

Example C:
George traveled 187 miles one day before lunch, then continued for another 290 miles in the afternoon. How many miles did he travel that day?

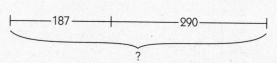

PROBLEM 1   Think of a situation in your life that requires addition (joining or combining). Make a sketch of the problem.

Look at the following problems. Don't try to find the answers—yet.

Example D:
A bag contained 14 oranges. How many are left after 5 are eaten?

Example E:
Maria had $18.00 in her purse. After she spends $7.00 in the grocery store, how much does she have left?

These problems involve **separating** or taking away objects. They require you to **subtract.**

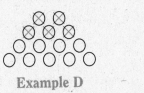

Example D

$ $ $ $ $ $
$ $ $ $ $ $
$ $ $ $ $ $

Example E

Another situation that requires subtraction is one that asks you to make a **comparison** or to find the **difference** between two quantities.

Example F:
George traveled 180 miles one day before lunch, then continued for another 290 miles in the afternoon. How many more miles did he travel in the afternoon than he did in the morning?

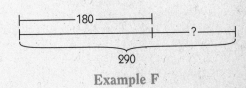

Example F

PROBLEM 2   Think of a personal situation that involves the difference between two quantities or distances. Make a sketch of the problem.

• • •
To understand a problem, get a mental picture or make a sketch.
• • •

2. Write the Problem

The order of the **addends** (numbers being added) does not matter. Because of this, the operation of addition is said to be **commutative**

After you "picture a problem," the next step is to write it mathematically.

Example:

Roberta has 5 children, and her sister Ronnie has 3. When their families get together, how many children are there in all?

This problem can be written mathematically in two ways:

$$5 + 3 \quad \text{or} \quad 3 + 5$$

PROBLEM 3 Write two addition problems for each picture.

a) 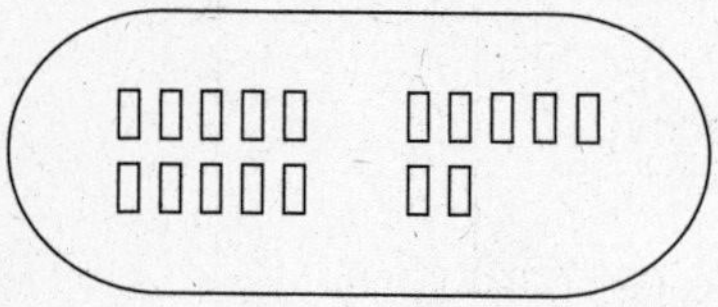

b) 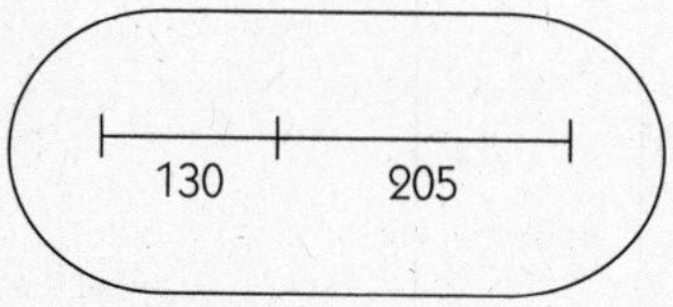

When you subtract, the order in which the problem is written **is** important. You **cannot** change the order of numbers in a subtraction problem.

Example:

A bag contained 14 oranges. How many are left after 5 are eaten?

This can **only** be written as $14 - 5$

The original number, the 14, **must** come first in the problem.

PROBLEM 4 Write a subtraction problem for each picture.

a) 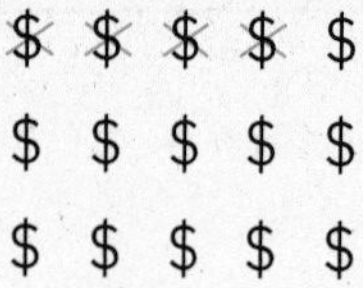

b) 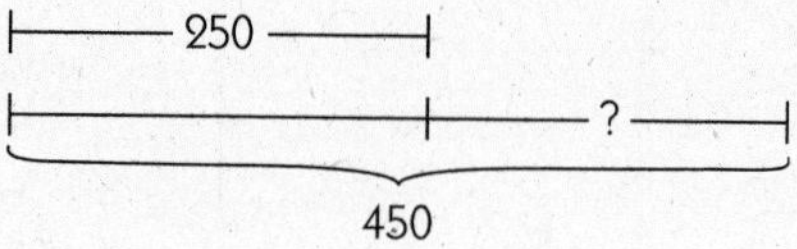

PROBLEM 5 Write either an addition or a subtraction problem based on these sketches.

a) 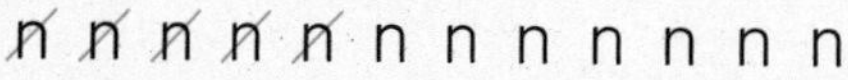

d) 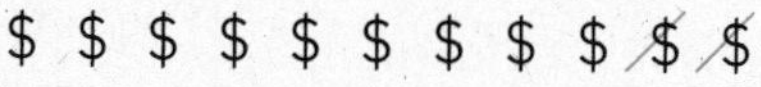

b) 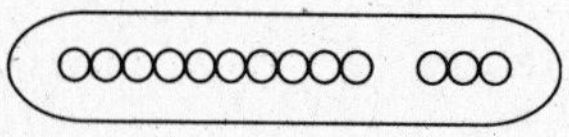

e) 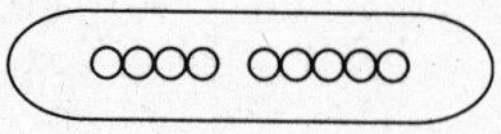

c) 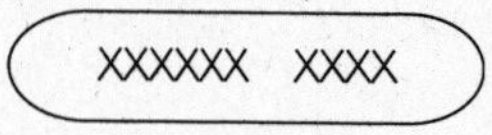

f) 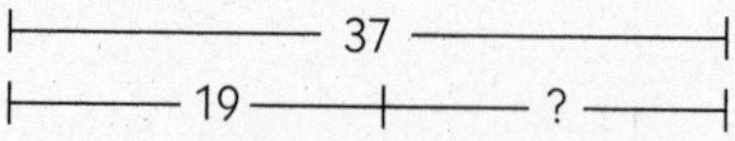

When you write an expression, you can use any letter to represent the unknown quantity.

Sometimes you use a letter in place of a number in a problem. The letter is called a **variable**—its value is unknown and may change from problem to problem.

Example:

Juan deposited $150 into his checking account. He was not sure how much money he originally had in the account, so at this point, he knew only that he had $150 more than his previous balance.

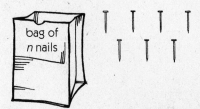

$150 + \text{balance}$ or $\text{balance} + \$150$

$\$150 + \boxed{?}$ $\boxed{?} + \$150$

$\$150 + x$ $x + \$150$

Notice that the x is the variable in this problem—it represents the original amount in Juan's account.

Example:

How many nails are left in a bag after 7 are used?

$$n - 7$$

↑ Original number of nails

bag of *n* nails

We don't know the number of nails in the bag.

Remember that the order is important in writing a subtraction problem. The number that is taken away comes second in the problem.

Study these examples of writing a problem:

four more than 5	$4 + 5$ or $5 + 4$
$\boxed{?} + 5$	$x + 5$ or $5 + x$
four more than Jane has (x)	$4 + x$ or $x + 4$
3 cm wider than the picture (p)	$3 + p$ or $p + 3$
the difference between 13 and 5	$13 - 5$
the difference between 13 and x	$13 - x$
nine less than 21	$21 - 9$
nine less than the maximum (m)	$m - 9$

PROBLEM 6 Write an expression for each of the following.

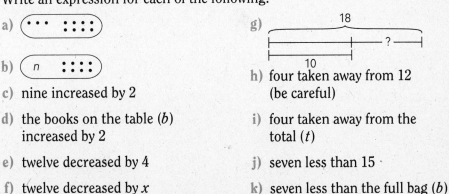

a) (image)

b) (n)

c) nine increased by 2

d) the books on the table (b) increased by 2

e) twelve decreased by 4

f) twelve decreased by x

g) (number line: 18, 10, ?)

h) four taken away from 12 (be careful)

i) four taken away from the total (t)

j) seven less than 15

k) seven less than the full bag (b)

3. Find the Answer ....

The focus of most math classes is to find the answer. But most students agree that to pass the GED Test and to use math in their lives, they must first

- picture the situation (understand the problem), and then

- write the problem.

Once you have the problem written down, you can decide *how* you will find the answer. Usually you have three choices:

1) **Figure it out by using mental math or estimation strategies.** This is the quickest and easiest method. You already use both in everyday life, and you can use them to pass the GED Test. To be good at the skills, however, you need to memorize the basic addition and subtraction facts as well as the multiplication tables. This book will give you lots of practice, but you may need to take some extra time to learn these basics so that you feel confident with your skills.

   - Do you estimate in your daily life? When?

   - Do you think you can estimate to find answers on the GED Test? Why or why not?

2) **Use paper and pencil calculations to figure out the answers.** You may think that there is only one "right" way to calculate. However, there are many methods that can be used. For example, on page 247 of the appendix, you can see some interesting ways to add without carrying and to subtract without borrowing. These may inspire you to invent some methods of your own. The method you choose may depend on which one is easier to remember or on the kind of problem you are facing.

   - Do you use paper and pencil to solve math problems? All of the time? Most of the time?

3) **Use a calculator.** Many people use calculators to solve problems that are too hard to do "in their heads." This is an acceptable choice. You are not "cheating" when you use a calculator. You have already done the most difficult parts of the problem before you start pushing the buttons. Even if you cannot use a calculator on the GED Test, you should have a calculator available as you work through this book.

   - Do you know how to use a calculator? If not, would you like to learn?

   - Do you ever use a calculator? At home? At work?

Adding and Subtracting Mentally ....

To improve your ability to work with numbers, you should learn some number patterns.

Using Zeros

The answer to an addition problem is called the **sum** of the numbers. Adding zero to a number gives the same number.

The answer to a subtraction problem is called the **difference**. Subtracting zero from a number gives the same number.

$$34 + 0 = 34 \qquad 0 + 49 = 49 \qquad\qquad 34 - 0 = 34 \qquad 49 - 0 = 49$$

Building on Basic Facts

Use the basic facts of addition and subtraction along with what you know about zeros to solve more problems in your head.

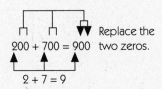

Replace the two zeros.

$200 + 700 = 900$

$2 + 7 = 9$

- Forget about the common zeros while you add or subtract the digits on the front.

- Then replace the zeros to get the answer.

PROBLEM 7   Add or subtract the digits that have the same place value—that is, add tens to tens, hundreds to hundreds, thousands to thousands, and so on.

a) $2 + 3 = 5$
$20 + 30 = 50$
$200 + 300 = 500$
$2,000 + 3,000 =$

b) $7 + 8 = 15$
$70 + 80 =$
$700 + 800 =$
$7,000 + 8,000 =$

c) $7 - 3 = 4$
$70 - 30 =$
$700 - 300 =$
$7,000 - 3,000 =$

d) $9 - 6 = 3$
$90 - 60 =$
$900 - 600 =$
$9,000 - 6,000 =$

Take the next step with more difficult numbers. Often, reading or saying the numbers will help you keep track when you find answers mentally.

$\underline{8}00 + \underline{1}80 =$ "$\underline{8}$ hundred plus $\underline{1}$ hundred 80 equals $\underline{9}$ hundred 80" (980)

PROBLEM 8
a) $740 - 200 =$
b) $740 - 700 =$
c) $430 + 300 =$

d) $100 + 920 =$
e) $420 - 300 =$
f) $300 + 710 =$

g) $2,100 + 400 =$
h) $8,400 - 300 =$

Other problems require you to focus on the endings of numbers. Again, you can use simple addition or subtraction facts as the basis for understanding harder problems.

PROBLEM 9   Notice the pattern and complete the following.

a) $6 + 8 = 14$
$36 + 8 = 44$
$56 + 8 = 64$
$86 + 8 = 94$
$126 + 8 =$

b) $11 - 7 = 4$
$31 - 7 = 24$
$61 - 7 =$
$91 - 7 =$
$101 - 7 =$

c) $4 + 9 = 13$
$24 + 9 =$
$74 + 9 =$
$94 + 9 =$
$234 + 9 =$

d) $12 - 3 = 9$
$52 - 3 =$
$72 - 3 =$
$102 - 3 =$
$552 - 3 =$

Rounding and Estimating

Sometimes you need to add or subtract numbers that are not as "nice" (easy to work with) as the ones on the previous page. Round them first, then add.

Example: 367 + 717

Where would you place the 367 on the number line below? How about the 717? Ask yourself, which *hundred* is each of the numbers closest to?

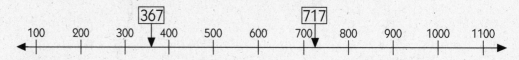

400 + 700 = 1100 is a fair estimate of the problem. (You **rounded** each number to the nearest hundred so that you could estimate mentally.)

367 + 717 ≈ **1100** (The symbol ≈ means "is approximately equal.")

Note: 1100 means the same as 1,100.

PROBLEM 10 Use the number line of 100s above to round the numbers and estimate the answers.

a) 488 + 577 ≈ 500 + 600 = 1100   d) 822 + 1088 ≈

b) 562 – 318 ≈   e) 1075 – 888 ≈

c) 98 + 612 ≈   f) 733 – 688 ≈

PROBLEM 11 Use the number line of 10s below and estimate the following.

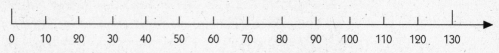

a) 56 + 32 ≈ 60 + 30 =   d) 119 – 42 ≈

b) 71 + 24 ≈   e) 98 – 59 ≈

c) 83 + 37 ≈   f) 64 – 31 ≈

· · ·
Whenever an estimated answer will do, estimate.
· · ·

Is estimation a valuable skill for the GED Test? Absolutely. Since the GED Test gives you five answer choices, you can look them over to see which choice is closest to your estimated answer. On the problem below, round the numbers and estimate. See how this can get you the right answer—and save time.

PROBLEM 12 On business, Sam traveled 671 miles last month and 913 miles this month. What is his total mileage for the two months?

(1) 121
(2) 242
(3) 1,584
(4) 2,255
(5) 3,168

Check Your Understanding

You may use your calculator on any problem for which it seems appropriate.

Write the problem (an **expression**) illustrated by the following.

1.

2.

3. ■ ■ ■ ■ ✕ ✕ ✕

4. $\vdash\!\!—14—\!\!\dashv$
   $\vdash—8—\vdash—?—\dashv$

5. six added to three

6. six added to those in the box (x)

7. eighteen reduced by 9

8. eighteen reduced by x

9. 10 less than 54

10. 10 less than x

11. 0.3 m farther than the record (r)

12. 15° higher than the day's low (l)

13. 8° less than the recorded high (h)

14. the amount in the bank (b) plus a deposit of $75

15. the amount in the bank (b) minus a withdrawal of $25

16. 7 more points than his average (a)

17. 7 fewer points than his average (a)

18. $25 more than last month's bill (b)

19. $25 less than the original price (p)

Find the answers to the following problems *mentally*.

20. 500 + 800 =

21. 1,300 − 700 =

22. 3,000 + 4,500 =

23. 7,800 − 2,000 =

24. 56 + 5 =

25. 86 + 5 =

26. 96 + 5 =

27. 236 + 5 =

28. 72 − 7 =

29. 92 − 7 =

30. 102 − 7 =

31. 452 − 7 =

Round the numbers to the closest 10, 100, or 1,000. Then estimate the answer *mentally*.

32. 37 + 78 ≈

33. 188 + 521 ≈

34. 79 − 43 ≈

35. 98 − 33 ≈

36. 188 + 703 ≈

37. 1,102 − 444 ≈

38. 976 − 622 ≈

39. 5,987 + 3,421 ≈

GED Practice

40. The Lincoln Adult School raised $815 at its fund-raiser. However, the students had $295 in expenses. How much money did the school make after paying the expenses?

    (1) $430
    (2) $520
    (3) $720
    (4) $1,050
    (5) $1,110

• LESSON 2 • Grouping to Add More than Two Numbers

Did you notice that each of the numbers above has ending digits that add to 10? This makes the numbers **compatible pairs** for addition. Compatible pairs can be grouped for easy mental addition. In this lesson, you will look for these compatible pairs and add them first to make the next step easier.

• Perimeters

The **perimeter** of a figure is the distance around it. The sum of the lengths of the sides of a figure is its perimeter.

A common use of adding more than two numbers is finding the **perimeter** of a figure.

Example:
How many feet of edging does Geraldo need to put around the garden?

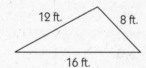
12 ft.   8 ft.
16 ft.

You can combine the three quantities in any order.

16 + 8 + 12

or 12 + 16 + 8

or 8 + 12 + 16

The order of the numbers (called addends) in an addition problem does not affect the answer. To add more than two numbers, start by adding any two of them, then add that answer to the next number, one step at a time.

16 + 8 + 12	or	12 + 16 + 8	or	8 + 12 + 16
24 + 12		28 + 8		20 + 16
36 ft.		36 ft.		36 ft.

Addition is **associative**. This means that the way that you group the addends does not affect the answer.

Notice that adding 8 and 12 first (in the third example) made the rest of the problem easier. You can use **parentheses** to indicate that these compatible numbers should be added first.

16 + (8 + 12)   Add these first.

16 + 20

36

You can use the associative property of addition to make problems easier to solve.

PROBLEM 1 The parentheses in the following problems are placed so that you first group the compatible pairs that add up to 10. Complete the problems.

a) $37 + (27 + 3)$ b) $(11 + 19) + 24$ c) $(6 + 14) + (13 + 7) + 56$

     $37 + 30$

PROBLEM 2 First place parentheses in the following problems to show the easiest order in which to complete the addition. Then find the answers by working one step at a time.

a) $56 + 99 + 1$ c) $17 + 3 + 24$ e) $15 + 5 + 26 + 4 + 32$

b) $56 + 4 + 37$ d) $15 + 9 + 21$ f) $22 + 8 + 3 + 37 + 24$

When a problem contains only addition, you can change the order of the addends, then group them. This example shows regrouping numbers into compatible pairs before adding:

$$12 + 15 + 8 + 17 + 5 \ = \ (12 + 8) + (15 + 5) + 17$$
$$20 \quad + \quad 20 \quad + 17$$
$$57$$

PROBLEM 3 Look for compatible pairs whose last digits add to 10. Rewrite each problem so that you can solve it easily, and then solve it.

a) $23 + 9 + 7 + 11 + 42$ c) $53 + 12 + 4 + 18 + 26$

b) $46 + 21 + 9 + 17 + 4$ d) $35 + 17 + 16 + 3 + 5$

Grouping with Variables

As you saw in Lesson 1, a letter is often used in a problem to indicate an unknown number. When a letter (variable) is one of the numbers being added, you cannot actually carry out that addition. You can only write an expression to indicate that the number and letter are to be added.

 | eight more than what's in the box | can be written as
$x + 8$ or $8 + x$

When there are more than two numbers and/or letters to be added, group the numbers together and add them. Then indicate the remaining addition in a single expression.

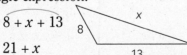

$8 + x + 13$ $x + 11 + y + 8$

$21 + x$ $19 + x + y$

PROBLEM 4 First write the problem. Then find the perimeter of each of these figures.

a) 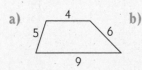   b)   c) 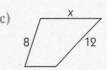   d)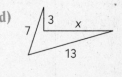

Evaluating Expressions

Example: What would the perimeter be if the value of x were 16?

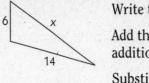

Write the problem.	$14 + 6 + x$
Add the numbers, and indicate the remaining addition.	$20 + x$
Substitute 16 for x in the expression.	$20 + 16$
Add.	36

PROBLEM 5 Find the perimeter of the triangle above.
a) Assume that x is 13. b) Assume that x is 18.

PROBLEM 6 Write an expression and find the perimeter for Figures A and B below, if the value of x is a) 6, b) 8, c) 11.

Figure A

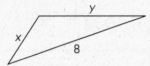

Figure B

PROBLEM 7 a) Express the perimeter of this triangle using the letters and numbers.

What would be the perimeter if

b) $x = 4$ and $y = 6$?

c) $x = 5$ and $y = 7$?

• How Much Is the Total Cost?
Estimating and Calculating ....

Read the following example:

> Doris had only $10 in her purse and stopped at a convenience store for a can of coffee ($5.99), a box of cereal ($2.79), and a loaf of bread ($1.49). Before she went to the cashier, she wondered if she had enough money for the items she had chosen.

Doris needed to **estimate** the total cost in order to avoid embarrassment at the checkout counter. To guess at the total, she focused on the first numbers, because these front-end digits gave her a general idea about how much each item costs. Since that front-end estimate came fairly close to her limit of $10, she needed a more accurate estimate. Doris took a second look, rounding the numbers to the nearest dollar, then adding.

Front-End Estimation	**Second Look (Rounding)**
$5.99 + $2.79 + $1.49	$5.99 is nearly $6.00
↓ ↓ ↓	$2.79 is closer to $3.00
5 + 2 + 1 = 8	These add to $9.00
	$9.00 plus $1.49 is about $10.50

Now you can use your calculator to find the exact total.

$$\boxed{5}\ \boxed{\cdot}\ \boxed{9}\ \boxed{9}\ \boxed{+}\ \boxed{2}\ \boxed{\cdot}\ \boxed{7}\ \boxed{9}\ \boxed{+}\ \boxed{1}\ \boxed{\cdot}\ \boxed{4}\ \boxed{9}\ \boxed{=}\ \boxed{10.27}$$

| decimal point | plus sign | decimal point | plus sign | decimal point | equals sign |

This shows that Doris's second look *was* important—$10 was not enough money.

If a front-end estimate leaves you uncertain, you can take a second look and round the numbers before you add.

PROBLEM 8   Do a front-end estimate of these totals, then take a second look by rounding to get closer. Finally, use your calculator to find the precise answer.

	Front End	**Second Look—Rounding**	**Calculator Answer**
a) $2.27 + $4. 07 + $1.49 ≈	☐	_____	_____
b) $7.16 + $11.99 + $ .99 ≈	☐	_____	_____
c) $6.49 + $1.79 + $1.99 ≈	☐	_____	_____

Grouping in Estimating

A third method of estimating is grouping to find easy numbers to work with. This is most useful when the original numbers are not very close to whole numbers.

Example: $ 7.29 + $1.68 + $ 2.50 = ☐ ? ☐

First, add the dollars.   ($7 + $1 + $2) $10.00
Then, group the cents   ($.29 + $.68 is nearly $1, plus $.50)   +   1.50
into dollar groups. $11.50
Finally, add the two sums.

You may want to group amounts that add to nice numbers that you can add mentally.

Example: $16.35 + $ 3.69 + $ 5.25 + $ 4.99 = ☐

           about $20   +   about $10   = about $30

PROBLEM 9   From the prices shown below, find pairs that group to about $5, about $10, and about $15. You may use prices more than once.

a) about $5   **b) about $10**   **c) about $15**

____ + ____   ____ + ____   ____ + ____

____ + ____   ____ + ____   ____ + ____

                     ____ + ____   ____ + ____

                     ____ + ____   ____ + ____

| • $4.21 | • $11.09 | • $5.89 | • $2.65 | • $2.12 |

| • $7.39 | • $.84 | • $9.15 | • $12.30 | • $7.68 |

Money and Decimals

In the last section on estimating, you worked problems with dollars and cents. Your familiarity with money can be the stepping-stone to understanding the value of decimal fractions. Why? Because one cent is one-hundredth of a dollar.

money form		pure decimal form
one cent is written	$.01	0.01
ten cents is written	$.10	0.10 or 0.1 (you can drop the 0 from the end)
Similarly,		
fifty cents is written	$.50	0.50 or 0.5 (you can drop the 0 from the end)
five cents is written	$.05	0.05

Example: Which is larger, 0.05 or 0.5?   0.01 or 0.1?

These questions may seem confusing, but by remembering what you know about money, you can answer them much more easily.

You know that: **so you also know that:**

fifty cents is more than five cents ⟶ 0.5 is larger than 0.05

ten cents is more than one cent ⟶ 0.1 is larger than 0.01

Locating the values of these coins on a decimal **number line** makes their relative size more obvious. (Numbers on a number line get larger as you move from left to right.)

Example: Can you find the location of $.19, $.20, $.38, and $.40 on the number line above?

By adding the labels of some marks in between, you get a better picture of where these values lie.

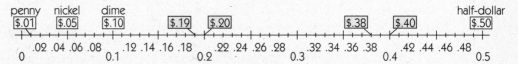

You can see by their location on the number line that 0.2 ($.20) is larger than 0.19 ($.19) and that 0.4 ($.40) is larger than 0.38 ($.38).

PROBLEM 10   On the number line below, write the approximate location of the following numbers. (The first one is done for you. **Think:** .09 is the same as $.09. That is less than .1, which is equivalent to $.10.)

a) 0.09   c) 0.25   e) 0.59   g) 0.8   i) 0.11

b) 0.1   d) 0.3   f) 0.6   h) 0.75   j) 1.1

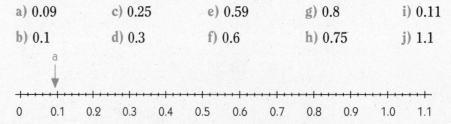

Comparing Decimal Numbers

Example: Which is larger?   0.45   OR   0.4?

- Add zeros to the end so that the numbers have the same number of digits after the decimal point.

  0.45   0.40

- Disregard the decimal point and choose the larger number.

  (45)   40

45 is larger, so 0.45 is larger than 0.4.

PROBLEM 11   Which number in each pair is larger?

a) 0.6 or .07   c) 0.04 or 0.2   e) 1.3 or 0.13   g) 2 or 0.5

b) 0.677 or 0.7   d) 3.9 or 3.09   f) 1.005 or 1   h) 70.8 or 7.08

Both the > and < signs open to the larger number.

These are three of the signs used in mathematics to tell the relationship between numbers:

< means "is less than"
= means "is equal to"
> means "is greater than"

PROBLEM 12   The following statements are true. Write them using the words above to understand their meaning.

Examples: 6 > 3 "6 is greater than 3"   2 < 4 "2 is less than 4"

a) 8 > 6   b) 6 < 8   c) 40 > 10   d) 10 < 40   e) 1.6 > .67   f) 7.2 < 10

PROBLEM 13   Insert one of the signs < , =, or, > between each pair of numbers to make true statements.

a) 0.45 ___ 0.7   c) 0.08 ___ 0.8   e) 0.7 ___ 0.70   g) 0.12 ___ 1.2

b) 3 ___ 3.00   d) 90 ___ 0.09   f) 0.69 ___ 0.7   h) 1 ___ 0.89

Now you can use your knowledge of decimals to solve this GED-type problem:

PROBLEM 14   Packages weighing .26 lb., .06 lb., .2 lb., and .6 lb. were taken to the post office. Which of the following arranges these weights in order from *smallest* to *greatest*?

(1) .2, .26, .6, .06
(2) .2, .26, .06, .6
(3) .06, .26, .2, .6
(4) .06, .2, .26, .6
(5) .2, .06, .6, .26

Reading Word Problems

To solve word problems, you must first be able to understand the situation that the words describe. This exercise will give you some ideas of questions to ask and techniques to use to fully understand what a problem is about.

PROBLEM 15   Marcus drove 10 miles farther than Ben.

a) Who drove the longer distance?

b) If Ben drove 15 miles, how far did Marcus drive?

c) Complete the table to the right.

Ben	Marcus
2	—
8	—
—	19
—	23
20	—

PROBLEM 16   Which statements below say the same thing as "Marcus drove 10 miles farther than Ben"? You will have more than one answer.

If you are not sure of your answer, use the values from the table above as a test of correctness.

a) Marcus drove 10 times as far as Ben.

b) Ben drove 10 miles less than Marcus.

c) The distance Marcus drove was 10 miles farther than the distance Ben drove.

d) Ben drove 10 times farther than Marcus.

e) The number of miles that Ben drove plus 10 equals the number of miles that Marcus drove.

PROBLEM 17   Which diagram "pictures the problem"?

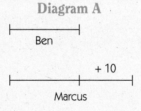

Diagram A

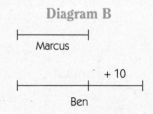

Diagram B

You may use your calculator on any problem for which it seems appropriate.

When adding, you can change both the order and grouping of the numbers without changing the answer. Rearrange the following expressions and place parentheses so that you can do all the adding, step by step, in your head. Then, add.

1. $45 + 8 + 5 + 12$

2. $21 + 3 + 9 + 16 + 17$

3. $36 + 15 + 15 + 4 + 29$

4. $19 + 8 + 32 + 56 + 11$

Find the perimeters of the following figures. Try to find the sums mentally by grouping first.

5.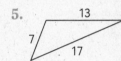

7.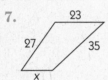

6.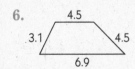

8.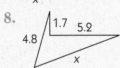

Problems 9 and 10 are based on this figure:

9. Write the perimeter as an expression.

10. What would be the perimeter if the value of x were

a) 16?

b) 13?

c) 17.7?

11. When manufactured material is put in a shipping box, you should allow 3 extra inches for packing. If an article were x inches high, write an expression for the height of the packing box.

12. Allowing 3 inches for packing, how high would a box be for an article that is

a) 24 inches high?

b) 32 inches high?

c) 18 inches high?

13. Estimate each total cost, using the method that seems best to you. Then find the precise answer.

a) $\$3.89 + \$2.12 + \$6.49 =$

b) $\$15.35 + \$22.98 + \$4.66 =$

c) $\$11.98 + \$5.04 + \$6.22 + \$1.75 =$

d) $\$2.75 + \$12.88 + \$7.30 + \$1.21 =$

14. Joe Swift jogged the following distances during one week:

Mon. — 7.8 km
Tue. — 10 km
Wed. — 4.1 km
Fri. — 12.05 km
Sat. — 5.9 km

a) Estimate the total number of kilometers he jogged.

b) Then find the precise answer.

15. Insert <, =, or, > to make these statements true.

a) 6 ___ 0.6

b) 0.3 ___ 2.3

c) 2.3 ___ 2.25

d) 10 ___ 10.00

e) 0.9 ___ 0.09

f) 50 ___ .05

g) 1.04 ___ 1.4

h) 0.33 ___ 0.3

GED Practice

16. On Monday, Sam's Service Station charged $1.47 for a gallon of Supreme Unleaded. On Thursday, Sam raised the price by $.03, and on Friday, he raised it $.04 more. What was the price of gas on Saturday?

(1) $1.40
(2) $1.45
(3) $1.50
(4) $1.53
(5) $1.54

• LESSON 3 • Equivalent Equations: Addition and Subtraction

Mental Math Exercises

What number is
1. 10 more than 49?
2. 5 less than 51?
3. 19 greater than 20?
4. 70 reduced by 3?
5. 7 fewer than 100?

In this lesson, you will expand on the expressions above and learn to make equations—full mathematical sentences—to solve problems such as this:

Example: How much milk did the baby drink?

BEFORE: 8 oz.   AFTER: 2.5 oz.

The basic relationship underlying the problem is:

| 2.5 oz. | **+** | ? | **=** | 8 oz. |

the amount left   the amount the   the full bottle
in the bottle   baby drank

To find the answer, you would usually rearrange this in your mind to say:

| ? | **=** | 8 oz. | **−** | 2.5 oz. |

the amount the   the full bottle   the amount left
baby drank   in the bottle

This lesson will show how you can write an equation for a problem and rearrange it so it is easy to solve.

• Writing Equivalent Equations . . . .

• • •
What addition does,
subtraction undoes.
• • •

An **equation** is a mathematical sentence that contains an equals sign. It says that whatever is on one side of the equals sign *has the same value as* what is on the other side.

Think about these equations involving addition and subtraction:

Addition   **Subtraction**

$6 + 9 = \boxed{15}$ $9 + 6 = \boxed{15}$ $\boxed{15} - 9 = 6$ $\boxed{15} - 6 = 9$

The four equations in this row are **equivalent**; the sentences are different, yet they say the same thing. If you know the addition fact $6 + 9 = 15$, then you also know the other three facts. These examples show how addition and subtraction are related.

PROBLEM 1 Using the addition and subtraction examples on page 18, write **three** equations that are equivalent to each of the following.

a) $7 + 8 = 15$ b) $9 + 3 = 12$ c) $6 + 7 = 13$ d) $7 + 9 = 16$

Using a variable (a letter in place of the number) in the equation makes writing the equations a bit more complicated. Notice the position of the boxed number in each equation below.

$$\textbf{Addition} \qquad\qquad\qquad\qquad \textbf{Subtraction}$$

$$x + 6 = \boxed{14} \qquad 6 + x = \boxed{14} \qquad\qquad \boxed{14} - x = 6 \qquad \boxed{14} - 6 = x$$

The number in the box is the **sum** of the addition problems and must be in the first position of the subtraction problems.

PROBLEM 2 Write one addition and two subtraction equations that are equivalent to each of the following.

a) $9 + x = \boxed{17}$ b) $7 + x = 12$ c) $x + 8 = 13$ d) $x + 6 = 14$

PROBLEM 3 Write two equivalent equations using subtraction for each of them:

Example: For $14 + x = 30$, write $30 - x = 14$ and $30 - 14 = x$.

a) $9 + 11 = 20$ d) $8 + x = 12$ g) $x + 45 = 100$

b) $7 = 6 + x$ e) $17 = x + 9$ h) $30 = x + 29.9$

c) $14 = 8 + x$ f) $15 = x + 12$ i) $81 + x = 100$

PROBLEM 4 Write two equivalent equations, one with subtraction and one with addition.

Example: For $x - 18 = 10$, write $x - 10 = 18$ and $10 + 18 = x$.

a) $13 - 7 = 6$ d) $17 - x = 9$ g) $x - 8 = 6$

b) $13 = 15 - x$ e) $15 = 20 - x$ h) $32 = x - 8$

c) $20 = 28 - x$ f) $x - 15 = 20$ i) $40 = 75 - x$

$\cdots$
You can reverse the order of equations. For example, $6 + x = 7$ is the same as $7 = 6 + x$.
$\cdots$

In the exercises above, you rearranged equations into equivalent ones. But in real situations, this is not the first step. First you must be able to write an equation that describes the situation. Follow the sequence of the pictures and the equations that follow them.

$$\boxed{\$20} \quad + \quad \boxed{x} \quad = \quad \boxed{\$25} \qquad \$20 + x = \$25$$

money in   money Jack   Jack's new
Jack's   found on the   total
pocket   dresser

 $\quad - \quad \boxed{x} \quad = \quad$ $\qquad 24 \text{ sodas} - x = 18$ sodas

case of   sodas that   case with 18
24 sodas   were finished   sodas left

Writing Equations to Solve Problems . . . .

In solving word problems, the most critical step is writing the equation. The following two techniques are helpful.

1. Describe the Action of the Problem

One way to describe the action in the problem is to simply *translate* from the English words into mathematical symbols.

Example:

When they were married, Roberto weighed 58 pounds more than his wife, Maria. If Roberto weighed 188 pounds, how much did Maria weigh?

— 58 lb.

1. Represent the unknown quantity with a letter.
   Let m = Maria's weight.

2. **Translate** the action sentence. Roberto weighed **58 lb. more than Maria** is the same as:
   $$188 \text{ lb.} = 58 \text{ lb.} + m$$

. . .

To write an equation for a word problem, you do not need to know in advance how to solve it, but you must understand what is going on in the problem.

. . .

The equation is a mathematical **translation** of the problem situation. Writing it did not require you to think ahead as to what you will do to find the answer. You merely translated. Later in this lesson, we will solve this equation for m (Maria's weight).

Example:

Joan, whose present weight is 166 pounds, wants to lose some weight so that she will weigh only 140 pounds. How much weight should she lose?

Since the question asks how much weight she should lose, this is the **unknown**.

Let x = how much weight Joan should lose.

The action of the problem is losing weight—a subtraction action. Think of this in **time order** (the order something happens) and then translate.

$$166 - x = 140$$

Joan starts at 166, loses some weight (x), then weighs 140.

PROBLEM 5   Write an equation that follows the action or time order in each of these problems.

a) Andy has already saved $500 to buy a used motorcycle. How much more does he have to save if the bike costs $1,125?

b) LaTonya starts on a shopping trip with $100. When she is finished shopping, she has $12 left. How much did she spend?

2. Use a Known Relationship as a Guideline

Your experience and prior knowledge are important when writing equations.

For example, consider a store owner who sells items at a higher price (**selling price**) than what he paid for them (**cost**) so that he can make a **profit**:

$$\text{cost} + \text{profit} = \text{selling price}$$

This is a simplified formula for the relationship.

Examples:

A furniture store buys a sofa for $525 and sells it for $750. The profit the store makes on the sofa is $225.

$$\text{cost} + \text{profit} = \text{selling price}$$
$$\$525 + \$225 = \$750$$

Lucille buys bracelets from a supplier for $.85 each. She personalizes them by putting people's names on them, then sells them for $2.50 each. What is her profit per item?

The question asks for the **profit**.

Use the formula

and **substitute** the values.

Let p = profit.

$$\text{cost} + \text{profit} = \text{selling price}$$
$$\$.85 + p = \$2.50$$

PROBLEM 6 Write an equation for each of the following problems by either (1) following the action or time order of the problem (translating) or (2) using a known relationship as shown in the examples above. Use any letter for the unknown. **Do not solve yet.**

a) Wade, who trades baseball cards, purchased a 1986 José Canseco rookie card for $8. He later sold it for $49. What was his profit on this card alone?

b) At the start of a trip, the odometer on Juan's car read 11,031.8 miles. At the end of the trip, it read 11,988.2 miles. How many miles did he drive on this trip? (Note: Write the equation in time order.)

c) After losing 32 pounds, Jim is back to his "fighting weight" of 185 pounds. How much did he weigh before he lost the weight?

d) A used-car dealer paid $850 for a car, shined it up, and then put it on his lot with a price of $1,099 on the windshield. If he sells it for that price, how much profit will he make?

PROBLEM 7 Write an equation to represent the types of problems that you saw in Lessons 1 and 2. **Do not solve yet.**

a) One side of a triangular lot measures 100 feet, another measures 80 feet. If the perimeter of the triangle is 230 feet, how long must the third side be?

b) The economy-size box of cereal weighs 121 grams more than the regular size box. If the economy size weighs 567 grams, how much does the regular size weigh?

Solving Equations . . . .

Use Guessing

To *solve* an equation that has a variable in it, find the numerical value for the letter that makes the equation true.

It is very simple to solve some equations. You can just look at an equation and know the answer.

You can replace x with a number that makes the following equations true.

	Ask Yourself	**Solution**
$x + 5 = 12$	What added to five results in 12?	$x = 7$
$3 + x = 13$	Three plus what number equals 13?	$x = 10$
$15 - x = 7$	Subtracting what number from 15 leaves 7?	$x = 8$
$20 - x = 12$	20 minus what number leaves 12?	$x = 8$

By using your mental addition skills, you can solve even more complicated equations with this guessing method.

PROBLEM 8 Solve these equations by the method described above. The solution is the number that makes the equation true.

a) $7 + x = 13$
   $x = $ ___

c) $x + 15 = 20$
   $x = $ ___

e) $17 - x = 9$
   $x = $ ___

g) $20 - x = 9$
   $x = $ ___

b) $35 + x = 95$
   $x = $ ___

d) $x + 125 = 200$
   $x = $ ___

f) $50 - n = 30$
   $n = $ ___

h) $870 - p = 800$
   $p = $ ___

Write an Equivalent Equation

Sometimes it is difficult to guess at a solution. A second method requires you to rearrange an equation so that it is easier to solve.

Compare these two equivalent equations by trying to solve each of them. Which seems easier to solve? Why?

$$45 + x = 96 \qquad 96 - 45 = x$$

It is usually easier to solve an equation when the variable (the letter) is alone on one side of the equals sign. Compare these. Which is easier to solve? Why?

$$99 - x = 35 \qquad 99 - 35 = x$$

Because the second equation tells you exactly what to do, it is easier for most people to solve.

PROBLEM 9 Rearrange these problems to make them easier to solve. Then solve them.

a) $100 + x = 125$

c) $x + 100 = 225$

e) $p + 30 = 56$

b) $100 - x = 70$

d) $x - 100 = 225$

f) $56 - p = 30$

Now you will review some problems from earlier in this section. In each case, you will follow these steps:

Step 1: Picture the situation.

Step 2: Write an equation that follows the action.

Step 3: Write an equivalent equation that is easy to solve.

Example A:

When they were married, Roberto weighed 58 pounds more than his wife, Maria. If Roberto weighed 188 pounds, how much did Maria weigh?

Step 1: Roberto weighed 58 pounds more than Maria.

Step 2: $188 = 58 + m$

Rearrange the equation.

Step 3: $m = 188 - 58$
$m = 130$ pounds

Maria weighed 130 pounds.

Example B:

Joan, whose present weight is 166 pounds, wants to lose some weight so that she will weigh only 140 pounds. How much weight should she lose?

Step 1: present weight − loss = desired weight

Step 2: $166 - w = 140$

Step 3: $w = 166 - 140$
$w = 26$ pounds

Joan should lose 26 pounds.

Example C:

Lucille buys bracelets from a supplier for $.85 each. She personalizes them by putting people's names on them, then sells them for $2.50 each. What is her profit per item?

Step 1: cost + profit = selling price

Step 2: $.85 + p = 2.50

Step 3: $2.50 - $.85 = p$
$1.65 = p$

Lucille's profit is $1.65.

The key to solving all of these problems is to picture the problem, write the equation (rewrite it if necessary), and solve it.

Make Sure Your Answer Makes Sense

Can you find the error in this problem?

William, who is 45 inches tall, is 14 inches taller than his 5-year-old sister, Rebecca. How tall is Rebecca?

Incorrect Solution

Step 1: 45 inches tall is 14 inches taller than Rebecca.

Step 2: $45 = 14 + x$

Step 3: $x = 45 + 14 = $**59 inches**

Hold it! Rebecca should be shorter than 45 inches, not taller! The equivalent equation should have been written as $x = 45 - 14 = 31$ inches.

PROBLEM 10 Go back to problems 6 and 7 on page 21. Solve the equations you wrote. Then reread each problem to make sure your answer makes sense.

Another Way to Subtract

You can change subtraction problems that are difficult into easy ones:

26 ADD 1	27		32 ADD 3	35		76 ADD 2	78
− 9 ADD 1	− 10		− 17 ADD 3	− 20		− 38 ADD 2	− 40
17	17		15	15		38	38

Because you added the same number to both, you didn't change the answer. Notice that you add to the top whatever is needed to make the second number easy to subtract.

PROBLEM 11 Use the method shown above to subtract these. Can you do them mentally?

a) 23 − 8   c) 62 − 38   e) 51 − 19   g) 75 − 48

b) 35 − 7   d) 33 − 15   f) 46 − 29   h) 143 − 96

On page 247 of the Appendix, you will find some other ways to subtract without borrowing.

● More Practice with Equations . . . .

So far in this lesson, you have learned to

* write equations to solve problems

* change to equivalent equations to simplify problems

* test answers to see if they make sense

On the GED Test, you may need to choose the equation that could be used to correctly solve a problem. The correct answer may not be the equation that you would have come up with, but it will be an equivalent equation. You must be able to recognize when an equation is merely a rearrangement of yours. Practice with these problems below.

PROBLEM 12

A repairman bought a part for $78. He charged his customer $109 for the same part. Which of the following equations shows how much profit he made on the part?

(1) $78 − p = $109
(2) $78 + $109 = p
(3) $109 + p = $78
(4) $109 − $78 = p
(5) p − $78 = $109

PROBLEM 13

Rachel rides her bike 15 miles each evening for exercise. She follows the same triangular route each time so she knows how far she's gone. Part of her route is 5 miles and another is 7 miles. Which equation shows the length of the third part of her route?

(1) $m = 15 + 5 + 7$
(2) $15 = 5 + 7 + m$
(3) $15 + m = 5 + 7$
(4) $m − 5 = 15 − 7$
(5) $m = 15 − 5 + 7$

You may use your calculator on any problem for which it seems appropriate.

1.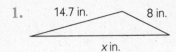

   a) Write an expression for the perimeter of this figure.

   b) Write an equation if the perimeter were 30 inches.

   c) Write an equivalent equation using subtraction so that x is alone on one side of the equals sign.

   d) Solve this equation.

2. At her annual physical, Mrs. Slimbody weighed in at 106 pounds. Her physician mentioned that for her height and frame, the ideal weight would be 125 pounds. How many pounds would she need to gain to achieve the ideal weight?

   a) Let w = the number of pounds to gain. Write an equation that follows the action in the problem.

   b) Write an equivalent subtraction equation that places the w alone on one side of the equation.

   c) Solve for w. Then, ask yourself, "Is this answer reasonable?"

3. A football player lost 41 pounds getting in shape for the season. After losing this weight, he weighed 299 pounds. How much did he weigh previously?

   a) Choose a letter for the unknown, and write the equation suggested by the time order in the problem. (Hint: It is a subtraction action.)

   b) Rewrite the equation so it is easier to solve. Use addition.

   c) Solve the equation.

4. After owning a house in which they invested $46,500 for 7 years, the Johnsons sold it for $90,000. What was their profit?

   a) Fit the information into the known formula, letting a letter stand for the unknown.

   b) Rewrite the equation.

   c) Solve the equation.

5. Write a subtraction sentence that is equivalent to each addition equation. Make sure the variable is alone on one side of the equation. (Remember that the sum of the addition problem becomes the first number of the subtraction problem.)

   a) $4 + x = 15$ c) $45 = x + 15$

   b) $y + 9 = 20$ d) $35 = 30.5 + n$

6. Following the example below, show the steps in finding the solution to the following equations. (Remember, you can change the subtraction problems into easier ones.)

   Example: $74 - n = 19$
   $\qquad\quad 74 - 19 = n$ (Think: 75 – 20)
   $\qquad\qquad\;\; 55 = n$

   a) $23 - a = 15$ d) $t - 49 = 61$

   b) $54 + x = 75$ e) $104 = p + 85$

   c) $s + 39 = 68$

7. Nancy is a sales representative. On her last road trip, she covered 855 miles in three days. She drove 327 miles the first day and 288 miles the third day. Which of the following expressions shows how many miles she covered the second day?

   (1) $x = 327 + 288$
   (2) $x = 855 - 288$
   (3) $x = 855 - 327 + 288$
   (4) $855 = 327 + x + 288$
   (5) $855 = 327 + 288 - x$

• Part One

In Lessons 1–3 you covered a lot of ground. Before going on, use the following exercises to maintain your skills. If you are having difficulty, this is a good time to go back and review.

1. Write an expression for each of the following problems.

a)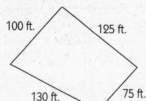

d) 1,250 more than the minimum (m)

b) $23 more than Hilary's salary (s)

e) 9 inches wider than the frame (f)

c) $10 off the original price (p)

f)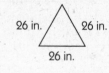

2. Write an expression for the distance around the figures shown below. Group the numbers in the easiest way to add wherever possible.

a) parking lot

100 ft. 125 ft. 130 ft. 75 ft.

b) garden

12 m 6 m 10m 8m

c) coffee table

26 in. 26 in. 26 in.

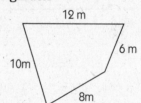

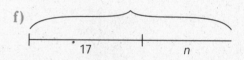

3. Write a subtraction equation that is equivalent to each addition equation. Make sure the variable is alone on one side of the equation.

a) $650 + x = 1,000$ b) $y + 99 = 470$ c) $300 + x = 430$

4. Write equations and solve the problems below.

a) After she drove 300 miles, Belinda only had 675 miles left to go to her grandmother's house. How long was her entire trip?

b) Samantha sold a painting for $200 more than she had paid for it. If she sold it for $925, how much did she pay for it?

c) Todd's grocery bill came to $78 after he was credited $7 for coupons. What would his bill have been without coupons?

• Part Two . . . .

Now put your skills to work on some GED-type math problems.

1. There are 5 boxes on Kim's shelf. They weigh .2 lb., .15 lb., .17 lb., 1.1 lb., and 1.2 lb. Which box is the lightest?

    (1) .2 lb.
    (2) .15 lb.
    (3) .17 lb.
    (4) 1.1 lb.
    (5) 1.2 lb.

2. Estimate the total of this bill to the nearest dollar.

    (1) $2
    (2) $3
    (3) $6
    (4) $13
    (5) $20

Date:	11/18
Server:	Joan
Pizza	9.75
Pitcher	
Coke	1.80
Tax	.90

Problems 3 and 4 are based on the chart below.

	RYAN	KELLEY
Precinct 1	1,215	930
Precinct 2	672	1,177
Precinct 3	829	990

3. In all, how many people voted for Ryan?

    (1) 672
    (2) 829
    (3) 1,215
    (4) 2,716
    (5) 3,087

4. How many more votes did Kelley receive than Ryan in Precinct 2?

    (1) 161
    (2) 285
    (3) 405
    (4) 505
    (5) 1,849

5. A sketch of part of Hank's neighborhood is shown below. Hank's school is 8 blocks from his home. How many blocks does Hank travel from school to the grocery store?

    (1) 6
    (2) 8
    (3) 10
    (4) 20
    (5) 22

14 blocks

home   school   grocery
                               store

6. An assembly line produced 855 defective valves during its three shifts. The first shift produced 190 and the second shift produced 475. Which of the following show the number of defects produced by the third shift?

    (1) $855 + 190 + 475$
    (2) $855 + 190 - 475$
    (3) $855 = 475 - 190 - x$
    (4) $855 = 475 + 190 - x$
    (5) $855 = 190 + 475 + x$

7. Caroline worked 12 hours on Wednesday. This was 5 more hours than she worked on Thursday. How many hours did she work on Thursday?

    (1) 5
    (2) 7
    (3) 17
    (4) 20
    (5) 60

8. How many centimeters of weatherstripping does a maintenance engineer need to put around the window shown at right?

    (1) 57
    (2) 400
    (3) 557
    (4) 657
    (5) 15,000

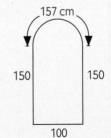

157 cm

150   150

100

Mental Math Exercises

1. $40 + n = 180$
2. $35 + x = 180$
3. $85 + p = 180$
4. $44 + n = 100$
5. $78 + c = 100$

You could easily solve the equations above mentally. In previous lessons, you wrote equations like these based on word problems that described real situations. In this lesson, you will write more equations as you study geometry topics. After you learn the vocabulary involved and some special geometry relationships, you will be able to write the equations and solve them.

• Angles

You see angles every day around you.

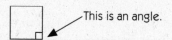

This is an angle.   This is an angle.

An **angle** is formed between two sides when they extend from one point. The point is called the **vertex**.

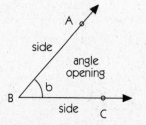

Angles can be named in three ways. For example, this angle can be named
1) ∠ ABC or ∠ CBA (Note: the *B* is in
2) ∠ B   the middle.)
3) ∠ b

The **measure** of an angle depends on the size of the opening between its sides. The unit of measure for angle openings is the **degree** (°).

The size of the opening of an angle is measured with a protractor. On the GED Test, you will not need a protractor.

The lengths of an angle's sides have nothing to do with how large it is. The size of the angle is based only on the opening.

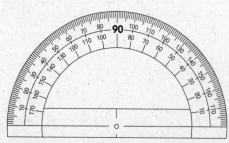

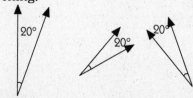

All three of these angles have the same measure (20°).

You should know the measures of these common angles for the GED Test.

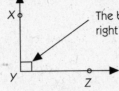

A **right angle** has a measure of 90°.

The box in the vertex indicates that this is a right angle. Think of the term *square corner*.

Right Angle (90°)

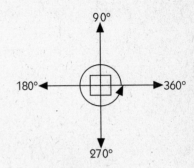

Straight Angle (180°)

Since this angle results in a straight line, the name is easy to remember.

90° + 90° = 180°

Circle (360°)

If you started at 0° and continued full circle around a point, you would pass through 360°. There are 360° in a **circle**.

90° + 90° + 90° + 90° = 360°

Acute angles have smaller openings than right angles. Their measure is between 0° and 90°.

An **obtuse angle** is one whose measure is greater than 90° but less than 180°. These angles have larger openings than right angles, but smaller openings than straight angles.

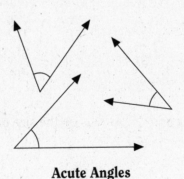

Acute Angles

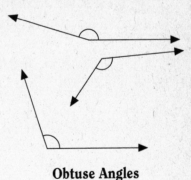

Obtuse Angles

PROBLEM 1   Identify the following angles as acute, right, obtuse, or straight.

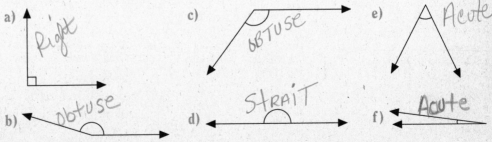

a) Right

b) Obtuse

c) Obtuse

d) Strait

e) Acute

f) Acute

Complementary and Supplementary Angles

Two angles are **complementary** if the sum of their measures is 90°.

The following pairs of angles are complementary. Their total measure is 90°.

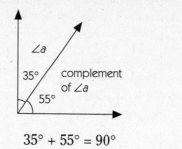

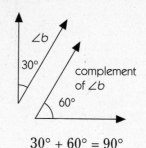

$$35° + 55° = 90°$$

$$30° + 60° = 90°$$

PROBLEM 2 If a pair of angles is complementary, each angle must be _____. (acute, right, obtuse, straight)

Two angles are **supplementary** if the sum of their measures is 180°.

The following pairs of angles are supplementary. Their total measure is 180°.

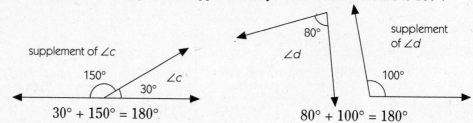

$$30° + 150° = 180°$$

$$80° + 100° = 180°$$

PROBLEM 3 Two angles are both supplementary and equal to each other. They must both be _____ angles. (acute, right, obtuse, straight)

Now, combine this new vocabulary with the equation-writing skills you learned in Lesson 3.

Example 1:
Find the complement of an angle whose measure is 35°.

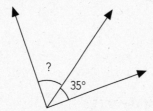

Let x = unknown angle.

$$35° + x = 90°$$
$$x = 90° - 35°$$
$$x = 55°$$

Write an equation to describe the relationship.

Rearrange the equation to get the unknown alone.

Solve to find the value of the variable.

Example 2:
Find the supplement of an angle whose measure is 65°.

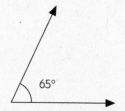

Let n = unknown angle.

$$65° + n = 180°$$
$$n = 180° - 65°$$
$$n = 115°$$

"Seeing" How to Solve a Problem

Both solutions below are correct. However, Solution 2 skipped the first step. Sometimes you can "see" how to solve the problem, and you can write an equation that you do not need to rearrange.

Example:

A brace makes an angle of 40° with the post it supports. What is the measure of the second angle formed?

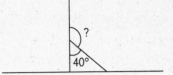

Solution 1

$40° + x = 180°$

$x = 180° - 40°$

$x = 140°$

Solution 2

$x = 180° - 40°$

$x = 140°$

PROBLEM 4   Write an equation to find the complement of the angle shown, then do the same to find the supplement of the angle. (**Note:** Some angles may have only a supplement.) Solve.

Examples: For an angle of 30°.

Complement

$x = 90° - 30°$

$x = 60°$

Supplement

$x = 180° - 30°$

$x = 150°$

a)

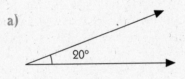

c)

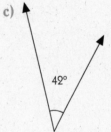

b)

d)

PROBLEM 5   Josh had to replace a piece of tile that was part of a design on his bathroom floor. Find the size of the angle the tile must have in order to fit in the design.

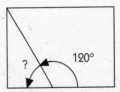

PROBLEM 6   After completing the problems above, you can see that the *complement* of an angle whose measure is $b°$ can be expressed as $90° - b°$. Write an expression for the measure of the *supplement* of an angle that measures $m°$.

. . .
The sum of the measures
of the angles that make up
a triangle is always 180°.
. . .

• Triangles

Triangles are closed figures made up of three angles.

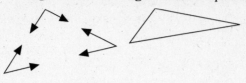 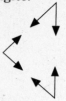 

You can use the fact that the angles of any triangle add up to 180° to solve the problem.

Example:

Find the measure of angle b in this triangle.

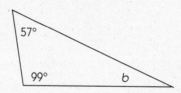

Solution 1		Solution 2

$$57° + 99° + b = 180° \qquad\text{OR}\qquad 180° - (57° + 99°) = b$$
$$156° + b = 180° \qquad\qquad\quad 180° - 156° = b$$
$$b = 180° - 156° \qquad\qquad\quad 24° = b$$
$$b = 24°$$

PROBLEM 7 A tile setter cut a square tile on the line shown. If one of the new angles formed is 30°, what is the measure of the other new angle?

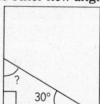

PROBLEM 8 Find the measure of angle m in each of the following triangles:

a)

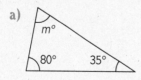

c)

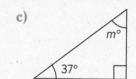

b)

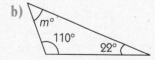

PROBLEM 9 Which expression could be used to find the third angle of this triangle?

(1) $180° - x°$
(2) $180° - (90° - x°)$
(3) $180° - (90° + x°)$
(4) $180° - 90°$
(5) $90° + x°$

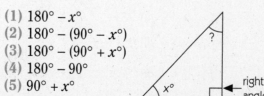

Special Types of Angles . . . .

Parallel and Perpendicular Lines

Two lines are **parallel** (//) if they lie on the same plane and do not meet.

When two lines form right angles, the two lines are said to be **perpendicular** (⊥) to each other.

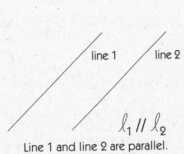

Line 1 and line 2 are parallel.

Line 1 and line 2 are perpendicular.

PROBLEM 10   Name one place where you can see parallel lines.

PROBLEM 11   Name one place where you can see perpendicular lines.

Angles Formed by Intersecting Lines

Look at the diagram below. Two lines have been drawn to form 4 angles. These angles have special relationships.

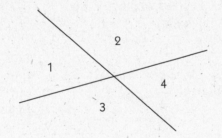

Opposite angles have the same measure.

For example:

$\angle 1 = \angle 4; \quad \angle 2 = \angle 3$

These are called **vertical angles**.

Pairs of angles on a straight line equal 180°.

$\angle 1 + \angle 2 = 180°$
$\angle 3 + \angle 4 = 180°$

You know these as supplementary angles.

PROBLEM 12   For the lines shown here:

a) List the two pairs of angles that are equal to each other.

b) List the 4 pairs of angles that equal 180°.

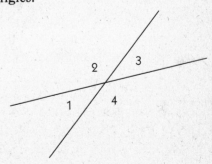

Corresponding Angles Are Equal

In the diagram below, a third line has been drawn across two parallel lines. The 8 angles are numbered on the sketch.

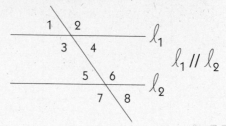

Look at a pair of angles, ∠2 and ∠6.

Angles that occupy the same position on parallel lines have the same measure.

Both ∠2 and ∠6 lie above a parallel and to the right of the intersecting line. They form a pair of **corresponding angles** that are equal to each other.

Problems 13–15 are based on the sketch below.

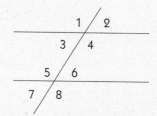

PROBLEM 13

Name the pairs of corresponding angles on the drawing above.

Example:
∠1 and ∠5

a) ∠2 and _____.

b) ∠3 and _____.

c) ∠4 and _____.

PROBLEM 14

If ∠5 = 140°, what is the measure of

a) ∠1?

b) ∠6?

c) ∠7?

d) ∠8?

PROBLEM 15

If ∠5 = 140°, which expression shows how to find the measure of ∠6?

(1) 180° + 140°
(2) 180° − 140°
(3) 140° − 90°
(4) 140° + 90°
(5) 180° + 90°

You may use your calculator on any problem for which it seems appropriate.

1.

Write three ways to name this angle.

2.

Which pairs of angles are supplementary?

3.

a) $\angle D = 95°$ and $\angle E = 51°$.
   Write an expression to find $\angle F$.

b) What is the measure of $\angle F$?

c) $\angle D = 95°$ and $\angle E = x°$.
   Write an expression to find $\angle F$.

d) If $\angle D$ is a right angle and $\angle F = 27°$,
   what is the measure of $\angle E$?

e) If $\angle D$ is a right angle, what do you know
   about the pair of remaining angles?

4. Main Street crosses Walnut Avenue and forms the
intersection shown in the sketch below.

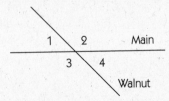

If corner 4 measures 45°, how many degrees does
corner 2 measure?

5.

a) What is the measure of the complement of
   $\angle NOP$?

b) What is the measure of the supplement of
   $\angle NOP$?

6.

a) What is the measure of $\angle 3$?

b) Assuming that $\angle 1 = 130°$, find the measure
   of $\angle 2$.

c) What is the reason that you know that
   $\angle 2 + \angle 3 + \angle 5 = 180°$?

d) How do you know that
   $\angle 4 + \angle 5 + \angle 6 = 180°$?

7.

Pine Bluff Drive connects Woodlawn and Ashland
avenues as shown in the illustration above. If
Woodlawn is parallel to Ashland, what is the value
of $\angle B$, the acute angle that Pine Bluff makes with
Woodlawn?

(1) 23°
(2) 67°
(3) 87°
(4) 90°
(5) 113°

LESSON 5 • The Number Line and the Coordinate Graph

• The Number Line

You already know about *positive* and *negative numbers* on a thermometer.

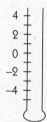

The positive numbers are *above zero* (2°, 4°, etc.) and the negative numbers are *below zero* (–2°, –4°, etc.).

A number line looks something like a thermometer on its side. On a number line, such as the one below, the negative numbers are to the left of zero.

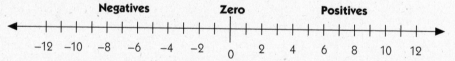

Numbers on a number line get larger as you move to the right. You can see that

- The values of all negative numbers are less than 0.

- Since 8 is to the right of 6, 8 > 6 (8 is greater than 6).

- Since –2 is to the right of –10, –2 > –10 (–2 is greater than –10).

PROBLEM 1 In each pair of numbers, decide which is larger. For help, think of either the thermometer or the number line.

   a) 8 or –10   b) 0 or –25   c) –50 or –25   d) –6 or –5.6

PROBLEM 2 Insert the symbol >, <, or = to make each statement true. Remember, > means "is greater than," and < means "is less than."

   a) –9 ___ –8   c) 5 ___ –6   e) 2 ___ –2   g) –5.4 ___ –5.5

   b) 5 ___ 6   d) –5 ___ –6   f) 5.4 ___ 5.5   h) –2 ___ –1.2

• Adding and Subtracting on the Number Line ....

We can show addition and subtraction as movements on a number line.

Examples:

To *add* a number to another, start at the first number and move the second number of spaces *to the right*.

To *subtract* a number, move that many spaces to the *left*.

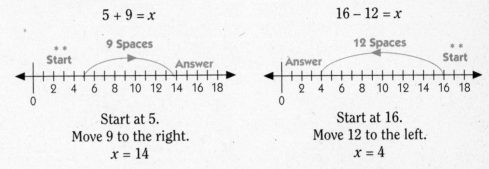

$$5 + 9 = x$$

$$16 - 12 = x$$

Start at 5.
Move 9 to the right.
$x = 14$

Start at 16.
Move 12 to the left.
$x = 4$

If you think of the number line as extending to the left of zero, you can picture subtracting a larger number from a smaller one.

$$7 - 18 = x$$

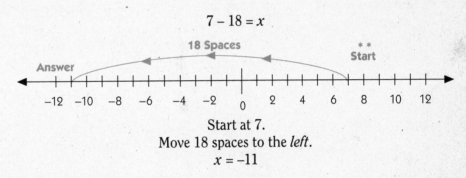

Start at 7.
Move 18 spaces to the *left*.
$x = -11$

Problems like the one above make more sense if you attach a real situation to them.

Examples:

Imagine the zero as the original line of scrimmage in a football game. On the first play, your team gains 7 yards, and on the second play it loses 18 yards. Where is your team now with respect to the original line of scrimmage?

You may prefer to think in terms of money. Imagine earning $7 in the same hour that you spend $18. The hour ends with a net loss of $11.

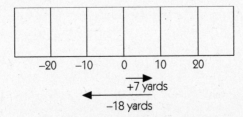

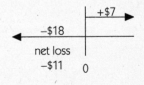

This can be expressed as
$7 - 18 = -11$

This can be expressed as
$\$7 - \$18 = -\$11$

You can also picture problems that start at negative numbers.

$$(-8) + 13 = x$$ $$(-2) - 5 = x$$

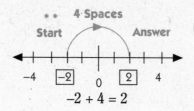

Start at –8.
Move 13 spaces to the *right*.
$x = 5$

Start at –2.
Move 5 spaces to the *left*.
$x = -7$

THINK: a loss of 8 followed by a gain of 13

THINK: a loss of 2 followed by a loss of 5

PROBLEM 3   Write the problem illustrated by each of the following diagrams.

Example:

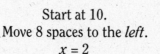

$$-2 + 4 = 2$$

a)
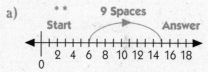

c)
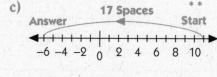

b)
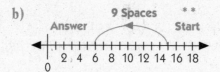

d)
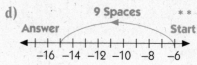

. . .
Adding a negative number has the same result as subtracting a positive number.
. . .

The equation $10 + (-8) = x$ can be written as $10 - 8 = x$ and solved in the same way as before.

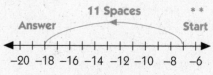

Start at 10.
Move 8 spaces to the *left*.
$x = 2$

Think of two money losses, first a loss of $7 and then a loss of $11. They can be written in an equation as $(-7) + (-11) = x$, which is the same as:

$$(-7) - 11 = x$$

Start at –7.
Move 11 spaces to the *left*.
$x = -18$

Take the time to "see" what you are doing with these problems. If you do, you will not forget as easily as when you just memorize rules. Strive to understand each problem, even if you must take longer to solve it.

Whenever you can, use common sense rather than rules to solve problems.

On the GED Test, problems using negative numbers will be based on real-life situations. A thermometer provides a perfect example of a number line in daily use. You will find the following problems easier to solve because of your life experience.

Example:
Saturday morning it was –2°. By afternoon, the temperature had dropped 3°. What was the new temperature?

Picture the problem on a thermometer—or draw a picture of a number line.

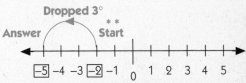

The new temperature is –5°.

The **windchill temperature** depends on both the actual recorded temperature and the wind speed. The following table is a record of some winter temperatures. Use it for problem 4 below.

	S	M	T	W	T	F	S
Recorded temps (° F)	20	12	–3	–1			5
Windchill temps (° F)	3	–10		–24	–29	–20	–8

PROBLEM 4
Use the thermometer at the left to help you "picture the problem."

What was the difference between the recorded temperature and the windchill temperature

a) on Sunday?

b) on Monday? (Picture the numbers on the thermometer and determine the number of spaces between them.)

c) on Wednesday?

d) If the windchill temperature was 13° lower than the recorded temperature on Tuesday, what was the windchill temperature? (Write the mathematical sentence first.)

PROBLEM 5
Solve the following equations. Remember that it is more important to understand the problem than to be speedy in solving it. (To help yourself, "picture the problem" on a thermometer or number line.)

a) $15 - 27 = x$

b) $47 + (-67) = x$

c) $-9 + 27 = m$

d) $-32 + 16 = b$

e) $(-34) + (-44) = n$

f) $(-22) - 33 = k$

If you laid a thermometer on its side, you could see a number line.

The Coordinate Graph . . . .

Placing two number lines perpendicular to each other so that they intersect at the zeros creates a **coordinate plane**.

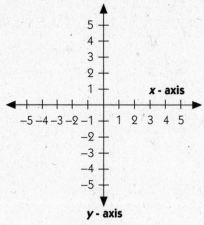

Coordinate Plane

This is a pair of **axes**.

The horizontal axis is called the **x–axis**, and the vertical axis is the **y–axis**.

The point at which they meet is called the **origin** and represents 0 for both axes.

Note that on the *x*–axis, the positive numbers are to the right of the origin and the negatives are to the left of the origin.

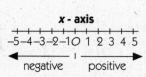

Likewise, on the *y*–axis, the positives are above the origin and the negatives below.

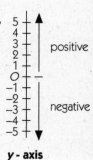

The axes are used to pinpoint the position of any point on a plane.

Example:

Find the distance from point *A* to each of the axes.

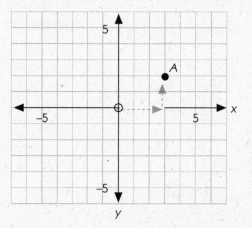

Starting at the origin, move to the right (or left) until you are directly under (or over) the point. How far to the right (or left) did you move? Count the lines.

You moved 3 spaces to the right. That is +3 (or just 3) on the *x*-axis.

Then move up (or down) until you reach the point, counting the units as you go. How far up (or down) did you go?

You moved 2 spaces up. That is +2 (or just 2) on the *y*-axis.

To find the point (*x*, *y*) on a graph, start at the origin, move *x* units to the left or right, then move *y* units up or down.

The position of this point is called (3, 2). These numbers are called the **coordinates** of point *A*. The first number of the pair tells how far to the left or right the point is; it is called the **x-coordinate**. After the comma, the second number—the **y-coordinate**—tells how far up or down the point is. Think of this as the point (*x, y*).

Example:

Compare the positions of points *A* (3, 6) and *B* (–3, 6).

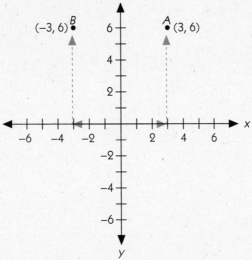

Both of these points have a positive *y*-value. They both lie above the *x*-axis.

Look at the first number of each of these points.

The first number tells you how far *to the left or right* of the origin to move.

If the first number is negative, move to the left. If it is positive, move to the right.

Example:

Compare the positions of points *C* (–5, 2) and *D* (–5, –2).

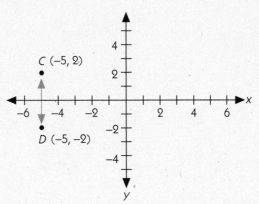

Both of these points have a negative *x*-value because they are located to the left of the *y*-axis.

Now look at the second number of both of these points.

The second number tells you how far *up or down* to move.

If the second number is positive (as in point *C*), *move up* from the *x*-axis. If it is negative (as in point *D*), *move down*.

Write the coordinates of the following points.

Example: The coordinates of *A* are (3, 6).

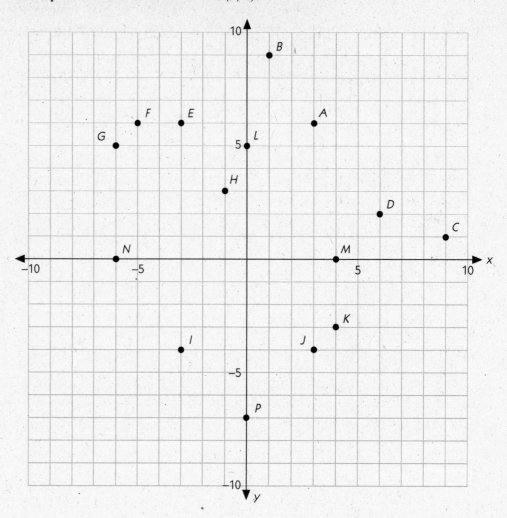

You may use your calculator on any problem for which it is appropriate.

1. Insert one of the following symbols: <, =, or > to make each statement true.

   a) 7 ___ 2

   b) –7 ___ –2

   c) –3 ___ –4

   d) 0 ___ 9

   e) 0 ___ –9

   f) 7 ___ 6.5

   g) –7 ___ –6.5

   h) –7 ___ 6.5

2. Some high and low temperatures of cities around the United States on a winter day are recorded in the following table. All temperatures are given in degrees Fahrenheit.

	High	Low
FARGO, ND	–7	–18
CHICAGO, IL	8	–8
WASHINGTON, DC	15	
DENVER, CO		–4
BUFFALO, NY	–2	

   a) In Washington, the temperature fell 18° from the high to the low. What was the low temperature that day? (Write the equation first.)

   b) What was the difference between Chicago's high and low temperatures?

   c) What is the difference between Fargo's high and low temperatures? (Picture the numbers on a thermometer and determine the number of spaces between them.)

   d) Denver's low temperature occurred at 4:00 A.M. By 2:00 P.M., the temperature had risen 31° to the high for the day. What was the high temperature? (Write the equation first.)

   e) If Buffalo's low temperature was $n°$ lower than the high, how would you represent the low temperature?

3. Solve the following equations. Picture the problems on a number line.

   a) $25 - 34 = k$

   b) $57 + (-45) = m$

   c) $-7 + 21 = n$

   d) $-39 + 13 = x$

   e) $-48 + (-48) = n$

   f) $(-72) - 28 = p$

4. Write the coordinates of each lettered point.

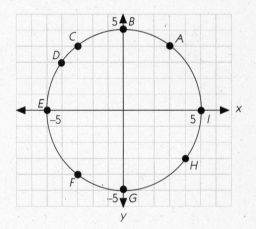

GED Practice

5. Which one of the following statements is true?

   (1) $-13 > -4$
   (2) $-4 > -.03$
   (3) $-4 > 0$
   (4) $-4 > -2$
   (5) $-4 > -14$

6. Today's temperature rose to 10°F. This was 13° higher than yesterday's high temperature. What was the high temperature yesterday?

   (1) $-13°$
   (2) $-10°$
   (3) $-3°$
   (4) $3°$
   (5) $23°$

Mental Math Exercises

1. 600 + 700		**6.** 600 – 700	
2. 87 – 9		**7.** 87 + 9	
3. 100 – 16		**8.** 100 – 135	
4. 340 – 200		**9.** 340 + 200	
5. 246 + 50		**10.** 50 – 70	

Were you able to do all of the problems mentally? If so, you have already made a lot of progress. The rest of this lesson will help you check how much you have learned so far.

So far, you have learned how to apply the operations of addition and subtraction to solve many kinds of problems, including everyday problems.

Chris intended to complete the 488-mile trip from Boise, Idaho, to Seattle, Washington, in one day. By noon, she had driven 203 miles. How much farther did she have to go?

1. Understand the problem.

Remember what the operations do.

Addition combines or joins.
Subtraction compares or separates.

You can help yourself understand the problem by sketching the situation.

Boise ———— 203 ———— ? ———— Seattle
———————————— 488 ————————————

2. Write the problem.

The relationship in the problem can be represented as the equation

$$203 + x = 488$$

You can write an equivalent equation where x is alone on its side of the equation: $488 - 203 = x$

If you were able to see the path to the answer immediately, you could write the problem as

$$x = 488 - 203$$

3. Find the answer.

In all cases, estimate first:

203 is close to 200; 488 is nearly 500.

500 – 200 is approximately **300 miles**.

Do you need a precise answer? If so, how will you find it—mentally, with paper and pencil, or with a calculator? You can subtract these precisely: 488 – 203 = **285 miles**.

4. Check that your answer is reasonable.

What if you had mistakenly added, so that you got 488 + 203 = 691? It doesn't make sense that the remainder of a trip would be longer than the entire trip. You can avoid costly mistakes by taking a moment to ask yourself, "Does this answer make sense?"

● Two Problem-Solving Tips . . . .

Estimation in the GED Math Test

For many of the problems on the GED Math Test, good estimation skills are sufficient. All of the problems on the test are multiple choice, so you may be able to choose the correct answer by making an estimate and comparing your estimate to the choices given. Besides being easier than actually computing an answer, estimating can save you time for the problems that require more thought or a precise solution.

The diagram below shows how you can approach many math problems and particularly problems on the GED Test.

GED Problem–Solving Model

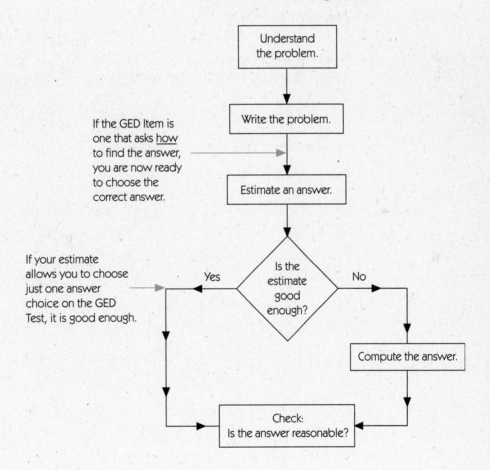

Take a look at how you can use your skills with estimation for two different GED-type problems.

Example A:

A woman read 68 pages of her biology book, 123 pages of literature, and 80 pages of psychology. How many pages did she read in all?

(1) 28

(2) 43

(3) 148

(4) 191

(5) 271

Estimate: 68 is about 70.
123 is about 120.

70 + 120 + 80 = 270

Compare: 270 is very close to choice **(5)** and not close at all to the other choices.

Choose: **(5)** 271

Example B:

Angel spent $35.85 on a new hairdryer. If her purchase came to $37.80 including tax, how much tax did Angel pay?

(1) $.65

(2) 1.55

(3) 1.95

(4) 2.05

(5) 73.65

Estimate: $35.85 is about $36
$37.80 is about $38

$38 − $36 = $2

Compare: $2 is very close to both choices **(3)** and **(4)**. Therefore, you will have to calculate an answer.

Calculate: $37.80 − $35.85 = $1.95

Choose: **(3)** $1.95

* REMEMBER: Estimate first. It may be all you need to do to choose the correct option.

Deciding When There Is Not Enough Information

On the GED Test, one possible answer choice may be "not enough information is given."

- It will be the correct answer choice for one or more of the problems on the test.

- Use caution and think twice before choosing the answer. Can you identify what information is missing? Be sure that there is no way for you to find an answer.

Example A:

Alicia drove 245 miles from Houston to Dallas. If she drove straight through and arrived at 6:00 P.M., how long did it take her to drive to Dallas?

(1) 4 hr.

(2) 4 hr. 30 min.

(3) 5 hr.

(4) 5 hr. 30 min.

(5) Not enough information is given.

The correct answer would be **(5)** Not enough information is given.

Since you don't know how fast Alicia drove or what time she left Houston, you can't find the solution.

Example B:

Roberto pays $400 per month in rent. How much rent does he pay in a year?

(1) $400

(2) $800

(3) $4,000

(4) $4,800

(5) Not enough information is given.

The correct answer choice is **(4)** $4,800.

$400 × 12 months = $4,800

At a quick glance, it may look like there is only one number in the problem—$400 per month. You might be inclined to jump to the conclusion that choice **(5)** *Not enough information is given* is correct.

However, you do know that there are 12 months in a year, and you can use this information to solve the problem. On the GED Test, you will be expected to know everyday math relationships and use them to solve real-life problems.

On the test below, try to solve as many problems as possible with mental math and estimating. You may use the formulas page (page 246), but the use of calculators is not allowed.

1. The following amounts are weights (expressed in pounds) of packages of cheddar cheese in the refrigerated section of the supermarket.

    1.01   0.9   1.2   0.95   1.11

   Which of the following sequences is arranged in order from *smallest* to *largest*.

   (1) 0.9, 0.95, 1.01, 1.2, 1.11
   (2) 1.2, 1.01, 1.11, 0.9, 0.95
   (3) 1.01, 1.2, 1.11, 0.9, 0.95
   (4) 0.9, 0.95, 1.01, 1.11, 1.2
   (5) 0.9, 0.95, 1.2, 1.01, 1.11

2. At the beginning of June, Ron's checking account balance was $233.12. During the month, he wrote checks for a total of $980.12 and made deposits of $1,180.00. Disregarding any interest or check charges, which expression below shows his balance at the end of the month?

   (1) 233.12 – 980.12 – 1,180.00
   (2) 233.12 + 1,180.00 – 980.12
   (3) 233.12 + 1,180.00 + 980.12
   (4) 1,180.00 – 980.12 – 233.12
   (5) 1,180.00 – 233.12 + 980.12

Problem 3 refers to the following diagram.

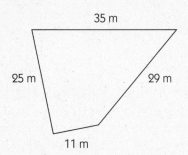

3. How many meters of fencing would be necessary to fence in the irregularly shaped lot pictured above?

   (1) 20
   (2) 100
   (3) 200
   (4) 875
   (5) Not enough information is given.

4. Elizabeth's present weight is x pounds. She is trying to lose 35 pounds. Which of the following expressions represents her target weight?

   (1) $35x$
   (2) $35 + x$
   (3) $x + 35$
   (4) $x - 35$
   (5) $35 - x$

5. From the tip of an antenna on top of a high-rise apartment building to the ground is a drop of 331 feet. The floor of the sub-basement of the same building is 37 feet *below* the ground. How far is it from the top of the antenna to the bottom of the sub-basement?

   (1) 257 ft.
   (2) 294 ft.
   (3) 368 ft.
   (4) 405 ft.
   (5) Not enough information is given.

6. The manufacturer's suggested retail price on a new automobile was $9,782. With the factory rebate and the dealer's discount, Rose was able to purchase the car for $7,990. Which of the following expressions represents the total of her savings?

   (1) $9,782 + $7,990
   (2) $9,782 − $7,990
   (3) $7,990 − $9,782
   (4) $\dfrac{\$9,782}{\$7,990}$
   (5) $7,990 × $9,782

Problems 7 and 8 refer to the following diagram.

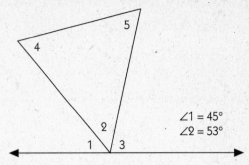

$\angle 1 = 45°$
$\angle 2 = 53°$

7. What is the measure of ∠ 3?

   (1) 45°
   (2) 53°
   (3) 82°
   (4) 98°
   (5) Not enough information is given.

8. If ∠ 2 = ∠ 4, what is the measure of ∠ 5?

   (1) 45°
   (2) 53°
   (3) 74°
   (4) 106°
   (5) Not enough information is given.

Self-Evaluation

After you have checked your answers, take the time to evaluate your progress and mistakes.

1. On how many problems did you estimate?

2. Could you have estimated successfully on more problems? Which ones?

3. Can you identify areas that you need to review?

Problems	Skill	Lessons
1	Decimal Comparisons	2
2, 4, 6	Recognizing expressions	1 & 3
5	Positive and negative numbers	5
3	Perimeter	2
7, 8	Angles	4

• LESSON 7 • "Seeing" Multiplication and Division

Mental Math Exercises
1. $2 + 2 + 2 + 2 = ?$
2. $5 + 5 + 5 = ?$
3. $4 + 4 + 4 + 4 + 4 = ?$
4. $7 + 7 + 7 + 7 = ?$
5. $10 + 10 + 10 + 10 + 10 = ?$

Adding the same number over and over can get to be tricky. This lesson introduces a much shorter way. You know it as multiplication.

• 1. Picture the Situation. . . . .

Consider these problems. Do not try to find the answers.

Example A:
A teacher bought 4 packages of pencils. Each package contained 3 pencils. How many pencils did the teacher buy?

Example B:
When the men's choir performs, the men line up in 4 rows. There are 9 men in each row. How many men are in the choir?

Both of these problems ask you to **combine** groups that are the same size.

$3 + 3 + 3 + 3$ $9 + 9 + 9 + 9$

Now think about the following situations. Do not try to find the answers.

Example C:
How many 8-passenger vans are necessary to transport 24 people to the ball game?

This problem asks, "How many groups of 8 are there in 24?"

Example D:
Sal needs to cut a 54-inch-long piece of wood into 6 stakes. How long should each piece be?

This problem asks, "How long is each of the 6 stakes?"

Both of these situations ask you to **separate** large groups into smaller, equal-sized groups.

2. Write the Problem . . . .

Examples A and B can both be thought of as adding the same number over and over. However, it is shorter to think of the process as **multiplying**.

4×3 is a shorter method than $3 + 3 + 3 + 3$. 4×9 is shorter than $9 + 9 + 9 + 9$.

In Example C on page 50, you could have subtracted 8 over and over. However, **division** is a shorter way to do repeated subtractions.

$24 \div 8$ asks the same question as "How many times can you subtract 8 from 24?"

$$24 \div 8 = 3$$

$$24 - 8 = 16 \ \text{(once)}$$
$$16 - 8 = 8 \ \text{(twice)}$$
$$8 - 8 = 0 \ \text{(three times)}$$

You can see by these sketches that the order of the numbers in a multiplication problem does not affect the result.

$3 \times 5 = 15$ is the same total number as $5 \times 3 = 15$

But the order *is* very important when you divide. The problem $54 \div 6$ is read as 54 <u>divided by</u> 6 (or 6 <u>divided into</u> 54). It asks, "How many 6s are there in 54?"

Example: Enter these two problems into your calculator and compare the answers. Are they different?

⑤④÷⑥= ____   ⑥÷⑤④= ____

The answers *are* different—the order does affect the result when you divide.

> Multiply when you want to combine or join groups of the same size.

> Divide when you want to separate a large group into smaller, equal-sized groups.

> With multiplication and addition, the order **does not** affect the result. They are said to be commutative. Subtraction and division are not commutative. The order **is important** when you subtract or divide.

PROBLEM 1 Think of a situation in your life that would require the use of multiplication. Draw a picture or tell how it fits the description of multiplying as combining equal groups.

PROBLEM 2 Draw a picture or describe a situation that requires division. Does it fit into the description of division as separating into equal groups?

PROBLEM 3 Write a mathematical expression for Example D on page 50.

PROBLEM 4 Solve the following pairs of problems **with your calculator**, and compare the answers. Which pairs of answers indicate that the order is important?

a) $695 + 42$ $42 + 695$ e) $8,901 + 767$ $767 + 8,901$

b) 45×62 62×45 f) 498×711 711×498

c) $56 - 34$ $34 - 56$ g) $1,003 - 698$ $698 - 1,003$

d) $625 \div 25$ $25 \div 625$ h) $780 \div 13$ $13 \div 780$

Notation

You are already familiar with two ways to write a multiplication problem:

$$65 \qquad 65 \times 11 =$$
$$\underline{\times\, 11}$$

This same problem can also be written as: $65 \cdot 11$ or $(65)(11)$ or $65(11)$

When there is no sign next to the parentheses, multiply.

There are also many ways to write division problems. 56 <u>divided by</u> 8 can be written as:

$$56 \div 8 \quad \text{or} \quad 8\overline{)56} \quad \text{or} \quad \frac{56}{8} \quad \text{or} \quad 56/8$$

Note: The form $\frac{56}{8}$ is used most often on the GED Test and in this book. Remember, this is read as 56 <u>divided by</u> 8.

Using Variables

Example:

There are six desks in each row in a classroom. If there are n rows, how many desks are in the room?

This example describes a situation where there are n groups of equal size. The expression is written as:

$$6 \times n \quad \text{or} \quad 6(n) \text{ or, more simply, just } 6n$$

Whenever a number and letter are next to each other without a sign between them, it indicates multiplication ($4y$ means 4 times y). This also is true for two letters (mn means m times n).

Example:

There are x pieces of candy in a package. If Fran shares the bag with 3 other friends, how many pieces will each get?

The large group is made up of x objects to be split up into 4 equal groups. (Fran and her friends.)

$$x \div 4 \quad \text{or} \quad \frac{x}{4}$$

PROBLEM 5 Write each problem in an equivalent form, then in numbers and words.

Examples: 4(5) $\underline{4 \cdot 5}$ $\underline{4 \text{ times } 5}$

$\frac{6}{m}$ $\underline{6 \div m}$ $\underline{6 \text{ divided by } m}$

a) $21 \div 7$ _____   _____

b) $(21) - (7)$ _____   _____

c) $20x$ _____   _____

d) $\frac{m}{3}$ _____   _____

e) $4 + (15)$ _____   _____

f) $6\overline{)36}$ _____   _____

Translating Words to Problems:

As you have seen, writing a mathematical expression is key to solving problems. Read through the expressions below to prepare to write your own expressions. Notice that these expressions use numbers and variables.

4 more than 7 .... $4 + 7$	6 less than 15 .... $15 - 6$
4 more than y .... $4 + y$	x less than 15 .... $15 - x$
4 times as great as 5 .... 4×5	the number of 6s in 42 .... $\frac{42}{6}$
4 times as great as n .... $4n$	the number of 6s in p .... $\frac{p}{6}$
the number of doughnuts in 3 dozen .... $12(3)$	the number of 5-member teams formed from 40 people .... $\frac{40}{5}$
the number of doughnuts in d dozen .... $12d$	the number of x-member teams formed from 40 people ... $\frac{40}{x}$
98 divided by 7 .... $\frac{98}{7}$	
98 divided into 7 .... $\frac{7}{98}$	

PROBLEM 6 Write a mathematical expression for each problem. Think about why some problems seem harder than others.

Example: 63 divided by 9 $\frac{63}{9}$ $63 \div 9$, or $9\overline{)63}$

a) 32 divided by 8

b) 32 divided into 8

c) 32 divided by b

d) x divided into 8

e) 6 times as much as 3

f) 6 more than 3

g) the number of 3s in 6

h) 3 less than 6

PROBLEM 7 Translate the following situations into mathematical expressions. It will help if you ask yourself, "Am I *combining* equal amounts or *separating into* equal amounts?" Write your reason after the expression.

Examples:	Expression	Reason
the number of cents in 4 nickels (5¢)	5×4	combining
the number of nickels (5¢) in 75¢	$\frac{75}{5}$	separating
a) the number of cents in 10 nickels	_____	_____
b) the number of nickels in 20 cents	_____	_____
c) the number of 12s in 36	_____	_____
d) the number of feet in y yards	_____	_____
(Note: 3 feet = 1 yard)		
e) the number of months in 2 years	_____	_____
(Note: 12 months = 1 year)		
f) the number of months in x years	_____	_____
g) the number of 25s in 100	_____	_____
h) the number of quarters (25¢) in 125¢	_____	_____

3. Find the Answer—Mentally . . . .

Multiplying and Dividing by 1

When you multiply or divide any number by 1, the answer is the same as the original number.

The answer to a multiplication problem is called the **product**. When you multiply any number by 1, the product is that same number back again. This is also true when you multiply variables by 1.

$$7 \times 1 = 7 \quad 1 \cdot 578 = 578 \quad 1(149) = 149 \quad 1 \cdot a = 1a = a$$

In some situations, you may have to think of a variable alone as being 1 times that variable.

(For example, $x = 1x$, $b = 1b$, $y = 1y$)

When you *divide by 1*, the answer is the same as the number you were dividing into.

$$7 \div 1 = 7 \quad \frac{67}{1} = 67 \quad \frac{625}{1} = 625 \quad \text{BUT} \quad \frac{1}{625} = 0.0016$$

(You are dividing by 625, not by 1.)

Multiplying and Dividing with 0

Whenever you multiply by 0, the product is 0. Try the examples below on your calculator.

$$9(0) = 0 \quad 0 \times 58 = 0 \quad 489 \times 0 = 0 \quad 0(1,025) = 0$$

Division is a bit more complicated. There are two separate cases to learn:

When you multiply or divide 0 by any number, the answer is 0. However, do not *divide by 0*.

1) When you *divide into 0* (that is, when 0 is the top number), the **quotient** (answer) is always 0, no matter what the divisor is.

$$\frac{0}{9} = 0 \quad \frac{0}{39} = 0 \quad \frac{0}{529} = 0 \quad \frac{0}{2,376} = 0$$

2) However, when you *divide by 0*, you run into trouble. Division by 0 is **undefined**. In other words, it is not allowed in our system of arithmetic. 0 cannot be the bottom number in a problem.

$$\frac{67}{0} \quad 49 \div 0 \quad 0\overline{)38} \quad 23/0$$

PROBLEM 8 Find the answers mentally. When a problem can't be done, write "undefined."

a) $10,000 \times 1 = $ _____   i) $1 \div 10,000 = $ _____

b) $10,000 \times 0 = $ _____   j) $0 \div 10,000 = $ _____

c) $10,000 + 0 = $ _____   k) $0 \times 10,000 = $ _____

d) $10,000 - 1 = $ _____   l) $0 + 10,000 = $ _____

e) $10,000 \div 0 = $ _____   m) $n \times 1 = $ _____

f) $10,000 + 1 = $ _____   n) $n \div 1 = $ _____

g) $10,000 \div 1 = $ _____   o) $n \times 0 = $ _____

h) $10,000 - 0 = $ _____   p) $0 \div n = $ _____

Building on Basic Facts

Multiplication

Working with multiples of 10 (10; 100; 1,000; etc.) is easy to do in your head.

$4 \times 1\underline{0} = 4$ tens $= 4\underline{0}$ $4 \times 1\underline{00} = 4$ hundreds $= 4\underline{00}$ $4 \times 1,\underline{000} = 4$ thousands $= 4,\underline{000}$

1) Think of the problems in this way: Ignore the trailing zeros while you multiply the digits at the front. Then replace the trailing zeros in the answer. Now you can do even more problems mentally.

$6 \times 200 = 1,200$	$3 \times 90 = 270$	$500 \times 7 = 3,500$	$700 \times 6 = 4,200$
$6 \times 2 = 12$	$3 \times 9 = 27$	$5 \times 7 = 35$	$7 \times 6 = 42$

2) When both multipliers have trailing zeros, forget about all of them while you multiply the digits at the front ends. Then replace all the zeros in the answer.

	90×60	80×600	900×700	$50 \times 4,000$
Think:	$9 \times 6 = 54$	$8 \times 6 = 48$	$9 \times 7 = 63$	$5 \times 4 = 20$
Replace 0s:	5,400	48,000	630,000	200,000
	two 0s	three 0s	four 0s	four 0s

Division

1) The process is the same when you divide. Ignore the trailing zeros that are not involved with the division, then replace them in the answer.

$\dfrac{800}{4} = 200$	$\dfrac{3600}{4} = 900$	$\dfrac{640}{8} = 80$	$\dfrac{4000}{8} = 500$
$8 \div 4 = 2$	$36 \div 4 = 9$	$64 \div 8 = 8$	$40 \div 8 = 5$

2) When both numbers in a division problem have trailing zeros, cancel the ones they have in common. Then proceed as before.

	$\dfrac{6,000}{30} = \dfrac{6,000}{30}$	$\dfrac{180,000}{200} = \dfrac{180,000}{200}$	$\dfrac{3,000,000}{60} = \dfrac{3,000,000}{60}$
Cancel:			
Think:	$6 \div 3 = 2$	$18 \div 2 = 9$	$30 \div 6 = 5$
Replace 0s:	200	900	50,000

PROBLEM 9   Find the answers to the problems below using the techniques you have learned.

a) $4 \times 300 =$ _____

b) $70 \times 6 =$ _____

c) $700 - 70 =$ _____

d) $600 \times 9 =$ _____

e) $80 \times 40 =$ _____

f) $640 \div 8 =$ _____

g) $1,500 \div 5 =$ _____

h) $50 \times 600 =$ _____

i) $900 \times 800 =$ _____

j) $900 + 800 =$ _____

k) $9,000 \div 30 =$ _____

l) $4,900 \div 700 =$ _____

m) $800 \times 500 =$ _____

n) $40,000 \div 80 =$ _____

Rounding and Estimating . . . .

Why do you need to develop your estimating skills to pass the GED Test? As you saw in earlier lessons, estimating is often all you need to solve a problem.

Look at the problem below. While you could multiply to find an exact answer, a quick overview of the answer choices shows that an estimate would be sufficient.

Example:

Pam is collecting trading stamps from her grocery store for a new set of dishes. Each book of stamps has 38 pages that can hold 30 stamps per page. How many stamps does each book hold?

(1) 68
(2) 114
(3) 126
(4) 570
(5) 1,140

By simply estimating the problem to be 30×40, you can see the answer has to be near 1,200. Only choice **(5)** 1,140 is close to your estimate.

Multiplication

Rounding one factor	**Rounding both factors**

Estimate 7×582.

Estimate $58(321)$.

Think: 582 is between 500 and 600 but closer to 600.

Think: 58 is close to 60, and 321 is close to 300.

$7 \times 600 = 4,200$

$60(300) = 18,000$ is easy to do.

So, $7 \times 582 \approx 4,200$

So, $58(321) \approx 18,000$

PROBLEM 10   Use rounding to estimate answers to the following problems.

a) $3 \times 49 \approx$ e) $92 \times 39 \approx$

b) $8 \times 411 \approx$ f) $27 \times 63 \approx$

c) $769 \times 7 \approx$ g) $\$6.18 \times 43 \approx$

d) $53 \times 78 \approx$ h) $\$24.75 \times 105 \approx$

Now use estimating to solve the sample GED problem below.

PROBLEM 11   To complete a construction project, 18 workers each worked 120 hours. How many hours did the project take?

(1) 108
(2) 138
(3) 216
(4) 2,160
(5) 6,666

Division

You can also round numbers to make division easier. Look at the two problems below.

Example: Which is easier to divide?

$\frac{628}{3}$ OR $\frac{600}{3}$

At a glance, you know that $\frac{600}{3}$ is easier. That is because $6 \div 3 = 2$, so $\boxed{\frac{600}{3}} = 200$.

Example: Which is easier to divide?

$\frac{318}{5}$ OR $\frac{300}{5}$

Again, you know that $\frac{300}{5}$ is easier because $30 \div 5 = 6$, so $\boxed{\frac{300}{5}} = 60$.

To estimate with division, you can round to the nearest ten, hundred, or thousand—whichever will help to make your work easier. Look at the GED-type problem below.

Example:

Sam's Car Wash shared \$315 in tips evenly among its 5 employees. How much will each worker receive?

(1) \$6
(2) \$43   Estimate: $\frac{\$315}{5} \approx \frac{\$300}{5} = \$60$
(3) \$63
(4) \$430   \$60 is closest to choice **(3)** \$63.
(5) \$630

A quick rounding helps you select the right answer without having to do the long division. When you estimate with division, you often have to think ahead before you divide so that you create an easy problem to work with.

PROBLEM 12 First, circle the rounded number that will make these problems easier to divide. Then, find an estimated solution.

		Round to:		**Solve**
		nearest 10	**nearest 100**	
Example:	$\frac{152}{3}$	$\left(\frac{150}{3}\right)$	$\frac{200}{3}$	$\boxed{\frac{150}{3}} = 50$
a)	$\frac{213}{4}$	$\frac{210}{4}$	$\frac{200}{4}$	
b)	$\frac{877}{8}$	$\frac{880}{8}$	$\frac{900}{8}$	
c)	$\frac{1,157}{60}$	$\frac{1,160}{60}$	$\frac{1,200}{60}$	
d)	$\frac{1,574}{40}$	$\frac{1,570}{40}$	$\frac{1,600}{40}$	

PROBLEM 13 Estimate answers to the following division problems.

a) $\dfrac{418}{7}$ d) $\dfrac{779}{4}$ g) $\dfrac{1,221}{40}$

b) $\dfrac{1,823}{3}$ e) $\dfrac{1,486}{50}$ h) $\dfrac{1,221}{400}$

c) $\dfrac{537}{9}$ f) $\dfrac{1,486}{500}$ i) $\dfrac{12,211}{4,000}$

Compatible Numbers for Division

・・・
To find compatible pairs for division, you must know your multiplication and division facts very well.
・・・

Sometimes, rounding to the nearest 10, 100, or 1,000 will not give you easy numbers to work with. In that case, round to numbers that make it easy to divide. Numbers that are easy to divide are based on the multiplication and division facts. They are called compatible pairs for division.

If rounding to the nearest 10:

$\dfrac{349}{9}$ would round to $\dfrac{350}{9}$.

This is not easy to do in your head.

Instead, round to a number that 9 divides into:

$\dfrac{349}{9} \approx \dfrac{360}{9} = 40$ Why?

Because 36 ÷ 9 is an easy math fact to work with!

PROBLEM 14 Estimate answers to the following problems. Write the math fact you used to get each estimate.

	Problem	**Fact**
Example:	$\dfrac{418}{7} \approx \boxed{\dfrac{420}{7}} = 60$	$42 \div 7 = 6$

a) $\dfrac{230}{3} \approx \dfrac{240}{3} = ?$

b) $\dfrac{621}{8} \approx$

c) $\dfrac{1,823}{3} \approx$

d) $\dfrac{2,234}{3} \approx$

e) $\dfrac{3,816}{6} \approx$

PROBLEM 15 Choose the best way to find **the closest** estimated answer for each problem. Tell why you made each choice.

Example: $\dfrac{619}{7}$ $\dfrac{560}{7}$ OR $\dfrac{630}{7}$

$\dfrac{619}{7} \approx \dfrac{630}{7}$ is better, because 619 is closer to 630.

a) $\dfrac{91}{4}$ $\dfrac{80}{4}$ OR $\dfrac{120}{4}$? b) $\dfrac{662}{8}$ $\dfrac{640}{8}$ OR $\dfrac{720}{8}$? c) $\dfrac{1,399}{6}$ $\dfrac{1,200}{6}$ OR $\dfrac{1,800}{6}$?

Use the estimating techniques you learned in this lesson to solve the GED-type problem below.

PROBLEM 16 A rummage sale raised $6,270 for 5 neighborhood projects. If the money was divided evenly, how much went to each project?

(1) $125
(2) $655
(3) $1,254
(4) $1,395
(5) $1,500

You may use your calculator on any problem for which it seems appropriate.

1. Write a multiplication or division mathematical expression for each. Do not solve.

   a) the number of eggs in 2 dozen

   b) the number of 3s in 42

   c) the number of days in 21 weeks

   d) the number of years in 104 weeks (there are 52 weeks in a year)

   e) the number of chairs in each row when 72 chairs are arranged into 6 rows

   f) the number of centimeters (cm) in y meters (there are 100 cm in one meter)

   g) the number of shoes in p pair

2. A group of 10 workers won a lottery prize of $2,600,000. If the workers split the winnings evenly, how much will each worker get?

   a) Write the problem as a mathematical expression.

   b) Find the answer.

3. A ream of paper contains 500 sheets. What is the total number of sheets in 8 reams?

   a) Write the problem as a mathematical expression.

   b) Find the answer.

4. Bart ate a breakfast of 450 calories and a lunch of 350 calories. What is the total number of calories he consumed in those 2 meals?

   a) Write the mathematical expression.

   b) Find the answer.

5. How many $200 payments will be necessary to pay off a debt of $1,000?

   a) Write the mathematical expression.

   b) Find the answer.

6. What is the seating capacity of a restaurant that has 30 tables, each of which seats n persons? Write the mathematical expression.

7. Find the following answers mentally.

   a) 6×70

   b) $60(70)$

   c) 60×700

   d) $600(700)$

   e) $600 + 700$

   f) $300 \div 5$

   g) $\dfrac{3,000}{5}$

   h) $240 \div 8$

   i) $\dfrac{2,400}{80}$

   j) $24,000 \div 800$

   k) $\dfrac{24,000}{8}$

   l) $2,400 - 800$

   m) $5 \cdot 600$

   n) $5(6,000)$

8. Estimate the answers to the following problems:

   a) $7 \cdot 683 \approx$

   b) $3(926) \approx$

   c) $43 \times 68 \approx$

   d) $92(79) \approx$

   e) $98 \times 438 \approx$

   f) $\dfrac{566}{3} \approx$

   g) $4,188 \div 6 \approx$

   h) $733 + 319 \approx$

   i) $1,010 - 397 \approx$

GED Practice

9. Laura's new car gets 27 miles to the gallon. How many miles does she travel on 48 gallons of gas?

   (1) 96 miles
   (2) 960 miles
   (3) 1,296 miles
   (4) 2,096 miles
   (5) Not enough information is given.

10. Pete loads cartons onto a truck for shipping. Each carton weighs 40 pounds. One truck to be loaded has a load limit of 2,000 pounds. Which expression below tells how many cartons can be loaded on this truck?

    (1) $\dfrac{40}{2,000}$
    (2) $2,000(40)$
    (3) $40(2,000)$
    (4) $\dfrac{2,000}{40}$
    (5) $2,000 + 40$

LESSON 8 • Measurement: Multiplying More than Two Numbers

Mental Math Exercises

1. $0 + 589 =$	**4.** $589 \div 1 =$
2. $589 \times 1 =$	**5.** $589 \div 0 =$
3. $589 - 0 =$	**6.** $\frac{589}{589} =$

• Units of Measure ....

Two systems of measurement are used in the United States today. One is the English system, which commonly measures length as shown in the table below.

> 12 inches (in.) = 1 foot (ft.)
> 3 feet = 1 yard (yd.)
> 5,280 feet = 1 mile (mi.)

There is no fixed pattern to the relationships between the units in the English system. Therefore, to be able to change from one unit to another, you need to learn the equivalents.

Most of the rest of the world uses the metric system, in which the standard unit of length is the meter. The commonly used units are millimeter, centimeter, meter, and kilometer.

> 1,000 millimeters (mm) = 1 meter (m)
> 100 centimeters (cm) = 1 meter
> 1,000 meters = 1 kilometer (km)

To change from one unit to another in this system, you only need to multiply or divide by multiples of 10.

PROBLEM 1 Find the part of *your* hand that most closely represents the length of 1 inch. Suggestion: try the length of the last joint of a finger. Use the ruler on this page to measure and find some part of your hand that measures 1 centimeter. (Try the width of a nail.)

The units of **length** are the basis for other measurements as well.

One Dimension	Two Dimensions	Three Dimensions
Examples: in., ft., m, km	Area is measured in **square** units.	Volume is measured in **cubic** units.
length	To indicate squared units, write sq. in., sq. ft., cm², mm², etc. area	To indicate cubic units, write cu. ft., cu. yd., m³, cm³, etc. volume

PROBLEM 2 Use the chart above to tell which unit in the English system would most likely be used to make each of the following measurements:

a) how far it is from Minneapolis to Des Moines
b) how far it is from your car in the parking lot to the building
c) how much carpet to buy for the living room
d) how much storage room is in a public warehouse

Areas

Area is a two-dimensional measure of how much surface is inside a region. It is usually measured in square units. Think of the palm of your hand as such a unit. Put your palm on the top of your desk and estimate how many "palms" your desktop would contain. This is the area of the desk in "palm" units. Likewise, when you find the area of a figure, you find out how many *square units* are inside.

Rectangles

This rectangle has been divided into square units. There are 6 rows, and each row contains 8 squares.

Find the area of the rectangle.

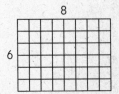

To find the answer, you could count the squares one by one, or you could add 8 six times. Or you could multiply 6×8 to find the number of squares. Any way that you do it, the area is 48 squares.

Note: Remember to **always** write area in square units, for example sq. ft., sq. in., m^2 (square meters).

PROBLEM 3 Multiply to find the area of each of the following rectangles. Write your answer in square units.

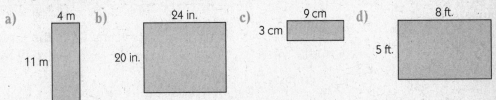

a) 4 m 11 m   b) 24 in. 20 in.   c) 9 cm 3 cm   d) 8 ft. 5 ft.

PROBLEM 4 On the formulas page of the GED Test and page 246 of this book, there is a formula for the area of a rectangle. It says:

$$A = lw \ (\text{area} = \text{length} \times \text{width}), \text{ where } l = \text{length and } w = \text{width}$$

Does this describe what you have been doing? How? (**Remember:** When two letters are next to each other, with no sign between them, you multiply.)

PROBLEM 5 A hallway measures 2.9 feet by 19.5 feet.

a) Estimate how many square feet of tile are needed to resurface the floor.

b) Use your calculator to find the precise number of square feet in the hallway.

c) Which answer would you use when you went to purchase the tile? Why?

PROBLEM 6 Sarah bought some plastic sheeting to cover her garden. Which expression represents the size of the plastic?

(1) $A = (5 + 2) + (5 + 2)$
(2) $A = 2(5 - 2)$
(3) $A = 2(5) + 2(2)$
(4) $A = 2 \times 5$
(5) $A = 5 - 2$

2 ft.   5 ft.

Parallelograms

These four-sided figures are called **parallelograms**

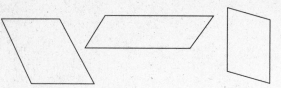

Their opposite sides are both equal and parallel. This is also true of rectangles. What feature of a rectangle makes it a special parallelogram?

The angles in the corners of a rectangle are all **right angles.**

How do you find the area of a parallelogram? Look at the example in the sketches below. When you picture a parallelogram on a grid (Figure 1), you notice that the slanted lines make it hard to see exactly how many square units are inside.

How can you make this parallelogram into a well-organized rectangle in order to find the area?

Cut off one slanted end and slide it over to the opposite side of the parallelogram. This makes it a rectangle. (Figure 2)

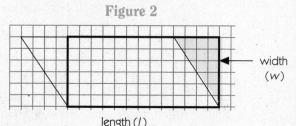

Figure 1   Figure 2

height (h)   base (b)   length (l)   width (w)

Did the area change when you "rearranged" the parallelogram? No. The area of the parallelogram (Figure 1) is the same as that of the rectangle (Figure 2).

Notice:

- The base (*b*) of the parallelogram is the same as the length (*l*) of the rectangle.

- The height (*h*) of the parallelogram is the same as the width (*w*) of the rectangle.

  (The height (*h*) of the parallelogram is not the slanted side; it is the perpendicular (⊥) distance between the opposite sides.)

Height can be indicated with a straight line inside or outside the parallelograms.

height   height

PROBLEM 7   Use what you have learned about parallelograms to find the area of these figures. Look carefully for the heights.

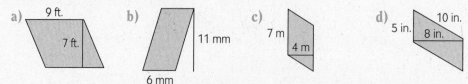

a) 9 ft.   7 ft.   b) 11 mm   6 mm   c) 7 m   4 m   d) 5 in.   10 in.   8 in.

PROBLEM 8   The formula for the area of a parallelogram is on the formulas page (page 246 of this book and included with the GED Test). It is:

$$A = bh; \text{ where } b = \text{base and } h = \text{height}$$

Does this fit with what you were doing to find the area of these figures? How?

PROBLEM 9

. . .

It is not necessary to memorize the formulas for area. You can refer to the formulas page during the GED Test.

. . .

Which of the following shows the difference between the areas of the two figures (Figure A − Figure B)?

(1) $(10 \times 7) - (10 \times 5)$
(2) $(10 \times 7) - (4 \times 5)$
(3) $(10 + 7) - (10 + 4)$
(4) $(10 + 7) - (10 + 5)$
(5) $(10 \times 7) - (10 \times 4)$

Figure A

Figure B

Triangles

How many square units are in a triangle?

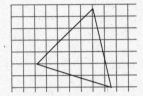

It is hard to tell by looking at the figure.

However, from the sketches below, it is easy to see that any triangle, if doubled, becomes a parallelogram.

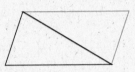 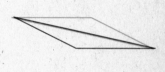

Using this fact, you can see that the area of a triangle would be half a parallelogram's area. On the formulas page, the formula for the area of a triangle appears as

$A = \frac{1}{2}bh$, where b = base and h = height

This confirms your discovery above. To find the area of a triangle, you find $\frac{1}{2}$ of the area of a parallelogram with the same base and height.

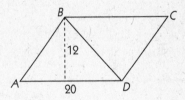

Area of parallelogram $ABCD$: $A = bh$
$$A = 20 \times 12 = 240$$

Area of triangle ABD: $A = \frac{1}{2}bh$
$$A = \frac{1}{2}(20 \times 12) = 120$$

Example:

To determine the amount of fertilizer to buy, Robert Lin must know the area of this triangular garden plot.

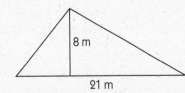

$A = \frac{1}{2}bh$
$A = \frac{1}{2} \times 21 \times 8$

Regrouping to Multiply

To find the answer when you multiply, you can **regroup** the numbers—as you did in addition.

Example: Which of these problems would be the easiest for Robert to multiply?

Note: Multiplying by $\frac{1}{2}$ is the same as dividing by 2.

$$(\tfrac{1}{2} \times 21) \times 8 \qquad \tfrac{1}{2} \times (21 \times 8) \qquad (\tfrac{1}{2} \times 8) \times 21$$

The third solution would be the easiest. You can even do this in your head.

$$(\tfrac{1}{2} \times 8) \times 21$$

$$4 \times 21 = 84 \text{ m}^2 \text{ or } 84 \text{ square meters}$$

PROBLEM 10 Find the area of each of the following triangles. Regroup when possible.

a)
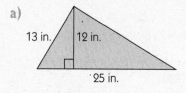

b)
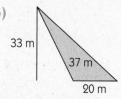

c)
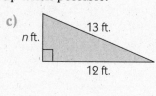

PROBLEM 11 What is the area of triangle *ABD* at the right?

(1) 10 sq. ft.
(2) 12 sq. ft.
(3) 15 sq. ft.
(4) 24 sq. ft.
(5) 30 sq. ft.

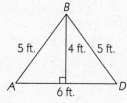

Irregular Figures

Shapes in your everyday experience may be combinations of the ones you have studied. You can find the area of these figures by dividing them into shapes you have already worked with.

Example:
One side of Gloria's house is sketched in the figure. How many square feet of surface is on this side of the house?

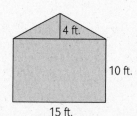

This shape consists of a rectangle plus a triangle.

$A = lw + \tfrac{1}{2}bh$
$A = (10 \times 15) + \tfrac{1}{2}(15 \times 4)$
$A = 150 + 30$
$A = 180$ sq. ft.

Example:
The shaded area in the sketch is to be sodded. How many square meters of sod will be necessary to cover it?

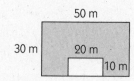

The shaded area is a rectangle minus a smaller rectangle.
$A = lw - lw$
$A = (50 \bullet 30) - (20 \bullet 10)$
$A = 1,500 - 200$
$A = 1,300 \text{ m}^2$

PROBLEM 12 Find the area of the <u>shaded</u> parts of the figures below. (Decide whether you need to add or subtract the two figures.)

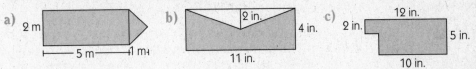

a) 2 m | 5 m | 1 m

b) 2 in. | 4 in. | 11 in.

c) 2 in. | 12 in. | 5 in. | 10 in.

• Volumes ....

You can think of perimeter by imagining fencing around a figure. You can think of area as the covering on a surface. Volume, then, can be thought of as packing inside a box or carton.

Example:

To find the volume of the figure at the right, you want to know how many cubes could be packed into the carton.

The bottom layer is shown. How many cubes are in one layer? (5×7)
How many of these layers will go into the box? (6)
What is the total number of cubes that can be packed into this box?
$6 \times 5 \times 7 = 210$ cubes

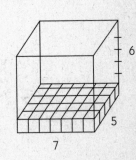

Note: Remember to write volume as cubic units: cu. ft., m³, etc.

Again, the formula on the formulas page (on page 246) confirms the commonsense method:
$$V = lwh, \text{ where } l = \text{length, } w = \text{width, and } h = \text{height}$$

PROBLEM 13 Find the volume of the following rectangular containers. If you cannot find a number answer, write an expression using numbers and letters.

Example: $V = (3 \text{ in.}) (6 \text{ in.}) (x \text{ in.}) = 18x$ cu. in.

a) 11 m | 4 m | 2 m

b) 5 ft. | 9 ft. | x ft.

c) 3 cm | 10 cm | 9 cm

d) n in. | 10 in. | 24 in.

PROBLEM 14 How many cubic feet of sand can be carried in this wagon if it is packed level with the top?

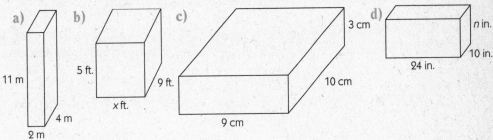

4 ft. | 2 ft. | 6 ft.

(1) 8 cu. ft.
(2) 24 cu. ft.
(3) 48 cu. ft.
(4) 480 cu. ft.
(5) Not enough information is given.

Finding the Answer Mentally............

Compatible Numbers for Multiplication

Finding areas of triangles and volumes of rectangular solids requires you to multiply three numbers, called *multipliers* or *factors*. By grouping *compatible factors* (those that are easy to compute with), you can make these problems easy to solve mentally.

$4 \times 13 \times 25$
$(4 \times 25) \times 13$ 4 and 25 are
100×13 compatible.
$1,300$

$8 \times 9 \times 5$
$(8 \times 5) \times 9$ 8 and 5 are
40×9 compatible.
360

$4 \times 11 \times 50$
$(4 \times 50) \times 11$ 4 and 50 are
200×11 compatible.
$2,200$

PROBLEM 15 Find a pair of compatible factors for each problem, then multiply.

a) $2 \times 57 \times 5$
b) $5 \times 13 \times 6$

c) $4 \times 89 \times 25$
d) $2 \times 44 \times 50$

e) $4 \times 5 \times 41$
f) $2 \times 15 \times 22$

Sometimes you can make compatible factors from those which did not appear to be compatible.

24×50
$12 \times 2 \times 50$
$12 \times (2 \times 50)$
$12 \times 100 = 1,200$

25×44
$25 \times 4 \times 11$
$(25 \times 4) \times 11$
$100 \times 11 = 1,100$

35×12
$7 \times 5 \times 2 \times 6$
$(5 \times 2) \times (7 \times 6)$
$10 \times 42 = 420$

PROBLEM 16 Discover compatible pairs of factors for each problem, then multiply.

a) 24×25
b) 16×50

c) 15×18
d) 28×500

e) 32×25
f) 45×18

Doubling and Halving

Some of the most common math in your everyday life requires you to double or to find half of a number. These exercises will help you to solve more of these problems mentally.

Double 36.
Break 36 up into its parts $(36 = 30 + 6)$, and double each of them.
Then add.

double 30: 60
double 6: 12
add: 72

In a similar way, you can mentally find half of an even number by breaking up the number into parts.

Halve 428, or find $\frac{428}{2}$.
Break up 428 $(428 = 400 + 20 + 8)$, and find half of each part.

half of 400:   200
half of 20:   10
half of 8:   4
add: 214

Halve 94, or find $94 \div 2$.
Break up 94 (into parts that can be halved easily) $(94 = 80 + 14)$.

half of 80:   40
half of 14:   7
add: 47

PROBLEM 17 Find the answers by using the methods shown above.

a) 58×2
b) $\frac{58}{2}$

c) 127×2
d) $\frac{284}{2}$

e) 177×2
f) $\frac{76}{2}$

You may use your calculator on any problem for which it seems necessary.

1. Fill in the blanks, using the equivalencies given on page 60.

   a) 1 yd. = _____ in.

   b) 1 mi. = _____ yd.

   c) 1 sq. ft. = _____ sq. in.

   d) 1 sq. yd. = _____ sq. ft.

   e) 1 cu. ft. = _____ cu. in.

2. Write an equation to find the area of each of the following figures. Solve if possible, or write an expression using letters and numbers.

   a)

   12 cm
   7 cm

   b)
   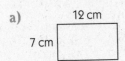
   8 in.
   15 in.

   c)
   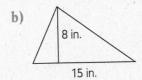
   11 m
   11 m

   d)

   15 m
   7 m
   12 m
   4 m

   e)
   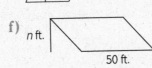
   25 m
   28 m

   f)
   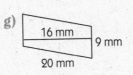
   n ft.
   50 ft.

   g)
   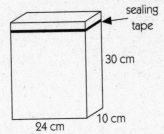
   16 mm
   9 mm
   20 mm

   h)
   10 ft.
   20 ft.
   25 ft.

3. What is the area of the shaded deck sketched below?

   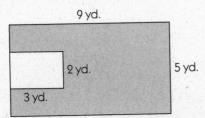
   9 yd.
   2 yd.
   5 yd.
   3 yd.

4. The sketch below shows the dimensions of a pennant that Trudy has agreed to sew for her son's soccer team.

   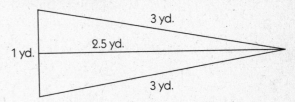
   3 yd.
   2.5 yd.
   1 yd.
   3 yd.

   a) How much trim will she need in order to bind around the edges of the pennant?

   b) What is the area of the pennant?

5. The sketch below shows a carton made to hold sugar.

   sealing tape
   30 cm
   24 cm
   10 cm

   a) How much sealing tape will be needed to encircle the carton as shown?

   b) How much shelf space will each carton take up if the cartons stand as shown in the sketch?

   c) What volume of sugar can this carton hold?

GED Practice

6. Which equation represents the volume of the container below?

   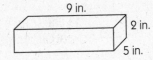
   9 in.
   2 in.
   5 in.

   (1) $V = 5 \times 2$
   (2) $V = 2 \times 9$
   (3) $V = 9 \times 5 \times 2$
   (4) $V = \dfrac{5 \times 9}{2}$
   (5) $V = \frac{1}{2}(5 \times 2)$

Equivalent Equations: Multiplication and Division

Mental Math Exercises

1. 54×2 **4.** 50×16
2. $684 \div 2$ **5.** 25×28
3. $5 \times 8 \times 9$ **6.** $2 \times 29 \times 50$

The above exercises refreshed your mental skills with multiplication and division. In this lesson, you will relate division to multiplication in a fundamental way by using two everyday relationships.

● Finding Total Cost . . . .

Example: A compact disc recording costs $14.

Follow the pattern in the chart below. If one CD costs $14, two would cost $(2 \times \$14)$, or $28.

number	cost
1	$14
2	$28
3	$42
4	$56
5	

Example — row 2

PROBLEM 1

a) What is the cost of 5 compact discs?

b) What is the cost of 10 CDs?

c) How did you find the total cost? Fill in the blank: To find the total cost, multiply 14 by _____

d) Paul has a collection of 70 CDs. How much has he spent on his collection?

As you can see from the problems above, to find the total cost of a number of similar items you multiply the **number of items** times the **price per item**. This is a formula from the formulas page (page 246).

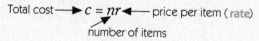

Total cost ──▶ $c = nr$ ◀── price per item (rate)
number of items

The information from the table has been pictured on this graph. The points lie on a straight line.

Example: How much do 3 CDs cost?

Find 3 on the horizontal (bottom) axis, and move straight up until you hit the line. From that point move across to the vertical (side) axis and estimate ($42).

PROBLEM 2

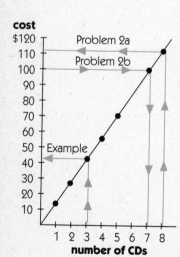

a) Estimate the total cost of 8 CDs by reading the graph.

b) Using the graph, estimate how many CDs can be purchased for $100.

c) How would you find the answer to problem 2b without the graph?

d) Fill in the blank: To find the number of CDs you can buy, divide _____ by 14.

• Finding Distance . . . .

Example: A small airplane can cruise at 250 mph.

The table below summarizes the flight of this airplane. Follow the pattern shown in the table.

If the airplane were flying for 2 hours at this rate, it would travel (2 × 250) or 500 miles.

PROBLEM 3

a) How far would the airplane travel in 5 hours?

b) How far would the airplane travel in 10 hours?

c) Think about what you did in problems 3a and 3b. Fill in the blank: To find the distance flown, multiply 250 by _____.

d) Write the expression for the distance it would travel if the airplane continued at this rate for *n* hours.

	time	distance
	1	250
2 hours	2	500
	3	750
	4	1,000
	5	

The airplane example shows that to find the distance traveled when moving at a constant rate, you multiply the rate (or speed) by the number of hours traveled. On the formulas page (page 246), this appears as:

distance ⟶ $d = rt$ ⟵ number of units of time
rate (how far it goes in one unit of time)

This graph pictures the information from the table above.

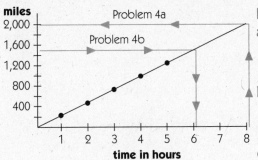

PROBLEM 4

a) Using the graph, estimate the number of miles this airplane would travel in 8 hours.

b) From the graph, estimate the number of hours it would take to travel 1,500 miles.

c) How would you have determined the answer without the graph?

d) Fill in the blank: To find the number of hours it would take this airplane to travel a certain distance, divide _____ by 250.

• Notice that the graphs of these two relationships ($c = nr$ and $d = rt$) were constructed to show what happens when you **multiply**.

• However, you also used them to **divide**—to find the number of CDs in problem 2b and the number of hours in problem 4b.

You can do this because multiplication and division are **inverse operations**—they have the same relationship as addition and subtraction. By using the idea of inverse operations, you can rewrite equations to solve many more problems.

The relationship between multiplication and division is shown by the following equivalent equations:

$$7 \times 8 = \boxed{56} \qquad 8 \times 7 = \boxed{56} \qquad \frac{56}{7} = 8 \qquad \frac{56}{8} = 7$$

Each of these equations is different, yet they say the same thing. Notice that the boxed number is the answer to the multiplication problems and is the top number in the division problems.

PROBLEM 5 Write two equivalent division sentences for each of these multiplication sentences.

Example: $6 \times 8 = \boxed{48}$ would be written as $\frac{48}{8} = 6$ and $\frac{48}{6} = 8$.

a) $8 \times 9 = 72$ c) $20 \times 5 = 100$ e) $24 \times 50 = 1,200$

b) $8 \times b = 72$ d) $m \times 5 = 100$ f) $24 \times 50 = d$

PROBLEM 6 Write one multiplication and one division equation equivalent to each of these division sentences.

Example: $\frac{32}{8} = 4$ is equivalent to $4 \times 8 = \boxed{32}$ and $\frac{32}{4} = 8$.

a) $\frac{54}{9} = 6$ c) $\frac{128}{2} = 64$ e) $\frac{3,000}{5} = 600$

b) $\frac{54}{n} = 6$ d) $\frac{128}{2} = t$ f) $\frac{p}{5} = 600$

PROBLEM 7 Write the equivalent equation to each of these placing the unknown alone on its side of the equation.

Examples: $10 = 4r$ would be written as $r = \frac{10}{4}$ and $11 = \frac{132}{n}$ would be written as $n = \frac{132}{11}$.

a) $45 = 9w$ d) $5x = 95$ g) $125 = \frac{m}{10}$

b) $8 = \frac{96}{k}$ e) $11 = \frac{99}{t}$ h) $21b = 105$

c) $39 = 13p$ f) $75 = 15n$ i) $\frac{w}{9} = 6$

Use the idea of equivalent equations to rewrite the two basic relationships from the last two pages.

cost relationship

$c = nr$ can be written as

$$n = \frac{c}{r} \quad \text{or} \quad r = \frac{c}{n}$$

Consider the situation where $28 is the cost of 2 CDs when each costs $14.

$$n = \frac{28}{14} = 2 \qquad r = \frac{28}{2} = 14$$

distance relationship

$d = rt$ can be written as

$$r = \frac{d}{t} \quad \text{or} \quad t = \frac{d}{r}$$

Consider the situation where 500 miles is the distance traveled by an airplane in 2 hours when it is traveling at 250 mph.

$$r = \frac{500}{2} = 250 \qquad t = \frac{500}{250} = 2$$

The basic formulas will be available to you on a formulas page during the GED Test. If you can rewrite these equivalent equations, you can handle many of the problems on the test.

Working with Equivalent Equations

When you do problems based on the cost relationship ($c = nr$) or the distance relationship ($d = rt$) on the GED Test, you can choose to

1) use the basic formula and write an equivalent equation, or

2) use the equivalent equations directly.

Example: Each gallon of gasoline costs $1.20. How many gallons did Tracy purchase with $4.80? Let n stand for the number of gallons.

1) The basic equation: $c = nr$

2) Or, begin with the equivalent equation: $n = \frac{c}{r}$

Substitute known values: $\$4.80 = n \times \$1.20$
Write an equivalent equation where the unknown is alone: $n = \frac{4.80}{1.20}$

Substitute values: $n = \frac{4.80}{1.20}$

Solve: $n = 4$ gallons

Solve: $n = 4$ gallons

Example: Rick wants to be at his destination, which is 350 miles away, in 7 hours. What would his average speed need to be? Let r stand for rate (the speed).

1) The basic equation: $d = rt$

2) Or, begin with the equivalent equation: $r = \frac{d}{t}$

Substitute known values: $350 = r \times 7$
Write an equivalent equation where the unknown is alone: $r = \frac{350}{7}$

Substitute values: $r = \frac{350}{7}$

Solve: $r = 50$ mph

Solve: $r = 50$ mph

For each problem below, write an equation and solve it.

Use $c = nr$, $d = rt$, or equivalent equations.

These real-life problems may contain more information than you need or not enough information to solve them. If not enough information is given, just write "not enough information" as your answer.

PROBLEM 8 A bicyclist can maintain a speed of 20 mph for long periods. At this rate, how long must he ride to travel 90 miles?

a) Decide: do you find distance, rate, or time?   b) Solve the problem.

PROBLEM 9 In 1990, Arie Luyendyk won the Indianapolis 500 (an auto race that is 500 miles long) with a speed close to 186 mph. At what time did he finish?

PROBLEM 10 A package of 25 nails costs 69¢. Find the price per nail to the nearest tenth of a cent.

a) Do you find total cost, number of nails, or price per nail?   b) Solve the problem.

PROBLEM 11 A jogger stays in shape by running an average of 8 hours a week. How far does he run if he maintains a pace of 8.5 km/hr. for 1.4 hr.?

What Happens When You Multiply?

Use the formula $c = nr$ to make some discoveries.

Consider this situation: The gas tank of a small automobile holds 12 gallons of gasoline. How much does it cost to fill the tank?

Let $n = 12$, and watch what happens to c (the total cost) as r (the price per gallon) changes: $c = 12r$

price per gallon (r)	total cost (c)
.50	$ 6.00
.75	
.85	
.99	
1.00	$12.00
1.50	
2.00	
3.00	

PROBLEM 12

Complete the table to show the changing cost of 12 gallons of gas. Use your calculator when necessary.

Use the table in problem 12 to solve problem 13.

PROBLEM 13

a) As the price per gallon increases, what happens to the total cost? Does it increase or decrease?

b) When the price was less than a dollar per gallon, the total cost was less than _____.

c) When the price was more than a dollar per gallon, the total cost was more than _____.

d) Complete these statements:

• When a number is multiplied by a value less than 1, the result is _____ than the original number.

• When a number is multiplied by a value greater than 1, the result is _____ than the original number.

Estimating Answers

PROBLEM 14 Use the principle you discovered in problem 13d to estimate whether the answer would be greater or less than the value given. Choose *greater* or *less than*.

a) 36×1.38 greater or less than 36?

b) 158×0.87 greater or less than 158?

c) 212×0.45 greater or less than 106?

d) 54×2.09 greater or less than 108?

e) 785×1.223 greater or less than 785?

PROBLEM 15 Complete, using the estimation ideas above.

Example: 43×0.95 is less than ___43___.

a) 97×0.88 is less than _____.

b) 522×1.04 is greater than _____.

c) 46×0.48 is less than _____.

d) 103×1.25 is greater than _____.

What Happens When You Divide?

Consider this situation: You have \$12 to spend on cheese. Various kinds of cheese have different prices per pound. The equation $n = \frac{c}{r}$ can be used to find the number of pounds of cheese you can buy. Let $c = \$12$, and watch what happens to n (the number of pounds) as the value of r (the price per pound) is changed: $n = \frac{\$12}{r}$

price per lb. (r)	number of lb. (n)
.50	24
.75	
1.00	
4.00	
6.00	
12.00	
24.00	

PROBLEM 16

Complete this table to show the changing number of pounds of cheese.

Use the table in problem 16 to solve problem 17.

PROBLEM 17

a) As the price per pound increases, the number of pounds you can buy with \$12 _____.

b) When the price per pound was less than a dollar, the number of pounds you could buy was _____ than 12.

c) When the price per pound was more than a dollar, the number of pounds you could buy was _____ than 12.

d) When the price per pound was greater than \$12, the number of pounds you could buy was less than _____.

e) Complete these statements: When a number is divided by a value less than 1, the result is _____ than the original number. When a number is divided by a value greater than 1, the result is _____ than the original number. When a number is divided by a value greater than itself, the result is less than _____.

Estimating Answers

When you divide, it may help to interpret the problem in this way:

$\frac{120}{99}$ asks the question "How many 99s are there in 120?" (Estimated answer: more than 1.)

PROBLEM 18 Decide whether the answer will be more or less than the value given. Choose *more* or *less than*.

a) $\frac{59}{0.92}$ more or less than 59?

b) $\frac{43}{1.19}$ more or less than 43?

c) $\frac{79}{80}$ more or less than 1?

d) $\frac{356}{311}$ more or less than 1?

PROBLEM 19 Complete, using the estimation ideas above.

Example: $139 \div 1.02$ is less than ___139___.

a) $152 \div 0.96$ is greater than _____.

b) $71 \div 1.17$ is less than _____.

c) $45 \div 40$ is greater than _____.

d) $150 \div 160$ is less than _____.

Problem Solving with Equations ....

Use your understanding of formulas, equivalent equations, and estimation to solve these problems.

Problems 20–22 are based on this information.

> It is 350 miles from Beloit to Randolph on the interstate highway.

PROBLEM 20

Which expression shows how long it will take Hazel to make the trip if she averages 54 miles per hour?

(1) $t = \frac{350}{54}$

(2) $t = \frac{54}{350}$

(3) $t = 54 \times 350$

(4) $t = 54 + 350$

(5) Not enough information is given.

PROBLEM 21

a) If Hazel averages 54 miles per hour, estimate whether she will take more or less than 7 hours to travel from Beloit to Randolph.

b) Explain your answer.

PROBLEM 22

If gas costs $1.20 per gallon, how much will Hazel pay for gas?

(1) $1.20
(2) $8.40
(3) $12.00
(4) $52.00
(5) Not enough information is given.

Problem 23 is based on this chart.

Price	Pounds of Apples
.79	1
1.58	2
2.37	3
?	4

PROBLEM 23

What would be the cost of 40 pounds of apples?

(1) $ .79
(2) $1.58
(3) $3.16
(4) $15.80
(5) $31.60

Problems 24–25 are based on this road sign.

> Gary   30 miles
> Chicago 60 miles

On the highway, Sandy saw this sign. She knows that Gary and Chicago are on the same road.

PROBLEM 24

Which of the following expressions tells how far it is from Chicago to Gary?

(1) 60 + 30
(2) 60 − 30
(3) 60 × 30
(4) $\frac{60}{30}$
(5) Not enough information is given.

PROBLEM 25

If you are driving 65 miles per hour, how long will it take you to get to Chicago from the sign Sandy saw?

(1) less than an hour
(2) exactly 1 hour
(3) 2 hours
(4) 4 hours
(5) Not enough information is given.

You may use your calculator on any problem for which it seems appropriate.

1. Write 2 equivalent division equations for $40 = 8 \times 5$.

2. a) Write an equation to find the cost (c) of 6 shirts at $24.99 each.

   b) Find the cost of the shirts (without tax).

3. a) Write an equation to find the price (r) of 1 shirt if 6 cost $186.

   b) Find the cost of each shirt.

4. A rectangle contains 84 sq. ft. If its length is 7 ft., what is its width?

   a) Write the formula for the area of a rectangle and substitute the known values.

   b) Write an equivalent equation so that the unknown is alone on one side of the equation.

   c) Find the precise answer.

5. Manny saves $50 a week from his paycheck. How many weeks does he have to save before he has savings of $1,000?

   a) Substitute values into

   Total savings = number of weeks × weekly savings.

   b) Write an equivalent equation and solve.

6. A package of hamburger meat contains 1.2 pounds of meat. The price per pound is $2.45.

   a) Substitute the values into the equation $c = nr$.

   b) Will the cost be more or less than $2.45? Support your answer.

7. Write expressions for each problem below.

   a) A trucker finds that he can average 50 mph on interstate highways. Write an expression to find how far he can travel (d) in k hours.

   b) Write an expression for the number of bottles (n) that can be purchased with $12.00 if each bottle costs $$b$.

   c) The cost of 12 ears of corn was $$n$. Write an expression for the price (c) of one ear (r).

8. A rental car company charges the rates shown in the table below. Continuing the pattern shown, determine the total cost for renting a car for 5 days.

Number of Days	Total Cost
1	$19.95
2	$39.90
3	$59.85
4	$79.80
5	

GED Practice

9. How long would it take an airliner traveling at 520 miles per hour to fly the 3,640 miles from New York to Paris?

   (1) 6 hours
   (2) 7 hours
   (3) 16 hours
   (4) 17 hours
   (5) Not enough information is given.

10. If x books, all the same price, cost $49.95, which expression tells you the price of one book?

   (1) $49.95 + x$
   (2) $49.95 - x$
   (3) $(49.95)(x)$
   (4) $\dfrac{49.95}{x}$
   (5) $(49.95)(49.95) x$

11. Tracy walks 0.8 of a mile to school. Which expression shows how far she walks to and from school in a five-day week?

   (1) $(.8)(2)$
   (2) $(.8)(2)(5)$
   (3) $(.8) + (2)(5)$
   (4) $(.8)(5)$
   (5) $(.8)(5) - (2)$

Multi-Step Problems

Mental Math Exercises

If it is true that:	Can it be true that:
1. $50 \times 75 = 3{,}750$	$45 \times 75 = 3{,}825$?
2. $5{,}700 \div 100 = 57$	$5{,}700 \div 95 = 60$?
3. $36 \times 10 = 360$	$36 \times 10.5 = 378$?
4. $100 \div 5 = 20$	$100 \div 5.5 = 22.5$?
5. $4.6 \times 2.5 = 11.5$	$4.42 \times 2.5 = 11.05$?

Until now, you have been working with problems that take one step to solve.

Example:

How much do 3 pounds of hamburger cost if one pound costs $2.45?

$c = 3 \times \$2.45$
$c = \$7.35$

The GED Test contains many problems that take more than one step to solve.

Example:

If you bought 3 pounds of hamburger at $2.45 a pound, how much change would you get back from $20?

$c = 3 \times \$2.45$
$c = \$7.35$ cost of hamburger
change = $\$20.00 - \$7.35 = \$12.65$

Before you can solve these multi-step problems, you need to learn how to write them.

• Order of Operations . . . .

What is the answer to this problem? $4 + 5 \times 6 = ?$

Is it 54? ($4 + 5 = 9$; $9 \times 6 = 54$)   OR   Is it 34? ($5 \times 6 = 30$; $30 + 4 = 34$)

Try it on your calculator. Just press the keys in order as you see them.

$\boxed{4}\ \boxed{+}\ \boxed{5}\ \boxed{\times}\ \boxed{6}\ \boxed{=}\ \boxed{}$ Some calculators will display the answer 54, and others will display 34.

Which answer should you believe? Only one of these can be the correct answer.

To avoid this kind of uncertainty when more than one operation is involved in a problem, mathematicians have agreed on an order of operations. Here are two parts of that agreement.

1) **Multiply and divide before you add and subtract.** Multiplication and division are at a higher level than addition and subtraction.

- So, in the problem above, multiply the 5×6 first.

$$4 + 5 \times 6$$
$$4 + 30 = 34$$

Examples:

$9 + 30 \div 3$ $100 - 25 \times 3$
$9 + 10 = 19$ $100 - 75 = 25$

2) Do each *level* of operations in order from left to right.

Notice in the following examples—multiplication and division are carried out, from left to right, before addition and subtraction.

$20 - 8 \div 2$ Divide first. $40 \div 2 \times 5$ Only multiplication
$20 - 4 = 16$ Then subtract. $20 \times 5 = 100$ and division. Work
                                       from left to right.

$12 - 8 - 3$ Only subtraction. $30 \div 6 + 24 \div 6$ Complete the
$4 - 3 = 1$ Work from left to $5 + 4 = 9$ divisions first. Then
                right.   add.

$8 \times 7 \times 5$ All multiplication. $32 + 5 + 25 + 8$ All addition.
$40 \times 7 = 280$ Regroup to make $30 + 40 = 70$ Choose the order
                it easier.   and grouping you
                                                    wish.

PROBLEM 1   Using the rules for order of operations, solve these problems.

a) $12 \div 4 + 2$ $5 + 2 \times 3$ $24 - 6 \div 2$ $32 \div 8 \div 2$

b) $12 + 3 \div 3$ $33 \div 3 + 8 \div 4$ $5 + 8 \div 4 - 3$ $6 \times 3 + 6 \times 2$

c) $5 \times 13 \times 4$ $17 + 16 + 3$ $15 - 3 + 3$ $49 \div 7 \times 7$

Parentheses and Division Bars

How do parentheses, ( ) or [ ] , fit into these rules about the order of operations? You have already seen that operations inside parentheses are done first.

For example, $34 + (7 + 43)$ The parentheses make the addition
$34 + 50 = 84$ easier by grouping compatible pairs.

In most cases, however, parentheses are placed in a problem for the purpose of *changing* the standard order of operations.

$7 \times (4 + 5)$ Without the parentheses, you would multiply first. $7 \times 4 + 5$
$7 \times 9 = 63$ With them, you add first. $28 + 5 = 33$

Parentheses have the highest priority. First do the operations within parentheses, then follow the standard order of operations.

There is another grouping symbol: the fraction line (or division bar). The line in a division problem means "divided by," but it also serves the same purpose as parentheses.

• • •
Complete operations within parentheses or on top and bottom of the division bar (fraction line) before anything else.
• • •

$\dfrac{24 - 6}{3}$ This means the same as $\dfrac{(24 - 6)}{3}$ $\dfrac{5 + 7}{4 - 2}$ This is the same as $\dfrac{(5 + 7)}{(4 - 2)}$

$\dfrac{18}{3}$ Do the operation on top first. $\dfrac{12}{2}$ Before you divide, do the operations above and below the line.

6 Divide. 6

PROBLEM 2   Do the indicated operations. Compare the answers of pairs grouped by the word *and*.

a) $12 - 6 \div 2$ and   b) $(12 - 6) \div 2$ g) $\dfrac{12 - 7}{5}$

c) $3 + 12 \times 2$ and   d) $(3 + 12) \times 2$ h) $\dfrac{21 - 7}{7 - 5}$

e) $6 \times 3 + 2$ and   f) $6 \times (3 + 2)$ i) $15 \div (6 - 4 + 1)$

The Distributive Property ....

In Lesson 8, you learned to find the areas of rectangles. Find these areas.

$6 \times (3 + 2)$
6×5
30

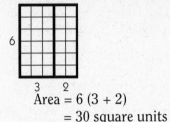

Area = 6 (3 + 2)
= 30 square units

$(6 \times 3) + (6 \times 2)$
$18 + 12$
30

Area = 6 • 3 + 6 • 2
= 30 square units

The **distributive property** of multiplication states that $a(b + c)$ is the same as $ab + ac$, and $a(b - c)$ is the same as $ab - ac$.

The answers to both problems are the same, just as both areas are the same. $(6(3 + 2) = 6 • 2 + 6 • 3)$ This is an example of the **distributive property** of multiplication over addition.

The distributive property allows you to work problems two ways. Sometimes one is easier than the other.

Example A:
$15 \times (20 + 3)$—also written as $15(20 + 3)$

Factored Form	Expanded Form (Easier)
$15 \times (20 + 3)$ Add first	$(15 \times 20) + (15 \times 3)$ Multiply first
15×23	$300 + 45$
345	345

Example B:
$13(15 + 5)$

Factored Form (Easier)	Expanded Form
$13(15 + 5)$	$13(15) + 13(5)$
$13(20)$	$195 + 65$
260	260

Writing the Expanded Form: $ab + ac$

The distributive property states that a number in front of parentheses is distributed to each of the numbers inside. This is the **expanded form**.

> We show this as:
> $a(b + c) = ab + ac$
> $a(b - c) = ab - ac$

$7 (15 - 9) = 7(15) - 7(9)$ Use the minus sign.

$2 (5 + 3) = 2(5) + 2(3)$ Use the plus sign.

$m (10 + 4) = 10(m) + 4(m)$ Multiply numbers and letters.

PROBLEM 3   Using the distributive property, write these expressions in expanded form.

Example: $12(40 + 6) = 12(40) + 12(6)$

a) $8 (2 + 5)$ c) $12 (10 - 5)$ e) $13 (x + 3)$

b) $34 (21 + 19)$ d) $5 (4 + 3 + 8)$ f) $k (8 - 3)$

Writing the Factored Form: $a(b + c)$

The distributive property says that if the same number (a) is a factor of both terms, you can write it outside of the parentheses.

We show this as:
$ab + ac = a(b + c)$
$ab - ac = a(b - c)$

This is the factored form.

$3(9) - 3(2) = 3(9 - 2)$ Use the minus sign.

$(7 \times 2) + (7 \times 8) = 7(2 + 8)$ Use the plus sign.

$5n + 6n = n(5 + 6)$ A letter can be a common factor.

The last example could also be written as: $5n + 6n = 11n$.

This shows an important principle of algebra:

To add or subtract terms that have the same letter, just add or subtract the numbers, and carry the letter along.

$4x + 13x = 17x$ $12b - 7b = 5b$ $4a + a = 5a$ (Remember, a means $1a$.)

$4 + 13 = 17$ $12 - 7 = 5$ $4 + 1 = 5$

PROBLEM 4 Use the distributive property to write these expressions in factored form.

a) $6 \cdot 8 + 6 \cdot 2$ c) $22 \times 10 - 22 \times 4$ e) $7x + 6x$

b) $12(7) + 12(3)$ d) $11 \cdot 17 - 11 \cdot 7$ f) $13n - 9n$

For the GED Test, it is essential that you recognize that the factored form and the expanded form are equal to each other. This type of item could appear on the GED Test.

Example:

Sam worked for 7 hours on Saturday for $6 per hour and also worked for 3 hours on Sunday for $6 per hour. Which expression shows how much Sam was paid for this work?

Your first thought might have been to set up the problem like this:

$6(7) + 6(3)$, which is the same as choice **(3)** $6(7 + 3)$

(1) $7 + 6 + 3 + 6$
(2) $7 \times 6 \times 3 \times 6$
(3) $6(7 + 3)$
(4) $7(6 + 3)$
(5) $3(7 + 6)$

PROBLEM 5 Which expression is equal to $5x + x - 2x$?

(1) 5
(2) 6
(3) $3x$
(4) $4x$
(5) $4x^3$

• Using Your Calculator . . . .

When multi-step problems are too complicated to do mentally, you may want to use a calculator. You have already discovered that different calculators handle problems in different ways and get different answers. You need to know what to expect from your own calculator when you press a sequence of keys.

Example: Which operation does your calculator do first?

Watch your calculator display as you key in each step of the following problem. Does it follow the one shown?

Key in: ⑶ ⊕ ⑵ ⊗ ⑷ ⊖ ⑸ ⊜

Display: | 3. | 3. | 2. | 2. | 4. | 11. | 5. | 6. |

If your calculator display followed the same pattern as the one printed, the order of operations rules have been programmed into your calculator, a feature that more advanced calculators have.

If your display did not follow the one printed, you will need to follow the standard order of operations as shown on pages 76 and 77.

For the example above, $3 + (2 \times 4) - 5 = ?$, you could:

1) **Enter the problem into the calculator in the correct order.** The multiplication must be done first, so enter it first.

⑵ ⊗ ⑷ ⊕ ⑶ ⊖ ⑸ ⊜   to get the correct answer of 6.

2) **Remember or write down the intermediate results as you proceed.**

By visualizing the problem as $3 + (2 \times 4) - 5$, you could do the multiplication first mentally.

Enter ⑶ ⊕ ⑻ ⊖ ⑸ ⊜ to get the correct answer of 6.

3) **Use the memory keys.**

If you want to use these keys, consult the instruction book that came with your calculator.

You must figure out what your calculator does and what you have to do with it to get the correct answers. The calculator can only make the computing easy; you will need to think about how to enter the problem.

Example A: $1,008 - (24 \times 11)$

Multiply. ⑵⑷ ⊗ ⑾ ⊜ 264
(Write down this partial answer.)

Subtract. ⑴⓪⓪⑻ ⊖ ②⑹⑷ ⊜ 744

Example B: $(45 \times 3) + (92 \times 8)$

Multiply once. ④⑤ ⊗ ⑶ ⊜ 135
(Write down the partial answer.)

Multiply again. ⑨② ⊗ ⑻ ⊜ 736
(Keep the second answer.)

Add to the second answer ⑺③⑹ ⊕ ①③⑤ ⊜ 871

PROBLEM 6 Find the answers to these problems, using whatever method works with your calculator.

a) $256 \div 32 \times 4$

b) $(437 + 78) \times 31$

c) $2,604 - 45 \times 32$

d) $\dfrac{650 + 376}{3}$

e) $30 \times 72 + 25 \times 43$

f) $\dfrac{1,364}{45 + 79}$

Solving Real Problems with Many Steps . . . .

Perimeters of Rectangles

When finding the perimeter (sum of the lengths of the sides) of a rectangle, you can use the distributive property.

There are 2 ways of writing the perimeter of the rectangle:

$P = (2 \times 8) + (2 \times 3)$ expanded form

$P = 2(8 + 3)$ factored form

In both cases, the perimeter is 22.

Checking the formulas page (page 246), you see that this example has followed the formula for the perimeter of a rectangle: $P = 2l + 2w$. This formula written in factored form would be $P = 2(l + w)$. You may use either form when solving problems.

Example A:

Find the perimeter of a rectangle whose length = 8.5 cm and whose width = 3.5 cm.

$P = 2(8.5) + 2(3.5)$ OR $P = 2 (8.5 + 3.5)$

$P = 17 + 7 = 24$ cm $P = 2(12) = 24$ cm

Example B:

How much fencing is required to enclose a rectangular garden that is b ft. long and 5 ft. wide?

$2 \cdot b + 2 \cdot 5$ OR $2(b + 5)$

$2b + 10$ $2b + 10$

Finding the Mean (Average)

Finding the average of a group of numbers is a way of computing one number that is typical of the group. To find the mean (average): (1) add all the numbers in the group, then (2) divide that sum by the number of numbers in the group.

Example C:

In four games of a tournament, a basketball player scored 25, 28, 19, and 35 points, respectively. On average, how many points did he score in a game?

Step 1: Add the scores. $25 + 28 + 19 + 35 = 107$

Step 2: Divide by 4, the number of scores. $\frac{107}{4} = 26.75$

The two steps in the problem above can be written as one equation:

$$\text{Mean} = \frac{25 + 28 + 19 + 35}{4} \longleftarrow \text{This means "divided by."}$$

Compare this example with the formula for the mean found on the formulas page (page 246). The formula should be easier to understand now that you have seen a specific example.

On the GED Test, you will see multi-step problems represented as one equation. Throughout the rest of this book, you will have practice recognizing and working with these set-up problems.

PROBLEM 7   For the perimeter of the rectangle to the right:

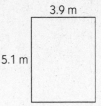
3.9 m

5.1 m

   a) Write an expression in expanded form: $P = 2l + 2w$
   b) Write an expression in factored form: $P = 2(l + w)$
   c) Find the perimeter of the rectangle, using the form that makes the computation easier.

PROBLEM 8

The high temperatures for five summer days were recorded as shown below.

M	T	W	Th	F
85°	90°	70°	80°	85°

   a) Write the expression for the average temperature as one equation.

   b) What was the average temperature?

PROBLEM 9

Last week Ramon worked on a research project for the number of hours shown on the chart. Which expression shows the average hours he worked per day?

(1) $\dfrac{4 + 5 + 6 + 3 + 4}{5}$

(2) $\dfrac{4 \times 5 \times 6 \times 3 \times 4}{5}$

(3) $\dfrac{(4 + 5) \times (3 + 4)}{6}$

Mon.	4 hr.
Tues.	5 hr.
Wed.	6 hr.
Thurs.	3 hr.
Fri.	4 hr.

Miscellaneous Many-Step Monsters

Before you try solving word problems that have more than one step, do some translating of expressions from English to mathematics. Remember that the **sum** is the answer when you add and the **product** is the answer when you multiply.

six times five increased by 8 $6 \times 5 + 8$

eight less than 4 times 12 $4 \times 12 - 8$ Order is important in subtraction.

three times the sum of 8 and x $3(8 + x)$ Needs parentheses to show that you add first

three more than the product of 8 and 7 $3 + 8 \times 7$ No parentheses necessary

44.99 divided by the sum of 5 and 6 $\dfrac{44.99}{5 + 6}$

PROBLEM 10   Choose the correct mathematical <u>expression</u> for each statement. **Do not solve.**

   a) 3 more than 4 dozen $(3 + 4) \times 12$ OR $3 + 4 \times 12$

   b) 3 quarters less than 5 dollars $5 - (3 \times .25)$ OR $(.3 \times .25) - 5$

   c) the number of legs on 5 birds and 3 dogs $5 + 2 + 3 + 4$ OR $5(2) + 3(4)$

   d) the number of shoes in 5 men's pairs and 8 women's pairs $5(2) + 8(2)$ OR $5(2 + 8)$

PROBLEM 11   Write these expressions mathematically. **Do not solve.**

   a) six more than three times seven

   b) 10 times the difference between 15 and 7

   c) 6 times the sum of 5 and 8

   d) half of the difference between 35 and 25

   e) 98.99 divided by the sum of 4 and 3

   f) the price of 5 25¢ stamps and 7 15¢ stamps

   g) the amount earned in 8 hours at $8 per hour and 3 hours at $12 per hour

More Multi-Step Problems

The first example shows two correct ways to solve the same problem.

Example A:

A small office purchased 20 boxes of computer paper in January and 9 boxes in September last year. If the cost of each box was $6.25, what was the total amount the office spent on computer paper that year?

How to plan it:
You could choose to add the 20 boxes and 9 boxes, then to multiply that sum by $6.25.

You could find the same answer by multiplying 20 boxes by $6.25 and 9 boxes by $6.25, then adding those products.

How to write it:
$t = 6.25 (20 + 9)$
$t = 6.25 (29)$
$t = \$181.25$

$t = 6.25 \cdot 20 + 6.25 \cdot 9$
$t = 125 + 56.25$
$t = \$181.25$

The second example shows the fraction line serving two purposes: it means "divided by," and it also is a grouping symbol indicating which operation to do first.

Example B:

A case of 12 cans of motor oil costs $11.50. For a limited time, a discount of $2.50 per case was given. What was the price per can at this special price?

How to plan it:
First, find the discounted price by subtracting $2.50 from $11.50. Divide the difference by 12, the number of cans.

How to write it:
$$p = \frac{11.50 - 2.50}{12}$$
$$p = \frac{9.00}{12}$$
$$p = \$.75$$

PROBLEM 12 For problem 12, write each problem in a single equation and solve. Compare your equation with those written by others in the class, and determine whether the expressions are equivalent.

a) The package on a coil of rope indicates that it is 50 ft. long. George cuts off 12 pieces, each of which is 3 ft. long. How long is the rope remaining in the coil?

b) The expenses of a trip were shared by four people. They spent $283 on gas and $165 on lodging. What was each person's share of the expenses?

c) What is the total cost of 3 cheeseburgers at $2.05 each, 3 orders of fries at $.70 each, and 3 medium soft drinks at $.85 each?

PROBLEM 13 How much change from 2 $20 bills should Bart receive if he purchased 2 shirts at $14.95 each, a belt at $7.50, and paid tax of $1.88?

(1) $.72
(2) $9.72
(3) $29.90
(4) $37.40
(5) $39.28

Example C shows how a multi-step problem can be written as one equation.

Example C:

A used car is priced at $4,500. Under a time payment plan, Carlos would make a down payment of $500 and 36 monthly payments of $150 each. How much extra would Carlos pay if he used the time payment plan?	**How to plan it:** Multiply 36 payments by $150, and add the sum to $500. Then subtract $4,500.	**How to write it:** $d = 36 \cdot 150 + 500 - 4,500$ $d = 5,400 + 500 - 4,500$ $d = 5,900 - 4,500$ $d = \$1,400$

Example D shows how to incorporate a quick mental subtraction (44 hours − 40 hours = 4 hours) into the process of writing a single equation.

Example D:

Sarah's regular rate of pay is $5.85 per hour for the first 40 hours that she works in a week. She is paid double that amount for each overtime hour that she works. How much will she be paid for a week in which she works 44 hours?	**How to plan it:** Mentally subtract 40 hours from 44. Then multiply 40 hours by $5.85 and 4 hours by (2 × $5.85). Finally, add those products together.	**How to write it:** $p = 40 \cdot \$5.85 +$ $\quad 4 \cdot (2 \cdot \$5.85)$ $p = 234 + 46.80$ $p = \$280.80$

PROBLEM 14 For problem 14, write each problem in a single equation. Estimate the answer. Then solve for the precise answer, using your calculator if necessary.

a) The Blackwells found some carpeting they liked for a price of $17.95 per sq. yd. installed. They need 50 sq. yd. If they purchase this carpet, how much of their redecorating budget of $2,000 will be left?

b) Ray earns a salary of $23,245 per year, and his wife, Rowena, earns $10,755 per year. What is their combined *monthly* income?

c) When driving on the highway, Betty averages 55 mph. If she drove for three hours in the morning and 4 hours in the afternoon, how far did she drive?

d) Vance earns $6.25 an hour for the first 8 hours he works each day. He is paid $10 an hour for each additional hour that he works. One day he worked 11.5 hours. How much did he earn that day?

PROBLEM 15 A gallon of paint should cover 400 sq. ft. Which of the following expressions shows how many gallons must be purchased to paint a side of a building that is 154 ft. long and 22 ft. high?

(1) $154 \times 22 \times 400$

(2) $(154 + 22) \times 400$

(3) $\dfrac{154 + 22}{400}$

(4) $\dfrac{154 \times 22}{400}$

(5) $\dfrac{400}{154 \times 22}$

You may use your calculator on any problem for which it seems appropriate.

1. Which pairs of expressions are equal to each other?

   a) $20 - 4 + 5$ $20 - (4 + 5)$

   b) $7 + k + 1$ $7 + (k + 1)$

   c) $8 \times 6 \div 6$ $8 \times (6 \div 6)$

   d) $(4)(m) + 2$ $4m + 2$

   e) $50 - (5 \cdot 3)$ $50 - 5 \times 3$

   f) $7 \times 6 + 8$ $7 \times (6 + 8)$

   g) $6 \cdot 3 + 4 \cdot 5$ $(6 \cdot 3) + (4 \cdot 5)$

   h) $10\,(8 + 7)$ $10 \cdot 8 + 10 \cdot 7$

   i) $6x + 3x$ $9x$

2. Using the rules for the order of operations, find the value of each of these expressions.

   a) $19 - 7 \div 7$

   b) $31 \div (6 - 5)$

   c) $48 \div 6 \times 2$

   d) $\dfrac{10 + 14}{8}$

   e) $\dfrac{22 - 6}{13 - 9}$

   f) $8 \cdot 9 + 8 \cdot 10$

3. Using your calculator, find the answer to each of these problems.

   a) $13 + 11 \times 12$

   b) $(13 + 11) \times 12$

   c) $30 \cdot 15 + 31 \cdot 16$

   d) $\dfrac{33 + 127}{5}$

   e) $176 - 148 \div 4$

4. Write a single mathematics expression that means the same as

   a) five times nine decreased by 3

   b) ten times the sum of 30 and 8

   c) 6 more than the product of 4 and b

   d) the sum of 12 and m divided by 15

5. Find the perimeter and the area of this rectangle.

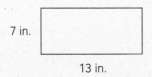

7 in.

13 in.

For problems 6–10:

   a) Write the problem in a single equation.

   b) Estimate the answer.

   c) Then solve, using your calculator if necessary.

6. How much change should Paul get from $10 if he bought 5 candy bars that cost $.35 each?

7. Barbara is paid $7.20 an hour for the first 40 hours she works during a week. If she works more than 40 hours, she is paid 1.5 times her normal rate for each hour over 40 that she works. How much should she be paid for a week in which she works 45 hours?

8. A car rental agency advertises a rate of $24 per day plus $.15 a mile for every mile driven. How much would the agency charge for a 2-day rental in which the car was driven 200 miles?

9. Four luxury cars were tested for fuel efficiency. The numbers of miles they got per gallon of gasoline were 23, 20, 27, and 21 respectively. What is the average fuel efficiency for these cars?

10. According to one source, an egg contains 26 mg of calcium, and a piece of toast contains 43 mg of calcium. How many mg of calcium are in a breakfast of 2 eggs and 3 pieces of toast?

GED Practice

11. Which expression indicates the total cost (disregarding tax) of an order of 5 lunch specials at $3.95 each and 5 coffees at $.50?

    (1) $5 + 3.95 + 5 + 0.50$ (4) $5 \times 3.95 \times 0.50$
    (2) $5(3.95 + 0.50)$ (5) $25(3.95 + 0.50)$
    (3) $10(3.95 + 0.50)$

12. Sue watches about 1.5 hours of television on Monday and Wednesday nights. On Tuesdays and Thursdays, she watches 2.5 hours of television. Choose the expression that shows how many hours of television she watches for these 4 days of the week.

    (1) $1.5 + 2.5 + 4$ (4) $2\,(1.5 + 2.5)$
    (2) $4\,(1.5 + 2.5)$ (5) $2\,(1.5 + 2.5 + 4)$
    (3) 1.5×2.5

• **Part One** . . . .

Before going on further in this book, use the following exercise to maintain your skills. If you are having difficulty, this is a good time to go back and review.

1. Write an <u>expression</u> for each of the following figures. **Do not solve.**

    a) area: _____   b) perimeter: _____   c) volume: _____

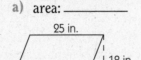 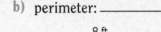 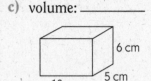

2. Write an expression for each of the following. Then solve.

    a) the number of weeks in 3 years

    b) the amount of money earned by each of 4 waitresses if $344 in tips is shared evenly amongst them

    c) the cost of 2 dozen cupcakes if one cupcake costs $.43

    d) the seating capacity of an auditorium with 50 rows of y seats

3. **Estimate** an answer to the following:

    a) $2,073 \div 500$ b) 8×189 c) $99(12)$ d) $187 \div 90$ e) $403 \div 7$

4. What is the area of the shaded floor sketched at right?

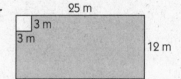

5. Continuing the pattern shown on the chart at right, how much does Gallagher Landscaping charge for 6 cubic feet of bark mulch?

Gallagher Mulch Prices	
1 cu. ft.	$22.50
2 cu. ft.	$45.00
3 cu. ft.	$67.50
4 cu. ft.	$90.00

6. Use the rules of order of operations to solve the following:

    a) $20 - 14 \div 2$ b) $(12 + 20) \div 4 + 102$ c) $\dfrac{74 - 50}{8}$

7. Write an equation to find the number of hours it would take to cycle 45 miles if you rode at a rate of 15 miles per hour. Then solve the equation.

Part Two

Now put your skills to work on some GED-type math problems.

1. A Jumboburger contains 1,119 grams of sodium. Large french fries contain 689 grams of sodium. Which of the following expressions gives the grams of sodium in 4 Jumboburgers and 4 large fries?

   (1) $1,119 + 689 + 4 + 4$
   (2) $\dfrac{1,119 + 689}{4}$
   (3) $4(1,119 + 689)$
   (4) $\dfrac{4}{1,119 + 689}$
   (5) $\dfrac{1,119 - 689}{4}$

2. MaryLou takes her work to be photocopied at QuikPrint. The store charges a $5.00 set-up fee, then $.07 per page. How much would MaryLou pay to copy a 96-page document?

   (1) $5.96
   (2) $6.72
   (3) $11.72
   (4) $480.00
   (5) $486.72

3. Which expression shows how many kilometers per hour a ship traveled if it covered 720 kilometers in h hours?

   (1) $720h$
   (2) $\dfrac{720}{h}$
   (3) $\dfrac{h}{720}$
   (4) $720 + h$
   (5) $720 - h$

4. How many level cubic feet of sand can be poured into the sandbox shown below?

   (1) 1
   (2) 25
   (3) 26
   (4) 130
   (5) 260

   2 ft.
   10 ft.
   13 ft.

5. Which expression tells you the number of centimeters of braid needed to trim the edges of the pillow pictured below?

   (1) $22 + 45$
   (2) 22×45
   (3) $\dfrac{(22 \times 45)}{2}$
   (4) $2 \times 22 \times 45$
   (5) $2(22 + 45)$

   22 m
   45 m

6. A forklift can hold up to 3,000 pounds per load. How many cartons, each weighing 150 pounds, can it hold at one time?

   (1) 15
   (2) 20
   (3) 1,500
   (4) 2,850
   (5) 450,000

7. Nina paid $2.76 for some peaches. If she bought 4 pounds, what was the price per pound?

   (1) $.19
   (2) $.69
   (3) $2.72
   (4) $2.80
   (5) $11.04

8. How many square feet of area is in the shaded area of the patio shown below?

   (1) 190
   (2) 150
   (3) 140
   (4) 110
   (5) 40

   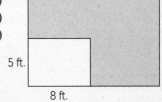

   15 ft.
   10 ft.
   5 ft.
   8 ft.

· LESSON 11 · Powers and Roots

Mental Math Exercises

1. 8 times itself = ?
2. 36 = ? times itself
3. 4 times itself = ?
4. 100 = ? times itself
5. ? = 12 times itself

The numbers that result from multiplying a number by itself are called perfect squares. In this lesson, you will learn some new ways to write these numbers and to use them to solve problems.

• Exponents ....

Remember that multiplication is a short way to do repeated addition:

$$\text{Instead of } \underbrace{7 + 7 + 7 + 7 + 7} \longrightarrow \text{write } 7 \times 5$$

five addends that are the same

There is also a shorthand way to write repeated multiplications:

$$\text{Instead of } \underbrace{2 \cdot 2 \cdot 2 \cdot 2} \longrightarrow \text{write } 2^4 \qquad 2 \text{ is the base, and 4 is the exponent}$$

four factors that are the same   read as "2 to the fourth power"

Example: 4^3

4 is the base. It is the factor that is going to be multiplied.

3 is the exponent. It tells how many 4s to multiply.

4^3 means to use 4 three times as a factor. It means $4 \cdot 4 \cdot 4$ and is equal to 64.

Example: 3^4

4 is the exponent.

$$3^4 = \underbrace{3 \cdot 3 \cdot 3 \cdot 3} = 81$$

3 is the base.   4 factors of 3

PROBLEM 1   Complete this table:

a) 6×6 6^2 "6 to the second power" or "6 squared" *
b) $5 \times 5 \times 5$ 5^3 "5 to the third power" or "5 cubed" *
c) $7 \times 7 \times 7 \times 7$ 7^4 "7 to the fourth power"
d) _____ 8^2 _____
e) _____   _____   "2 to the fifth power"
f) 5×5 _____   _____
g) _____   _____   "4 cubed"
h) _____ 8^4 _____
i) _____   _____   "4 to the eighth power"
j) $m \times m$ _____   _____

*Note that you can write numbers to the second and third powers in two different ways.

• Squares . . . .

Only two of the powers had special ways to be named—the squares and the cubes. These powers have special names because they can be represented by real things in our lives. This lesson will concentrate on the squares and their practical uses.

Remember that you found the area of a rectangle by multiplying its length by its width.

Area = lw

When all sides of a rectangle are equal, it is a square. To find the area of a square, you multiply a side by itself.

Area = s²

Examples:

Find the area of a square whose side is 11 m long.

$Area = s^2$
$A = 11^2 = 11 \times 11$
$A = 121 \text{ m}^2$

Remember from Lesson 8 that you find area in square units.

How many square inches are in a square foot?

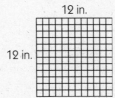

12 in.

12 in.

A square foot is a square whose sides are each 1 ft. (12 inches) long.

$Area = s^2$
$A = 12^2 = 12 \times 12$
$A = 144 \text{ sq. in. (in a square foot)}$

Some situations require you to change units as a step in solving the problem.

Example: How many <u>square yards</u> of carpet are necessary to cover a floor that measures 15 ft. by 12 ft.?

Solution 1: There are 3 ft. in one yard. In this problem, it is easy to change the feet to yards (divide each side by 3) before you begin to find the area.

Solution 2: Since there are 3 ft. in one yard, there are 3^2 or 9 sq. ft. in 1 sq. yd. You could find the area in sq. ft. first, then divide that by 9 to find the number of square yards.

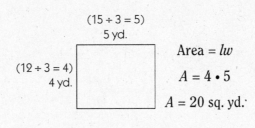

(12 ÷ 3 = 4)
4 yd.

(15 ÷ 3 = 5)
5 yd.

$Area = lw$
$A = 4 \cdot 5$
$A = 20 \text{ sq. yd.}$

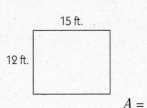

15 ft.

12 ft.

equation to find square yards

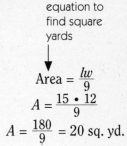

$Area = \dfrac{lw}{9}$
$A = \dfrac{15 \cdot 12}{9}$
$A = \dfrac{180}{9} = 20 \text{ sq. yd.}$

PROBLEM 2

a) Find the area of a square whose sides are each 15 mm long.

b) How many square <u>inches</u> are there in a square yard? (Hint: 1 yd. = 3 × 12 in. = ? in.)

c) A rectangular mirror measures 16 in. by 18 in. What is its area in square feet?

d) There are 10 millimeters in 1 centimeter. How many mm^2 are there in 1 cm^2?

e) A rectangular section of grip tape for a skateboard measures 25 cm by 30 cm. How many <u>mm^2</u> are covered by its surface? (There are 10 mm in 1 cm.)

Square Roots

In the last section, you worked with a new operation with numbers: taking them to a power. Specifically, you performed the operation of squaring—multiplying a number by itself. In this section, you will find **square roots**—the opposite operation of squaring.

The inverse operation of squaring would have to *undo* what squaring *does*.

Example: Because you know that   You also know that:
$6^2 = 36$ "6 squared is 36" $\longrightarrow$ $\sqrt{36} = 6$ "the square root of 36 is 6"
$4^2 = 16$ "4 squared is 16" $\longrightarrow$ $\sqrt{16} = 4$ "the square root of 16 is 4"
The equations $6^2 = 36$ and $\sqrt{36} = 6$ are **equivalent**

Examples: Find the following values:

$\sqrt{49}$ Think: "What number times itself equals 49?" $\sqrt{49} = 7$
$\sqrt{81}$ Think: "What number times itself equals 81?" $\sqrt{81} = 9$

What is the length of the side of a square whose area is 64 sq. in.?

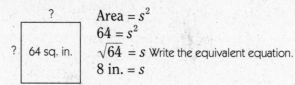

$Area = s^2$
$64 = s^2$
$\sqrt{64} = s$ Write the equivalent equation.
$8\ in. = s$

PROBLEM 3 Evaluate:
a) $\sqrt{16}$ b) $\sqrt{25}$ c) $\sqrt{100}$ d) $\sqrt{144}$

PROBLEM 4 Find the length of the side of a square whose area is 81 sq. ft.

Order of Operations

Where do these new operations fit into the order of operations? They are at a higher level than multiplication, so they must be completed before you multiply or divide. The entire set of rules for order of operations is as follows:

1. Complete the operations within **p**arentheses.
2. Do the operations with **e**xponents and radicals.
3. Complete the **m**ultiplications and **d**ivisions from left to right.
4. Complete the **a**dditions and **s**ubtractions from left to right.

A memorizing trick:
Please
Excuse
My **D**ear
Aunt **S**ally

$4(8) - 5^2$ No operations within parentheses, $200 - 10(4)^2$ The exponent applies only to
$4(8) - 25$ so square the five first, $200 - 10(16)$ the 4.
$32 - 25$ then multiply, $200 - 160$ Square the 4 first,
7 and finally subtract. 40 then multiply that by 10, and finally subtract.

When there is an operation to complete within parentheses, it must be done first:

$(3 + 4)^2 = 7^2 = 49$ $(3 \times 4)^2 = (12)^2 = 144$

PROBLEM 5 Evaluate:

a) $5 + 3^2$ $(5 + 3)^2$ $5 + 3(2)$
b) $2(3)^2$ $(2 \times 3)^2$ $2 \times 3(2)$
c) $5(6) + 4^2$ $5^2 - \sqrt{4}$ $\sqrt{16} + \sqrt{4}$

Pythagorean Theorem . . . .

A right triangle has one right angle (90°). The lengths of the sides of a right triangle have a relationship that was first proven to be true by the Greek mathematician Pythagoras.

This is his Pythagorean theorem:

> The square of the **hypotenuse** (longest side—opposite the right angle) of a right triangle is equal to the sum of the squares of the other two sides.

This formula is usually written as: $a^2 + b^2 = c^2$, where a and b are the two legs of a right triangle and c is the side opposite the right angle—the **hypotenuse.**

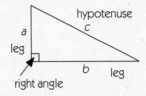

The Pythagorean theorem works both ways: if you have a right triangle, then you know that $a^2 + b^2 = c^2$. Also, if $a^2 + b^2 = c^2$, then you know that you have a right triangle.

Certain groups of whole numbers fit into this relationship nicely.

For example, $3^2 + 4^2 = 5^2$
                 $9 + 16 = 25$

Because they work in this formula, 3, 4, and 5 are called a **Pythagorean triple**.

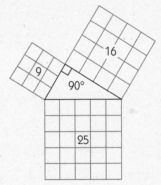

To decide whether 3 numbers can be sides of a right triangle, substitute them in the Pythagorean theorem: $a^2 + b^2 = c^2$.

Examples: Can the 3 numbers be sides of a right triangle?

2 in., 3 in., and 4 in.	30 m, 40 m, and 50 m
$2^2 + 3^2 \overset{?}{=} 4^2$	$30^2 + 40^2 \overset{?}{=} 50^2$
$4 + 9 \overset{?}{=} 16$	$900 + 1{,}600 \overset{?}{=} 2{,}500$
No, 13 *does not* equal 16.	Yes, $2{,}500 = 2{,}500$

PROBLEM 6 Decide whether these sets of numbers can be sides of a right triangle. You may wish to use your calculators.

a) 4, 5, and 6   d) 30, 40, and 50   g) 5, 12, and 13

b) 8, 15, and 17   e) 6, 11, and 12   h) 7, 24, and 25

c) 9, 12, and 15   f) 12, 16, and 20   i) 15, 20, and 25

The Pythagorean theorem allows you to find the length of the third side of a right triangle when you know the lengths of the other two sides. You can find the third side without actually measuring it.

Example: Find the length of side a.

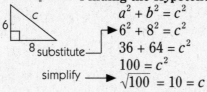

$a^2 + 8^2 = 10^2$ 6, 8, and 10 make a
$a^2 + 64 = 100$ Pythagorean triple because
$a^2 = 100 - 64$ $6^2 + 8^2$ equals 10^2
$a^2 = 36$ $36 + 64 = 100$
$a = \sqrt{36} = 6$

On the GED Test, you may have to find the missing side of a right triangle.

Examples: **Finding the Hypotenuse**

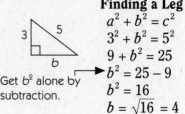

$a^2 + b^2 = c^2$
substitute — $6^2 + 8^2 = c^2$
$36 + 64 = c^2$
$100 = c^2$
simplify → $\sqrt{100} = 10 = c$

Finding a Leg

$a^2 + b^2 = c^2$
$3^2 + b^2 = 5^2$
$9 + b^2 = 25$
Get b^2 alone by → $b^2 = 25 - 9$
subtraction. $b^2 = 16$
$b = \sqrt{16} = 4$

Use the Pythagorean theorem to solve problems 7–9. Remember: This theorem applies only to right triangles.

PROBLEM 7 Sondra drives her 5-year-old son to school, following the route shown to the right. How many miles is it from the <u>school</u> to her <u>work</u>?

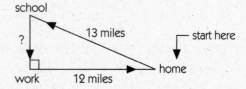

(1) 5 mi.
(2) 9 mi.
(3) 144 mi.
(4) 169 mi.
(5) 313 mi.

PROBLEM 8 The bridge across the pond is x ft. long. How long is the bridge?

(1) 5 ft.
(2) 10 ft.
(3) 40 ft.
(4) 50 ft.
(5) 250 ft.

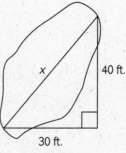

PROBLEM 9 Which of the following expressions can be used to find the length of side b?

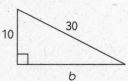

(1) $10^2 + 30^2 = b^2$
(2) $30^2 - 10^2 = b^2$
(3) $10^2 - b^2 = 30^2$
(4) $30^2 + b^2 = 10^2$
(5) $\sqrt{10} + \sqrt{30} = b$

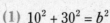

Estimating and Calculating Square Roots ....

What happens when you have to find the square root of a number that you don't know to be a perfect square? You can estimate the answer, or you can use your calculator to give you a more accurate answer.

To be a good estimator, you must know the squares of some key numbers.

Table of Squares

Number	Square
1	1
2	4
3	9
4	16
5	25
6	36
7	49
8	64
9	81
10	100
11	121
12	144
13	169
14	196
15	225
20	400
25	625
30	900
40	1,600
50	2,500
100	10,000

Example B: $\sqrt{55}$

Example A: $\sqrt{196}$

You already know the first 12 squares and square roots based on the multiplication tables. (See the table to the left.)

To **estimate**, notice one important feature on this table. As the numbers get larger, so do their squares.

You will use this table most often to find a square root.

Example A:
Find the square root of 196.

- Move down the "Square" column until you find 196.

- Look across to the left to find the 14.

How can you use the table to estimate the square roots of numbers that are not perfect squares?

Example B:
Estimate the square root of 55.

Move down the "Square" column until you come to the two numbers that 55 is between (49 and 64).

$\sqrt{55}$ is between $\sqrt{49}$ and $\sqrt{64}$ (7 and 8).
Estimated square root: between 7 and 8
Closer estimated square root: 7.5

Use the table for as long as you need it, but soon you will find that you can do this whole process mentally.

PROBLEM 10   Use the table to <u>estimate</u> these answers.

   a) The value of $\sqrt{50}$ is approximately ___.
   b) The value of $\sqrt{75}$ is between ___ and ___.
   c) The value of $\sqrt{500}$ is between ___ and ___.
   d) The value of $\sqrt{1,000}$ is between ___ and ___. It is closer to ___.
   e) The value of $\sqrt{2,000}$ is between ___ and ___. A good estimate is ___.
   f) The value of $\sqrt{30}$ is between ___ and ___. A good estimate is ___.
   g) The value of $\sqrt{125}$ is between ___ and ___. It is closer to ___.
   h) The value of $\sqrt{70}$ is between ___ and ___. A good estimate is ___.

Using the $\boxed{\sqrt{}}$ Key

The second way to find the square root of some number you don't recognize is to use your calculator. There is a $\boxed{\sqrt{}}$ key on most calculators. Use it to find $\sqrt{55}$.

Press: $\boxed{5}\boxed{5}\boxed{\sqrt{}}$ The display will immediately show the answer: $\boxed{7.4161984}$.

Example: Estimate and then find the exact square root of 200.

Estimate: 200 is between 196 and 225, so $\sqrt{200}$ is between 14 and 15. It is closer to 14.

Press: $\boxed{2}\boxed{0}\boxed{0}\boxed{\sqrt{}} = \boxed{14.142135}$

Can you think of a situation when you would need the answer to be as precise as the calculator answer? For most practical purposes, when you are figuring the length of a side of a triangle or square, your estimate is adequate. On the GED Test, you will have to find the exact square roots of numbers that are perfect squares, or you will choose an estimated square root.

Examples:

The area of a square piece of carpet is 90 sq. ft. What is the approximate length of each side?

$Area = s^2$
$90 = s^2$
$s = \sqrt{90}$
$s \approx$ halfway between 9 and 10 (estimate)
Why? Because $\sqrt{90}$ is between $\sqrt{81}$ and $\sqrt{100}$.
$s = 9.49$ (calculator answer rounded to the nearest hundredth)

A wire is attached to the top of a 15-foot pole and anchored at a spot 8 feet away from the base of the pole. How long must the wire be if the pole is perpendicular to the ground?

15 ft.   ?
8 ft.

$a^2 + b^2 = c^2$
$15^2 + 8^2 = c^2$
$225 + 64 = c^2$
$289 = c^2$
$c = \sqrt{289} = 17$ ft.

How many feet of picket fence will Natalie need to place along the longest edge of her flower bed as pictured?

4 ft.   ?
5 ft.

Caution! You cannot use the 3, 4, 5 triple.
$a^2 + b^2 = c^2$
$4^2 + 5^2 = c^2$
$16 + 25 = c^2$
$c^2 = 41$
$c = \sqrt{41} \approx$ between 6 ft. and 7 ft.

PROBLEM 11 How long is the side(s) of a square painting whose area is 169 cm^2?

s
$A = 169$ cm^2

PROBLEM 12
Find the length of side c in this triangle:

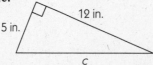
12 in.
5 in.
c

PROBLEM 13
Find the length of side b in this triangle:

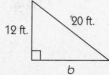
20 ft.
12 ft.
b

You may use your calculator on any problem for which it seems appropriate.

1. Evaluate the following:

   a) 7^2 g) $4(3)^2$

   b) 2^3 h) $(4 \cdot 3)^2$

   c) $\sqrt{25}$ i) $3(4)^2$

   d) $\sqrt{121}$ j) $17(10)^2$

   e) $3 + \sqrt{16}$ k) $8(5) + 6^2$

   f) $11 - 3^2$ l) $20^2 - 10^2$

2. Write an equivalent equation using exponents:

   Example: $\sqrt{100} = 10$; $10^2 = 100$

   a) $\sqrt{81} = 9$

   b) $\sqrt{361} = 19$

   c) $\sqrt{2,025} = 45$

3. Which of the following groups of numbers can be the sides of a right triangle? (Are they Pythagorean triples?)

   a) 3, 5, and 8

   b) 600, 800, and 1,000

   c) 16, 30, and 34

   d) 10, 24, and 26

4. Estimate the value of each expression. (You may use the table on page 93 if necessary.)

   a) $\sqrt{10}$

   b) $\sqrt{40}$

   c) $\sqrt{150}$

5. The area of the floor of a square tent is 196 sq. ft. How long is each side of the tent?

6. To get from her house to the subway station, Martha walks 3 blocks north and 4 blocks east. If she were able to "cut across" the blocks, how far would she have to walk?

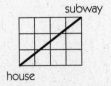

GED Practice

7. A ramp leads to a loading dock that is 4 feet above the ground. The ramp begins 8 feet away from the end of the dock. Approximately how long is the ramp?

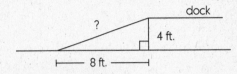

   (1) between 3 and 4 ft.
   (2) between 4 and 5 ft.
   (3) between 5 and 7 ft.
   (4) between 7 and 8 ft.
   (5) between 8 and 9 ft.

8. Roy and Elena found the carpet they liked priced at about $20 per <u>square yard</u>. This price includes padding and installation. Which of the following is a good estimate of the cost of carpeting their room, which measures 15 ft. by 18 ft.?

   (1) $270
   (2) $600
   (3) $1,200
   (4) $1,800
   (5) $5,400

9. Which of the following equations shows how to find the length of a?

   (1) $500 - 400 = a$
   (2) $500^2 - 400^2 = a^2$
   (3) $500 + 400 = a$
   (4) $500^2 + 400^2 = a^2$
   (5) $a^2 + 500^2 = 400^2$

• Radius and Diameter ....

You can find the shape of a circle in many things you see each day.

Circles involve a vocabulary all their own. You will need to be able to use these terms for the GED Test:

radius   diameter   circumference   pi (π)

The size of a circle is determined by its **radius** (r)—the distance from the center to the edge of the circle.

Every radius of a circle has the same length. $CD = CE$

The length of a circle's **diameter** (d) is double the length of its radius. The diameter is a line that extends from one side of a circle to the other and passes through the center.

The length of a diameter is the greatest distance you can measure across a circle.

Note: $r = \frac{1}{2}d$ and $d = 2r$

PROBLEM 1   What is the length of the <u>diameter</u> of each circle below?

a)    b)    c)    d)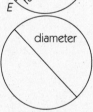

PROBLEM 2   What is the length of the <u>radius</u> of each circle below?

a)   b)   c)   d)

Circumference and Pi (π) . . . .

Circumference can be thought of as the perimeter of a circle. It answers the question, "How long would the circle be if it were broken and laid straight out?" Circumference measures length, so it is a one-dimensional measure.

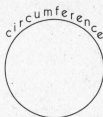

There is a special relationship between the diameter and the circumference of a circle.

The distance around the circle is a little more than 3 times the diameter, no matter what the size of the circle is.

Example: Estimate the circumference of this circle.

diameter = 4 cm
circumference is a little more than 3 times 4
c = a little more than 12 cm

The ancient Greeks named this value π (pronounced "pie"). As a result, the formula for the circumference of a circle is:

$C = \pi d.$ (In most cases, the value of π is estimated as 3.14.)

It is a good idea to estimate the circumference first, as done above, by using 3. Then find a more precise answer (if needed) with 3.14.

Example:
Find the circumference of this circle.

$C = \pi d$ (substitute 3.14 for π and 4 for d)
$C = 3.14(4)$
$C = 12.56$ cm

PROBLEM 3   First **estimate** the length of the circumference of each of these circles. Then find a more precise answer using π = 3.14. (You may wish to use your calculator.)

a)
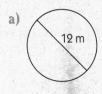
12 m

b)
5 in.

c)
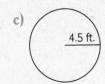
4.5 ft.

d)
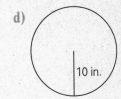
10 in.

PROBLEM 4   Many calculators have a special key for π. If yours has a π key, repeat the exercises in problem 3 using the key ⓟ.

For example, in **3a)** ① ② ⊗ ⓟ ⊜ (37.699112) Note that even when you use 3.14, your answer is an estimate.

PROBLEM 5   The diameter of a bicycle tire is 2.25 feet. How far will the bicycle travel when the wheel goes around one time?

a) Find the answer three ways: First, estimate by using 3 for π, then use 3.14 for π, and finally use the calculator key ⓟ.

b) If you needed the answer to be correct to the nearest foot, which of the above three ways would be the easiest to find, yet be accurate enough?

Using Equivalent Equations

In some situations, it is not easy to find the diameter, but you know the circumference. Using the idea of equivalent equations, you can rearrange the formula for circumference. When you know the circumference, you can find the diameter by dividing the circumference by π.

$$C = \pi d \text{ can be rewritten as } d = \frac{C}{\pi}$$

Example A:

A giant redwood tree is measured as 12 m around the base of the trunk. Approximately how thick is the tree (Hint: what is the length of the diameter?) at this point?

First, estimate:

$$d \approx \frac{12}{3}$$

Since you are dividing by a little more than 3, the answer will be a little less than 4.

Then, calculate. (You may use your calculator.)

$$d = \frac{12}{3.14}$$
$$d = 3.82$$

On the GED Test, you will find that the best first step is to estimate.

Example B:

Approximately how many feet of edging are required to go around this circular garden that has a radius of 4 ft.?

4 ft.

(1) 6.28
(2) 8
(3) 25.12
(4) 39.44
(5) 50.24

The distance around is the circumference.
$$C = \pi d \quad \text{or} \quad C = 2\pi r$$

You need the *diameter*, but are given the *radius*.
$d = 2r \quad d = 8$ ft.

First, estimate:
$C \approx 3 \times 8 = 24$ ft. Answer choice **(3)** 25.12 is the only one that is close.

PROBLEM 6   a) If the circumference of a circle is 6.28 m, what is the diameter?

b) What is the radius?

PROBLEM 7   The circular bottom of a lampshade has a diameter of 9.5 inches. To the nearest inch, how much trim is needed to go around the bottom of the lampshade?

a) Estimate the answer mentally.

b) Calculate the answer and round to the nearest inch.

PROBLEM 8   The circular garden sketched below is divided into equal plots by 6 spokes, each of which is 8 ft. long. Which of the following expressions indicates the approximate number of feet around this garden?

(1) 6×8
(2) $6 \times 8 \times 3.14$
(3) 8×3.14
(4) $2 \times 8 \times 3.14$
(5) $8 \times 8 \times 3.14$

8 ft.   8 ft.

8 ft.

PROBLEM 9   To fence in a circular track that has a diameter of 50 m would require how many meters of fencing?

(1) 15.92
(2) 78.5
(3) 100
(4) 157
(5) 314

● Area

In the last lesson, you learned to square numbers. To find the area of a circle, you need to square the radius. The formula for the area of a circle as found on the formulas page (page 246) is:

$$\text{Area} = \pi r^2$$

Area is measured in square units. Square units are found by multiplying one dimension by another. These facts give you an idea why the radius must be multiplied by itself to find the area. But it is more difficult to "see" the sense of this formula than it was with the area of a rectangle or square.

Remember that the circumference of a circle is equal to π times the diameter $(C = \pi d)$. Also remember that the diameter is twice as long as the radius. These two facts together allow us to write $C = 2\pi r$ as an alternate equation for the circumference. Follow the sequence of sketches to find out how the area formula makes sense.

 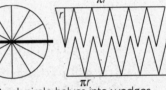 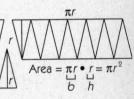

C of circle $= 2\pi r$ C of $\frac{1}{2}$ circle $= \pi r$ Break circle halves into wedges and rearrange.

To use this formula, remember that the order of operations says to <u>square</u> the radius before you multiply by π and that the value of π is usually estimated as 3.14.

Example A:
Find the area of a circle whose radius is 20 m long.

$\text{Area} = \pi r^2$
$A = 3.14 \times 20^2$ square radius first
$A = 3.14 \times 400$
$A = 1{,}256 \text{ m}^2$

Be alert to the possibility that the problem may not give you the dimension you need for the formula.

Example B:
The diameter of a circular table is 6 ft. long. What is the area of the surface of the table?

$\text{Area} = \pi r^2$
$A = 3.14 \times 3^2 \ (\frac{1}{2} d = 3)$
$A = 3.14 \times 9$
$A = 28.26$ sq. ft.

PROBLEM 10   Find the areas of the circles pictured below. Use your calculator if necessary.

a)   10 in.

b)   10 cm

c)   50 ft.

d)   50 m

Some irregular figures are made from joining parts of a circle to other figures.

Example:

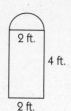

2 ft.

4 ft.

2 ft.

A window has a half-circle of glass above the usual rectangular window. What is the total area of the window at the left?

Total = rectangle + half-circle

Total area = $lw + \frac{1}{2}\pi r^2$

Area = $2 \times 4 + \frac{1}{2} \times 3.14 \times 1^2$

Area = $8 + 1.57 = 9.57$ sq. ft.

The diameter of the half-circle is 2 ft., so its radius is 1 ft.

On the GED Test, it is important to be able to decide which formula—for circumference or for area—the problem requires. Remember that area is two-dimensional and can be thought of as "covering." On the other hand, circumference is only length (one-dimensional) and can be thought of as "fencing."

For the following problems, first take time to decide which formula is required to find the missing quantity. Estimate first, when appropriate.

PROBLEM 11

How many yards of fringe are necessary to edge a circular tablecloth that measures 2.5 yards in diameter?

(1) 7.85
(2) 4.91
(3) 3.14
(4) 1.25
(5) Not enough information is given.

PROBLEM 12

A reflecting pool has the shape shown in the figure below. How many feet of sealing tape are necessary to seal the edge of this pool?

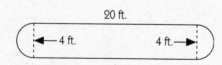

20 ft.

← 4 ft.   4 ft. →

(1) 24
(2) 26.28
(3) 46.28
(4) 52.56
(5) 92.56

PROBLEM 13

The gardener has divided a circular flower bed into three equal plots as shown. Which expression below indicates how many square meters are to be planted with <u>petunias</u>?

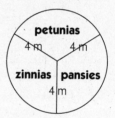

petunias

4 m   4 m

zinnias | pansies

4 m

(1) $3 \times \pi \times 4 \times 4$
(2) $3 \times \pi \times 4 \times 2$
(3) $3 \times \pi \times 4$
(4) $\dfrac{\pi \times 4 \times 4}{3}$
(5) $\dfrac{\pi \times 4 \times 2}{3}$

PROBLEM 14

Which expression shows the approximate number of square feet in a circular pool cover that measures 15 feet in diameter?

(1) (3.14)(15)(15)
(2) (3.14)(15)(2)
(3) (3.14)(15)
(4) (3.14)(7.5)(7.5)
(5) (3.14)(7.5)(2)

You may use your calculator on any problem for which it seems appropriate.

1. Estimate mentally and then calculate to find the circumference (to the nearest hundredth) of a circle whose

   a) diameter is 9.8 cm

   b) diameter is 47 ft.

   c) radius is 3.1 m

   d) radius is 47 ft.

2. Consider the equator of the earth to be a large circle. It is approximately 25,000 miles around the earth at the equator. Use this information to **estimate** the diameter of the earth at the equator.

3. What is the area of the circular region irrigated by a sprinkler that covers a radius of 3 meters?

4. A large pizza has a diameter of 16 inches, while a medium pizza has a diameter of 12 inches. How much more area does the large pizza cover?

GED Practice

5. The minute hand on the clock sketched below is 5 inches long. Through how many inches does its tip pass in one hour?

   (1) 15.7
   (2) 31.4
   (3) 78.5
   (4) 157
   (5) 314

Questions 6 and 7 are based on this diagram.

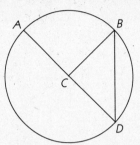

Point C is at the center of the *circle*.

6. Which of the following lines is a diameter of the circle?

   (1) *AC*
   (2) *AD*
   (3) *BC*
   (4) *BD*
   (5) *CD*

7. If the length of *AC* is 20 cm, which of the following expressions shows the number of cm^2 in the area of the circle.

   (1) $20\pi^2$
   (2) $40\pi^2$
   (3) 40π
   (4) $(20)(20)\pi$
   (5) $(40)(40)\pi$

_____

8. A pond, circular in shape, is ringed closely by a pathway. When James walked around it, he counted it to be 315 paces long. About how many of James's paces would equal the distance across the pond through its center?

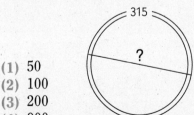

   (1) 50
   (2) 100
   (3) 200
   (4) 900
   (5) Not enough information is given.

• LESSON 13 • More Powers—Powers of 10

Mental Math Exercises

1. 35×10
2. 6×100
3. 925×10
4. $42 \times 1,000$
5. $691 \times 1,000$

• Powers of 10 and Place Value . . . .

Multiplying by 10, 100, and 1,000 in the problems above involved simply tacking on zeros. Why is it so easy? Because 10, 100, and 1,000 are powers of 10 and because our number system is based on 10. First study the powers of 10.

Notice that the place before the decimal point, the ones place, is labeled 10^0: $10^0 = 1$.

Exponent	Expanded	Long Way	Word Name
10^0	—	1	one
10^1	—	10	ten
10^2	10×10	100	one hundred
10^3	$10 \times 10 \times 10$	1,000	one thousand
10^4	$10 \times 10 \times 10 \times 10$	10,000	ten thousand
10^5	$10 \times 10 \times 10 \times 10 \times 10$	100,000	one hundred thousand
10^6	$10 \times 10 \times 10 \times 10 \times 10 \times 10$	1,000,000	one million
10^9	—	1,000,000,000	one billion
10^{12}	—	1,000,000,000,000	one trillion
10^{15}	—	1,000,000,000,000,000	one quadrillion

Raising 10 to powers is easy to do because our number system is based on 10—it is a **decimal system**. The powers of 10 provide the names for the places in our system. The chart below shows the place value names in our decimal system. Use it as a guide for the next section.

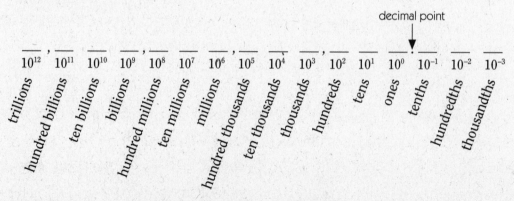

The places to the right of the decimal point are **decimal fractions**. The **negative exponents** tell you to divide by that number.

Examples: $10^{-1} = \frac{1}{10} = .1$ $10^{-2} = \frac{1}{10^2} = \frac{1}{100} = .01,$ $10^{-3} = \frac{1}{10^3} = \frac{1}{1,000} = .001$

You know that problems are sometimes easier to do mentally when you break the numbers up, digit by digit. The value of each digit in a number depends on which place it occupies. For example, the 3 in 3,456 has a value of 3 **thousand**, while the value of the 3 in 93,000,000 is 3 **million**.

A number can be expanded according to place value so that the value of each digit is shown.

Example A: $329 = 3(100) + 2(10) + 9(1)$ $56.28 = 5(10) + 6(1) + 2(.1) + 8(.01)$

For larger numbers, it is easier to use exponents for the place values.

Example B: $35,544,000 = 3(10^7) + 5(10^6) + 5(10^5) + 4(10^4) + 4(10^3)$

As you break up the numbers, notice these important facts:

1) When a power of 10 is written the long way, the number of zeros behind the 1 is the same as the exponent of the 10 when it is written in shorthand.

$$1\underline{0\,0} = 10^2 \qquad 1\underline{0\,0},\underline{0\,0\,0} = 10^5$$
two zeros ⤴   five zeros ⤴

2) The number of places between the digit and the decimal point is the same as the exponent of the 10 in the place value of that digit. Look at the 5s in both examples.

Example C:
5,040.2
Look at the 5. There are 3 places between it and the decimal point. Its place value is 10^3.

Example D:
57,300,000.9
Look at the 5. There are 7 places between it and the decimal point. Its place value is 10^7.

3) On the place value chart, the place value names do *not* center around the decimal point. They center around the *ones place*. The names to the left of the ones place match up with the names to the right.

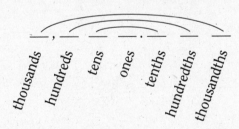

thousands   hundreds   tens   ones   tenths   hundredths   thousandths

PROBLEM 1   What is the value of the <u>8</u> in each of the following numbers?

a) 84.67   b) 209. 82   c) 38,009   d) 85,000,000   e) 0.08

PROBLEM 2   Expand each of the following numbers by place value. (See Examples A and B above.)

a) 380   b) 5,000.02   c) 60,400   d) 29,000,000   e) 100.004

PROBLEM 3   Write each of the following numbers as a digit times a power of 10.

Examples: $4,000,000 = 4(10^6)$ $600,000,000 = 6(10^8)$ $.06 = 6(10)^{-2}$

a) 50   c) 80,000   e) 0.09   g) 600,000,000   i) 30,000

b) 0.5   d) 800   f) 9,000   h) 0.006   j) 30,000,000

Multiplying and Dividing a Number by a Power of 10 . . . .

· · ·
To multiply a number by a power of 10, move the decimal point to the right the same number of places as the exponent.
· · ·

You have already seen how to carry trailing zeros along when you multiply by powers of 10.

$49 \times 100 = 4,900$

$49.00 \times 100 = 4,900.$

You can multiply by 100 (10^2) by moving the decimal point 2 places **to the right**. (Add 0s when necessary.)

Adding on the trailing zeros can also be thought of as moving the decimal point.

$325 \times 1,000 = 325,000$

$325.000 \times 1,000 = 325,000.$

You can multiply by 1,000 (10^3) by moving the decimal point 3 places **to the right**. (Add 0s when necessary.)

· · ·
To divide a number by a power of 10, move the decimal point to the left the same number of places as the exponent.
· · ·

Dividing by powers of 10 can be viewed in the same manner.

Remember that you canceled the common zeros when you divided mentally in Lesson 7.

$\frac{6,000}{100} = 60$

$6,000 \div 100 = 60.00$

To divide by 100 (10^2), move the decimal point 2 places **to the left**.

Instead of canceling common zeros, think of moving the decimal point—this time to the left.

$\frac{40,000}{10,000} = 4$

$40,000 \div 10,000 = 4.0000$

To divide by 10,000 (10^4), move the decimal point 4 places **to the left**.

How can you remember which direction to move the decimal point? Try to make sense of what you are doing:

- **By moving the decimal point to the right, you are making the number larger.** You already know that when you multiply a number by something larger than 1, it increases. (See the tables, "What happens when you multiply and divide?" on pages 72 and 73 in Lesson 9.)

- **By moving the decimal point to the left, you are making the number smaller.** You know that when you divide a number by something larger than 1, it decreases.

PROBLEM 4 Complete the table using the technique of moving the decimal point to multiply and divide:

Number	× 10	÷ 1,000	× 1,000
Examples: 308.5	3,085	0.3085	308,500
5.004	50.04	0.005004	5,004
a) 730.2	_____	_____	_____
b) 2.105	_____	_____	_____
c) 45	_____	_____	_____
d) 0.08	_____	_____	_____

Scientific Notation . . . .

The population of California in 1990 was estimated at 29,600,000.

Scientific notation is a method you can use to write large numbers like this, as well as small numbers, in a shorthand way. The number above is written as 2.96×10^7.

A. 5,000,000,000 in scientific notation would be 5×10^9.

This is merely breaking up the number into the digit times its place value. (Count the 0s.)

. . .
Scientific notation consists of two parts: a number with a value between 1 and 10 multiplied by a power of 10.
. . .

B. 0.004 in scientific notation would be 4×10^{-3}.

The 4 is in the thousandths place. Multiplying by 10^{-3} ($\frac{1}{1,000}$) is the same as dividing by 10^3 (1,000).

C. 8,200 in scientific notation would be 8.2×10^3.

Move the decimal point so that just one digit is to the left of it.	8200
How many places did you move it? In what direction?	3 to the left (divided)
Compensate for the division by multiplying by the same number.	8.2×10^3

D. 0.00029 in scientific notation would be 2.9×10^{-4}.

Move the decimal point so that there is just one digit to the left.	0.00029
How many places did you move it? In what direction?	4 to the right (multiplied)
Compensate for the multiplication by dividing by the same number.	2.9×10^{-4}

E. 4.39×10^7 written the long way would be 43,900,000.

The single digit 4 is before the decimal point. Add enough zeros so that the 4 is in the 10^7 place.

4 3 , 9 0 0 , 0 0 0   (The 10^7 place means that there are 7 digits between the 4 and the decimal point.)

PROBLEM 5   Write the following numbers in scientific notation.

a) 70,000	c) 800,000,000	e) 0.008	g) 0.000009
b) 300,000	d) 9,000,000,000	f) 0.00003	h) 0.0000002

PROBLEM 6   In 1980, major airlines flew 5,400,000 flights. Write the number of flights in scientific notation.

PROBLEM 7   In 1986, (1.25×10^{10}) was spent on state-run lotteries. Write this amount in long form.

PROBLEM 8   A pollen grain measures 0.0004 m in diameter. Write this measurement in scientific notation.

PROBLEM 9   The radius of the hydrogen atom is 10^{-8} cm. Write this in long form.

Estimating with Multiplication . . . .

This lesson reviews the technique of breaking up numbers by place value. You can use this idea to do front-end multiplication. Appendix page 248 explains this method in greater detail.

Example: $7(4,321) = 7(4,000) + 7(300) + 7(20) + 7(1)$

$$= 28,000 + 2,100 + 140 + 7 = 30,247$$

This method of finding a precise answer is also a valuable estimating tool, because your first multiplication tells you the most about the size of the answer. (The 28,000 in the above example made up most of the total answer.) This fact makes front-end multiplication especially effective when you take a test such as the GED Test.

Example: What is the cost of a fleet of 40 new compact cars, each of which cost $9,450?

(1) $23,625
(2) $37,800
(3) $236,250
(4) $378,000
(5) $409,450

- To find the exact answer: $9,450 × 40 = $378,000

- To estimate the answer:

  Start at the front end: $9,000 × 40 = $360,000
  This eliminates all but two choices: **(4)** and **(5)**

  For a closer estimate, round the remaining $450 to $500: $500 × 40 = $20,000

  $360,000 + $20,000 = $380,000 (closest to choice **(4)**)

The answer choices on the test will determine just how close an estimate you need. If you practice your estimation skills, you can use them to save precious time on the test.

Different problems lend themselves to different estimation techniques. You will need to take time to analyze problems and decide which estimating method will give an answer that is close enough. The following review covers the techniques that you have already studied.

Estimation Strategies

1) Multiplying a number by a power of 10 is the easiest strategy. Just carry the **trailing zeros** or move the decimal point.

$6,539 × 1,000 = 6,539,000$

When you see that a factor is close to a power of 10, round that factor and multiply.

$289 × 9.3 ≈ 289 × 10 = 2,890$

$4.92 × 103 ≈ 4.92 × 100 = 492$

2) Find **compatible pairs** for multiplication that are easy to compute. Multiplying by 50 is easy, since $2 × 50 = 100$.

Similarly, $4 × 25 = 100$.

$18 × 50 = 9 × (2 × 50) = 900$

$32 × 25 = 8 × (4 × 25) = 800$

If any of the factors are *close* to a compatible number for multiplication, round the factors to the numbers you can compute easily.

$24 × 48 ≈ 24 × 50 = 12 × (2 × 50) = 1,200$

$44 × 26 ≈ 44 × 25 = 11 × (4 × 25) = 1,100$

3) When you can't use either technique, **round the factors** so that you only have to multiply by a single digit. Sometimes you only have to round one factor, sometimes both.

Round one.

$$32 \times 37 \approx 32 \times 40 = 1{,}280$$

$$6.8 \times 8.9 \approx 7 \times 9 = 63^-$$

Round both.

This means the actual answer is **less than** the estimate.

You may need to know whether the actual answer is more or less than your estimate.

- If both factors are **rounded up**, the actual answer will be **less than** the estimate.
- When the numbers are about **halfway between**, you may want to **round one up and the other down** to get a closer estimate.

$$5.6 \times 9.5 \approx 6 \times 9 = 54$$

$$443 \times 549 \approx 400 \times 600 = 240{,}000$$

Here it is difficult to tell if the actual answer will be more or less than the estimate.

You will find that many techniques can apply to the same problem.

Example: 23×211 can be estimated by

$20 \times 200 = 4{,}000$ a good estimate

or by $20 \times 211 = 4{,}220$ a better estimate

or by $23 \times 200 = 4{,}600$ also a good estimate

Your estimated answers do not have to be the same as the ones listed in the answer key. There are times, particularly on timed tests, that it is more important to get a quick estimate than a close estimate.

PROBLEM 10   Decide on a strategy and **estimate** the answers to these problems.

a) $7 \times 467 \approx$ e) $52 \times 66 \approx$ i) $77 \times 22 \approx$

b) $9.7 \times 744 \approx$ f) $24 \times 88 \approx$ j) $102 \times 537 \approx$

c) $49.99 \times 8 \approx$ g) $97 \times 64.2 \approx$ k) $62 \times 38 \approx$

d) $1{,}049 \times 0.055 \approx$ h) $3.4 \times 5.5 \approx$ l) $98.95 \times 13.5 \approx$

PROBLEM 11   See if you can **estimate** the answers to <u>all</u> of these in less than two minutes.

a) $6 \times 8{,}352$ c) 300×49.99 e) $12 \times 1{,}500$

b) $\$98.95 \times 72$ d) 6.85×71.23 f) $365 \times \$103.50$

• • •

You estimate to find an answer that is "close enough" for each particular situation. As you estimate, there will always be a struggle between quickness and closeness. The situation will determine just how close the answer has to be.

• • •

Use estimation to solve the GED-type problems below.

PROBLEM 12

Rachel's payments on her new car were $189.50 for 48 months. How much were her total payments?

(1) $7,435
(2) $7,692
(3) $8,432
(4) $9,096
(5) $11,292

PROBLEM 13

Mike's office bought 12 new computer printers for $875 each. What was the total spent on printers (before tax)?

(1) $875
(2) $1,750
(3) $8,010
(4) $8,750
(5) $10,500

Estimating with Division ....

Long division is one part of mathematics that most of us like to avoid. Developing the division estimation skills that you began learning in Lesson 7 will help you to find answers that are close enough for many situations in your life. When you use your calculator to find a precise answer, you should use estimation to know whether the answer shown on the calculator display is reasonable. (You can make mistakes when you key in numbers on a calculator.)

Two steps are involved in estimating an answer for division.
1) Find the first digit.

2) Decide how many digits are in the answer.

With single-digit divisors, *round* to find a compatible number to divide into.

single-digit divisor

	Step 1	Step 2

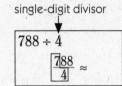

$788 \div 4$

$\frac{788}{4} \approx$

To find the first digit, divide 4 into 7. But 7 is not a multiple of 4, so it is *not compatible*. Which multiple of 4 is closest to 7?

$4 \times 2 = 8$

Estimate the problem as $\frac{800}{4}$.

$\frac{800}{4} = 200^-$

The actual answer will be less than 200. Why?

$571 \div 8$

$\frac{571}{8} \approx$

Since 8 cannot go into 5, think of dividing 8 into 57. But 57 is *not compatible* with 8. What is the nearest multiple of 8?

$8 \times 7 = 56$

Estimate the problem as:

$\frac{560}{8} = 70^+$

The answer will be greater than 70. Why?

You can do the same thing with some familiar double digit divisors.

	Step 1	Step 2

$499 \div 12$

$\frac{499}{12} \approx$

Think of dividing 12 into 49. What is the nearest multiple of 12?

$12 \times 4 = 48$

Estimate the problem as:

$\frac{480}{12} = 40^+$

The answer will be more than 40. Why?

$6,529 \div 22$

$\frac{6,529}{22} \approx$

What compatible number would you use instead of 65? It is easy to see that

$3 \times 22 = 66$

Estimate the problem as:

$\frac{6,600}{22} = 300^-$

The answer will be less than 300. Why?

PROBLEM 14   Write an estimate using compatible numbers, and **estimate** the answer. Then decide if the exact answer will be more or less than your estimate.

Example: $\frac{354}{9} \approx \frac{360}{9} = 40$

a) $\frac{362}{7}$ c) $\frac{622}{9}$ e) $\frac{815}{4}$

b) $\frac{371}{12}$ d) $\frac{872}{11}$ f) $\frac{47,033}{25}$

Sometimes you must first round the **divisor** (the number you are dividing <u>by</u>) to be able to make an estimate.

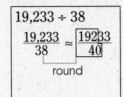

First round the divisor to 40, then find a compatible number to divide into that is close to 192.

$$40 \times 5 = 200$$

Estimate the problem as:

$$\frac{20,000}{40} = 500$$

Since you raised *both* numbers in the problem, you cannot tell whether the answer is over or under your estimate.

You can use these same techniques when a decimal point is part of the number you are dividing into. <u>Ignore</u> the decimal point until you have found your estimate. Then <u>insert</u> it into the estimate to keep the same number of places behind the decimal point.

$34.95 \div 6$

$\frac{34.95}{6} \approx$

The nearest compatible number to 34 is 36.

$$6 \times 6 = 36$$

Estimate the problem as:

$$\frac{36.00}{6} = 6.\underline{00} \text{ or } 6$$

$2.03 \div 7$

$\frac{2.03}{7} \approx$

21 is the nearest compatible number.

$$7 \times 3 = 21$$

Estimate the problem as:

$$\frac{2.10}{7} = 0.\underline{30} \text{ or } .3$$

$2.87 \div 150$

$\frac{2.87}{150} \approx$

300 is the nearest compatible number.

$$150 \times 2 = 300$$

Estimate the problem as:

$$\frac{3.00}{150} = 0.\underline{02}$$

PROBLEM 15 Choose the **estimated answer** that is reasonable.

Example: $\frac{7.87}{17}$ 40   4   .4 $\frac{7.87}{17} \approx \frac{8.00}{20} = .40 \text{ or } .4$

a) $\frac{922}{105}$ 9   90   900

c) $\frac{3.99}{19}$ 2   0.20   0.02

b) $\frac{3,525}{69}$ 5   50   500

d) $\frac{4.50}{75}$ 6   0.60   0.06

PROBLEM 16 Write an **estimate** using compatible numbers. Then **estimate** the answer.

Example: $\frac{1569}{375} \approx \frac{1600}{400} = 4$

a) $\frac{1,011}{31}$

c) $\frac{1,252}{19}$

e) $\frac{4.78}{25}$

b) $\frac{976}{52}$

d) $\frac{5.64}{3}$

f) $\frac{87.35}{4}$

PROBLEM 17 See if you can **estimate** the answers to *all* of these in less than two minutes.

a) $\frac{62}{11}$

c) $\frac{177}{16}$

e) $\frac{8.14}{97}$

b) $\frac{8.88}{3}$

d) $\frac{3,165}{78}$

f) $\frac{7,633}{26}$

Another Way to Divide

When you need an exact answer to a division problem and do not have a calculator available, you will need to rely on the long division process.

"Another Way to Divide" on page 249 in the appendix shows a method for long division that is simple; it doesn't involve a lot of rules. You may like it!

Problem Solving with Multiplication and Division

Sometimes, when you read a problem, it is hard to figure out whether to multiply or divide. Keep these ideas in mind:

- Am I looking for a larger combination of equal amounts? (Multiply.)
- Am I separating a large amount into smaller, equal-size pieces? (Divide.)
- Am I looking for the price or size of only 1 in a group? (Divide.)

Read the following problems carefully. First decide whether to multiply or divide. Then try to use estimating to find the answer.

PROBLEM 18

At Marina's Pizzeria, a large pizza serves 3–4 people. If the pizza is cut into 28 pieces and is divided equally among 4 people, how many pieces will each person get?

(1) 7
(2) 9
(3) 12
(4) 14
(5) 16

PROBLEM 19

A carton of fruit punch contains 8 eight-ounce servings. Each serving has 120 calories. Which of the following expressions shows how many calories are in a full carton?

(1) 8×8
(2) 8×120
(3) $8 \times 8 \times 120$
(4) $(8 + 8)120$
(5) $120 \div 8$

PROBLEM 20

Jan gets six hours of sleep five nights a week and about ten hours of sleep each of the other two nights. How many hours does she sleep in a week?

(1) 20
(2) 23
(3) 30
(4) 40
(5) 50

PROBLEM 21

A new car model can travel 522 miles on 1 tank of gas. The gas tank holds 9 gallons. Which expression shows how many miles per gallon the car gets?

(1) 522×9
(2) $522 \times 9 \times 1$
(3) 522×10
(4) $\frac{522}{9}$
(5) $\frac{522}{10}$

PROBLEM 22

Al bought 9.8 gallons of gas. The gas cost $1.189 per gallon. If he paid with a twenty-dollar bill, how much change did he receive?

(1) $8.35
(2) $9.90
(3) $10.20
(4) $10.99
(5) $11.65

PROBLEM 23

Michael works 40 hours a week at $9.60 an hour. Which expression represents how much money Michael makes in a <u>year</u> at this rate?

(1) $40 \times \$9.60$
(2) 40×12
(3) $40 \times \$9.60 \times 12$
(4) $\$9.60 \times 52$
(5) $40 \times \$9.60 \times 52$

You may use your calculator on any problem for which it seems appropriate.

1. What is the value of the <u>six</u> in each number?

   a) 561

   b) 78.6

   c) 6,329

   d) 560,489

   e) 44,744.26

2. Expand each of the following numbers by place value.

   Example: $133 = 1(100) + 3(10) + 3(1)$

   a) 78

   b) 4.73

   c) 5,003.9

   d) 62,000

   e) 93,000,000

3. Write the following numbers in scientific notation.

   a) 90,000

   b) 0.007

   c) 4,500,000

   d) 0.000029

   e) 88,000,000

4. In 1990, the budget deficit reduction plan was to trim $500 billion from the deficit. Write this figure in scientific notation.

5. Oprah Winfrey's salary as a TV talk show host was reportedly 3.5×10^6 for one year. Write this in long form.

6. To measure long distances in space, astronomers use a unit of measurement called a light-year. A light-year is approximately 5,880,000,000,000 miles long. Write this in scientific notation.

7. A googol is the name for the number 1 with 100 zeros behind it. Write 7 googols in scientific notation.

Do the problems 8–13 in three steps:

a) Write the equation.

b) Study the equation you have written, and decide on an appropriate **estimated answer** for the problem.

c) Find the **exact answer**. You may use your calculator.

8. A recreational vehicle averages 8 miles for each gallon of gasoline. How many gallons would be used on a trip of 550 miles?

9. Each six-pack of soda costs $1.49. How much would 4 six-packs cost?

10. A roll of 24-exposure film costs $2.95. What is the film's cost per exposure?

11. A package of 6 drinking glasses costs $4.39. What is the price of each glass?

12. Each gallon of milk contains 16 cups. How many gallons are needed to provide 100 cups of milk?

13. A computer printer can print 2 lines per second. How long would it take to print a page that contains 41 lines?

GED Practice

14. Sonja earns $1,500 a month on her job. How much does she earn each year?

   (1) $1,500
   (2) $1,600
   (3) $15,000
   (4) $18,000
   (5) Not enough information is given.

15. Sonja also pays $18.50 every two weeks for health insurance. How much does she pay for health insurance each year? (Hint: 52 weeks = 1 year.)

   (1) $222
   (2) $444
   (3) $481
   (4) $962
   (5) $1,924

It is time to apply the math skills that you have been learning to GED-type questions. By this point, you should have the following math skills:

- You know what each arithmetic operation does. (Addition and multiplication combine, while subtraction and division separate.)
- You can recognize which operations a word problem is describing.
- You can write an equation that summarizes what's going on in a problem. (If a formula covers the situation, that makes your job easier.)
- You can reorganize an equation to make it easy to find the missing value.
- You can estimate to find a close-to-precise answer.

What more do you need? When you take a standardized test such as the GED Test, chances are very good that the problems on the test will not be exactly like the ones you have been practicing. In fact, since the GED is a **problem-solving** test, it is meant to be that way. So can you use the basics that you have learned in order to solve a problem that you've never seen before?

<u>Yes, you can.</u> First, read the problems and explanations on the next page. Then refer to them again as you read the tips below.

• Test-Taking Tips . . . .

1) **General Relationships.** You are expected to know some general relationships from daily life. For example, in previous lessons, you explored the relationship between cost, selling price, and profit. In **problem 1** on the next page, you must recognize that the cost of materials gets added to the **labor** and the **overhead** costs to reach a total cost.

   You also are expected to remember some of the **measurements** (for example, 12 inches = 1 foot) and **geometric relationships** (for example, 180° in a triangle) you have learned in this book. Do not expect these relationships to be spelled out in each problem. Remember that many basic relationships are summarized on the formulas page of the test.

2) **Extra Information.** Some problems will include more information than you need to find the answer. You will need to choose just the information necessary to solve a problem. In **problem 2** on the next page, the number of hours the Quik Lube stayed open is not needed to find out how many quarts of oil the business uses each hour. When you notice that the problem gives information that you haven't used, step back and look at the problem again to be sure that you haven't missed something.

3) **Not Enough Information.** To determine whether a problem gives you all the information needed to find the answer, you must have a good understanding of the problem and process involved in finding the answer. See **problem 3** on the next page.

   When you think that some necessary information is missing, try to name that quantity. For example, "I need the *number of hours*," or "I need to know the *selling price*." Then analyze the information given, looking for ways that you might be able to figure out the missing quantity. **Be careful!** Do not assume anything. When you are sure that there is no way to find the answer with the information given, choose response **(5)** *Not enough information is given*. Expect a few of this type of problem on the GED Math Test.

Problems 1, 2, and 3 are based on the following information.

Some problems on the test are part of a set. More than one question is asked about a single situation.

Art's Quik Lube specializes in oil changes for automobiles. An oil change involves changing the oil (4 quarts) and replacing the filter. Art's has 5 stations, each of which averages 3 oil changes an hour. The business stays open 10 hours a day.

Read the passage well enough to know the situation—more than once if necessary. Do not anticipate the kind of question that will be asked.

General Relationships

1. The charge for an oil change at Art's is $23.95. If it costs Art $4.00 for each filter and $.75 for each quart of oil that he uses, how much of that money is left to cover labor costs and overhead?

   (1) $4.75
   (2) $7.00
   (3) $10.00
   (4) $16.95
   (5) $19.20

You need to have some sense of what is going on. The fee must cover the cost of materials plus the labor and overhead costs (and hopefully leave some profit). Each oil change uses 1 filter and 4 quarts of oil. Let x stand for what's left.

$$\$23.95 = \$4 + 4 \times (.75) + x$$

To find the answer, you must subtract the total cost of materials from the $23.95. Your equation will look like this:

$$\$23.95 - (4 + 4 \times .75) = x$$

The materials total $7, leaving **(4)** $16.95.

Extra Information

2. If each oil change requires 4 quarts of oil, how much oil must Art have in stock for each hour of operation?

   (1) 12
   (2) 15
   (3) 60
   (4) 150
   (5) 600

What mathematical operation is involved? Each station does 3 oil changes an hour, so you are combining equal amounts—multiplication! Each change requires 4 quarts—multiplication again.

Write the equation: $x = (5 \times 3) \times 4$

Do you need to consider the 10 hours a day? The 10 hours is extra information, not involved in this question.

You can rearrange the numbers to do the problem easily:

$$x = (5 \times 3) \times 4 = (5 \times 4) \times 3 = 20 \times 3 = \textbf{(3)}\ 60 \text{ quarts}$$

Not Enough Information

3. Manuel is a mechanic who works at Art's. His weekly take-home pay is $275. How much is he being paid an hour?

   (1) $4.58
   (2) $5.50
   (3) $6.87
   (4) $8.25
   (5) Not enough information is given.

To find an answer here, you need to know how many hours Manuel works each week.
Is that information given? *No*.

Can you figure it out from something else that is given? You know that Art's stays open 10 hours a day. Does Manuel work all 10 hours? How many days a week does he work?

Don't assume anything. You don't know enough about Manuel, so you don't have enough information to solve this problem—choice **(5)**.

On the test below, try to solve as many problems as possible with mental math and estimating. You may use the formulas page (page 246), but the use of calculators is not allowed.

1. The value of $\sqrt{72}$ is between which of the following pairs of numbers?

   (1) 6 and 7
   (2) 7 and 8
   (3) 8 and 9
   (4) 9 and 10
   (5) 70 and 80

2. What is a train's rate of speed in miles per hour if it travels 375 miles in 2.5 hours?

   (1) 55
   (2) 65
   (3) 90
   (4) 150
   (5) 937.5

3. A gallon of paint for patios can cover 400 sq. ft. of cement surface. How many gallons would Sam need to buy to cover the patio (shaded area) sketched below?

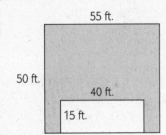

   (1) 2
   (2) 4
   (3) 5
   (4) 6
   (5) 21.5

4. One auto-transport trailer holds 7 vehicles. Which expression below tells how many such trailers it would take to transport 48 vehicles from the port of entry to a dealership 1,050 miles away?

   (1) $\dfrac{7}{48}$

   (2) $\dfrac{48}{7}$

   (3) $\dfrac{1,050 - 48}{7}$

   (4) $\dfrac{1,050}{48 \times 7}$

   (5) $\dfrac{1,050 \times 7}{48}$

5. A self-service storage company charges $.10 per month for each cu. ft. of space rented. Martin and Gloria rented a rectangular unit that measures 5 ft. by 5 ft. All the units in the building are 8 ft. high. How much was their monthly rent?

   (1) $20
   (2) $25
   (3) $40
   (4) $50
   (5) $200

6. Which expression below should be used to find the number of meters of fencing that would be required to surround the circular area pictured?

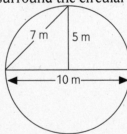

   (1) 3.14×5
   (2) 3.14×7
   (3) 3.14×10
   (4) $3.14 \times (5)^2$
   (5) $3.14 \times (10)^2$

7. In the sketch below, angle *COD* is a right angle, and angle *BOD* measures 115°. What is the measure of angle *AOB*?

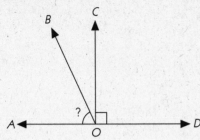

(1) 15°
(2) 25°
(3) 65°
(4) 90°
(5) Not enough information is given.

8. A breakfast order of 2 coffees and 3 Danish rolls cost a total of $4.95 before tax. Each of the rolls cost $1.25. What was the price of each coffee?

(1) $.25
(2) $.60
(3) $1.20
(4) $1.35
(5) Not enough information is given.

9. The cost of renting a Rototiller is a fee of $15 plus $2 for each hour that it is rented. Which expression below tells how many dollars it would cost to rent the Rototiller for *n* hours?

(1) $15 + 2 + n$
(2) $(15)(2)(n)$
(3) $\dfrac{15}{2n}$
(4) $15 + 2n$
(5) $\dfrac{15 + 2}{n}$

10. The high temperature for the 5 days of the Browns' vacation was 92° F. The low temperature that occurred was 64° F. What was the average daily temperature during the family's five-day vacation?

(1) 31.2°
(2) 64°
(3) 78°
(4) 92°
(5) Not enough information is given.

11. What are the coordinates of the intersection of lines *a* and *b* in the sketch below?

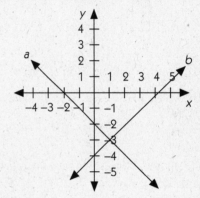

(1) (1, 3)
(2) (3, 1)
(3) (−1, −3)
(4) (−3, 1)
(5) (1, −3)

12. The total amount Richard is paid each month is $1,950. But his employer deducts $360 each month for taxes and social security. How much pay does Richard take home for the <u>year</u>?

(1) $1,590
(2) $2,310
(3) $15,900
(4) $19,080
(5) $27,720

13. As the sketch of a map indicates, to travel by road from Centerville to Gotham, one must go 9 miles north and 12 miles east. How many miles would it be if one could go directly ("as the crow flies") from Centerville to Gotham?

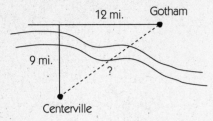

(1) 3
(2) 15
(3) 18
(4) 24
(5) Not enough information is given.

14. Find the value of h in the following equation if $t = 3$.

$$h = t^2 + t$$

(1) 3
(2) 6
(3) 9
(4) 12
(5) 18

15. For each mile that Bernie walks, he estimates that he burns 100 calories. He walked 6 miles on Tuesday, 3 on Wednesday, and 7 on Friday. Which expression below shows the number of calories he burned walking those three days?

(1) $100(6 + 3 + 7)$
(2) $100(6 \times 3 \times 7)$
(3) $6(100) \times 3(100) \times 7(100)$
(4) $(6 + 100) \times (3 + 100) \times (7 + 100)$
(5) $\dfrac{6 + 3 + 7}{100}$

16. What is the height of this triangle if its area is 30 cm²?

(1) 6 cm
(2) 10 cm
(3) 12 cm
(4) 20 cm
(5) 60 cm

Self-Evaluation

Check your answers and compare your solutions to those given in the answer key. When you compare solutions, you can learn another way to do the problem and adopt the new way if you like it better than yours.

Review the questions again, trying to gain some insight into the kinds of problems you can expect on the GED Test.

1. How many of the problems *required* you to use paper-and-pencil computations to find the answer? Could you have answered any of these by estimating instead?

2. For which questions would you have used your calculator if it had been allowed?

3. For how many questions did you refer to the formulas page?

4. Can you identify any areas that you need to study?
   - use of formulas for areas and volumes
   - squares and square roots
   - multi-step problems

Problems	Skills	Lessons
1	Squares	11
2	Finding distance/Equivalent equations	9
3	Areas	8
4	"Seeing" multiplication and division	7
5	Volumes/Multi-step problems	8 & 10
6	Circumference and π	12
7	Complementary and supplementary angles	4
8, 9, 12	Multi-step problems	10
10	Not enough information	6
11	Coordinate graphs	5
13	Pythagorean theorem	11
14	Powers and roots	11
15	Distributive property	10
16	Areas/Equivalent equations	8 & 9

• LESSON 15 • Size of Fractions

What happens when you divide?

1. $\frac{12}{12}$ 4. $\frac{12}{3}$

2. $\frac{12}{6}$ 5. $\frac{12}{2}$

3. $\frac{12}{4}$ 6. $\frac{12}{1}$

While finding the answers to the above division problems, you may have noticed that as the divisors (the numbers on the bottom that you were <u>dividing by</u>) got smaller, the answers got larger. You also saw this mathematical principle in Lesson 9. It will be very important to remember that principle as you learn about fractions in this lesson.

Fractions are not as important in people's lives as they once were. In the United States, fractions are still used in some measurements, but in many cases, the decimal form has replaced fractions.

When the Hensons saw this sign,   the odometer in their car read

```
┌─────────────────┐
│   REST STOP     │
│   1¼ mi.        │
└─────────────────┘
```

```
┌─┬─┬─┬─┬─┬─┐
│7│5│4│8│1│.6│
└─┴─┴─┴─┴─┴─┘
```

To figure out what the odometer will read by the time the Hensons get to the rest stop, you need to know about the relationship between common and decimal fractions, the main topic of this lesson.

• What Does a Fraction Mean? . . . .

2 ◄ The number on top is called the **numerator**.
5 ◄ The number on the bottom is called the **denominator**.

A fraction can be thought of as part of a whole.

The denominator (bottom number) tells how many *equal* parts the whole is divided into.

The numerator (top number) tells how many of those parts are shaded.

This rectangle has 5 equal parts.   This rectangle pictures the fraction $\frac{2}{5}$.

A fraction can also be thought of as a division problem.

The line in a fraction means "divided by," just as it did in the division problems in previous lessons.

The fraction $\frac{3}{4}$ can be read as "3 divided by 4." The fraction $\frac{6}{2}$ can be read as "6 divided by 2."

By carrying out division, using your calculator, you will find the decimal value of a fraction.

This decimal value will name the same point on a number line as the fraction does.

Example:

Use your calculator to compare the values of the fractions $\frac{4}{5}$ and $\frac{5}{4}$. Show their position on a number line.

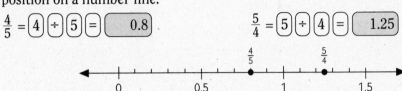

$\frac{4}{5}$ = [4] [÷] [5] [=] ☐ 0.8 $\frac{5}{4}$ = [5] [÷] [4] [=] ☐ 1.25

- - -
If a fraction has a numerator that is equal to its denominator, it is equal to 1.
- - -

Fractions Close to 1

What is the value of $\frac{5}{5}$? of $\frac{4}{4}$? When a number is divided by itself, the answer is 1.

For example, $\frac{5}{5} = 5 \div 5 = 1$; $\frac{523}{523} = 523 \div 523 = 1$

PROBLEM 1   Use your calculator to find the value of the following fractions. Show where they fall on the number line. The first one is done for you.

a) $\frac{1}{4} = 0.25$ d) $\frac{4}{2}$ g) $\frac{12}{5}$

b) $\frac{1}{5}$ e) $\frac{4}{16}$ h) $\frac{12}{8}$

c) $\frac{1}{8}$ f) $\frac{4}{20}$ i) $\frac{12}{15}$

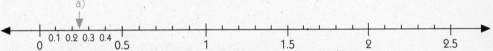

PROBLEM 2   Notice the fractions in problem 1 whose value is **greater than** 1.
Their numerators (numbers on top) are *larger* than their denominators.

Finish this statement about the fractions that are **less than** 1.
A fraction whose value is less than 1 has a numerator (top number) that is _____ than its denominator (bottom number).

PROBLEM 3   Which of the fractions below are less than 1 in value? Which fractions are greater than 1? What is the value of the remaining fractions?

a) $\frac{2}{3}$ d) $\frac{5}{2}$ g) $\frac{4}{4}$

b) $\frac{6}{5}$ e) $\frac{3}{7}$ h) $\frac{10}{11}$

c) $\frac{7}{6}$ f) $\frac{7}{8}$ i) $\frac{11}{11}$

PROBLEM 4   Insert numbers into the following fractions so that they are very close to, but less than, 1.

Example: $\frac{7}{8}$

a) $\frac{}{12}$ b) $\frac{}{6}$ c) $\frac{}{20}$ d) $\frac{3}{}$ e) $\frac{13}{}$ f) $\frac{9}{}$

A fraction whose value is greater than 1 can be written as a mixed number. A mixed number tells how many ones the number contains (the whole number part) as well as what remains (the fractional part).

Examples: Rewrite $\frac{5}{3}$ and $\frac{24}{5}$ as mixed numbers.

$\frac{5}{3}$ can be written as $1\frac{2}{3}$.

(1 one ($\frac{3}{3}$) with $\frac{2}{3}$ remaining)

$\frac{24}{5}$ can be written as $4\frac{4}{5}$.

(4 ones ($\frac{20}{5}$) with $\frac{4}{5}$ remaining)

You can also change a fraction to a mixed number by simply carrying out the division mentally.

$\frac{5}{3} = 5 \div 3 = 1$ with 2 remaining $= 1\frac{2}{3}$

$\frac{24}{5} = 24 \div 5 = 4$ with 4 remaining $= 4\frac{4}{5}$

PROBLEM 5 Write the following fractions as mixed numbers. Use either of the methods shown above.

Example: $\frac{7}{3} = \frac{6}{3} + \frac{1}{3} = 2\frac{1}{3}$ or $7 \div 3 = 2$ with 1 remaining $= 2\frac{1}{3}$

a) $\frac{4}{3}$ c) $\frac{7}{4}$ e) $\frac{7}{3}$ g) $\frac{17}{6}$

b) $\frac{5}{2}$ d) $\frac{10}{7}$ f) $\frac{11}{5}$ h) $\frac{20}{3}$

Fractions Close to $\frac{1}{2}$

What is the value of $\frac{4}{8}$? of $\frac{3}{6}$? of $\frac{7}{14}$? If you enter these fractions into your calculator as division problems, the display will read 0.5 for each answer. They are all equal to $\frac{1}{2}$. Half of the bottom number equals the top number.

If the numerator of a fraction is greater than $\frac{1}{2}$ of the denominator, the value of the fraction is greater than $\frac{1}{2}$.

PROBLEM 6 Each of the following fractions is equal to or close to $\frac{1}{2}$ in value. Which fractions are exactly $\frac{1}{2}$ in value? Which are greater than $\frac{1}{2}$?

a) $\frac{3}{5}$ d) $\frac{6}{11}$ g) $\frac{35}{70}$

b) $\frac{2}{4}$ e) $\frac{7}{13}$ h) $\frac{51}{100}$

c) $\frac{5}{10}$ f) $\frac{5}{9}$ i) $\frac{20}{39}$

PROBLEM 7 Choose the fractions below each sketch that <u>could be</u> an estimate of how much is shaded. (More than one answer is possible.)

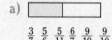

a) $\frac{3}{7}$ $\frac{5}{6}$ $\frac{5}{11}$ $\frac{6}{7}$ $\frac{9}{19}$ $\frac{9}{10}$

b) $\frac{1}{9}$ $\frac{8}{9}$ $\frac{4}{9}$ $\frac{1}{12}$ $\frac{11}{12}$ $\frac{14}{15}$

c) $\frac{1}{10}$ $\frac{1}{2}$ $\frac{8}{15}$ $\frac{1}{15}$ $\frac{14}{15}$ $\frac{1}{20}$

PROBLEM 8 For a sewing project, Sasha needs a length of fabric at least $\frac{1}{2}$ yard long. Which length should she choose?

(1) $\frac{1}{8}$ yd.

(2) $\frac{3}{8}$ yd.

(3) $\frac{9}{16}$ yd.

(4) $\frac{1}{3}$ yd.

(5) $\frac{1}{4}$ yd.

Which Fraction Is Larger? . . . .

This question can always be answered precisely by entering the fractions into your calculator as division problems, then comparing the resulting decimals.

Example:
Which is larger, $\frac{3}{7}$ or $\frac{5}{11}$?

$\boxed{3}\,\boxed{\div}\,\boxed{7}=\boxed{0.42857}$, $\boxed{5}\,\boxed{\div}\,\boxed{1}\,\boxed{1}=\boxed{0.45455}$

By comparing decimal equivalents, you can see that $\frac{5}{11}$ is larger.

You can also reason mentally about the size of certain fractions by understanding more about them.

Compare fractions with the same denominator:

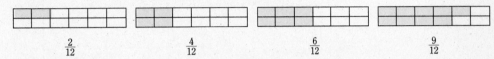

The diagrams above show that as the *numerators get larger*, more of the pieces are shaded, and the size of the shaded region *increases*.

Therefore, if two fractions have the same denominator, the one with the larger numerator has the larger value.

Compare fractions with the same numerator:

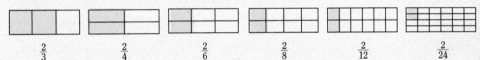

These diagrams show that as the *denominators get larger*, the size of the pieces gets smaller, and the size of the shaded region *decreases*.

Therefore, if two fractions have the same numerator, the one with the smaller denominator has the larger value.

Sometimes you can reason in other ways to help you decide.

Example: Which is larger, $\frac{8}{15}$ or $\frac{9}{19}$?

Neither the numerators nor the denominators are the same. But the values of both fractions are *close to* $\frac{1}{2}$. $\frac{8}{15}$ is greater than $\frac{1}{2}$, and $\frac{9}{19}$ is less. So $\frac{8}{15}$ is larger.

PROBLEM 9 Decide which fraction in each pair is <u>larger</u>. Try to do all of these mentally. You can check your reasoning with your calculator.

a) $\frac{4}{5}$ or $\frac{4}{7}$ e) $\frac{9}{10}$ or $\frac{10}{9}$

b) $\frac{8}{11}$ or $\frac{7}{11}$ f) $\frac{13}{5}$ or $\frac{13}{10}$

c) $\frac{5}{6}$ or $\frac{5}{8}$ g) $\frac{3}{11}$ or $\frac{6}{11}$

d) $\frac{5}{8}$ or $\frac{4}{9}$ h) $\frac{5}{9}$ or $\frac{8}{17}$

Hint: How
do these
relate
to $\frac{1}{2}$?

Decimal and Fractional Equivalents

It is important to know all you can about the common fractions that occur regularly in everyday life. One crucial aspect of these fractions is their decimal equivalents. If you can remember which decimals and fractions are equal, you will be able to solve everyday problems more easily.

Just as in Lesson 2, you have a head start in learning the equivalents because of what you already know about money.

You know:	Because:
$\frac{1}{2}$ = 0.50 or 0.5	$\frac{1}{2}$ of a dollar is $.50
$\frac{1}{4}$ = 0.25	one quarter is $.25
$\frac{3}{4}$ = 0.75	three quarters are $.75
$\frac{1}{10}$ = 0.10 or 0.1	one dime is $.10
$\frac{1}{100}$ = 0.01	one penny is $.01

You may not have realized that you know another fraction:

$\frac{1}{5}$ = 0.20   (there are five $.20 in a dollar)

But you do know that: So the two fractions are equal to each other:

$\frac{2}{10}$ = 0.20   (two dimes is $.20) $\frac{2}{10} = \frac{1}{5}$ = 0.20

PROBLEM 10 Use the equivalents above to find the following:

a) 3 dimes = $.____ $\frac{3}{10}$ = ____   e) 6 dimes = $.____ $\frac{6}{10} = \frac{3}{5}$ = ____

b) 7 dimes = $.____ $\frac{7}{10}$ = ____   f) 8 dimes = $.____ $\frac{8}{10} = \frac{4}{5}$ = ____

c) 9 dimes = $.____ $\frac{9}{10}$ = ____   g) 2 quarters = $.____ $\frac{2}{4} = \frac{1}{2}$ = ____

d) 4 dimes = $.____ $\frac{4}{10} = \frac{2}{5}$ = ____   h) 5 dimes = $.____ $\frac{5}{10} = \frac{1}{2}$ = ____

These exercises show that if you remember what you know about money, you know the decimal equivalents of the halves, fourths, fifths, and tenths.

Now learn the thirds:

Enter $\frac{1}{3}$ into your calculator.   Enter $\frac{2}{3}$ into your calculator.

The display reads [0.3333333]   The display reads [0.6666666]

These numbers are called **repeating decimals** because the same digit (or pattern of digits) keeps repeating itself and <u>never</u> comes out evenly. Rather than write out so many digits, you can show that a decimal is a repeating decimal by

(1) placing a line or a dot above the   (2) placing three dots after the digits
     digits that repeat

$\frac{1}{3} = 0.\dot{3} = 0.\overline{3}$ $\frac{2}{3} = 0.66$•••

You should learn all of these equivalents—halves, thirds, fourths, fifths, and tenths—just as you learned the addition and multiplication facts.

PROBLEM 11 Quiz yourself by finding <u>decimal</u> <u>equivalents</u> for the fractions or <u>fraction</u> <u>equivalents</u> for the decimals.

a) $\frac{4}{5}$ = ___

f) 0.2 = ___

k) 0.66••• = ___

b) $\frac{1}{3}$ = ___

g) 0.25 = ___

l) 0.6 = ___

c) $\frac{3}{10}$ = ___

h) 0.7 = ___

m) $\frac{9}{10}$ = ___

d) $\frac{3}{4}$ = ___

i) 0.1 = ___

n) $\frac{10}{10}$ = ___

e) $\frac{1}{2}$ = ___

j) 0.4 = ___

o) $\frac{11}{10}$ = ___

PROBLEM 12 Which of the following is equal to .75?

(1) $\frac{1}{2} + \frac{1}{4}$
(2) $\frac{1}{2} + \frac{1}{8}$
(3) $\frac{1}{2} + \frac{3}{4}$
(4) $\frac{1}{2} + \frac{1}{2}$
(5) $\frac{3}{4} + \frac{3}{4}$

• Equal Fractions . . . .

Reading a ruler can help you learn about equal fractions, and learning about equal fractions can help you read a ruler.

Think of a ruler as a number line that starts at zero. The inch marks are labeled as a number line.

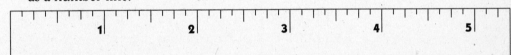

Find the half-inch marks. Finish labeling them as on the ruler below.

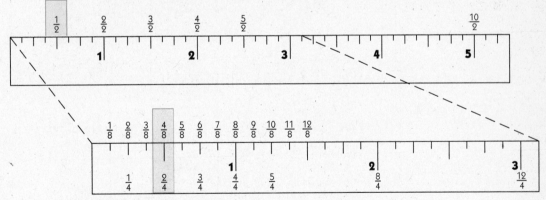

• • •
Fractions that name the same mark on the ruler are equal to each other.
• • •

Finish marking the fourth-inch marks and the eighth-inch marks on the blown-up version of the ruler above.

Notice that many ruler marks are getting more than one label. For example, the $\frac{1}{2}$ mark is also labeled $\frac{2}{4}$ and $\frac{4}{8}$.

By blowing up the ruler a little more, we can show the sixteenths.

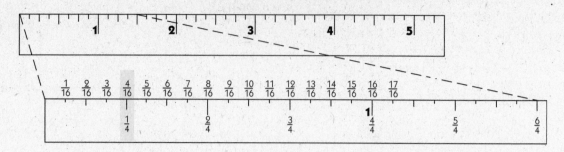

Since $\frac{4}{16}$ and $\frac{1}{4}$ are both labeling the same point, you can <u>see</u> that they are equal. You can confirm that this is true by entering both into your calculator as division problems: $\frac{4}{16} = 0.25$, and $\frac{1}{4} = 0.25$.

It is also important to see an important fact about fractions that are equal. Notice that these fractions are multiplied (and divided) by fractions equal to 1 ($\frac{2}{2}$ and $\frac{4}{4}$).

$\frac{12}{16}$ and $\frac{6}{8}$ are equal.

$$\frac{6 \times 2}{8 \times 2} = \frac{12}{16} \qquad \frac{12 \div 2}{16 \div 2} = \frac{6}{8}$$

$\frac{12}{8}$ and $\frac{3}{2}$ are equal.

$$\frac{12 \div 4}{8 \div 4} = \frac{3}{2} \qquad \frac{3 \times 4}{2 \times 4} = \frac{12}{8}$$

In fact, this relationship is so important in the study of fractions that it should have a name. We can call it the Fundamental Principle of Equal Fractions.

. . .
If both the numerator and denominator of a fraction are multiplied or divided by the same number, the result is an equal fraction.
. . .

Fundamental Principle of Equal Fractions.

You can see from the problems above that this principle is based on another fundamental principle: multiplying or dividing by 1 creates a number of equal value.

PROBLEM 13 Complete the following equalities. For help, look back at the ruler markings on pages 123 and 124.

a) $\frac{4}{16} = \frac{?}{8}$

b) $\frac{3}{4} = \frac{?}{8}$

c) $\frac{10}{8} = \frac{?}{4}$

d) $\frac{6}{4} = \frac{?}{8}$

e) $\frac{18}{16} = \frac{?}{8}$

f) $\frac{1}{8} = \frac{?}{16}$

g) $\frac{1}{2} = \frac{?}{16}$

h) $\frac{6}{16} = \frac{?}{8}$

i) $\frac{5}{8} = \frac{?}{16}$

j) $\frac{5}{2} = \frac{?}{4}$

k) $\frac{5}{4} = \frac{?}{16}$

l) $\frac{32}{16} = \frac{?}{4}$

PROBLEM 14 If you remember which fractions are equal, you can determine which are greater or less than another. Insert >, <, or = to make the following expressions true. Use the rulers again to help you.

Example: $\frac{5}{16} \boxed{>} \frac{1}{4}$. Remember that $\frac{1}{4} = \frac{4}{16}$, so $\frac{5}{16} >$ (is greater than) $\frac{1}{4}$.

a) $\frac{5}{8} \square \frac{1}{2}$

b) $\frac{7}{8} \square \frac{3}{4}$

c) $\frac{3}{8} \square \frac{1}{4}$

d) $\frac{3}{8} \square \frac{1}{2}$

e) $\frac{5}{16} \square \frac{3}{8}$

f) $\frac{1}{2} \square \frac{9}{16}$

You may use your calculator on any problem for which it seems appropriate.

$$\frac{1}{2}, \frac{1}{3}, \frac{2}{3}, \frac{1}{4}, \frac{3}{4}, \frac{1}{5}, \frac{2}{5}$$

1. Which of the common fractions above is a good estimate of a basketball player's performance if she:

   a) made 5 of 9 shots? (Hint: $\frac{5}{9} \approx \frac{5}{10}$)

   b) made 11 of 30 shots? (Hint: $\frac{11}{30} \approx \frac{10}{30}$)

   c) made 15 of 21 shots?

   Which would be a good estimate of a baseball player's performance if he:

   d) hit 9 of 28 times at bat?

   e) hit 4 of 25 times at bat?

   f) hit 12 of 49 times at bat?

   Which would be a good estimate of a quarterback's performance if he

   g) completed 7 of 20 passes?

   h) completed 15 of 31 passes?

   i) completed 11 of 53 passes?

2. Arrange the following numbers in order from <u>smallest</u> to <u>largest</u>. Use your calculator to change fractions to decimals.

   $$0.6, \frac{1}{2}, 0.2, \frac{5}{8}$$

3. Gloria found two fabric remnants that she liked at the store. One was marked $\frac{1}{2}$ yd., and the other was marked $\frac{3}{8}$ yd. Which piece is longer?

4. English wrench sizes are given in fraction form. Which one of each pair is the <u>larger</u>?

   a) $\frac{3}{16}$ or $\frac{1}{4}$ d) $\frac{7}{8}$ or $\frac{3}{4}$

   b) $\frac{5}{8}$ or $\frac{1}{2}$ e) $\frac{13}{16}$ or $\frac{3}{4}$

   c) $\frac{5}{16}$ or $\frac{1}{4}$ f) $\frac{9}{16}$ or $\frac{1}{2}$

5. The following fractions all have applications in money or on a ruler. Complete each statement to make equal fractions.

   a) $\frac{1}{2} = \frac{}{10}$ d) $\frac{1}{10} = \frac{}{100}$

   b) $\frac{1}{4} = \frac{}{16}$ e) $\frac{3}{4} = \frac{}{16}$

   c) $\frac{2}{5} = \frac{}{10}$ f) $\frac{3}{5} = \frac{}{100}$

6. What is the length of the shaded region?

7. The assembly instructions say to drill a hole that is 0.25 inch in diameter. If Hank has a set of drill bits containing the following sizes, which bit should he choose to do the job?

   (1) $\frac{1}{16}$ in.
   (2) $\frac{1}{8}$ in.
   (3) $\frac{1}{4}$ in.
   (4) $\frac{3}{8}$ in.
   (5) $\frac{1}{2}$ in.

8. In the process of cutting a recipe in half, Laura found that she needs $\frac{3}{8}$ cup of sugar. This amount is halfway between

   (1) 0 and $\frac{1}{4}$
   (2) $\frac{1}{4}$ and $\frac{1}{2}$
   (3) $\frac{1}{2}$ and $\frac{3}{4}$
   (4) $\frac{1}{2}$ and 1
   (5) Not enough information is given.

• LESSON 16 • Adding and Subtracting Fractions

Mental Math Exercises

Which is greater?

1. $\frac{1}{3}$ or $\frac{1}{5}$? **3.** $\frac{1}{4}$ or $\frac{3}{16}$?

2. $\frac{5}{7}$ or $\frac{5}{8}$? **4.** $\frac{1}{2}$ or $\frac{7}{15}$?

Determining which fraction is larger than another is an important part of estimating with fractions. In this lesson, you will learn to add and subtract precisely with a small number of common fractions. You will also learn to estimate the answers to other addition and subtraction problems.

• Picturing Fractions ....

One important part of adding and subtracting fractions is to be able to rename one fraction with another that is equal to it. This fraction table will help you to picture which of the common fractions are equal. Each line is a **number line** marked off in fractions having the same denominator.

Fraction Table

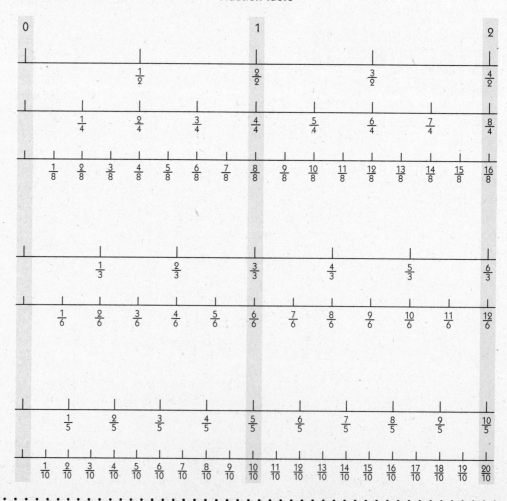

Use the fraction table on page 126 to answer the following.

PROBLEM 1 Find which fractions are equal to each other. Use the straight edge of your paper for accuracy.

Example: $\frac{1}{4} = \frac{2}{8}$

a) Name all the fractions shown that are equal to $\frac{1}{2}$.

b) Name all the fractions shown that are equal to $\frac{2}{3}$.

c) Name all the fractions shown that are equal to 1. What do they all have in common?

PROBLEM 2 Notice which fraction is larger than the other. (Again use a straight edge.) Place a > (greater than) or < (less than) sign to make the following true.

a) $\frac{1}{4} \;\square\; \frac{1}{5}$ c) $\frac{1}{4} \;\square\; \frac{1}{10}$ e) $\frac{1}{6} \;\square\; \frac{1}{3}$ g) $\frac{1}{2} \;\square\; \frac{3}{5}$

b) $\frac{5}{6} \;\square\; \frac{7}{8}$ d) $\frac{7}{8} \;\square\; \frac{9}{10}$ f) $1 \;\square\; \frac{11}{10}$ h) $\frac{15}{10} \;\square\; \frac{10}{8}$

PROBLEM 3 Rename as mixed numbers these fractions whose values are greater than 1.

Example: $\frac{6}{5} = 1\frac{1}{5}$

a) $\frac{5}{4}$ b) $\frac{5}{3}$ c) $\frac{13}{8}$ d) $\frac{19}{10}$ e) $\frac{15}{8}$

Renaming and Simplifying Fractions

If you do not have the fraction table at hand for reference, you can rename fractions using the Fundamental Principle of Equal Fractions.

· · ·
To find a fraction that is equal to another, multiply (or divide) both the numerator and denominator by the same number.
· · ·

Examples:

Rename $\frac{3}{4}$ so that it has a denominator of 8.
THINK: 4 is multiplied by 2 to get 8.
DO: Multiply both top and bottom by 2.

$$\frac{3}{4} = \frac{3 \times 2}{4 \times 2} = \frac{6}{8}$$

Multiplying by 1 results in an equal number.

Rename $\frac{2}{5}$ so that it has a denominator of 15.
THINK: To get 15, 5 must be multiplied by 3.
DO: Multiply both top and bottom by 3.

$$\frac{2}{5} = \frac{2 \times 3}{5 \times 3} = \frac{6}{15}$$

Write $\frac{4}{16}$ in simplest terms.
THINK: Both 4 and 16 can be divided by 4.

$$\frac{4}{16} = \frac{4 \div 4}{16 \div 4} = \frac{1}{4}$$

Dividing by 1 results in an equal number.

Write $\frac{15}{20}$ in simplest form.
THINK: 5 divides evenly into both 15 and 20.

$$\frac{15}{20} = \frac{15 \div 5}{20 \div 5} = \frac{3}{4}$$

PROBLEM 4 Rename these fractions with the denominators shown. Show the multiplication involved. Parts a and b are started.

a) $\frac{2}{3} \times \frac{2}{2} = \frac{}{6}$ b) $\frac{5}{6} \times \frac{3}{3} = \frac{}{18}$ c) $\frac{3}{5} = \frac{}{20}$ d) $\frac{1}{4} = \frac{}{32}$ e) $\frac{5}{8} = \frac{}{16}$ f) $\frac{3}{16} = \frac{}{32}$

PROBLEM 5 Write these fractions in simplest terms by dividing the top and bottom by the same number. Show the division involved. Parts a and b are started.

a) $\frac{4}{6} \div \frac{2}{2} =$ b) $\frac{4}{12} \div \frac{4}{4} =$ c) $\frac{12}{16}$ d) $\frac{16}{32}$ e) $\frac{5}{10}$ f) $\frac{5}{20}$

PROBLEM 6 Can you rename $\frac{1}{4}$ as a fraction that has a denominator of 7? Why or why not?

Adding Fractions . . . .

First, add using the ruler to picture the problem.

Think about this problem.

Robin sewed a stripe on a place mat by placing two pieces of ribbon next to each other. One ribbon is $\frac{1}{2}$ inch wide, and the other is $\frac{1}{8}$ inch wide. What is the total width of the stripe?

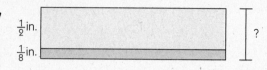

To find the answer, you must add two fractions. The most sensible way to discover the answer is to remember the work with rulers from the last lesson and picture the stripe next to the ruler. Which ruler mark does the total width come to?

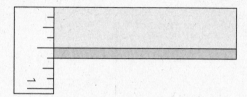

The final mark is one of the "eighth" marks.

Count the number of eighths **down** to this mark.

The width of the stripe is $\frac{5}{8}$ in.

PROBLEM 7 Use this blown-up picture of a ruler to determine the sum of the following fractions. You may find it helpful to mark off the lengths on a piece of paper.

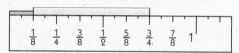

Example: $\frac{1}{8} + \frac{5}{8} = \frac{3}{4}$ (shown by the shading on the ruler)

a) $\frac{1}{4} + \frac{1}{4}$ c) $\frac{1}{4} + \frac{1}{8}$ e) $\frac{5}{8} + \frac{1}{8}$ g) $\frac{1}{2} + \frac{1}{16}$ i) $\frac{3}{16} + \frac{1}{2}$

b) $\frac{1}{4} + \frac{1}{2}$ d) $\frac{3}{8} + \frac{1}{8}$ f) $\frac{5}{8} + \frac{1}{4}$ h) $\frac{1}{16} + \frac{1}{4}$ j) $\frac{3}{16} + \frac{1}{4}$

Next, use a picture to make sense of the rule for addition of fractions.

To add two fractions with the same denominator, $\frac{a}{c} + \frac{b}{c} = \frac{a+b}{c}$.

Example: $\frac{1}{2} + \frac{1}{8}$

Rename $\frac{1}{2}$ as $\frac{4}{8}$.

1) Rewrite the problem so that both fractions have the same denominator.

The problem now is $\frac{4}{8} + \frac{1}{8}$

2) Add the numerators (top numbers) of the two fractions.

$$4 + 1 = 5$$

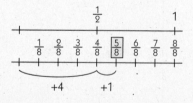

When both fractions have the same denominator, both are on the same number line where all the intervals are the same length.

3) Place the sum over the same denominator.

$$\frac{4}{8} + \frac{1}{8} = \frac{5}{8}$$

For some problems, an additional step may be needed.

Example: $\frac{1}{8} + \frac{5}{8} = \frac{6}{8}$

You will need to write the answer in simplest form.

$$\frac{6}{8} = \frac{6 \div 2}{8 \div 2} = \frac{3}{4}$$

$$\frac{1}{8} + \frac{5}{8} = \frac{6}{8} = \frac{3}{4}$$

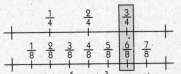

On the fraction table, $\frac{6}{8}$ and $\frac{3}{4}$ name the same point.

Looking back over the process, notice that there are only two complicated steps involved with adding fractions—first, **renaming** fractions so that they have the same denominator, and second, writing the answer in **simplest form**. Both of these steps require you to know about equal fractions.

Sometimes both fractions in the addition problem need to be renamed. Then you must first decide what denominator will work for both fractions. Do this by "building" equal fractions.

Example: $\frac{1}{5} + \frac{2}{3}$

You build equal fractions by multiplying each fraction in turn by $\frac{2}{2}$, $\frac{3}{3}$, $\frac{4}{4}$, $\frac{5}{5}$, etc. Watch for the same denominator to occur.

$$\boxed{\frac{1}{5}} = \frac{2}{10} = \boxed{\frac{3}{15}} = \frac{4}{20} = \frac{5}{25} \qquad \boxed{\frac{2}{3}} = \frac{4}{6} = \frac{6}{9} = \frac{8}{12} = \boxed{\frac{10}{15}}$$

$$(\times \tfrac{2}{2}) \quad (\times \tfrac{3}{3}) \quad (\times \tfrac{4}{4}) \quad (\times \tfrac{5}{5}) \qquad\qquad (\times \tfrac{2}{2}) \quad (\times \tfrac{3}{3}) \quad (\times \tfrac{4}{4}) \quad (\times \tfrac{5}{5})$$

Use $\frac{3}{15} + \frac{10}{15}$ as the problem, and you get $\frac{13}{15}$ as the answer.

PROBLEM 8   Find the answers to the following problems, using the techniques shown above. Then go back and try to picture the problems, step by step, on a ruler or a number line. Simplify your answer if necessary.

a) $\frac{3}{8} + \frac{1}{8}$ c) $\frac{1}{4} + \frac{1}{16}$ e) $\frac{5}{8} + \frac{1}{16}$ g) $\frac{2}{5} + \frac{3}{10}$ i) $\frac{1}{4} + \frac{2}{5}$

b) $\frac{1}{2} + \frac{1}{4}$ d) $\frac{3}{8} + \frac{1}{16}$ f) $\frac{3}{8} + \frac{3}{16}$ h) $\frac{1}{2} + \frac{1}{5}$ j) $\frac{2}{3} + \frac{1}{4}$

You may need to add fractions to solve math problems.

PROBLEM 9
Jack spent $\frac{1}{3}$ of an hour on the phone in the morning and $\frac{1}{2}$ of an hour on the phone in the afternoon. How much time did he spend on the phone altogether?

(1) $\frac{1}{5}$ hour

(2) $\frac{1}{3}$ hour

(3) $\frac{2}{5}$ hour

(4) $\frac{5}{6}$ hour

(5) 1 hour

PROBLEM 10
Tracy ate 3 slices of this pizza and Brian ate 2 slices. What fraction of the pizza did they eat?

(1) $\frac{1}{4}$

(2) $\frac{3}{8}$

(3) $\frac{5}{8}$

(4) $\frac{3}{4}$

(5) $\frac{7}{8}$

Subtracting Fractions . . . .

First, picture subtraction by using a ruler.

The basic ideas in subtracting fractions are nearly the same as in adding. As in addition, one way to find the answer to a subtraction problem is to **picture it** on a ruler or a number line.

A seamstress normally makes seams that are $\frac{5}{8}$ in. wide. A seam $\frac{3}{4}$ in. wide is required on a tailoring job. How much wider is this than the normal seam?

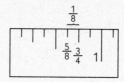

By locating these two fractions on a ruler and looking at the difference between them, it is easy to see that

$$\frac{3}{4} - \frac{5}{8} = \frac{1}{8}$$

PROBLEM 11 Sketch a ruler and picture the following problems on it to find the answers.

a) $\frac{1}{2} - \frac{1}{4}$ c) $\frac{3}{4} - \frac{5}{8}$ e) $\frac{3}{4} - \frac{1}{2}$ g) $\frac{3}{4} - \frac{3}{8}$ i) $\frac{7}{8} - \frac{3}{8}$

b) $\frac{3}{8} - \frac{1}{8}$ d) $\frac{7}{8} - \frac{3}{4}$ f) $\frac{3}{4} - \frac{5}{8}$ h) $\frac{9}{16} - \frac{1}{2}$ j) $\frac{11}{16} - \frac{7}{16}$

Or use a picture to make sense of the rule:

$\frac{a}{c} - \frac{b}{c} = \frac{a-b}{c}$ (subtracting fractions with the same denominator)

Example:

$\frac{7}{10} - \frac{1}{5}$ Write both fractions with the

$\frac{7}{10} - \frac{2}{10}$ same denominator.

$\frac{5}{10} = \frac{1}{2}$ Write the answer in simplest terms.

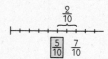

PROBLEM 12 Use the technique illustrated in the example above to find the answers to these problems. Then picture the steps on a number line or ruler so that you can "see" the process. Simplify if necessary.

a) $\frac{1}{2} - \frac{1}{8}$ c) $\frac{3}{4} - \frac{3}{16}$ e) $\frac{3}{4} - \frac{3}{8}$ g) $\frac{1}{4} - \frac{1}{5}$ i) $\frac{2}{3} - \frac{1}{2}$

b) $\frac{1}{2} - \frac{1}{16}$ d) $\frac{5}{8} - \frac{5}{16}$ f) $\frac{7}{10} - \frac{1}{2}$ h) $\frac{1}{3} - \frac{1}{4}$ j) $\frac{2}{3} - \frac{3}{5}$

Subtracting a fraction from 1—that is, taking part of something away from the whole thing—happens often in everyday life.

How much is left?

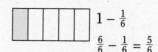 $1 - \frac{1}{4}$

$\frac{4}{4} - \frac{1}{4} = \frac{3}{4}$

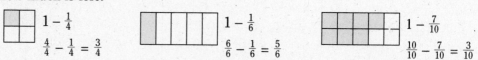 $1 - \frac{1}{6}$

$\frac{6}{6} - \frac{1}{6} = \frac{5}{6}$

$1 - \frac{7}{10}$

$\frac{10}{10} - \frac{7}{10} = \frac{3}{10}$

By thinking of 1 as being all of the parts that the whole contains (for example, $\frac{4}{4}$, $\frac{6}{6}$, $\frac{10}{10}$), it is easy to find the number of remaining parts. Use whichever name for 1 that the problem suggests.

Example: $1 - \frac{3}{8}$ is $\frac{8}{8} - \frac{3}{8} = \frac{5}{8}$

PROBLEM 13 Find the answers.

a) $1 - \frac{3}{5}$ b) $1 - \frac{3}{8}$ c) $1 - \frac{6}{11}$ d) $1 - \frac{11}{12}$ e) $1 - \frac{13}{20}$

• Adding and Subtracting Mixed Numbers . . . .

Different names for 1 are again used with mixed numbers. Remember that 1 can be named by any fraction whose numerator and denominator are the same ($\frac{2}{2}$, $\frac{4}{4}$, $\frac{5}{5}$, $\frac{8}{8}$, $\frac{10}{10}$, etc.). The name that you use will depend on the problem. For help with renaming mixed numbers as fractions, use the fraction table on page 126.

Example: On one day of training, Jamie swam $\frac{1}{2}$ mile, and on the next day he swam $\frac{3}{4}$ mile. How many miles did he swim over the two days?

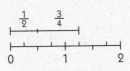

Count the number of fourths to the end mark. The answer is $\frac{5}{4}$, or $1\frac{1}{4}$ mi.

Or rewrite the problem:
$\frac{2}{4} + \frac{3}{4} = \frac{5}{4}$, or $1\frac{1}{4}$ miles.

To write the answer as a mixed number, you had to remember that $1 = \frac{4}{4}$ and that $\frac{5}{4} = \frac{4}{4} + \frac{1}{4}$ or $1 + \frac{1}{4}$.

Renaming 1 as all of its parts is often necessary in order to subtract.

Example: Ron ran $1\frac{1}{2}$ miles on one day, then ran $\frac{7}{8}$ mile the next day. How much farther did he run the first day than the second?

Count the number of eighths between the marks. The answer is $\frac{5}{8}$.

Or rename $1\frac{1}{2}$ as eighths:
$1\frac{4}{8} = \frac{8}{8} + \frac{4}{8} = \frac{12}{8}$

Rewrite the problem:
$\frac{12}{8} - \frac{7}{8} = \frac{5}{8}$

When larger values are involved, it is important to remember the commutative and the associative properties of addition: **the order and grouping of numbers can be changed when you add.**

$3\frac{1}{2} + 5\frac{5}{8}$

$(3 + \frac{1}{2}) + (5 + \frac{5}{8})$ This is the meaning of a mixed number.

$(3 + 5) + (\frac{1}{2} + \frac{5}{8})$ The properties allow putting
$8 + \frac{9}{8}$ the whole numbers together and the fractions together.

$8 + 1\frac{1}{8} = 9\frac{1}{8}$ Rename in simplest form. $(\frac{9}{8} = \frac{8}{8} + \frac{1}{8})$

This same problem can be written in a vertical format.

$$3\frac{1}{2} = 3\frac{4}{8}$$
$$+5\frac{5}{8} = +5\frac{5}{8}$$
$$8\frac{9}{8} = 9\frac{1}{8}$$

Subtracting can be just as easy for some problems.

$$21\frac{7}{8} = 21\frac{7}{8}$$
$$-16\frac{1}{4} = -16\frac{2}{8}$$
$$5\frac{5}{8}$$

But it can get more complicated when you have to "borrow."

$$10\frac{1}{4} = 10\frac{2}{8} = 9 + \frac{8}{8} + \frac{2}{8} = 9\frac{10}{8}$$
$$-3\frac{5}{8} \qquad\qquad\qquad = -3\frac{5}{8}$$
$$6\frac{5}{8}$$

PROBLEM 14   Using any of the methods discussed above, solve the following problems.

a) $\frac{3}{4} + \frac{3}{4}$ d) $3\frac{1}{8} + 5\frac{3}{4}$ g) $7\frac{1}{10} + 4\frac{3}{5}$ j) $10 - 5\frac{3}{4}$

b) $1\frac{1}{4} - \frac{7}{8}$ e) $4\frac{5}{16} - 2\frac{1}{4}$ h) $9 - 2\frac{1}{8}$ k) $66\frac{2}{3} + 12\frac{1}{2}$

c) $5\frac{1}{2} - \frac{3}{4}$ f) $8\frac{1}{5} + 10\frac{1}{4}$ i) $3\frac{7}{8} + 8\frac{1}{4}$ l) $37\frac{1}{2} - 16\frac{2}{3}$

• Estimating When Adding and Subtracting Fractions . . . .

Strategy 1: Compare to an easy problem.
Some of the easiest problems involve 0, $\frac{1}{2}$, and 1.

$$\tfrac{1}{2} + \tfrac{1}{2} = 1 \qquad 1 + \tfrac{1}{2} = 1\tfrac{1}{2} \qquad 1 + 1 = 2$$

By knowing these simple facts plus the fractions that are close to 0, $\frac{1}{2}$, and 1, you can estimate.

<u>The following fractions are close to 0.</u>	<u>These are close to 1.</u>	<u>These are close to $\frac{1}{2}$.</u>
$\frac{1}{9}, \frac{3}{17}, \frac{2}{13}, \frac{3}{50}, \frac{4}{65}$	$\frac{8}{9}, \frac{9}{11}, \frac{14}{15}, \frac{21}{20}, \frac{43}{40}$	$\frac{3}{8}, \frac{9}{17}, \frac{6}{11}, \frac{10}{21}, \frac{26}{50}$

To estimate, round the fractions to 0, $\frac{1}{2}$, or 1. Then add or subtract. Try to determine whether the actual answer will be higher or lower than your estimate.

> • • •
> When an estimated answer is written as $1\frac{1}{2}^-$ it means that the **exact answer** is **less than** the estimate $1\frac{1}{2}$.
> • • •

Examples:

$\frac{9}{10} + \frac{5}{11} \approx 1\frac{1}{2}^-$

$\boxed{1 + \tfrac{1}{2}}$

Both fractions are less than the estimates.
The exact answer will be less than your estimate.

$\frac{9}{16} - \frac{1}{11} \approx \frac{1}{2}$

$\boxed{\tfrac{1}{2} - 0}$

Both are over the estimate, but this is subtraction.

PROBLEM 15   Estimate, using 0, $\frac{1}{2}$, and 1 for each fraction.

Example: $\frac{2}{7} + \frac{5}{9} \approx 0 + \frac{1}{2} = \frac{1}{2}$

a) $\frac{8}{9} + \frac{1}{11}$ c) $\frac{4}{9} + \frac{7}{15}$ e) $\frac{14}{15} - \frac{5}{9}$ g) $\frac{9}{20} - \frac{2}{13}$

b) $\frac{11}{12} - \frac{6}{7}$ d) $\frac{25}{49} + \frac{1}{15}$ f) $\frac{5}{6} + \frac{19}{20}$ h) $\frac{5}{7} + \frac{6}{11}$

Strategy 2: Look for other easy problems to use as references when estimating.

What is an estimate of $\frac{1}{5} + \frac{1}{4}$?

$\boxed{\tfrac{1}{4} + \tfrac{1}{4} = \tfrac{1}{2}}$

Since $\frac{1}{5}$ is less than $\frac{1}{4}$, the actual answer is less than the estimate $\frac{1}{2}$ (written as $\frac{1}{2}^-$).

1) Think of an easy problem to compare it with.

2) Use common sense to adjust the answers.

What is an estimate of $\frac{15}{16} - \frac{2}{7}$?

$\boxed{1 - \tfrac{2}{7} = \tfrac{5}{7}}$

Since $\frac{15}{16}$ is less than 1, the difference is less than the estimate $\frac{5}{7}$ (written as $\frac{5}{7}^-$).

PROBLEM 16   Compare these to easy problems so that you can refine the estimates.

a) $\frac{1}{4} + \frac{2}{3}$, more or less than 1?   d) $\frac{5}{8} - \frac{1}{10}$, more or less than $\frac{1}{2}$?

b) $\frac{3}{4} + \frac{1}{5}$, more or less than 1?   e) $\frac{13}{15} - \frac{1}{2}$, more or less than $\frac{1}{2}$?

c) $\frac{1}{5} + \frac{1}{6}$, more or less than $\frac{1}{2}$?   f) $\frac{3}{16} - \frac{1}{10}$, more or less than $\frac{1}{4}$?

PROBLEM 17   **Estimate** the following answers. Decide whether the exact answer would be more or less than your estimate.

a) $\frac{8}{17} + \frac{1}{4}$ b) $\frac{9}{10} + \frac{1}{16}$ c) $\frac{5}{6} + \frac{1}{5}$ d) $\frac{1}{2} - \frac{11}{40}$ e) $\frac{19}{20} - \frac{2}{5}$

• Estimating with Mixed Numbers . . . .

Strategy 1: Compare to an easy problem with 0, $\frac{1}{2}$, or 1.
The first technique for estimating with mixed numbers follows closely what you did when you found the precise answers.

Example:
$8\frac{4}{5} + 10\frac{1}{9}$

$8 + 10 = 18$

$\frac{4}{5} + \frac{1}{9}$

$\boxed{1 + 0 = 1}$

$18 + 1 = 19$

Answer is close to 19.

1) Add the whole numbers.

2) Round the fractions and add.

3) Combine the amounts.

Example:
$2\frac{11}{13} + 6\frac{4}{9}$

$2 + 6 = 8$

$\frac{11}{13} + \frac{4}{9}$

$\boxed{1^- + \frac{1}{2}^-} = 1\frac{1}{2}^-$

$8 + 1\frac{1}{2} = 9\frac{1}{2}^-$

Answer is less than $9\frac{1}{2}$.

. . .
When an estimated answer is written as $6\frac{1}{12}^+$ it means that the **exact answer** is more than the estimate of $6\frac{1}{12}$.
. . .

Strategy 2: Round to the nearest whole number.
When the fraction part of one number is close to 1, a second method works well with addition. But this method is especially useful with subtraction because it avoids the hassle of borrowing.

Example:
$8\frac{6}{7} - 5\frac{1}{6}$

$8\frac{6}{7} - \boxed{5^+}$

Round the <u>second</u> number to the nearest whole number.

Estimate: $3\frac{6}{7}^-$
(Answer is less than $3\frac{6}{7}$.)

Subtract mentally.

Example:
$10\frac{1}{12} - 3\frac{5}{7}$

$10\frac{1}{12} - \boxed{4^-}$

Estimate: $6\frac{1}{12}^+$
(Answer is more than $6\frac{1}{12}$.)

PROBLEM 18   Choose from the methods above to **estimate** the following answers.

a) $3\frac{2}{3} + 9\frac{7}{8}$ c) $10\frac{1}{2} + 3\frac{6}{7}$ e) $18\frac{1}{3} - 5\frac{4}{5}$ g) $9\frac{11}{12} - 3\frac{1}{5}$

b) $6\frac{1}{5} + 3\frac{1}{4}$ d) $40\frac{3}{8} + 16\frac{9}{10}$ f) $20\frac{3}{5} - 9\frac{1}{7}$ h) $11\frac{1}{4} - 7\frac{7}{8}$

It is not difficult to apply the estimating techniques for fractions and mixed numbers to problems in which you must add more than two numbers.

Examples: $\frac{3}{5} + \frac{5}{6} + \frac{3}{7}$

1) Add whole numbers.

$\boxed{\frac{1}{2}^+} + \boxed{1} + \boxed{\frac{1}{2}}$

Estimate: 2

2) Estimate fractions.

3) Combine for estimate.

$5\frac{5}{12} + 8\frac{9}{10} + 6\frac{7}{8}$

$5 + 8 + 6 = 19$

$\frac{5}{12} + \frac{9}{10} + \frac{7}{8}$

$\boxed{\frac{1}{2}} + \boxed{1} + \boxed{1} \approx \boxed{2\frac{1}{2}}$

$19 + 2\frac{1}{2} = 21\frac{1}{2}$

PROBLEM 19   Estimate an answer for each of the following sums.

a) $\frac{2}{5} + \frac{5}{8} + \frac{1}{16}$ c) $\frac{7}{8} + 6\frac{3}{8} + \frac{1}{16}$ e) $8\frac{1}{2} + 7\frac{1}{6} + 6\frac{7}{8}$

b) $\frac{1}{4} + 3\frac{2}{3} + 4\frac{1}{2}$ d) $3\frac{1}{7} + 5\frac{1}{10} + 2\frac{1}{3}$ f) $14\frac{4}{5} + 3\frac{3}{10} + 2\frac{4}{7}$

Adding and Subtracting Fractions in Real Situations ....

The situations that require you to add and subtract fractions are likely to be ones that involve measurement. Some will require a precise answer.

Example:
What is the total length of the bolt in the drawing?

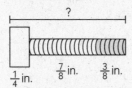

$\frac{1}{4}$ in. $\frac{7}{8}$ in. $\frac{3}{8}$ in.

For you to add, all fractions must have the same denominator.
$(\frac{1}{4} = \frac{2}{8})$

$$\frac{2}{8} + \frac{7}{8} + \frac{3}{8} = \frac{12}{8} = 1\frac{4}{8} = 1\frac{1}{2} \text{ in.}$$

In other situations, an estimate is all you need to proceed.

Example: Franco has a piece of PVC pipe that is 10 inches long. Is that long enough to cut two pieces, one $5\frac{3}{8}$ in. and the other $4\frac{1}{2}$ in.?

Add the whole numbers first.
$$(5 + 4 = 9)$$
Do the fractions add to more or less than 1?
($\frac{3}{8}$ is less than $\frac{1}{2}$, so the total is less than 1.)
Yes, the 10-inch pipe is long enough.

In problems 20 and 21, decide whether a **precise answer** or an **estimate** is appropriate for the situation. Then find the necessary value.

PROBLEM 20   How much sugar does Mabel need to bake both a batch of cookies that requires $\frac{3}{4}$ cup sugar and a loaf of banana bread that requires $\frac{1}{2}$ cup sugar?

PROBLEM 21   In the deli section of a supermarket at the beginning of the day, a tube of salami weighed $5\frac{5}{8}$ pounds. At inventory time at the end of the day, the remaining salami weighed $1\frac{1}{4}$ pounds. How much salami was sold that day?

Try to choose the correct answer to problems 22 and 23 by estimating.

PROBLEM 22
What is the diameter of the hole in the gasket below?

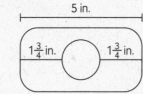

5 in.

$1\frac{3}{4}$ in. $1\frac{3}{4}$ in.

(1) $1\frac{1}{2}$ in.
(2) $3\frac{1}{2}$ in.
(3) 5 in.
(4) $6\frac{3}{4}$ in.
(5) $8\frac{1}{2}$ in.

PROBLEM 23
On Monday, George jogged $2\frac{1}{2}$ miles. On Wednesday, he jogged $1\frac{3}{4}$ miles, and on Thursday, he jogged $3\frac{1}{8}$ miles. How many total miles did he jog?

(1) 3
(2) $3\frac{3}{4}$
(3) $5\frac{1}{2}$
(4) $7\frac{3}{8}$
(5) $8\frac{1}{2}$

You may use your calculator on any problem for which it seems appropriate.

1. Find a **precise answer** to each of the following problems. Try to "see" the answer on a number line or ruler.

   a) $\frac{1}{2} + \frac{3}{8}$

   b) $\frac{3}{4} + \frac{1}{2}$

   c) $\frac{5}{8} - \frac{1}{4}$

   d) $\frac{5}{8} + \frac{13}{16}$

   e) $\frac{1}{2} + \frac{15}{16}$

   f) $\frac{1}{2} - \frac{3}{10}$

   g) $\frac{2}{5} + \frac{7}{10}$

   h) $\frac{2}{3} - \frac{1}{4}$

   i) $\frac{1}{3} + \frac{3}{5}$

2. **Estimate** an answer for each of the following problems. Decide whether the actual answer is more or less than your estimate.

   a) $\frac{3}{7} + \frac{4}{5}$

   b) $\frac{11}{12} + \frac{13}{15}$

   c) $\frac{1}{5} + \frac{1}{4}$

   d) $\frac{15}{16} - \frac{1}{20}$

   e) $\frac{15}{16} - \frac{2}{5}$

3. How much rope is left on a 50-ft. coil after $4\frac{1}{3}$ ft. is cut off?

4. The drapes made for Elaine's window will extend $1\frac{1}{2}$ ft. on each side of the window frame. If the window frame measures $6\frac{1}{3}$ ft., how long should the drapery rod be?

5. Estimate the following answers.

   a) $7\frac{1}{4} + 4\frac{1}{3}$

   b) $10\frac{1}{3} - 5\frac{13}{16}$

   c) $4\frac{8}{9} + 2\frac{5}{11}$

   d) $6\frac{2}{3} + \frac{5}{16}$

   e) $30\frac{2}{5} - 10\frac{7}{12}$

GED Practice

6. Thomas, a painter, can reach to a height of $7\frac{3}{4}$ ft. while he is painting with a roller. How high will he be able to reach if an extension of $2\frac{1}{2}$ ft. is added to the handle of his roller?

   (1) $3\frac{3}{4}$ ft.

   (2) $5\frac{1}{4}$ ft.

   (3) $9\frac{1}{4}$ ft.

   (4) $10\frac{1}{4}$ ft.

   (5) 14 ft.

7. Find the perimeter of the figure below.

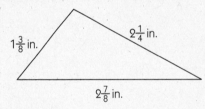

   (1) $4\frac{21}{64}$ in.

   (2) $5\frac{11}{20}$ in.

   (3) $6\frac{1}{4}$ in.

   (4) $6\frac{1}{2}$ in.

   (5) $9\frac{1}{16}$ in.

- ## Part One . . . .

Before going further in this book, use the following exercise to maintain your skills. If you are having difficulty, this is a good time to go back and review.

1. Find an **exact answer** to the following problems.

   a) $\frac{1}{2} - \frac{1}{8}$ c) $\frac{2}{3} + \frac{1}{3}$ e) $\frac{1}{3} + \frac{1}{4}$

   b) $\frac{3}{4} + \frac{1}{16}$ d) $\frac{3}{4} + \frac{3}{8}$ f) $\frac{2}{5} - \frac{2}{10}$

2. **Estimate** an answer to the following problems.

   a) $\frac{5}{6} - \frac{1}{3}$ c) $\frac{3}{4} - \frac{1}{5}$ e) $\frac{12}{13} - \frac{1}{2}$

   b) $\frac{1}{10} + \frac{8}{9}$ d) $\frac{1}{2} + \frac{1}{8}$ f) $\frac{4}{5} + \frac{9}{10}$

3. Arrange the following numbers in order from <u>smallest</u> to <u>largest</u>.

   a) $\frac{14}{15}$ 0.1   0.8 $\frac{3}{5}$ $\frac{1}{3}$

   b) 0.5 $\frac{4}{5}$ $\frac{3}{10}$ 1.0   0.9

4. Circle the larger fraction in each pair.

   a) $\frac{1}{2}$ OR $\frac{4}{9}$

   b) $\frac{4}{5}$ OR $\frac{9}{10}$

   c) $\frac{3}{16}$ OR $\frac{1}{4}$

   d) $\frac{7}{8}$ OR $\frac{3}{4}$

   e) $\frac{5}{6}$ OR $\frac{2}{3}$

5. Natasha bought a curtain rod that measures $36\frac{3}{8}$ inches across. The window measures exactly $36\frac{1}{4}$ inches across. Which is wider, the rod or the window?

6. Using the chart at right, estimate the total number of inches of wire used to assemble circuit board A.

Assembly Specifications	
Circuit Board A	
Side 1:	$21\frac{3}{4}$ in.
Side 2:	$19\frac{1}{16}$ in.
Side 3:	$12\frac{7}{8}$ in.
Side 4:	$11\frac{2}{5}$ in.

• Part Two

Now practice your skills with the following GED-type problems.

1. The chart below hangs on the wall at Ronda's plant. She wants to estimate each measurement to the nearest quarter inch. What would be a good estimate for the #A37 bolt?

Length of Bolts #A35–#A40	
#A35	1.25 in.
#A36	1.3 in.
#A37	1.48 in.
#A38	1.7 in.
#A39	1.8 in.
#A40	1.86 in.

(1) $1\frac{1}{4}$ in.
(2) $1\frac{3}{8}$ in.
(3) $1\frac{1}{2}$ in.
(4) $1\frac{3}{4}$ in.
(5) 2 in.

2. How much change should a customer receive from a $10 bill if she purchases a $3.89 bottle of shampoo and pays $.22 tax?

(1) $4.11
(2) $5.89
(3) $6.11
(4) $9.78
(5) $14.11

3. Which of the fractions listed below is a good estimate of a baseball player's hit record if he got 11 hits in 31 times at bat?

(1) $\frac{1}{8}$
(2) $\frac{1}{4}$
(3) $\frac{1}{3}$
(4) $\frac{1}{2}$
(5) $\frac{3}{5}$

4. A cleaning crew uses $10\frac{3}{8}$ quarts of the 20 quarts of floor polish it had on hand. How many quarts are left?

(1) $9\frac{5}{8}$
(2) $10\frac{3}{8}$
(3) $11\frac{5}{8}$
(4) $20\frac{3}{8}$
(5) $30\frac{3}{8}$

5. Which of the following represents the order of the distances listed below, from <u>largest</u> to <u>smallest</u>?

A.	0.2 mile
B.	$\frac{3}{8}$ mile
C.	$\frac{1}{4}$ mile
D.	0.5 mile

(1) D, A, B, C
(2) A, D, B, C
(3) B, A, D, C
(4) D, B, C, A
(5) D, B, A, C

6. Find the perimeter of the figure below in feet.

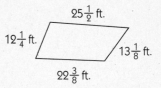

(1) 73
(2) $73\frac{1}{8}$
(3) $73\frac{1}{4}$
(4) $75\frac{1}{2}$
(5) $75\frac{3}{4}$

·LESSON 17· Multiplying and Dividing Fractions

Mental Math Exercises
More or less than 1?

1. $\frac{1}{2} + \frac{2}{3}$
2. $\frac{2}{3} + \frac{1}{4}$
3. $\frac{1}{4} + \frac{5}{8}$
4. $\frac{5}{8} + \frac{3}{16}$

What does "half of" something mean? Is it different from something "divided in half"? When you "divide something in thirds," are you doing the same thing as when you find a third of something? If they are the same, what operation are you using—multiplication or division?

... *When using fractions, "of" means times.* ...

Finding "half of" 30 means <u>multiplying</u>: $\frac{1}{2} \times 30$. However, remember from Lesson 8 that this also means the same as dividing 30 by 2. This lesson will show how these two ideas are related.

• Finding a Fraction of a Fraction . . . .

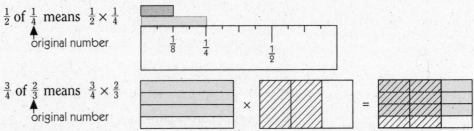

$\frac{1}{2}$ of $\frac{1}{4}$ means $\frac{1}{2} \times \frac{1}{4}$
↑
original number

$\frac{3}{4}$ of $\frac{2}{3}$ means $\frac{3}{4} \times \frac{2}{3}$
↑
original number

Note in the sketches above that the answers were <u>less than</u> the original numbers. Why? Because you were multiplying by a number less than 1. (Refer to Lesson 9, page 72.)

The technique for multiplying fractions is easy: you just multiply numerators and denominators straight across.

$\frac{1}{2}$ of $\frac{1}{4} = \frac{1}{2} \times \frac{1}{4} = \frac{1 \times 1}{2 \times 4} = \frac{1}{8}$ In formula form:

$\frac{3}{4}$ of $\frac{2}{3} = \frac{3}{4} \times \frac{2}{3} = \frac{3 \times 2}{4 \times 3} = \frac{6}{12} = \frac{1}{2}$ $\frac{a}{b} \times \frac{c}{d} = \frac{ac}{bd}$
(answer in simplest form)

PROBLEM 1   Multiply these fractions. Assure yourself that the answer is <u>less than</u> the original number.

a) $\frac{1}{2}$ of $\frac{3}{4}$ c) $\frac{1}{4}$ of $\frac{3}{8}$ e) $\frac{1}{2}$ of $\frac{2}{3}$ g) $\frac{3}{4}$ of $\frac{1}{6}$
       ↑
    original
    number

b) $\frac{1}{3}$ of $\frac{5}{8}$ d) $\frac{2}{3}$ of $\frac{4}{5}$ f) $\frac{3}{4}$ of $\frac{1}{5}$ h) $\frac{1}{8}$ of $\frac{4}{5}$

Finding a Fraction of a Number . . . .

Most often in everyday experience, you will be asked to find a fractional part of a number. It happens so often that you already know the answers to these problems.

- What is $\frac{1}{2}$ of an hour?

- What is $\frac{3}{4}$ of an hour?

- What is $\frac{1}{4}$ of a dollar?

Even though you know the answers, apply the method of multiplying fractions to these problems.

$\frac{1}{2}$ of 60 means $\frac{1}{2} \times 60$. To write 60 as a fraction, write it as $\frac{60}{1}$.

(When you divide by 1, the number remains the same.) —↰

$\frac{1}{2} \times \frac{60}{1} = \frac{1 \times 60}{2 \times 1} = \frac{60}{2} = 30$ minutes

Similarly, the second problem is	And finally,
$\frac{3}{4} \times \frac{60}{1} = \frac{3 \times 60}{4 \times 1} = \frac{180}{4} = 45$ minutes	$\frac{1}{4} \times \frac{100}{1} = \frac{1 \times 100}{4 \times 1} = \frac{100}{4} = 25$ cents

This next familiar example shows the advantages of **canceling**.

$$\frac{3}{4} \times 100 = \frac{3 \times 100}{4 \times 1} = \frac{300}{4} \quad \text{STOP!}$$

You can make this problem easier by dividing the numerator and denominator by the same number **before** you carry out the multiplication.

$\frac{3}{4} \times \frac{\overset{25}{\cancel{100}}}{\underset{1}{1}} =$ Here, the top and bottom numbers were divided by 4.

                  (100 ÷ 4 = 25; 4 ÷ 4 = 1)

$\frac{3 \times 25}{1} = \frac{75}{1} = 75$ The remaining computation is easy.

Did you recognize the Fundamental Principle of Equal Fractions at work again? It says that you can multiply or divide both numerator and denominator by the same number and keep an equal fraction. This allows you to cancel during a multiplication problem as well as to simplify the answer.

Examples:

$\frac{2}{3}$ of $60 = \frac{2 \times \overset{20}{\cancel{60}}}{\underset{1}{3} \times 1} = 40$ (Both top and bottom are divided by 3.) $\frac{3}{10}$ of $150 = \frac{3 \times \overset{15}{\cancel{150}}}{\underset{1}{10} \times 1} = 45$ (Both top and bottom are divided by 10.)

PROBLEM 2   Find the following fractional parts. Cancel when possible.

a) $\frac{1}{2}$ of 48   d) $\frac{2}{3}$ of 12   g) $\frac{1}{8}$ of 56   j) $\frac{1}{5}$ of 60

b) $\frac{1}{4}$ of 48   e) $\frac{2}{3}$ of 24   h) $\frac{3}{8}$ of 56   k) $\frac{1}{10}$ of 60

c) $\frac{1}{3}$ of 48   f) $\frac{2}{3}$ of 48   i) $\frac{5}{8}$ of 56   l) $\frac{3}{5}$ of 60

PROBLEM 3   A quart of milk weighs 32 ounces. How many ounces are in $\frac{1}{4}$ quart (1 cup)?

PROBLEM 4   A sale advertised $\frac{2}{5}$ off on all merchandise. How much did Rick save when he bought a jacket originally priced at $60?

You can also cancel when you are multiplying one fraction by another. It not only makes the problem easier because you can compute with smaller numbers, but it also eliminates the need to simplify the answer at the end. Compare these methods.

Examples:

Without canceling (need to simplify)

$$\frac{2}{5} \text{ of } \frac{7}{8} = \frac{2 \times 7}{5 \times 8} = \frac{14 \div 2}{40 \div 2} = \frac{7}{20}$$

$$\frac{2}{3} \text{ of } \frac{9}{10} = \frac{2 \times 9}{3 \times 10} = \frac{18 \div 6}{30 \div 6} = \frac{3}{5}$$

With canceling

$$\frac{2}{5} \text{ of } \frac{7}{8} = \frac{\overset{1}{2} \times 7}{5 \times \underset{4}{8}} = \frac{7}{20}$$

$$\frac{2}{3} \text{ of } \frac{9}{10} = \frac{\overset{1}{2} \times \overset{3}{9}}{\underset{1}{3} \times \underset{5}{10}} = \frac{3}{5}$$

CAUTION: You can cancel <u>only</u> when multiplying fractions.

PROBLEM 5 Multiply these fractions.

a) $\frac{3}{5}$ of $\frac{1}{6}$ c) $\frac{1}{2}$ of $\frac{4}{5}$ e) $\frac{3}{4}$ of $\frac{8}{9}$ g) $\frac{2}{5}$ of $\frac{3}{8}$

b) $\frac{2}{3}$ of $\frac{1}{4}$ d) $\frac{1}{3}$ of $\frac{3}{4}$ f) $\frac{5}{6}$ of $\frac{9}{10}$ h) $\frac{2}{3}$ of $\frac{3}{8}$

Estimating Fractional Parts . . . .

In your daily life, you probably will want to know approximate answers to problems like the ones below. For example, you may need to know what kind of number to expect when a cashier rings up a sale.

DELICATESSEN					
Corned Beef	$5.75 /lb.	Salami	$3.69 /lb.	Pepperoni	$4.18/lb.
Honey Ham	$4.80 /lb.	Bologna	$3.89 /lb.	Cheddar	$3.99 /lb.

• How much would you expect to pay for $\frac{1}{4}$ lb. of honey ham?

$$\frac{1}{4} \text{ of } \$4.80 = \frac{1 \times \overset{1.20}{4.80}}{\underset{1}{4} \times 1} = \$1.20$$

• How much for $\frac{1}{8}$ lb. of corned beef?

$$\frac{1}{8} \text{ of } \$5.75 = \frac{1 \times 5.75}{8 \times 1} \approx \frac{5.60}{8} = \$.70$$

You need a number that is compatible with 8. ($5.60)

• About how much for $\frac{3}{4}$ lb. of salami?

$$\frac{3}{4} \text{ of } \$3.69 = \frac{3 \times 3.69}{4 \times 1}$$

Look at the denominator before you round!

$$\approx \frac{3 \times \overset{.90}{3.60}}{\underset{1}{4} \times 1} = \$2.70$$

• What would you expect to pay for $\frac{3}{8}$ lb. of pepperoni?

$$\frac{3}{8} \text{ of } \$4.18 = \frac{3 \times 4.18}{8 \times 1}$$

(8 divides into 40 evenly.)

$$\approx \frac{3 \times \overset{.50}{4.00}}{\underset{1}{8} \times 1} = \$1.50$$

PROBLEM 6   The following sign appears on the window of a hardware store that is going out of business.

> $\frac{1}{3}$ **Off All Marked Prices**

Round each dollar amount to **estimate** how much you would save on the following items.

a) a blender marked at $23.95

b) an outdoor thermometer marked at $8.25

c) a trash can marked at $16.95

d) a faucet replacement set marked at $126.75

e) a lawn mower marked at $207.25

Practice estimating like this every time this kind of situation comes up in your life. Notice how much more powerful it makes you feel when you know the kind of number to expect.

• Multiplying Mixed Numbers . . . .

Multiplying mixed numbers is like applying the distributive property. (Refer to Lesson 10, page 78.) Each part of one mixed number (both the whole number part and the fractional part) must be multiplied by each part of the other mixed number.

Study the following two sketches and the problems they picture. Are the shaded fractional parts equally important to both pictures?

$$3\tfrac{1}{5} \times 1\tfrac{1}{2} \qquad\qquad\qquad 10\tfrac{1}{3} \times 8\tfrac{1}{2}$$

$$(3 + \tfrac{1}{5}) \times (1 + \tfrac{1}{2}) \qquad\qquad (10 + \tfrac{1}{3}) \times (8 + \tfrac{1}{2})$$

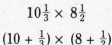

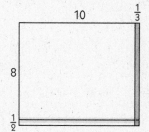

Compare the size of the rectangle picturing $\frac{1}{2} \times 3$ to the size of the rectangle that pictures 1×3.

Now compare the sizes of the rectangles for $\frac{1}{2} \times 10$ and for 8×10.

You can see that the sizes of the fractional parts of the pictures depend on the sizes of the whole numbers. They are *less important* when the whole numbers are larger.

• When you have <u>small</u> mixed numbers, it will be important to find the areas of all the rectangles. (Therefore, you will <u>use</u> the fractional parts.)

• When the numbers are <u>large</u>, the fractional parts are less important in relation to the size of the answer. (Therefore, you will <u>round</u> the mixed numbers.)

Because of this, you must know (1) a method to find precise answers for when you are multiplying small mixed numbers and (2) estimating techniques for when the numbers are large.

Renaming Mixed Numbers

When you are multiplying mixed numbers in which the whole number parts are small, it is easiest to **rename** them as single fractions and then multiply as before.

Example A:

$2\frac{1}{2} \times 1\frac{3}{4}$

$(\frac{4}{2} + \frac{1}{2}) \times (\frac{4}{4} + \frac{3}{4})$

$\frac{5}{2} \times \frac{7}{4} = \frac{35}{8} = 4\frac{3}{8}$

Estimate: $2\frac{1}{2} \times 2 = 5$

Rename as single fractions.

Example B:

$4\frac{2}{3} \times 1\frac{1}{8}$

$(\frac{12}{3} + \frac{2}{3}) \times (\frac{8}{8} + \frac{1}{8})$

$\frac{14}{3} \times \frac{9}{8} = \frac{21}{4} = 5\frac{1}{4}$

Estimate: $5 \times 1 = 5$

Both exact answers are close to your estimates.

The two methods used in checking the problems above are the two methods recommended for estimating with larger numbers.

Method 1: Round one number to a whole number. Multiply it by both the whole number part and the fraction part of the other. Add the results.

$7\frac{7}{8} \times 9\frac{1}{4} \approx$

Estimate: $8 \times (9 + \frac{1}{4})$ (Multiplication distributes over addition.)

$(8 \times 9) + (8 \times \frac{1}{4})$

$72 + 2 = 74^-$

(Exact answer will be less than the estimate.)

$10\frac{1}{5} \times 34\frac{1}{2} \approx$

Estimate: $10 \times (34 + \frac{1}{2})$

$(10 \times 34) + (10 \times \frac{1}{2})$

$340 + 5 = 345^+$

(Exact answer will be more than the estimate.)

Method 2: Round both numbers to the nearest whole number and multiply.

$5\frac{2}{3} \times 8\frac{5}{8} \approx$

Estimate: $6 \times 9 = 54^-$ (Exact answer will be less.)

$99\frac{1}{2} \times 35\frac{3}{8} \approx$

Estimate: $100 \times 35 = 3,500$

PROBLEM 7 **Estimate** an answer to each of these problems. Then find an **exact answer** to those starred.

a) $3\frac{1}{3} \times \frac{3}{4}^*$

b) $\frac{7}{8} \times 3\frac{1}{5}^*$

c) $1\frac{4}{5} \times 3\frac{1}{3}^*$

d) $12\frac{1}{8} \times 5\frac{1}{4}$

e) $9\frac{3}{4} \times 16\frac{5}{6}$

f) $7\frac{7}{8} \times 6\frac{1}{2}$

PROBLEM 8 A bag of fertilizer weighs $15\frac{1}{2}$ pounds. Larry loaded 30 bags onto a truck. How many pounds did he lift doing that job?

(1) $14\frac{1}{2}$

(2) $45\frac{1}{2}$

(3) 465

(4) $565\frac{1}{2}$

(5) Not enough information is given.

Dividing Fractions . . . .

Example:

The problem **$6 \div \frac{1}{4}$** asks, "How many $\frac{1}{4}$s are there in 6?"

Picture the problem first.

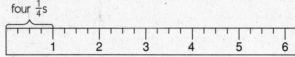

four $\frac{1}{4}$s

You know that there are four $\frac{1}{4}$s in 1.

Then it makes sense to multiply 6×4 to find the answer.

Your answer is *larger* than either of the numbers because you are finding many quarters.

Analyze what you did.

To divide by $\frac{1}{4}$, you multiplied by 4.

$$6 \div \frac{1}{4} = \frac{6}{1} \times \frac{4}{1} = 24$$

($\frac{4}{1}$ is the reciprocal of $\frac{1}{4}$.)

Example:

The problem $\frac{7}{8} \div \frac{1}{2}$ asks, "How many $\frac{1}{2}$s are there in $\frac{7}{8}$?"

Picture the problem first.

If asked to estimate, you would answer, "About 2."

Using the same technique as in the last problem,

$$\frac{7}{8} \div \frac{1}{2} = \frac{7}{8} \times \frac{2}{1} = \frac{7}{4} = 1\frac{3}{4}$$

($\frac{2}{1}$ is the **reciprocal** of $\frac{1}{2}$.)

This answer fits the estimate.

. . .
To divide by a fraction, multiply by its reciprocal.
. . .

You find the reciprocal of a fraction by simply turning it over. The reciprocal of $\frac{2}{3}$ is $\frac{3}{2}$, the reciprocal of $\frac{3}{4}$ is $\frac{4}{3}$, etc.

Example A: $\frac{1}{4} \div \frac{3}{4}$

$\frac{1}{4} \div \frac{3}{4}$ asks, "How many $\frac{3}{4}$s are in $\frac{1}{4}$?

Picture these on the fraction table.

$$\frac{1}{4} \div \frac{3}{4} = \frac{1}{4} \times \frac{4}{3} = \frac{1}{3}$$

The answer is exactly $\frac{1}{3}$.

Example B: $20 \div \frac{5}{8}$

$20 \div \frac{5}{8}$ asks, "How many $\frac{5}{8}$s are in 20?"

$\frac{5}{8}$ is between $\frac{1}{2}$ and 1. $20 \div \frac{1}{2} = 40$, and $20 \div 1 = 20$.

$$20 \div \frac{5}{8} = \frac{20}{1} \times \frac{8}{5} = 32$$

The answer is between 20 and 40.

PROBLEM 9

For each problem below, insert the numbers into this question: "How many ___s are there in ___?" Picture an answer first. Then find the answer as shown above. Check to see if your answer is reasonable.

Example: $6 \div \frac{2}{3}$ asks "How many $\frac{2}{3}$ are in 6?"

$$6 \div \frac{2}{3} = 6 \times \frac{\overset{3}{3}}{\underset{1}{2}} = 9$$

a) $\frac{7}{8} \div \frac{1}{8}$ d) $\frac{3}{4} \div \frac{1}{2}$ g) $10 \div \frac{5}{6}$

b) $8 \div \frac{1}{3}$ e) $\frac{3}{4} \div \frac{1}{8}$ h) $3 \div \frac{3}{4}$

c) $8 \div \frac{2}{3}$ f) $\frac{3}{4} \div \frac{7}{8}$ i) $20 \div \frac{2}{3}$

When to Multiply or Divide . . . .

To solve real problems involving fractions, the first step is to decide which operation to use. When the situations involved whole numbers, you chose multiplication if the problem involved **combining equal groups** and division if **separating into equal groups** was involved. You can use these same ideas with fractions.

In addition, this lesson has pointed out that if you need to find a fractional **part of** something, this means you have to multiply.

Example:

A survey found that $\frac{3}{4}$ of employed young people own a VCR. Of these, $\frac{1}{4}$ also own a video camera. What fraction of VCR owners also own a video camera?

To find the answer, you need to find $\frac{1}{4}$ **of** $\frac{3}{4}$. This means $\frac{1}{4} \times \frac{3}{4} = \frac{1 \times 3}{4 \times 4} = \frac{3}{16}$.

This lesson has also emphasized that division problems can ask the question "How many ___s are there in ___?" Use this question to determine whether to use division in a situation.

Example:

A manufacturer has 27 yards of batik fabric. It takes $1\frac{1}{8}$ yd. to trim the front of one shirt. How many shirts can he trim with the fabric he has?

Ask yourself if this situation can be interpreted as asking, "How many $1\frac{1}{8}$s are there in 27?"

Indeed it can, and the problem is $27 \div 1\frac{1}{8}$. (Since you are **dividing by** $1\frac{1}{8}$, it comes second.)

$$27 \div \frac{9}{8} = \frac{27}{1} \times \frac{8}{9} = 24 \ \text{(Make } 1\frac{1}{8} \text{ a single fraction before you find the reciprocal.)}$$

PROBLEM 10   If you maintain a speed of 60 mph for $3\frac{3}{4}$ hr., how far have you traveled in that time?

PROBLEM 11   A stack of plywood measures 25 inches high. Each sheet of plywood is $\frac{5}{8}$ inch thick. How many sheets are in the stack?

PROBLEM 12   The gasoline tank in Barry's car holds $16\frac{1}{2}$ gallons. When it is $\frac{1}{2}$ full, how many gallons does it contain?

PROBLEM 13   A ribbon $20\frac{1}{4}$ inches long is to be cut into 9 equal pieces. How long will each piece be?

    (1) $2\frac{1}{4}$ in.
    (2) $4\frac{1}{2}$ in.
    (3) 10 in.
    (4) $11\frac{1}{4}$ in.
    (5) $29\frac{1}{4}$ in.

You may use your calculator on any problem for which it seems appropriate.

1. Find the following fractional parts.

   a) $\frac{1}{5}$ of 120

   b) $\frac{1}{8}$ of 96

   c) $\frac{2}{3}$ of 45

   d) $\frac{5}{6}$ of 66

   e) $\frac{9}{10}$ of 80

   f) $\frac{3}{8}$ of 120

2. An after-Christmas sale gave $\frac{1}{4}$ off the marked prices of all Christmas decorations.

   Estimate how much was saved on each of the following items.

   a) a tinsel garland marked $1.99

   b) a wreath marked $5.79

   c) a tree ornament marked $9.59

   d) a box of cards marked $12.75

   e) a treetop ornament marked $19.50

3. The recipe for Betty's Seafood Casserole says that it will serve 12 people. Norma needed to make enough to serve 4 people, so she had to find $\frac{1}{3}$ of each of the amounts in the recipe. The recipe called for the following amounts of ingredients (among others). How much of each should Norma put in?

   a) 1 cup mayonnaise

   b) $1\frac{1}{2}$ cups finely chopped celery

   c) 2 cups crushed potato chips

   d) $\frac{1}{2}$ cup chopped green pepper

   e) $\frac{3}{4}$ lb. each of lobster, crab, and shrimp

4. Using the estimating techniques of this lesson and the previous lesson, **estimate** the answers to the following expressions.

   a) $4\frac{1}{10} + 6\frac{4}{7}$

   b) $7\frac{1}{2} \times 4\frac{5}{6}$

   c) $33\frac{1}{3} - 12\frac{1}{2}$

   d) $15\frac{3}{4} \div \frac{1}{2}$

   e) $9\frac{7}{8} \times 12\frac{1}{5}$

5. A stock was priced at $58\frac{7}{8}$ points at the beginning of the week, and by week's end it had dropped to $51\frac{1}{2}$. How many points did it lose that week?

GED Practice

6. A developer owns a 36-acre parcel, which he intends to partition into home lots. Each lot must be at least $\frac{3}{4}$ acre. How many homes can be built on this parcel?

   (1) 9
   (2) 12
   (3) 27
   (4) 48
   (5) 72

7. Every month, $\frac{2}{5}$ of the Normans' total income is spent on their mortgage payment. This year, $\frac{7}{8}$ of that amount pays interest on the loan. What fraction of their income is spent on home loan interest each month?

   (1) $\frac{2}{5}$
   (2) $\frac{3}{4}$
   (3) $\frac{7}{8}$
   (4) $\frac{7}{20}$
   (5) Not enough information is given.

• LESSON 18 • Making Connections

Mental Math Exercises

1. $\frac{1}{2}$ of $\frac{1}{4}$ 4. $\frac{1}{2}$ of $\frac{3}{5}$
2. $\frac{1}{2}$ of $\frac{1}{8}$ 5. $\frac{1}{2}$ of $\frac{3}{10}$
3. $\frac{1}{2}$ of $\frac{1}{3}$ 6. $\frac{1}{2}$ of $\frac{2}{6}$

Did you notice a pattern while doing the mental math exercises? Did you notice that multiplying a fraction by $\frac{1}{2}$ resulted in the doubling of the denominator? Noticing patterns and relationships is an important part of mathematics. The focus of this lesson will be to point out some of the connections between things you have already learned.

• Decimals and Fractions . . . .

Remember that fractions and decimals can be used to name the same numbers.

$\frac{1}{4} = 0.25$ $\frac{1}{5} = 0.20$ $\frac{1}{10} = 0.10$ $\frac{3}{4} = 0.75$ $\frac{1}{3} = 0.3$••• *(repeating decimal)*

The following reasoning will add to the list of fraction and decimal equivalents that you know.

. . .
Review these and the other equivalents by using the fraction table on page 126. Next to each fraction in the table, see if you can write the decimal equivalent. Check by using your calculator.
. . .

1) You know that
   $\frac{1}{2}$ of $\frac{1}{4} = \frac{1}{8}$.

2) You can reason that
   $\frac{1}{2}$ of $0.25 = 0.12\frac{1}{2}$ or 0.125.

3) So now you know that
   $\frac{1}{8} = 0.12\frac{1}{2}$ or 0.125. **(Learn this!)**

4) You can now figure out the value of the following fractions:

   $\frac{3}{8} = \frac{1}{4} + \frac{1}{8} = 0.25 + 0.125 = 0.375$

   $\frac{5}{8} = \frac{1}{2} + \frac{1}{8} = 0.50 + 0.125 = 0.625$

   $\frac{7}{8} = \frac{3}{4} + \frac{1}{8} = 0.75 + 0.125 = 0.875$

   You won't use these as often as the equivalents you learned before, but you can figure them out when you need them.

In solving problems, use either fraction or decimal form. Sometimes using fractions is the easiest.

Example:
After purchasing $\frac{7}{8}$ yd. of handwoven fabric, Doreen realizes that she can make two place mats from $\frac{1}{2}$ yd. How much fabric will she have left?

$\frac{7}{8} - \frac{1}{2}$

$\frac{7}{8} - \frac{4}{8} = \frac{3}{8}$ yd.

Other situations can be more easily solved using decimals.

Example:
The odometer in George's car reads 44,322.4 mi. after he has already traveled $10\frac{1}{2}$ miles on a trip. What should he record as the beginning odometer reading for this trip?

Odometer readings are expressed in decimals. You can easily change $10\frac{1}{2}$ miles to 10.5:

$44,322.4 - 10.5 = 44,311.9$ miles

Sometimes a combination works well. Use fractions for estimating, then decimals and your calculator for the precise answer.

Example:

Hard salami costs $3.49 a pound at the deli. What would you pay for $\frac{3}{4}$ of a pound?

Estimate: $\frac{3}{4}$ of $3.49 \approx$

$$\frac{3}{4} \times \frac{\$3.60}{1} = \$2.70$$

With calculator: $3.49 \times .75 = \$2.6175$
$\approx \$2.62$

How would you have entered the previous problem into the calculator if it had asked for the price of $\frac{2}{3}$ pound of hard salami?

How do you enter 0.66••• into the calculator? Simply enter the fraction as a division problem. Enter ②÷③×③·④⑨=. Watch the display as you enter the values. The answer, 2.3266667, can be rounded to $2.33.

When you are multiplying fractions, your calculator is easy to use in this way. Sometimes it may be a disadvantage that all answers appear in decimal form on the calculator. Choose the method you use according to the kind of answer you need.

$\frac{5}{8} \times \frac{2}{3} =$ 0.4166666 on the calculator, while $\frac{5}{8} \times \frac{2}{3} = \frac{5}{12}$ when you use fraction methods.

Caution: It is not as easy to add and subtract fractions with a calculator. Look at the following.

$8\frac{7}{8} + 4\frac{1}{6}$ could be entered into the calculator this way:

⑦÷⑧+⑧= M+ ①÷⑥+④= M+ MRC Display reads 13.041666

Check the manual that came with your calculator to find the procedure that works best.
Note: This uses the memory keys on your calculator.

Notice that if you had estimated the answer to the above problem by rounding $8\frac{7}{8}$ to 9 and $4\frac{1}{6}$ to 4, your estimate would be 13. Frankly, in most situations, the estimate is just as helpful as the precise answer—and a lot easier to find!

PROBLEM 1 Solve these problems in two ways—(1) with fractions and (2) with decimals. Use your calculator when necessary. Compare the answers, and decide which method worked best for you.

a) Roger has two lengths of pipe; one is $13\frac{3}{4}$ in. long, and the other is $9\frac{1}{2}$ in. long. What is their total length?

b) A bolt whose shaft is $3\frac{1}{2}$ in. long is placed through a beam that is $2\frac{3}{8}$ in. thick. How far does the bolt extend on the other side of the beam?

c) A coil of rope 50 feet long is to be cut into pieces $4\frac{1}{2}$ feet long. How many pieces of this length can be cut?

d) Marnie earns $64 a day. If she works only $\frac{5}{8}$ of the day, what will she earn?

e) Cheddar cheese costs $2.35 per pound. What is the price of $\frac{7}{8}$ of a pound?

PROBLEM 2 The number π is usually estimated using 3.14. However, another estimate for π is $3\frac{1}{7}$ or $\frac{22}{7}$.

a) Find the circumference of a circle whose diameter is 14 m using both the decimal and the fraction form of π.

b) Which form is easier—the fraction form or the decimal form? Why?

Fraction and Decimal Operations . . . .

Fractions and decimals can name the same numbers and can be interchanged in problems. Is there also a similarity in the methods you have learned to carry out the operations with these numbers? A careful examination of the methods can help to show *why* they work and to show that everything "fits" or connects in mathematics.

Remember that decimal fractions are really just special fractions with denominators that are powers of 10.

$$0.7 = \frac{7}{10} \quad 0.23 = \frac{23}{100} \quad 0.003 = \frac{3}{1,000} \quad 20.89 = 20\frac{89}{100} \quad 135.3 = 135\frac{3}{10}$$

Equal Fractions and Equal Decimals

Why is 0.5 equal to 0.50 and 0.500? What allows you to forget the trailing zeros in a decimal?

$$0.5 = \frac{5}{10} \qquad 0.50 = \frac{50}{100} \qquad 0.500 = \frac{500}{1,000}$$

Write the decimals as fractions.

$$\frac{50 \div 10}{100 \div 10} = \frac{50}{100} = \frac{5}{10} \qquad \frac{500 \div 100}{1,000 \div 100} = \frac{500}{1,000} = \frac{5}{10}$$

Rename them in simplest form. Cancel the common zeros.

Why? Because the Fundamental Principle of Equal Fractions allows you to divide both numerator and denominator by the same number.

Adding and Subtracting

When you added and subtracted fractions, you had to be sure that the denominators were the same before you carried out the operation.

$$\frac{1}{8} + \frac{1}{2} = \frac{1}{8} + \frac{4}{8} = \frac{5}{8} \qquad\qquad \frac{3}{4} + \frac{1}{5} = \frac{15}{20} + \frac{4}{20} = \frac{19}{20}$$

With decimals, you only had to be sure that the decimal points were lined up when you wrote the problem down.

$$8.03 + 9.165 = \quad \begin{array}{r} 8.03 \\ +9.165 \\ \hline 17.195 \end{array} \qquad\qquad 35.01 + 4,040 + 3.78 = \quad \begin{array}{r} 35.01 \\ 4,040. \\ + \quad 3.78 \\ \hline 4,078.79 \end{array}$$

How are these methods connected? When the decimal points are lined up, the digits in each column have the same denominator. When you add by columns, all the digits you add *do* have the same denominator (tenths, hundredths, thousandths, etc.).

Multiplying

By writing decimals as fractions and multiplying them, you can discover the rule for multiplying with decimals.

$$0.0\underline{8} \times 0.0\underline{7} = \frac{8}{100} \times \frac{7}{100} = \frac{56}{10,000} = 0.0\underline{0}\,\underline{5}\,\underline{6}$$

$$0.0\underline{3} \times 0.\underline{6} = \frac{3}{100} \times \frac{6}{10} = \frac{18}{1,000} = 0.\underline{018}$$

2 places 1 place   3 places

Because you have to multiply *both* the tops and bottoms, the denominators get larger.

· · ·

When you are multiplying with decimals, the number of decimal places in the answer is the sum of the number of decimal places in the multipliers.

· · ·

PROBLEM 3   **Do not** use a calculator to find the answers for problem 3.

  a) Which weighs more, a package of cheese weighing 0.6 lb. or one weighing $\frac{5}{8}$ lb.?

  b) How much change would you expect from $5 when your purchase totaled $3.12?

  c) After a 7.1 m length of rope is cut from a 15 m coil, how much is left?

  d) The side of a square measures 0.6 m. What is the area of the square?

Dividing with Decimals
Example:

One wooden pencil costs 8¢. How many can you buy with $3.20?

This problem asks: "How many 8¢ are there in $3.20?"

This could be written
$$\frac{\$3.20}{\$.08}$$

If both numbers were in cents, it would be:
$$\frac{320¢}{8¢} = 40 \text{ pencils}$$

Now look at the same problem using a fraction.
$$\$3.20 \div \frac{8}{100}$$
$$= 3.20 \times \frac{100}{8} = 40 \text{ pencils}$$

The traditional rule for division of decimals involves the following steps:

1) Move the decimal point of the *divisor* to the end of the number.
$$\frac{3.20}{.08} \quad \text{2 places}$$

2) Move the decimal point of the numerator the same number of places. Remember the Fundamental Principle of Equal Fractions!
$$\frac{3.20}{.08} \quad \text{2 places}$$

3) Now divide as before.
$$\frac{320}{8} = 40 \text{ pencils}$$

Notice that all the methods shown come to the same final step, $\frac{320}{8}$.

Another example using the traditional rules:
$$35 \div 0.005 = \frac{35}{.005} = \frac{35.000}{.005}$$
$$= \frac{35,000}{5} = 7,000$$

You need to add three zeros so that you can move the decimal point the *same number* of places.

PROBLEM 4   Each of these everyday problems requires you to divide with decimals. Choose the method of solution that works best for the problem. Do not use your calculator.

  a) How many 25¢ stamps can you buy with $12.50?

  b) Each aluminum can weighs 0.04 lb. How many cans would you need in order to have 5 lb. of cans to recycle?

  c) A pork roast weighing 3.5 lb. costs $7.35. How much does it cost per pound?

  d) One nail weighs 0.025 oz. How many of these nails are there in 16 oz. (1 pound)?

Multi-Step Problems ....

The first kind of problem in this section will show the connections between a number of skills you learned in this lesson. These skills are brought together in a kind of problem that occurs often in everyday life.

Discount and Sale Price

Example:

A certain model of TV set is marked "$\frac{1}{4}$ OFF" during a clearance sale. The original price was $240. What is the sale price of this TV set?

What is the relationship between the important words in this problem?

original price (or marked price) = sale price + discount

Often this needs to be rearranged to say,

"sale price = original price – discount."

This is one of those general relationships that you are expected to know to pass the GED Test. (See Lesson 14.) It is the underlying equation of problems of this type.

Method 1: Find the amount of discount and subtract.

How to plan it:	How to write it:
	sale price = original price – discount
First, find the discount ($\frac{1}{4}$ of $240).	$s = 240 - (\frac{1}{4} \times 240)$ (Do what is in the parentheses first!)
Subtract the discount from the original price ($240) to find the sale price.	$s = 240 - 60$ $s = \$180$

There is another way to find the answer to this problem. First examine the relationship again.

Think of the original price as being this rectangle.

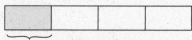

The original price is the *whole* thing.

Picture the discount as part of this rectangle.

The discount is $\frac{1}{4}$ of the whole.

The remainder of the rectangle must be the sale price.

The sale price is $\frac{3}{4}$ of the whole.

Method 2: Find the sale price directly.

How to plan it:	How to write it:
If the discount is $\frac{1}{4}$ of the original price, the sale price must be $\frac{3}{4}$ of the original price. $(1 - \frac{1}{4} = \frac{3}{4})$ To find the sale price, find $\frac{3}{4}$ of $240.	sale price = $(1 - \frac{1}{4}) \times$ original price $s = \frac{3}{4} \times 240$ (You could find $\frac{3}{4}$ mentally.) $s = \frac{3}{4} \times \frac{\overset{60}{240}}{\underset{1}{1}} = \$180$

Example:

An outlet store advertises "$\frac{1}{3}$ off Retail Prices." How much would the store charge for a coat that has a retail price of $174.80?

How to plan it:	How to write it:
The retail price is the original price. Using Method 2, subtract: $1 - \frac{1}{3} = \frac{2}{3}$ Then find $\frac{2}{3}$ of $174.80.	sale price $= (1 - \frac{1}{3}) \times 174.80$ $s = \frac{2}{3} \times \frac{174.80}{1}$ (An estimate of $\frac{2}{3} \times 180$ gives $120.) $s = 116.53333$ (on the calculator) $s = \$116.54$ (A merchant will take *a* fraction of a cent.)

PROBLEM 5 **Estimate** the price someone would have to pay for the following articles during the sale advertised here.

> **One-Day Sale—$\frac{1}{4}$ off Everything!**

a) student desk $119.97

b) table lamp   18.88

c) electric shaver   47.88

d) tea kettle   31.99

e) hair dryer   14.94

PROBLEM 6 Use your calculator to find the precise amount the store would charge for the articles listed in problem 5. Add to round to nearest cent.

PROBLEM 7 Which of the following equations could be used to find the sale price (on the day of the sale above) of a washing machine marked at $400?

(1) $s = \frac{1}{4} \times 400$

(2) $s = 400 - \frac{1}{4}$

(3) $s = 400 - \frac{1}{4}(400)$

(4) $s = \frac{1}{4}(400) + 400$

(5) $s = (1 + \frac{1}{4})400$

• More Miscellaneous Multi-Step Monsters . . . .

Example:

The bus traveling the interstate highway averaged 63 mph for 2 hours and 20 minutes. How far did it travel in that time?

How to plan it:	How to write it:
To find distance, multiply rate by time.	distance = rate $\times$ time ($d = rt$)
First, change the minutes to a fraction of an hour.	$d = 63 \times 2\frac{1}{3}$ (2 hours and 20 minutes = $2\frac{20}{60} = 2\frac{1}{3}$)
Then, find the distance.	$d = \frac{63}{1} \times \frac{7}{3} = 147$ miles

Example:

The gas tank on Portia's car holds 16.3 gallons. When the gas gauge reads $\frac{1}{4}$ full, how many gallons should be necessary to fill it up?

How to plan it:	**How to write it:**
Portia needs to fill $(1 - \frac{1}{4})$ or $\frac{3}{4}$ of the tank.	$n = \frac{3}{4}$ of 16.3 (estimate: $\frac{3}{4} \times 16 = 12$) $n = 0.75 \times 16.3 = 12.225$ gal.

Example:

What is the measure of the third angle of a triangle if the other two measure $32\frac{1}{2}°$ and $100\frac{1}{4}°$?

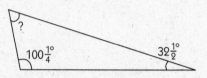

How to plan it:	**How to write it:**
The sum of all three angles is 180°.	$180° = a + 100\frac{1}{4}° + 32\frac{1}{2}°$
To find the answer, add the two angles that are given ($100\frac{1}{4}°$ and $32\frac{1}{2}°$), then subtract that sum from 180°.	$a = 180° - (100\frac{1}{4}° + 32\frac{1}{2}°)$ $a = 180° - 132\frac{3}{4}°$ $a = 47\frac{1}{4}°$

PROBLEM 8   Write a single equation to solve each of the following problems. Then solve, using your calculator if necessary.

a) How much change would you receive from a $10 bill if you purchased $1\frac{1}{2}$ pounds of corned beef priced at $5.60 a pound?

b) What is the measure of the third angle of a triangle in which the other two angles measure $50\frac{1}{4}°$ and $51\frac{3}{4}°$?

c) Ronald stopped to fill the gas tank of his car when the gauge indicated that the tank was about $\frac{1}{8}$ full. If the tank holds 15.2 gallons, how many gallons should Ronald need in order to fill the tank?

d) A truck driver noted that he had driven 144 miles in 2 hours and 15 minutes. What rate of speed did he average during that period of time?

e) A circular flower bed measuring 7 yd. in diameter is to be edged with material that sells for $1.69 a yd. How much will the material cost for this job? (Use $\pi = \frac{22}{7}$.)

You may use your calculator on any problem for which it seems appropriate.

Problems 1–3 are based on the following information.

Batting averages in baseball are figured by dividing:

$$\frac{\text{number of hits}}{\text{number of times at bat}}.$$

This fraction is then converted into a 3-decimal place number. So, if someone made 1 hit in 4 times at bat, the player's average would be $\frac{1}{4} = 0.250$.

1. Cincinnati's Barry Larkin's average coming into the last game of the 1990 World Series was 0.357. In the last game, he hit 1 time in 3 at-bats. Was this record higher or lower than his previous average?

2. Chris Sabo hit 3 out of 4 times during the last game but hit 9 out of 16 for the series. What are these averages?

3. Who had the higher average for the series, Rijo with 1 hit and 3 times at bat or Davis with 4 hits and 14 times at bat?

_____

4. A triangle whose base is 5 ft. has a height of $3\frac{1}{4}$ ft. What is the area of this triangle?

$3\frac{1}{4}$ ft.

5 ft.

5. A rectangle measures 2 feet 4 inches in width and 5 feet in length. How many square feet are in the area of this rectangle?

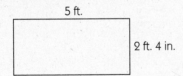

5 ft.

2 ft. 4 in.

6. Mrs. Hall divided a cake into three parts so that each of her sons would get an equal share. Paul ate half of his share in one day. What fractional part of the cake did Paul eat that one day?

7. The following list shows the regular prices of some items in a department store.

   a) bath towel $6.00

   b) hand towel   4.50

   c) washcloth   3.00

   During a white sale, all prices were $\frac{1}{3}$ off. What was the sale price of each of these items?

8. A finished piece of cross-stitch (a form of needlework) is 10 inches wide. If each stitch is $\frac{1}{11}$ in. wide, how many stitches are in each row? (Hint: This asks, "How many $\frac{1}{11}$s there are in 10?")

GED Practice

9. A group of 6 people ate 2 large pizzas. If each person ate the same amount, what fractional part of a pizza did each eat?

   (1) $\frac{1}{12}$

   (2) $\frac{1}{8}$

   (3) $\frac{1}{6}$

   (4) $\frac{1}{3}$

   (5) $\frac{1}{2}$

10. A customer gave a clerk a $20 bill to purchase four pints of cream. The cream was priced at $.69 per pint. How much change should the customer receive?

   (1) $.20
   (2) $2.76
   (3) $17.24
   (4) $19.31
   (5) $22.76

Checkpoint III

It is time for a check-up again. It is also time for you to reassure yourself that you are getting closer to your goal of passing the GED Test. Now that you've finished this section, you can

- compare the size of fractions,
- name numbers using either fractions or decimals,
- determine if two fractions are equal (using the Fundamental Principle),
- add, subtract, multiply, and divide fractions and mixed numbers,
- estimate the results of problems dealing with fractions, and
- solve everyday problems that include fractions.

This checkpoint contains problems covering all the concepts that you have learned so far in the book. However, since this one comes immediately after the fraction lessons, it will contain more fraction problems than on the GED Test. The real GED Math Test is not likely to have as many fraction problems.

• Test-Taking Tips: Multi-Step Problems . . . .

On most good multiple-choice tests, the answer choices that are given for each item correspond to mistakes that students tend to make. When the problem is one that requires more than one step to find the answer, students often stop after they finish only the first step. So you can expect to see the partial answers listed—ready to tempt you to make this error.

Example:

A refrigerator is priced at $980. The dealer offers a time payment plan under which Ron and Julia can pay $250 as a down payment and then make monthly payments of $80 a month for 12 months. How much more will they pay if they choose the time payment plan instead of paying the full price in cash?

(1) $1,210
(2) $960
(3) $730
(4) $230
(5) $70

You can avoid choosing partial solutions by writing a multi-step problem as a single equation, as you learned in Lesson 10. For the problem above, you could have written:

difference = $(250 + 80 \times 12) - 980$

After you have found an answer, <u>check</u> to see that it answers the question that is asked and is a reasonable solution.

Caution! Do not pick the first answer that appears in your work!

First: Put in your own words what the problem is asking: "How much more will the time payment plan cost?"

The first step in the solution of this problem is to multiply to find the total monthly payments.

80×12 months = $960.
This partial answer is choice (2).

Next, this amount must be added to the down payment to find the amount paid under this plan.

$960 + $250 = $1,210
This partial answer is choice (1).

Finally, subtract the cash price from the total cost of the time payment plan.

$1,210 − $980 = $230
The final answer is choice (4).

1. How much change would you expect from a $10 bill if you purchased 5 rolls of paper towels at $.69 each?

   (1) $3.45
   (2) $4.31
   (3) $5.69
   (4) $6.55
   (5) $9.31

2. Which of the following drill bit sizes would you choose to drill a hole 0.125 inch in diameter?

   (1) $\frac{1}{16}$ in.
   (2) $\frac{1}{8}$ in.
   (3) $\frac{3}{8}$ in.
   (4) $\frac{1}{2}$ in.
   (5) $\frac{9}{16}$ in.

3. Which expression below shows how many <u>square feet</u> make up the area of a sidewalk that is 3 ft. wide and m <u>yards</u> long?

   3 ft. | m yds.

   (1) $\frac{3}{m}$
   (2) m
   (3) $3m$
   (4) $9m$
   (5) $\frac{9}{m}$

4. Attendance figures showed that the stadium was filled to only $\frac{3}{5}$ its capacity for the 35 weeknight games during the season. How many seats were empty at each game?

   (1) 14
   (2) 21
   (3) 12,000
   (4) 16,000
   (5) Not enough information is given.

5. How many yards of fabric are needed to make 5 cheerleaders' skirts if one skirt requires $1\frac{1}{4}$ yards?

(1) $3\frac{3}{4}$ yd.
(2) 4 yd.
(3) $5\frac{1}{20}$ yd.
(4) $6\frac{1}{4}$ yd.
(5) $9\frac{1}{5}$ yd.

6. Which value of p makes the following equation true?
$3p - 7 = 17$

(1) $\frac{17}{3}$
(2) $\frac{17}{7}$
(3) $\frac{10}{3}$
(4) 8
(5) 10

7. An isosceles triangle has two sides that are equal. The two angles that are opposite these sides also are equal to each other. What is the measure of the equal angles at X and Z?

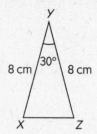

(1) 16°
(2) 50°
(3) 75°
(4) 150°
(5) Not enough information is given.

8. In 1928, Babe Ruth set a World Series batting record with a .625 average. Billy Hatcher broke that record by hitting 9 times out of 12 times at bat during the 1990 World Series. What was Hatcher's record?

(1) .900
(2) .750
(3) .666
(4) .333
(5) Not enough information is given.

9. During a time trial, Robert cycled 5.25 km in 10 minutes. During the same period, Thomas cycled one-tenth of a kilometer farther than Robert. How far did Thomas cycle?

(1) 52.5 km
(2) 5.35 km
(3) 5.26 km
(4) 5.15 km
(5) 0.525 km

10. The automotive industry spent $889 million in advertising on network TV for the first half of 1990. Which of the following expressions gives this number in scientific notation?

(1) 8.89×10^2
(2) 8.89×10^5
(3) 8.89×10^6
(4) 8.89×10^8
(5) 8.89×10^{10}

Problems 11 and 12 refer to the following information:

This graph shows the relationship between the number of pounds of aluminum cans submitted for recycling and the amount paid for them at a recycling center. That relationship is also shown by the formula $d = 0.75n$.

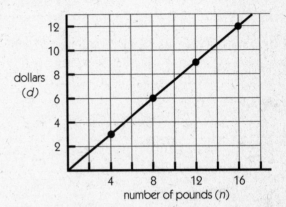

11. How much is paid for 12 pounds of cans?

(1) $16
(2) $12
(3) $9
(4) $8
(5) Not enough information is given.

12. How many pounds of cans are needed to be worth $10?

(1) 6
(2) $7\frac{1}{2}$
(3) 10
(4) $13\frac{1}{3}$
(5) 15

13. The following amounts are interest rates on savings offered by various investments. Which is the highest rate?

   (1) $7\frac{3}{4}$%
   (2) 7.46%
   (3) $7\frac{7}{8}$%
   (4) 7.77%
   (5) $7\frac{1}{2}$%

14. In a sample of cross-stitch on gingham, each stitch is $\frac{1}{8}$ in. wide. How many stitches will there be across a border that is $2\frac{1}{2}$ in. wide?

   (1) 20
   (2) $3\frac{1}{5}$
   (3) $2\frac{5}{8}$
   (4) $2\frac{3}{8}$
   (5) $\frac{5}{16}$

15. A 40-acre parcel of land is being developed for housing. Roads will take up 8 acres, and 4 acres of parkland are planned. Into how many $\frac{2}{3}$-acre home sites can the remaining acreage be divided?

   (1) 18
   (2) 21
   (3) 28
   (4) 32
   (5) 42

Problems 16 and 17 are based on the following diagram.

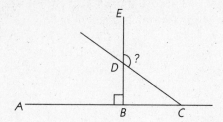

16. If angle *BDC* measures 45°, what is the measure of angle *EDC*?

   (1) 45°
   (2) 90°
   (3) 120°
   (4) 135°
   (5) Not enough information is given.

17. What kind of angle is angle *ABD*?

   (1) left
   (2) right
   (3) acute
   (4) obtuse
   (5) straight

_____

18. A rice and sauce mix weighs 127 g. The nutrition information on the package says that it contains 100 g of carbohydrates. Approximately what fractional part of the mix is carbohydrates?

   (1) $\frac{1}{27}$
   (2) $\frac{1}{5}$
   (3) $\frac{4}{5}$
   (4) $\frac{6}{5}$
   (5) $\frac{27}{10}$

19. For each hour that Belinda works at her part-time job, she earns $8.50. On Monday she worked $4\frac{1}{2}$ hours, on Tuesday she worked $1\frac{1}{2}$ hours, and on Wednesday she worked 3 hours. Which of the following expressions shows the number of dollars she earned during those 3 days?

    (1) $(4\frac{1}{2} \times 1\frac{1}{2} \times 3)(8.50)$
    (2) $9(8.50)$
    (3) $3(8.50)(10)$
    (4) $10(8.50)$
    (5) $4.5(8.50) \times 1.5(8.50) \times 3(8.50)$

20. For 1 hour and 10 minutes, a cyclist maintained a pace of 30 km per hour. How far did she travel in that time?

    (1) 25 km
    (2) 27 km
    (3) 31 km
    (4) 33 km
    (5) 35 km

Self-Evaluation

Check your answers and compare your solutions with those given in the answer key. When you compare solutions, you can learn another way to do the problem and adopt the new way if you like it better than yours.

Review the questions again, trying to gain some insight into the problems you can expect on the GED Test.

1) How many questions could you solve by estimating?

2) For which questions would you have used a calculator if it had been allowed?

3) For how many questions did you refer to the formulas page?

Problems	Skills	Lessons
1	Multi-step problems	10
2	Decimals and fractions	18
3	Areas	8, 11
4	Not enough information	6
5	Dividing fractions	17
6	Equivalent equations	9
7	Triangles	4
8, 13	Decimals and fractions	15, 18
9	Decimals	2
10	Scientific notation	13
11, 12	Finding cost/Equivalent equations	9
14	Dividing fractions	17
15	Dividing fractions/Multi-step problems	17 & 18
16	Complementary and supplementary angles	4
17	Angles	4
18	Equal fractions	15
19, 20	Multi-step problems	18

• LESSON 20 • Comparisons: Fractions as Ratios

Mental Math Exercises

Are the two fractions equal?

1. $\frac{1}{2}$ and $\frac{5}{10}$?   4. $\frac{1}{8}$ and $\frac{8}{32}$?

2. $\frac{1}{3}$ and $\frac{2}{9}$?   5. $\frac{1}{5}$ and $\frac{5}{20}$?

3. $\frac{1}{4}$ and $\frac{25}{100}$?   6. $\frac{1}{10}$ and $\frac{5}{50}$?

To compare the fractions in the Mental Math Exercises, you may have simplified one fraction. In this lesson, you will learn another way to decide when two fractions are equal.

• Using Fractions to Compare . . . .

There are twice as many men as women in this class.
The ratio of men to women is 2 to 1,   2:1,   OR $\frac{2}{1}$.

Each table seats 6 people. We need 1 table for each group of 6 people.
The ratio of tables to people is 1 to 6,   1:6,   OR $\frac{1}{6}$.

6 cans of soda cost $1.49.
The ratio of cans to cents is 6 to 149,   6:149,   OR $\frac{6}{149}$.

7 out of the 20 candies are red
The ratio of red candies to the total is 7 to 20,   7:20,   OR $\frac{7}{20}$.

Each fraction compares one number to another. When a fraction is used to compare numbers, it is called a ratio. A ratio is a comparison by division. You need 2 numbers to write a ratio. Notice that the order of the numbers in the fraction reflects the order of the words in the statement:

There are 11 students for each teacher.

The ratio of <u>students to teachers</u> is 11 to 1, OR $\frac{11}{1}$. The ratio of <u>teachers to students</u> is 1 to 11, OR $\frac{1}{11}$.

PROBLEM 1   Write each of the following comparisons using a ratio. Use the fraction format.

a) 2 aluminum cans for 5¢: Write the ratio of <u>cans</u> to <u>cents</u>.

b) 25 miles in 3 hours: Write the ratio of <u>miles</u> to <u>hours</u>. (Leave this as a single fraction. Ratios are not changed to mixed numbers.)

c) 3,300 miles in 5 days: Write the ratio of <u>miles</u> to <u>days</u>.

d) length of 10 m compared to a width of 7 m: Write the ratio of <u>width</u> to <u>length</u>.

e) one gallon of paint for 400 sq. ft.: Write the ratio of <u>gallons</u> to <u>square feet</u>.

f) $4 for 3 lb. of hamburger: Write the ratio of <u>pounds</u> to <u>dollars</u>.

• Rates . . . .

Some ratios can be thought of as rates. You have already learned a lot about one rate that we also call **speed**. Recall from Lesson 9 that rate = $\frac{distance}{time}$. When the distance is measured in miles and the time in hours, this becomes $\frac{miles}{hour}$ (miles per hour).

Cheryl can walk 4 miles in an hour.

Her <u>rate</u> of speed is $\frac{4 \text{ miles}}{1 \text{ hour}}$ (4 miles per hour), or simply 4 mph.

An average person's heart beats 72 times a minute.

This heart <u>rate</u> is $\frac{72 \text{ beats}}{1 \text{ minute}}$ (72 beats per minute).

A compact car can travel 34 miles on a gallon of gasoline.

Its mileage is $\frac{34 \text{ miles}}{1 \text{ gallon}}$ (34 miles per gallon), or 34 mpg.

Rates are often expressed using the word *per*. Think of *per* as saying "for each." Thus, 8 mpg says 8 miles <u>for each</u> gallon, 90 km/hr says 90 kilometers <u>for each</u> hour, and so on.

Unless you are told differently, you can assume that a rate is given in terms of 1 unit of measure. As in the examples above, you will have to provide the 1 so that there are 2 numbers to compare:

34 miles per gallon = $\frac{34 \text{ miles}}{1 \text{ gallon}}$ OR $\frac{34}{1}$

PROBLEM 2   Write each statement as a rate, using the word *per* to express the comparison.

Example: Barb can type 35 words in a minute.

35 words per minute

a) A rental car company charges $25 a day for renting a compact car.

_____

b) There are 4 glasses of milk in each quart.

_____

c) The speed limit on some interstate highways is 65 miles an hour.

_____

d) Warren earns $9.50 for each hour that he works.

_____

e) A high-speed train can travel 320 miles in one hour.

_____

f) The bank charges a monthly fee of $3.00.

_____

g) Jasmine paid $32 for each concert ticket.

_____

h) Each can of soda costs $.75 from the vending machine.

_____

• Ratios Compare by Division.....................

Why use fractions to express ratios? You know that the line in a fraction means "divided by." For example, $\frac{1}{2}$ means the same as $1 \div 2$. Similarly, ratios and rates compare two numbers by using division as the basis for the comparison.

How can you tell that a situation is using division to compare two numbers?

Division is the operation to use when something is separated into equal groups. Look for clues that indicate this relationship. When the word *per* (meaning "for each") is used to describe a relationship, it means that the quantity is being considered in equal groups.

Use 3 cups of flour *for each* package of yeast.

The ratio of <u>flour</u> to <u>yeast</u> is 3:1, or $\frac{3}{1}$.

Ratios can also be used to describe a relationship where multiplication is involved. Remember, multiplication is the inverse of division.

The window's width is twice its height.

The ratio of <u>width</u> to <u>height</u> is 2 to 1, or $\frac{2}{1}$.

However, you **cannot** use ratios when things are being compared by subtraction.

Martha finished the assignment in 2 hours less time than it took Harry.

This comparison does not use division; it uses subtraction to compare.

If Harry took h hours, Martha took $h - 2$ hours to finish.

For example, if Harry took 6 hours, Martha took 4 hours.

PROBLEM 3 Decide whether each of the following situations can be described using a ratio. If it can, write the ratio in fraction form.

Example: Ramona painted 4 rooms in 3 hours—$\frac{4}{3}$.

a) It is 4 miles farther to Grove City than it is to Raymond.

b) The solar car was able to go 40 miles in one hour.

c) The height of the triangle was 5 times the length of its base.

d) The height of the triangle was 5 inches longer than its base.

e) Add 3 parts red pigment to 2 parts yellow pigment.

f) Add 3 cups more cereal than peanuts.

g) Duane is 5 years older than his sister, Luann.

h) Thomas is 5 times as old as his son, Ted.

i) 9 out of 10 doctors use this product.

j) The vote count in the council was 19 for, 10 against the measure.

Percent

Percent is a ratio that is used nearly every day in our lives. The word **percent** literally means "per hundred" or "for each hundred."

A 6% sales tax means that for every $100 you spend, you must pay $6 in tax.

6% is expressed as a ratio by $\frac{6}{100}$ (6 out of a hundred).

A 9% interest rate means that $100 in savings will earn $9 a year in interest.

The ratio $\frac{9}{100}$ (9 out of a hundred) is the same as 9%.

PROBLEM 4   In a typical paragraph written in the English language, the letter *e* occurs most frequently. This list gives the percent frequency of some letters in ordinary English passages.

Letter	Frequency
e	13%
t	9%
a, o	8%
n	7%
i, r	6.5%
s, h	6%

a) How many *t*'s would you expect to find in a passage containing 100 letters?

b) How many *e*'s would you expect to find in a passage of 100 letters?

c) How many *n*'s in 100 letters?

d) How many *n*'s in 200 letters?

e) How many *s*'s in 100 letters? in 300 letters? in 1,000 letters?

Slopes

• • •
The slope of a line is the ratio $\frac{rise}{run}$.
• • •

A ratio that tells how steeply a line is leaning is called the **slope** of that line. The ratio compares how far up (or down) the line goes to how far across it goes from *left* to *right*.

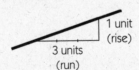

1 unit (rise)

3 units (run)

Sketching a right triangle under this line makes it easy to see that the line **rises** 1 unit while it **runs** 3 units.

The slope of this line is $\frac{rise}{run} = \frac{1}{3}$.

PROBLEM 5   Find the slope of each of these lines. Use the ratio $\frac{rise}{run}$.

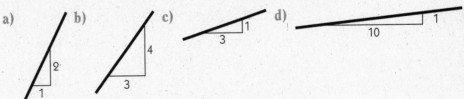

a) b) c) d)

2 1 4 3 1 3 10 1

PROBLEM 6   A road sign states that there will be a steep downgrade of 6% ahead. How many yards will the road descend for every 100 yards that it crosses?

• Expressing Ratios in Simplest Form. . . . .

There are 8 red candies out of 24.

What is the ratio of red candies to the total? $\frac{8}{24} = \frac{1}{3}$ The ratio is 1:3 or $\frac{1}{3}$.

Once a ratio is expressed as a fraction, you can apply the Fundamental Principle of Equal Fractions to write that fraction (ratio) in its simplest form. It is in simplest form when no number (other than 1) can be divided into *both* the numerator and the denominator.

$$\frac{5}{20} = \frac{5 \div 5}{20 \div 5} = \frac{1}{4} \qquad \frac{15}{21} = \frac{15 \div 3}{21 \div 3} = \frac{5}{7} \qquad \frac{90}{120} = \frac{90 \div 30}{120 \div 30} = \frac{3}{4}$$

PROBLEM 7 Write each of these comparisons as ratios in simplest terms.

a) Franz drove 360 km in 3 hours.

b) 250 people out of 1,000 surveyed favored the proposition.

c) Naomi earned $80 for working 8 hours.

d) Al paid $100 for 5 tickets.

e) One box weighs 14 oz., and the other weighs 7 oz.

f) Of 80 kernels in the bag, 12 remained unpopped.

Equal Ratios Are Proportions

A statement that says two ratios are equal is called a proportion. There are interesting patterns to notice in proportions. First notice the relationship you used when you expressed the ratios in simplest terms in the problems above.

$$\frac{16}{20} = \frac{4}{5}$$
proportion

Look *across* the proportion from numerator to numerator and denominator to denominator. Notice that 16 ÷ 4 = 4 and 20 ÷ 4 = 5. This is the pattern you have learned as the Fundamental Principle of Equal Fractions.

$$\frac{16 \div 4}{20 \div 4} = \frac{4}{5}$$

Use this relationship to build equivalent ratios the way you built equal fractions in Lesson 16.

A recycling center pays 5¢ for 2 aluminum cans.

Cans	2	4	6	8	10	12	14
Cents	5	10	15	20	25	30	35

The table is filled in by building equal fractions, using the Fundamental Principle of Equal Fractions.

$$\frac{2}{5} = \frac{4}{10} = \frac{6}{15} = \frac{8}{20} = \frac{10}{25} = \frac{12}{30} = \frac{14}{35}$$

$\left(\frac{2}{5} \times \frac{2}{2}\right) \quad \left(\frac{2}{5} \times \frac{3}{3}\right) \quad \left(\frac{2}{5} \times \frac{4}{4}\right) \quad \left(\frac{2}{5} \times \frac{5}{5}\right) \quad \left(\frac{2}{5} \times \frac{6}{6}\right) \quad \left(\frac{2}{5} \times \frac{7}{7}\right)$

In problems 8 and 9, complete the tables using the pattern shown on page 164.

PROBLEM 8
For $2, you can buy a package of 3 rolls of paper towels.

$	2			8	10	12
Rolls	3	6	9			

PROBLEM 9
The ratio of length to width of certain rectangles is 5 to 3.

Length	5			20	25	30
Width	3	6	9			

The statement 6:12 :: 3:6 is read as "6 is to 12 as 3 is to 6."

The second pattern in proportions occurs when a proportion is written in the manner of an analogy (a statement that tells that two relationships are equal). To notice the pattern, look from top to bottom of the same fraction.

1 is to 5 as 3 is to 15.
1:5 :: 3:15
$\frac{1}{5} = \frac{3}{15}$

What you did (× or ÷) to 1 to get 5 is the same thing you do to 3 to get 15.

8 is to 80 as 3 is to 30
8:80 :: 3:30.
$\frac{8}{80} = \frac{3}{30}$

The relationship (× or ÷) between 8 and 80 is the same as between 3 and 30.

PROBLEM 10 Complete the following statements.

a) 9 is to 1 as ☐ is to 2.

b) 8 is to 16 as ☐ is to 10.

c) 4 is to 5 as 400 is to ☐.

d) 5 is to 50 as 10 is to ☐.

e) 9 is to 45 as 12 is to ☐.

f) 100 is to 25 as ☐ is to 15.

The third pattern in proportions is less apparent than the other two, but it can be applied in all proportion situations. When a pattern is so dependable that you can always fall back on it, it becomes a mathematical principle or law.

The **Law of Proportionality** says that

$$\text{If } \frac{a}{b} = \frac{c}{d}, \text{ then } ad = bc.$$

In words, it says that if 2 ratios (fractions) are equal, their cross products are equal. The **cross products** are the answers you get when you multiply the numerator of each fraction by the denominator of the other.

$\frac{2}{3} = \frac{8}{12}$ So:
$2 \times 12 = 8 \times 3$
$24 = 24$

$\frac{3}{5} = \frac{9}{15}$ So:
$3 \times 15 = 9 \times 5$
$45 = 45$

Like some other laws you have learned, this one works both ways. That is, if the cross products are equal, the ratios (fractions) are equal. You can use this fact as a test to determine whether 2 ratios (fractions) are equal.

$\frac{5}{6} \overset{?}{=} \frac{25}{36}$ $5 \times 36 \overset{?}{=} 6 \times 25$
$180 \neq 150$ No, they are not equal.

$\frac{9}{12} \overset{?}{=} \frac{15}{20}$ $9 \times 20 \overset{?}{=} 15 \times 12$
$180 = 180$ Yes, they are equal.

(≠ means "is not equal to.")

PROBLEM 11 Use the Law of Proportionality to determine whether each pair of ratios is equal.

a) $\frac{3}{4} \overset{?}{=} \frac{9}{16}$

b) $\frac{4}{5} \overset{?}{=} \frac{12}{15}$

c) $\frac{3}{4} \overset{?}{=} \frac{15}{20}$

d) $\frac{3}{5} \overset{?}{=} \frac{9}{25}$

e) $\frac{4}{6} \overset{?}{=} \frac{7}{9}$

f) $\frac{6}{10} \overset{?}{=} \frac{27}{45}$

g) $\frac{4}{9} \overset{?}{=} \frac{16}{54}$

h) $\frac{8}{3} \overset{?}{=} \frac{72}{27}$

i) $\frac{3}{4} \overset{?}{=} \frac{9}{25}$

j) $\frac{3}{4} \overset{?}{=} \frac{75}{100}$

k) $\frac{3}{5} \overset{?}{=} \frac{60}{100}$

l) $\frac{5}{20} \overset{?}{=} \frac{20}{100}$

When to Use Proportions . . . .

Remember that ratios are used to compare two quantities by division, and that two equal ratios are called a proportion. A proportion problem provides one complete ratio.

Examples:

5 cents for 2 cans

$$\frac{5 \text{ cents}}{2 \text{ cans}}$$

55 miles per hour

$$\frac{55 \text{ miles}}{1 \text{ hour}}$$

A proportion problem also provides information for a similar ratio. This ratio will have a missing value. Substitute a letter in place of the missing value when setting up a proportion.

How much money would you receive for 100 cans if you get 5 cents for 2 cans?

$$\frac{5 \text{ cents}}{2 \text{ cans}} = \frac{x \text{ cents}}{100 \text{ cans}}$$

At 55 miles per hour, how long would it take to travel 500 miles?

$$\frac{55 \text{ miles}}{1 \text{ hour}} = \frac{500 \text{ miles}}{t \text{ hours}}$$

> The ratios in a proportion must be set up in the same order. Labeling the ratios will help maintain the correct order.

Sometimes it's hard to recognize ratios and proportions in everyday problems. First, decide whether or not a comparison is being made. If it is, you can then try to use a proportion to organize the information and solve the problem.

> Often a problem will state *at this rate* to indicate that the ratios are equal and a proportion is appropriate.

Example: Sarah bought a rug that measures 4 ft. by 7 ft. What total area does the rug cover?

A comparison is not being asked for. You would choose a different method of solution.

Decide if using proportions to solve problems 12 and 13 is appropriate. If the answer is yes, decide what is being compared, and set up a proportion, labeling the ratios to keep the values in the same order.

PROBLEM 12 Andy has made 9 of 12 free-throw attempts. If he continues at this rate, how many shots will he make in 16 attempts?

a) Can a proportion be used to solve the problem?

b) If yes, label the ratios and set up the proportion.

PROBLEM 13 A cake takes 45 minutes to bake. If the cake was put in the oven at 2:00, at what time was it done?

a) Can a proportion be used to solve the problem?

b) If yes, label the ratios and set up the proportion.

The order of numbers must be the same in both ratios of a proportion. Choose the answers that keep the ratios in the same order.

PROBLEM 14 Four out of 5 doctors surveyed recommended Brand Y aspirin. This was based on a survey of 200 doctors. Which of the proportions below could be used to find the number of doctors who recommended Brand Y? (More than one answer is possible.)

a) $\frac{4}{5} = \frac{d}{200}$

c) $\frac{5}{4} = \frac{200}{d}$

e) $\frac{4}{d} = \frac{5}{200}$

b) $\frac{4}{5} = \frac{200}{d}$

d) $\frac{5}{4} = \frac{d}{200}$

You may use your calculator on any problem for which it seems appropriate.

1. The following people were in a classroom one evening:
   1 teacher, male
   8 students, 3 male, 5 female

   What is the ratio (in fraction form)

   a) of <u>students</u> to <u>teachers</u>?

   b) of <u>male students</u> to <u>female students</u>?

   c) of male students to total students?

   d) of female students to total students?

   e) of males to females (total)?

2. Willie used 10 gallons of gasoline for a trip of 250 miles. What is the rate of miles traveled per gallon of gas? (Write as a simplified ratio.)

3. In one game, Byron attempted 12 free throws and made 10 of them. Write the ratio of free throws *missed* to those attempted.

4. A driver's manual recommends certain distances to maintain between your car and the one ahead so that there is room to stop if necessary. It recommends that you leave 1 car length for every 10 mph of speed at which you are driving. Complete this table:

Speed (mph)	20	30	40	50	60
Car Lengths					

5. The dropout rate for the class of 1986 in the Inglewood, California, schools was 31%. By 1989, the dropout rate was down to 11%. If the 1989 rate were maintained, how many people from a class of 100 would you expect to drop out before graduation?

6. What is the slope of the line sketched below?

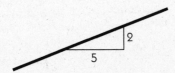

7. The ratio between the circumference and the diameter of every circle is the same:

   $$\frac{\text{circumference}}{\text{diameter}} = \pi$$

   Complete the following table.

c	22			88
d	7	14	21	

8. Complete the following statements:

   a) 4 is to 20 as 20 is to ☐.

   b) 2 is to 12 as 12 is to ☐.

   c) 5 is to 25 as 11 is to ☐.

   d) 8 is to 11 as 80 is to ☐.

   e) 99 is to 9 as ☐ is to 2.

   f) 6 is to 42 as ☐ is to 49.

9. Use the Law of Proportionality to determine which of the following ratios are equal.

   a) $\frac{7}{8} \overset{?}{=} \frac{56}{64}$

   b) $\frac{5}{9} \overset{?}{=} \frac{25}{81}$

   c) $\frac{4}{5} \overset{?}{=} \frac{45}{55}$

   d) $\frac{10}{15} \overset{?}{=} \frac{24}{36}$

   e) $\frac{3}{8} \overset{?}{=} \frac{31}{81}$

GED Practice

10. The Indianapolis 500 is a race that runs for 200 laps of the track. The 1990 winner, Arie Luyendyk, led for 35 laps. What is the ratio of the number of laps in which Luyendyk led to the total number of laps?

    (1) 7:100
    (2) 7:40
    (3) 2:5
    (4) 5:2
    (5) 100:7

• LESSON 21 • Proportions

Mental Math Exercises

Are the fractions equal?

1. $\frac{1}{3}$ and $\frac{3}{15}$?   4. $\frac{3}{4}$ and $\frac{16}{20}$?

2. $\frac{1}{2}$ and $\frac{60}{120}$?   5. $\frac{9}{11}$ and $\frac{18}{33}$?

3. $\frac{3}{5}$ and $\frac{10}{15}$?   6. $\frac{4}{5}$ and $\frac{16}{25}$?

• Proportions in Real Problems ....

Your daily experiences are full of situations that require you to decide whether two rates or ratios are equal. The first step is to write a proportion that describes the situation.

Example: An over-the-counter cold medication is available in 2 package sizes. A package of 25 tablets costs $3.00, while a package of 10 tablets costs $1.20. Is this the same price per tablet?

There are many ways to set up a proportion for this problem. The important thing is to keep the order the same in both ratios. Labeling the values can help you to keep corresponding values across from each other in the proportion.

$$\frac{\text{tablets}}{\text{cents}} \cdot \frac{25}{300¢} \overset{?}{=} \frac{10}{120¢} \qquad \frac{\text{cents}}{\text{tablets}} \cdot \frac{300¢}{25} \overset{?}{=} \frac{120¢}{10} \qquad \frac{\text{large pkg.}}{\text{small pkg.}} \cdot \frac{300¢}{120¢} \overset{?}{=} \frac{25}{10}$$

To decide whether these are **true proportions**, that is, whether the ratios are indeed equal, find the cross products. For each possible setup above, the multiplications remain the same.

$$25 \times 120 = 300 \times 10$$

(true proportion; the ratios are equal)

PROBLEM 1 Set up a proportion that fits each situation. Then, <u>test</u> to see if it is true.

a) Javier traveled 165 miles in 3 hours. Is this an average speed of 55 mph?

b) Oranges are priced at 2 for $.35. Will 8 oranges cost $1.50?

c) Each table seats 6 people. To seat 64 people, 16 tables are needed.

d) At the recycling center, 5¢ is paid for 2 aluminum cans. To get $10.00, you need to have 200 cans.

e) To mix the fuel for a 2-cycle engine, you combine 1 part oil with 10 parts gasoline. If you start with 5 cups of gasoline, you need 2 cups of oil.

f) A recipe serving 6 people asks for 2 lb. of ground beef. To serve 24 people, you need 8 lb. of ground beef.

g) In a state with a 6% sales tax, a buyer would pay $.30 tax on a $5.00 purchase.

h) If 2 out of 5 students are men, you would expect 12 <u>women</u> in a class of 20.

i) If the ratio of men to women in a class is 2 to 3, you would expect 8 men in a class of 20. (Remember to label the ratios.)

Finding a Missing Number in a Proportion . . . . . .

Before going on to solve proportions, take time to review how you solved equations involving variables earlier in the book.

Sometimes you could guess the correct answer.

$3c = 18$ says that *something* times 3 is 18. What is that something? It is 6.

Other times you wrote an **equivalent equation** in which the variable was alone.

$3n = \boxed{81}$ can also be written as $n = \frac{81}{3}$, and this equals 27.

> The product (answer to the multiplication problem) becomes the top number of the division problem.

PROBLEM 2 Solve these equations by first writing an equivalent equation.

a) $4 \cdot b = 40$ c) $7x = 140$ e) $25s = 450$

b) $5 \cdot t = 100$ d) $10d = 75$ f) $11y = 143$

Now, on to solving proportions. If you are given three of the numbers in a proportion, you can find the fourth one. Use a letter for the missing number, and find which value makes the proportion true.

Example: $\frac{n}{5} = \frac{12}{20}$

$20 \cdot n = 5 \cdot 12$

Step 1: Cross multiply. You get an equation with a variable in it.

$n = \frac{5 \cdot 12}{20} = \frac{60}{20}$

Step 2: Write the equivalent equation in which n is alone on its side of the equation.

$n = 3$

Step 3: Carry out the division.

$\frac{3}{5} = \frac{12}{20}$

$\frac{3 \times 4}{5 \times 4} = \frac{12}{20}$

$\frac{12}{20} = \frac{12}{20}$

Step 4: Check your answer. Put the *3* in place of the *n* in the original proportion. Look for another one of the relationships in the proportion that you can check mentally.

Compare Method 1 and Method 2 below. Method 2 is easier because you reduce before carrying out the multiplication of the numbers.

Method 1:

$\frac{12}{y} = \frac{6}{24}$

$6 \cdot y = 12 \cdot 24$

$6y = 288$

$y = \frac{288}{6} = 48$

Method 2:

$\frac{12}{y} = \frac{6}{24}$

$6 \cdot y = 12 \cdot 24$

$y = \frac{\overset{2}{12} \cdot 24}{\underset{1}{6}} = 48$

Check: $\frac{12}{48} = \frac{6}{24}$

Look for the other relationships in this proportion:

Top to bottom:
$12 \times 4 = 48$, and
$6 \times 4 = 24$.

Across:
6 is half of 12, and 24 is half of 48.

PROBLEM 3 Solve these proportions. Be sure to check your answers.

a) $\dfrac{c}{5} = \dfrac{24}{30}$ c) $\dfrac{5}{8} = \dfrac{p}{88}$ e) $\dfrac{t}{9} = \dfrac{10}{6}$ g) $\dfrac{6}{15} = \dfrac{10}{w}$

b) $\dfrac{8}{m} = \dfrac{20}{30}$ d) $\dfrac{4}{15} = \dfrac{20}{b}$ f) $\dfrac{10}{c} = \dfrac{25}{100}$ h) $\dfrac{3}{11} = \dfrac{k}{121}$

Fractions and Mixed Numbers

Fractions and mixed numbers can be terms of a proportion. The solutions will not always be whole numbers.

$\dfrac{1}{6} = \dfrac{b}{3}$

$6b = 3$

$b = \dfrac{3}{6} = \dfrac{1}{2}$

> **Check:**
> $\dfrac{1}{6} = \dfrac{\frac{1}{2}}{3}$
> Look across the example:
> $6 = 2 \times 3$, and $1 = 2 \times \frac{1}{2}$

$\dfrac{\frac{1}{4}}{3} = \dfrac{v}{36}$

$3 \cdot v = \dfrac{1}{4} \cdot 36$

$3v = 9$

$v = 3$

> **Check:**
> $\dfrac{\frac{1}{4}}{3} = \dfrac{3}{36}$
> Look across the example:
> $3 \times 12 = 36$, and $\frac{1}{4} \times 12 = 3$.

This method of solving proportions (using cross multiplication) works in every case, with all numbers. However, that does not mean that you *must* use it every time. If you recognize the **pattern** in the proportion and can solve it mentally, the problem becomes easier.

> **Look down each fraction.**
>
> Take time to examine the relationships.
>
> 14 is 2×7. ◄─── $\dfrac{7}{14} = \dfrac{12}{s}$ ───► so, s is 2×12.
>
> The bottom number is 2 times the top. Therefore,
>
> $s = 24$
>
> This completes the pattern, since $24 = 2 \times 12$.

> **Look across the proportion.**
>
> Can you simplify the ratio first?
>
> $12 \div 4 = 3$ ──► $\dfrac{12}{20} = \dfrac{9}{d}$
> $20 \div 4 = 5$ ──►
>
> Both 12 and 20 are divisible by 4.
>
> Now, look across ──► $\dfrac{3}{5} = \dfrac{9}{d}$
>
> The pattern across is apparent:
> 3×3 is 9, so $5 \times 3 = d$.
>
> $d = 15$

PROBLEM 4 Solve these proportions using the method that seems best for the problem.

a) $\dfrac{4}{5} = \dfrac{12}{b}$ f) $\dfrac{3}{7} = \dfrac{d}{28}$ k) $\dfrac{1.2}{z} = \dfrac{4.8}{8}$

b) $\dfrac{k}{12} = \dfrac{6}{8}$ g) $\dfrac{n}{25} = \dfrac{48}{100}$ l) $\dfrac{1.5}{9} = \dfrac{s}{12}$

c) $\dfrac{3}{8} = \dfrac{r}{64}$ h) $\dfrac{3}{7} = \dfrac{r}{10}$ m) $\dfrac{\frac{1}{4}}{6} = \dfrac{\frac{1}{8}}{n}$

d) $\dfrac{3}{v} = \dfrac{7}{28}$ i) $\dfrac{44}{4} = \dfrac{d}{11}$ n) $\dfrac{\frac{1}{5}}{20} = \dfrac{c}{4}$

e) $\dfrac{8}{32} = \dfrac{n}{100}$ j) $\dfrac{5}{8} = \dfrac{n}{100}$ o) $\dfrac{2\frac{1}{2}}{5} = \dfrac{100}{a}$

You have learned that the order of numbers must be the same in both ratios of a proportion. When proportions are set up for you on the GED Test, you must choose the answer that keeps the ratios in the same order.

• Using Proportions to Solve Real Problems . . . .

You have already seen some of the wide variety of problems that can be described by using a proportion. But there are many more!

In problems that involve rates, people often have trouble deciding whether to multiply or divide. When you use a proportion, that question is answered for you.

Example:

The GED Testing Service reports that one out of every six high school diplomas awarded in the United States each year is based on the GED Test. If 375,000 people passed the GED Test in 1989, what was the total number of high school diplomas earned in the United States that year?

Step 1: Set up the proportion.

$$\frac{GED}{Total} : \frac{1}{6} = \frac{375,000}{n}$$

Step 2: Cross multiply.

$$n = 6 \cdot 375,000 = 2,250,000$$

(*n* means the same thing as 1•*n*)

Step 3: Check. $\frac{1}{6} = \frac{375,000}{2,250,000}$

In Lesson 7, you may have had trouble deciding whether to multiply or divide in problems like this.

Example:

How many feet are there in 7 yards? (There are 3 feet in 1 yard.)

As the given ratio use the equivalency 3 ft. = 1 yd.

$$\frac{feet}{yards} : \frac{3}{1} = \frac{f}{7} \quad \text{Cross multiplying leaves}$$
$$f = 21. \text{ Check it.}$$

Instead of using the formulas $c = nr$ and $d = rt$, you can arrange the information into a proportion.

Example:

It is 350 miles on the interstate from Chicago to Des Moines. If Miriam can average 56 mph, how long will it take her to make the trip?

$$\frac{miles}{hours} : \frac{56}{1} = \frac{350}{h}$$
$$56 \cdot h = 350$$
$$h = \frac{350}{56} = 6.25 \text{ hours}$$

PROBLEM 5 Solve the following problems by using proportions.

a) Of the 12 people in one department, 7 are women. If this ratio holds true for the entire company, how many women work in this company of 96 people?

b) Oranges are priced at 2 for $.35. How much will it cost for a dozen oranges?

c) A recipe that calls for $\frac{1}{2}$ cup of sugar makes 4 servings. How many cups of sugar would you need to make 10 servings?

d) In a state that has a 7% sales tax, how much tax would you pay on a purchase of $200?

e) David earns a salary of $540 per week. If he works 5 days a week, how much does he earn in 1 day?

f) The manufacturer of a compact car states that the car can average 52 miles per gallon in highway driving. At that rate, how much gas will it take to travel 611 miles?

Similar Triangles . . . .

When two triangles are exact copies of one another, they are *congruent*.

Since △*ABC* ≅ (is congruent to) △*DEF*, all the corresponding parts are equal.

∠*A* = ∠*D*, ∠*B* = ∠*E*, ∠*C* = ∠*F*

side *AB* = side *DE*, side *AC* = side *DF*, side *BC* = side *EF*

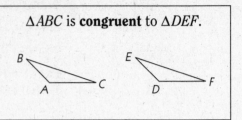

△*ABC* is **congruent** to △*DEF*.

When two triangles have the same shape but different sizes, they are *similar*.

Since △*KLM* ~ (is similar to) △*OPQ*, the corresponding angles are equal:

∠*K* = ∠*O*, ∠*L* = ∠*P*, ∠*M* = ∠*Q*

The corresponding sides are *proportional*.

$$\frac{\text{side } KL}{\text{side } OP} = \frac{\text{side } KM}{\text{side } OQ} = \frac{\text{side } LM}{\text{side } PQ}$$

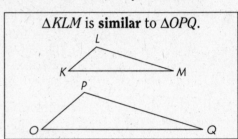

△*KLM* is **similar** to △*OPQ*.

Example:

If the length of *KL* is 5 inches and the length of *LM* is 8 inches, while in the other triangle the length of *OP* is 15 inches, what is the length of *PQ*?

Here are two ways that you can set up the proportion:

$$\frac{\text{side } KL}{\text{side } LM} = \frac{\text{side } OP}{\text{side } PQ} \quad \text{OR} \quad \frac{\text{side } KL}{\text{side } OP} = \frac{\text{side } LM}{\text{side } PQ}$$
$$\frac{5}{8} = \frac{15}{s} \qquad\qquad\qquad \frac{5}{15} = \frac{8}{s}$$

From either proportion, the answer is *s* = 24.

The next example shows how knowing about similar triangles allows you to figure the length of a side of a triangle that you cannot measure directly.

Example:

At the same time that a tall tree casts a shadow of 80 feet, a 6 ft. post casts a shadow of 10 ft. How tall is the tree?

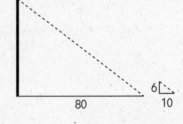

$$\frac{\text{tree}}{\text{post}} : \frac{t}{6} = \frac{80}{10}$$

$$10 \cdot t = 80 \cdot 6$$

$$t = \frac{80 \cdot 6}{10} = 48 \text{ ft.}$$

Check: $\frac{48}{6} = \frac{80}{10}; \frac{8}{1} = \frac{8}{1}$

PROBLEM 6

△*DON* ~ △*KEY*

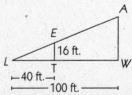

a) Find the length of side *DN*.

b) If ∠*D*=35° and ∠*N*=75°, what is the measure of ∠*O*?

PROBLEM 7

△ *LET* ~ △ *LAW*

What is the length of side *AW*?

(Look carefully for the similar triangles.)

• Using Similar Figures . . . .

The idea of similarity between figures is not only for triangles. Any figure is similar to another if their corresponding sides are in proportion.

When a drawing is enlarged or reduced in size, the figures are *similar*.

Example A:

A drawing that is 3 in. high and 5 in. wide will be blown-up in size so that it is 8 inches wide. How high will the enlarged drawing be?

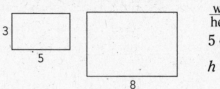

$$\frac{\text{width}}{\text{height}} \quad \frac{5}{3} = \frac{8}{h}$$

$$5 \cdot h = 24$$

$$h = \tfrac{24}{5} = 4\tfrac{4}{5} \text{ in.}$$

Scale drawings such as blueprints for construction projects are *similar* to the actual object.

Example B: The following notation is found on a blueprint for a warehouse:

$$1 \text{ in.} = 1\tfrac{1}{2} \text{ ft.}$$

a) A warehouse door is to be 12 ft. wide. How wide should it be on the blueprint?

$$\frac{\text{blueprint}}{\text{warehouse}} : \frac{1 \text{ in.}}{\tfrac{3}{2} \text{ ft.}} = \frac{b}{12 \text{ ft.}}$$

$$\tfrac{3}{2}b = 12$$

$$b = 12 \div \tfrac{3}{2} = 12 \times \tfrac{2}{3} = 8 \text{ in.}$$

b) If a wall on the blueprint is 9 inches long, how long will it be in the warehouse?

$$\frac{\text{blueprint}}{\text{warehouse}} : \frac{1 \text{ in.}}{\tfrac{3}{2} \text{ ft.}} = \frac{9 \text{ in.}}{w}$$

$$w = \tfrac{3}{2} \cdot \tfrac{9}{1} = \tfrac{27}{2} = 13\tfrac{1}{2} \text{ ft.}$$

A map is a special kind of scale drawing. Since lines for highways are rarely straight, you need to estimate when using maps.

Example C: One United States road map has the following scale:

$$1 \text{ in.} = \text{approximately 135 miles or 215 km}$$

a) On the map, Albuquerque is about 2 inches from Amarillo. Approximately how many miles apart are they?

$$\frac{\text{map}}{\text{actual}} : \frac{1 \text{ in.}}{135 \text{ mi.}} = \frac{2}{m}$$

$$m = 2 \cdot 135 = 270 \text{ mi.}$$

b) Dallas is 403 miles from Jackson, Mississippi. Approximately how many inches (to the nearest inch) apart will they be on the map?

$$\frac{\text{map}}{\text{actual}} : \frac{1 \text{ in.}}{135 \text{ mi.}} = \frac{n}{403}$$

$$135n = 403$$

$$n = 2.985 \approx 3 \text{ in.}$$

PROBLEM 8 A 3 × 4–inch snapshot is enlarged so that its shorter side is 9 inches. How long will the longer side be?

PROBLEM 9 On the warehouse blueprint in Example B, a window is 4 inches wide. How wide will it be in the warehouse?

PROBLEM 10 A plot map whose scale is 1 in. = 100 ft. shows the length of a lot to be $3\tfrac{1}{2}$ inches. How long is the actual lot?

PROBLEM 11 Nashville is 208 miles from Memphis. How many inches (to the nearest half inch) apart would they be on the map in Example C?

• Best Buys: Comparing Prices . . . .

Most people want to get the most for their money, and they take the time to compare prices to be sure that they do. In the supermarket, comparing prices is easy only when the containers are the same size. Of course, they seldom are, and it is rarely easy.

Unit price: To compare prices, find each price for 1 unit.

Write the ratio of the number of dollars to the number of ounces or pounds. Then divide to find the price for 1 ounce or pound.

Example A:

It costs 73¢ for a 10 oz. box of frozen cut corn. A 16 oz. bag of the same brand of frozen cut corn is 89¢. Which has the lowest unit price?

What is the **unit price** of each? $\frac{73}{10}$ = 7.3¢ per oz. $\frac{89}{16}$ = 5.5625¢ per oz.

The bag is less expensive per ounce, so it will give you more for your money.

Finding the unit prices and then comparing them is *always* a reliable way to compare prices. To do it accurately usually requires a calculator. To assist you, many supermarkets place the unit price below each item on the shelf.

Use compatible numbers to estimate unit prices.

Even without the calculator or unit pricing on the shelves, you can try to determine which is the better buy by estimating.

Example B:
The box of corn contains 10 oz. To find the price per oz., you divide by 10. Move the decimal point 1 place to the left.

$$\frac{73}{10} = 7.3¢$$

Example C:
The bag of corn contains 16 oz. Round this to 15 so that you can divide mentally.

$$\frac{89}{16} \approx \frac{90}{15} = 6¢$$

If the unit prices are so close that estimating cannot reveal a difference, then the savings may not be worth the time and effort to find with the calculator.

PROBLEM 12

Try to decide which is the better buy by **estimating**. (Check yourself by finding the unit prices with your calculator.)

a) A bottle of 24 pain-reliever tablets costs $2.79. Compare this to a bottle containing 100 tablets, which is marked $6.49.

b) Dishwashing liquid in the 22 oz. container costs $1.59, while the 32 oz. container costs $2.49.

c) A box of 30 disposable diapers costs $10.99, while a box of 64 costs $19.99.

d) An 8 oz. container of yogurt costs $.63, while a 32 oz. container costs $1.79.

e) A special promotion of snack-packs of raisins offers a package of six $1\frac{1}{2}$-ounce boxes for $.88. The regular price of a 9-ounce box is $1.09.

You may use your calculator on any problem for which it seems appropriate.

1. A high-speed train in Europe established a speed record of 320 mph in 1990. At that rate, how long would the train take to travel 1,280 miles?

2. Kiwi fruit are on sale at 4 for $1.00. How much would 10 kiwi cost?

3. How many ounces are there in $3\frac{1}{2}$ pounds? (1 lb. = 16 oz.)

4. During the first game of the season, LaTanya made 6 of the 9 free throws she tried. If she continues at this rate, how many shots does she have to try in order to make 100 of them?

5. The record distance jumped by a frog in the Calaveras County Frog Jumping Jubilee was $21\frac{1}{2}$ feet. This distance was covered in 3 jumps. If a frog could keep up this rate, how far would it travel in 12 jumps?

6. A dip recipe calls for a 3 oz. pkg. of cream cheese and 2 teaspoons of dill weed. How much dill weed would you add if you used an 8 oz. pkg. of cream cheese?

7. A marathon runner finished the race (a distance of about 26 miles) in $3\frac{1}{4}$ hours. How many miles per hour did she average?

8. The slope of this ramp is $\frac{1}{20}$. How far does it rise for each 50 feet that it crosses?

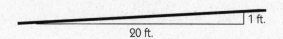
20 ft.   1 ft.

9. The quarterback from State U. completed 20 out of 32 passes in a game against Crimson College. The quarterback from Crimson completed 6 fewer passes than his opponent. How many passes did he complete?

10. Juanita inspects parts on an assembly line. On the average, 1 out of 20 parts she inspects is defective. On a day that she inspects 500 parts, how many of them are *acceptable*?

11. The shadow of a light pole is 55 feet long at 4 P.M., the same time that the shadow of a fence post is 11 feet long. What is the ratio of the length of the light pole to the length of the fence post?

12. A photo that measures 5 inches by 7 inches is in a frame that is 8×10 inches. Are the two rectangles *similar*?

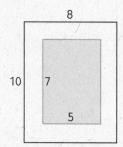

13. Which is the better buy, a package of 2 rolls of paper towels at $1.99 or a package of 3 rolls (of the same kind) for $2.67?

14. How many hours are there in 200 minutes? (1 hour = 60 min.)

15. On Wednesdays, tacos are 2 for $.99. On other days, each taco is $.59. Approximately how much do you save per taco on Wednesdays?

GED Practice

16. A map has the scale of 2 in. = 75 mi. How many actual miles apart are 2 cities that are 10 inches apart on the map?

(1) 750 mi.
(2) 375 mi.
(3) 150 mi.
(4) 100 mi.
(5) Not enough information is given.

Percent I

Mental Math Exercises

Which common fraction equals . . .

1. 0.50?   5. 0.60?
2. 0.75?   6. 0.40?
3. 0.20?   7. $0.33\frac{1}{3}$?
4. 0.10?   8. $0.12\frac{1}{2}$?

Each decimal in the Mental Math Exercises has 2 decimal places; the decimals are hundredths. **Percent** also means hundredths. This means that you can set the fractions equal to the percents.

$$\frac{1}{2} = 0.50 = 50\% \qquad \frac{3}{4} = 0.75 = 75\% \qquad \frac{1}{5} = 0.20 = 20\% \qquad \frac{1}{10} = 0.10 = 10\%$$

50 percent

50 hundredths

• Quick and Easy Everyday Percents . . . .

100% of a number is *all* of it. 0% is *none* of it.

$$100\% = \frac{100}{100} = 1 \text{ OR } 1.00 \qquad 0\% = \frac{0}{100} = 0$$

100% of 30	If 100% of a number *equals* the number, any % less than 100% of it will be less than the number.	0% of 56
$\frac{100}{100}$ of 30 = 30		$0 \times 56 = 0$

10% of a number is $\frac{1}{10}$ of it.

$$10\% = \frac{10}{100} = \frac{1}{10} \text{ OR } 0.10$$

To find 10% of a number, you can divide it by 10.

10% of 50	Remember that you can divide by 10 easily by moving the decimal point 1 place to the *left*.	10% of 155
$\frac{1}{10}$ of 50 = 5		$\frac{1}{10}$ of 155 = 15.5
OR		OR
$0.10 \times 50. = 5$	The digits remain the same.	$0.10 \times 155. = 15.5$

1% of a number is $\frac{1}{100}$ of it.

$$1\% = \frac{1}{100} \text{ OR } 0.01$$

To find 1% of a number, you can divide it by 100.

1% of 20	Remember that to divide by 100 easily, move the decimal point 2 places to the *left*.	1% of 511
$\frac{1}{100}$ of 20 = 0.2 OR		$\frac{1}{100} \times 511 = 5.11$ OR
$0.01 \times 20. = 0.2$		$0.01 \times 511. = 5.11$

PROBLEM 1 Complete the following equations by filling in the blanks.

| 40 | 500 | 2,000 |

a) 100% of 40 = _40_

   10% of 40 = ___

   1% of 40 = ___

c) 100% of 500 = ___

   10% of 500 = ___

   1% of 500 = ___

e) 100% of 2,000 = ___

   10% of 2,000 = ___

   1% of 2,000 = ___

| 80 | 300 | 1,500 |

b) ___% of 80 = 80

   ___% of 80 = 8

   ___% of 80 = 0.8

d) 100% of ___ = 300

   10% of ___ = 30

   1% of ___ = 3

f) 100% of 1,500 = ___

   ___% of 1,500 = 150

   1% of 1,500 = ___

PROBLEM 2 Use the patterns shown above to solve the following equations.

a) 10% of 90 = x

b) 10% of 91 = g

c) 10% of 89 = p

d) 1% of 70 = n

e) 1% of 71 = h

f) 1% of 69 = k

g) x% of 250 = 25

h) n% of 25 = 25

i) p% of 900 = 9

• More Easy Everyday Percents ....

50% of a number is $\frac{1}{2}$ of it.

$$50\% = \frac{50}{100} = \frac{1}{2} \quad \text{OR} \quad 0.50$$

To find 50% of a number, you can divide it by 2.

50% of 32

$\frac{1}{2}$ of $\overset{16}{\cancel{32}}$ = 16   OR

$0.5 \times 32 = 16$

Multiplying a number by $\frac{1}{2}$ is the same as dividing it by 2.

50% of 800

$\frac{1}{2}$ of $\overset{400}{\cancel{800}}$ = 400   OR

$0.5 \times 800 = 400$

25% of a number is $\frac{1}{4}$ of it.

$$25\% = \frac{25}{100} = \frac{1}{4} \quad \text{OR} \quad 0.25$$

To find 25% of a number, you can divide it by 4.

25% of 80

$\frac{1}{4}$ of $\overset{20}{\cancel{80}}$ = 20   OR

$0.25 \times 80 = 20$

Multiplying a number by $\frac{1}{4}$ is the same as dividing it by 4.

25% of 420

$\frac{1}{4}$ of $\overset{105}{\cancel{420}}$ = 105   OR

$0.25 \times 420 = 105$

20% of a number is $\frac{1}{5}$ of it.

$$20\% = \frac{20}{100} = \frac{1}{5} \quad \text{OR} \quad 0.20$$

To find 20% of a number, you can divide it by 5.

20% of 30

$\frac{1}{5}$ of $\overset{6}{\cancel{30}}$ = 6   OR

$0.20 \times 30 = 6.00$

Multiplying a number by $\frac{1}{5}$ is the same as dividing it by 5.

20% of 105

$\frac{1}{5}$ of $\overset{21}{\cancel{105}}$ = 21   OR

$0.20 \times 105 = 21$

PROBLEM 3 Complete the following equations by filling in the blanks.

20   120   ☐

a) 100% of 20 = ___   b) 100% of 120 = ___   c) 50% of ___ = 40

   50% of 20 = ___   ___% of 120 = 60   25% of ___ = 20

   25% of 20 = ___   25% of 120 = ___   20% of ___ = 16

PROBLEM 4 Solve the following percent equations by using the patterns shown above.

a) 25% of 16 = x d) 20% of 40 = c g) x% of 30 = 15

b) 50% of 16 = b e) 50% of t = 20   h) n% of 60 = 15

c) 50% of 12 = n f) 50% of w = 30   i) p% of 500 = 100

More than 100% of a number

$$200\% = \frac{200}{100} = 2 \qquad\qquad 300\% = \frac{300}{100} = 3$$

To find 200% of a number, multiply it   To find 300% of a number, multiply it
by 2.   by 3.

PROBLEM 5 Complete the following equations by filling in the blanks.

a) 100% of 30 = ___   b) 100% of ___ = 9   c) 100% of 150 = ___

   200% of 30 = ___   200% of 9 = ___   ___% of 150 = 300

   300% of 30 = ___   ___% of 9 = 27   ___% of 150 = 450

Other common fractions

$33\frac{1}{3}\% = \frac{1}{3}$ $30\% = \frac{30}{100} = \frac{3}{10}$ $75\% = \frac{75}{100} = \frac{3}{4}$

$33\frac{1}{3}\%$ of 15 = ___   30% of 60 = ___   75% of 48 = ___

$\frac{1}{3}$ of 15 = 5 $\frac{3}{10}$ of 60 = 18 $\frac{3}{4}$ of 48 = 36

                        $(\frac{1}{10} \times 60 = 6 \quad 6 \times 3 = 18)$ $(\frac{1}{4} \times 48 = 12 \quad 12 \times 3 = 36)$

PROBLEM 6 Solve the following percent equations using the patterns shown above.

a) 100% of 32 = 32   c) 100% of 60 = 60

   50% of 32 = c ___% of 60 = 6

   25% of 32 = d ___% of 60 = 12

   75% of 32 = n ___% of 60 = 18

   200% of 32 = t ___% of 60 = 30

   400% of 32 = x ___% of 60 = 15

b) 100% of 20 = 20   ___% of 60 = 45

   10% of 20 = m d) 100% of 300 = 300

   20% of 20 = b $33\frac{1}{3}\%$ of 300 = ___

   110% of 20 = p $66\frac{2}{3}\%$ of 300 = ___

   120% of 20 = s 300% of 300 = ___

                                         600% of 300 = ___

Writing the Percent Equation as a Proportion . . .

So far you have been able to solve many percent problems mentally by noticing the patterns. You should always look first for this possibility; when the numbers are "nice" and the patterns are obvious, find the answer without using pencil and paper. However, you do need a method to solve more difficult percent problems. The good news is that you already know the method: using proportions.

A percent equation involves 3 numbers.

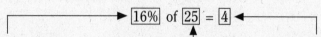

| The percent is easily recognized by the % sign. It tells the **rate** (number per 100). | Another number is the **base** or "whole." It is the number that comes after the word *of* because it is what the percent is based on. | The third number is difficult to label. In some cases, it is the **part**, but it is more correctly called the **percentage**. |

Make a proportion from these 3 numbers by setting up 2 equal ratios.

$$\text{rate} \quad \dfrac{\text{number}}{100} = \dfrac{\text{percentage}}{\text{base}}$$

1) One fraction comes from the **rate**. Place the number over 100 to make a fraction. (100 is the number that percent is based on.)

2) The other 2 numbers make up the second fraction. The **base** or "whole" goes on the bottom to correspond with the 100. (The number after the word *of* in the percent equation is always the denominator of the fraction.)

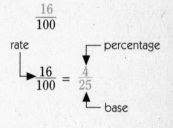

3) Check the proportion to see if it is true. First try to find patterns.

$$\dfrac{16 \div 4}{100 \div 4} = \dfrac{4}{25}$$
$$\dfrac{16}{100} = \dfrac{4}{25}$$
true proportion

- Can you simplify either fraction?

- Look across the proportion as well as up and down to locate a pattern.

- If you can't find a pattern, cross multiply and compare the products. If the cross products are equal, the fractions are equal; it is a true proportion.

PROBLEM 7 Write these percent sentences as proportions. Check to see if they are true or false. Look for patterns before you cross multiply.

Example: 50% of 60 is 30.

proportion: $\dfrac{50}{100} = \dfrac{30}{60}$

check: $\dfrac{50 \div 50}{100 \div 50} = \dfrac{1}{2}$ $\dfrac{30 \div 30}{60 \div 30} = \dfrac{1}{2}$ $\dfrac{1}{2} = \dfrac{1}{2}$ true proportion

a) 90% of 10 is 9.

b) 75% of 96 is 70.

c) 6 is 15% of 40.

d) 30 is 40% of 75.

e) 2% of 90 is 18.

f) 110% of 40 is 50.

g) 200% of 40 is 20.

h) 36 is 300% of 12.

Solving Percent Problems with Proportions . . . . .

A percent problem is a **percent sentence** with 1 of the 3 numbers missing. If you know 2 of the numbers, you can find the third one. Use a letter in place of the missing number when you set up the proportion, then solve the proportion just as you did in the last lesson.

30% of 80 = ___

$\dfrac{30}{100} = \dfrac{p}{80}$ 80 is the *base*.

$p = 24$

55% of ___ = 33

$\dfrac{55}{100} = \dfrac{33}{n}$ The *base* is missing.

$n = 60$

100 = ___% of 80

$\dfrac{x}{100} = \dfrac{100}{80}$ The *base* is after "of."

$x = 125$; the rate is 125%.

Always put your answer back into the percent sentence to see if it makes sense.

30% of 80 = 24
Since 80 is less than 100, 30% of it should be less than 30.

55% of 60 = 33
The part, 33, should be a little more than half of the whole, 60.

100 = 125% of 80
100 is $\frac{1}{4}$ more than 80.

Try to simplify the percent fraction first; you will end up with an easier problem. But remember that you can *always* solve a proportion by cross multiplying.

PROBLEM 8   Write each of these percent sentences as a proportion. Using your calculator if necessary, solve for the missing value. Then put your answer back into the problem to see if it makes sense.

a) 65% of 120 is what?

b) 70 is what % of 105?

c) 75% of what is 45?

d) 35% of 80 is what?

e) 105% of what is 42?

f) 9 is what % of 72?

g) 52% of 150 is what?

h) 250% of what is 10?

i) 252 is 36% of what ?

j) 200 is what % of 125?

Writing the Percent Equation for a Situation

Before you can actually use what you have learned about percent, you must know how to write the **percent equation** for a problem. The percent equation has places for 3 numbers. If a situation has enough information, it will give 2 of these numbers and ask you to find the third one.

$\underset{\text{rate}}{\underline{\hspace{1.5em}}}$ % of $\underset{\text{base}}{\underline{\hspace{1.5em}}}$ = $\underset{\text{percentage}}{\underline{\hspace{1.5em}}}$ OR $\underset{\text{percentage}}{\underline{\hspace{1.5em}}}$ = $\underset{\text{rate}}{\underline{\hspace{1.5em}}}$ % of $\underset{\text{base}}{\underline{\hspace{1.5em}}}$

Example: To earn a *C* on a certain test, Miguel needs to answer at least 70% of the questions correctly. If there are 40 questions on the test, what is the smallest number of correct answers that will earn him a *C*?

You need to decide which of the 3 numbers is missing. rate? base? percentage?

The <u>rate</u> is easiest to spot, since it has a % sign.

$\underset{\text{rate}}{\underline{70\%}}$ of $\underset{\text{base}}{\underline{\hspace{1.5em}}}$ = $\underset{\text{percentage}}{\underline{\hspace{1.5em}}}$

The <u>base</u> is the number of questions.
("70% *of* the questions")

$\underset{\text{rate}}{\underline{70\%}}$ of $\underset{\text{base}}{\underline{40}}$ = $\underset{\text{percentage}}{\underline{\hspace{1.5em}}}$

The percent equation that represents this situation is   **70% of 40 = *n***

Example:

On a test that had 25 questions, Marla answered 16 correctly. What % of the questions did she get right?

You can see immediately that it is the <u>rate</u> that is missing. You only need to determine which of the other 2 numbers is the <u>base</u>.

Look at the second sentence of the problem. "What % <u>of</u> the questions. . ." How many questions were there on the test? 25 is the <u>base</u>.

$$\underset{\text{rate}}{\underline{}\% \text{ of }} \underset{\text{base}}{\underline{25}} = \underset{\text{percentage}}{\underline{}}$$

$$\underset{\text{rate}}{\underline{}\% \text{ of }} \underset{\text{base}}{\underline{25}} = \underset{\text{percentage}}{\underline{16}}$$

That leaves the 16 to be the percentage.

The percent equation for this situation is **x% of 25 = 16 OR 16 = x% of 25**

Example:

Mannie answered 45 questions correctly on a test. This was 60% correct. How many questions were on the test?

This example requires you to know something about tests and percents to set up the equation.

You can see that the <u>rate</u> is given.

Is 45 the <u>base</u> or the <u>percentage</u>?

$$\underset{\text{rate}}{\underline{60\%} \text{ of }} \underset{\text{base}}{\underline{}} = \underset{\text{percentage}}{\underline{}}$$

$$\underset{\text{rate}}{\underline{60\%} \text{ of }} \underset{\text{base}}{\underline{}} = \underset{\text{percentage}}{\underline{45}}$$

Percent correct on tests is <u>based</u> on the total number of questions, which is what the problem asks for. The <u>base</u> is missing. 45 is the <u>percentage</u>.

The percent equation for this situation is **60% of w = 45 OR 45 = 60% of w.**

Write the percent equation for each of the following situations. Use one of these formats as a guide. **Do not solve—yet.**

$$\underset{\text{rate}}{\underline{}\% \text{ of }} \underset{\text{base}}{\underline{}} = \underset{\text{percentage}}{\underline{}} \qquad \text{OR} \qquad \underset{\text{percentage}}{\underline{}} = \underset{\text{rate}}{\underline{}\% \text{ of }} \underset{\text{base}}{\underline{}}$$

PROBLEM 9

a) A 46 oz. can of fruit drink is labeled "10% fruit juice." How many ounces of real fruit juice are in that can?

b) Jesse paid $1.47 sales tax on a shirt that cost $21.00. What is the sales tax rate that he paid?

c) The newspaper reports that 11% of the working-age population of the city is unemployed. Later in the same article, it says that 2,200 people in the city are unemployed. What is the working-age population of the city?

d) To purchase a home for $80,000, the Jacobs were required to make a down payment of $12,000. The down payment was what percent of the total?

e) An electronics store advertised a discount of 20% off on all merchandise. How much discount would you get on a telephone that was priced at $85?

f) What percent of his shots did Bo make if he made 12 out of 30 attempts?

Solving Percent Problems Using Equation Solving . . . .

Instead of setting up proportions, you can solve the percent equations directly. Again, the good news is that you already know how to do this by solving equations.

Example: Examine a percent equation: **60% of 95 = 57**

Percent *problems* arise if any one of the three numbers is missing.

Step 1: Write the percent equations using a variable in place of the missing number.

$$60\% \text{ of } 95 = m \qquad 60\% \text{ of } n = 57 \qquad x\% \text{ of } 95 = 57$$
percentage missing   base missing   rate missing

Step 2: Write the % as a fraction or a decimal. Replace *of* with *times*.

$$\tfrac{3}{5} \times 95 = m \qquad .60 \cdot n = 57 \qquad x\% \cdot 95 = 57$$

Step 3: Use regular equation-solving methods. Rewrite, if necessary, to get the variable alone.

$$m = \frac{3}{\underset{1}{5}} \times \frac{\overset{19}{95}}{1} = 57 \qquad n = \tfrac{57}{.60} = 95 \qquad x\% = \tfrac{57}{95} = 0.60 \text{ OR } 60\%$$

Step 4: Check by replacing the letter with your answer in the original equation.

$$60\% \text{ of } 95 = 57 \qquad 60\% \text{ of } 95 = 57 \qquad 60\% \text{ of } 95 = 57$$

You may prefer to use this method for some problems and the proportion method for others.

PROBLEM 10   Use the equation-solving method to solve these percent problems.

a) 90% of $150 = c$ d) $2{,}000 = n\%$ of $1{,}600$

b) 125% of $48 = x$ e) $80 = 33\tfrac{1}{3}\%$ of y

c) $55 = x\%$ of 88 f) 250% of $b = 50$

Using the Percent Key on Your Calculator . . . .

Once the equations are written so that the variable is alone on its side of the equation, you can use your calculator to find the answers. If you press the (%) key *after* you have entered the numbers and the operation, the calculator will place the decimal point in the correct position for you.

Examples:

54% of $860 = n$ 8 6 0 × 5 4 % $\boxed{464.4}$

85% of $c = 136$ 1 3 6 ÷ 8 5 % $\boxed{160}$
$c = \tfrac{136}{85\%}$

                                     * On some calculators you may need to press the (=) key after the (%) key.

$36 = x\%$ of 90 3 6 ÷ 9 0 % $\boxed{40}$
$x\% = \tfrac{36}{90}$

PROBLEM 11   Use your calculator to find the answers to problems 9a–f on page 181.

Check Your Understanding

You may use your calculator on any problem for which it seems appropriate.

1. Try to solve these equations mentally (or with the least amount of paper and pencil work).

   a) 100% of 35 = _____

   b) 25% of 48 = _____

   c) 50% of 150 = _____

   d) $33\frac{1}{3}$% of 60 = _____

   e) 0% of 67 = _____

   f) 500% of 25 = _____

   g) 1% of 450 = _____

   h) 10% of 450 = _____

   i) 20% of 400 = _____

   j) 75% of 16 = _____

2. Set up each of these percent equations as a proportion. Decide whether each equation is true or false.

   a) $4 \stackrel{?}{=} 20\%$ of 20

   b) $9 \stackrel{?}{=} 30\%$ of 30

   c) $16 \stackrel{?}{=} 40\%$ of 40

   d) 80% of $45 \stackrel{?}{=} 35$

   e) 10% of $215 \stackrel{?}{=} 2.15$

   f) $30 \stackrel{?}{=} 250\%$ of 12

   g) 1% of $3,000 \stackrel{?}{=} 3$

   h) 110% of $85 \stackrel{?}{=} 95$

   i) $8 \stackrel{?}{=} 75\%$ of 12

For problems 3–10, write a percent equation that describes the situation. Then solve it using whichever method seems best to you.

3. The Jacksons had to pay 6% of the selling price of their home as commission to their real estate broker. If they sold their home for $90,000, how much commission did they owe?

4. During a sale where all merchandise was discounted by 25%, Thomasina bought a dress that was marked down from $78.00. How much discount was taken?

5. By getting 20 answers correct on a test, Bob got a score of 80%. How many questions were on the test?

6. Rosie works as a sales representative and gets paid a commission of 5% of the amount of merchandise that she sells. How much does she have to sell in order to earn $200 in commissions?

7. A survey of 250 people found that 175 of them wished that they had a better education. What percent of those surveyed was this?

8. Each week, $88 of Rich's pay is deducted for taxes. If his salary is $400 a week, what percent of his pay is deducted?

9. A builder estimates that Pat would save 40% of her heating costs if she installed new insulation. Pat's present heating costs are $900 per year. How much could she expect to save each year?

10. Earvin's free-throw percentage for the preseason was 90%. If he *made* 36 free throws, how many did he attempt?

GED Practice

11. In 1989, families in the United States saved about 5% of their take-home pay. Ed and Sherrie save $50 each week from their combined paychecks, which total $500. What percent do Ed and Sherrie save?

    (1) 1%
    (2) 5%
    (3) 10%
    (4) 15%
    (5) 90%

- ## Part One

Before going on further in this book, use the following exercise to maintain your skills. If you are having difficulty, this is a good time to go back and review.

Questions 1–6 refer to the following information:

At Hitech Corporation, there are 120 employees—45 women and 75 men. Twenty percent of the employees are at the executive level. Thirty percent of the employees are minorities. Two out of every three employees favor a new insurance plan.

1. What is the ratio, in fraction form, of women to men at Hitech?

2. What is the ratio, in fraction form, of women to total employees?

3. How many minority employees are there at Hitech?

4. How many executives are there?

5. What is the ratio, in fraction form, of executives to total employees?

6. How many employees favor a new insurance plan?

---

7. A builder estimates that she needs 3 gallons of paint for every two rooms in an apartment complex. Complete the chart at right.

gallons paint	3	$4\frac{1}{2}$				
# rooms	2	3	4	5	6	7

8. Fill in the equivalent measurements below. (Remember: 1 lb. = 16 oz., 1 cup = 8 oz., and 2 cups = 1 pt.)

   a) $1\frac{1}{2}$ cups = _____ oz.

   b) 3 cups = _____ pints

   c) 40 oz. = _____ lb.

   d) 36 oz. = _____ cups

   e) 2 pints = _____ cups

9. Circle T (true) or F (false) for each of the following percent equations:

   a) 10% of 250 = 25   T   F

   b) 30 = 15% of 200   T   F

   c) 24 = 25% of 6   T   F

   d) 80% of 60 = 48   T   F

10. Out of 1,150 labels coming off an assembly line, 30% were found to be defective. How many labels were defective?

Part Two

Now practice your skills with the following GED-type problems.

1. The measurement scale on a builder's blueprint reads "$\frac{3}{4}$ in. = 1 ft." If a hallway shows a width of 3 inches on the blueprint, how many feet wide will it be?

   (1) $\frac{3}{4}$
   (2) 1
   (3) 2
   (4) 3
   (5) 4

2. An army unit has a *total* of 120 people (enlisted personnel and officers). Which of the following is the ratio of enlisted people to officers if there are 20 officers in the unit?

   (1) 1:6
   (2) 5:1
   (3) 1:5
   (4) 1:7
   (5) 134:20

3. A quality-control check reveals that there is an average of one malfunctioning transistor in every 35 that come off the assembly line. How many defective transistors are produced in a day when 7,000 transistors come off the line?

   (1) 1
   (2) 29
   (3) 35
   (4) 200
   (5) 245,000

4. If 3 lb. of tomatoes cost $2.88, choose an equation that could be used to find the price of 5 lb. of tomatoes.

   (1) $\frac{3}{5} = \frac{x}{2.88}$
   (2) $\frac{3}{5} = \frac{2.88}{x}$
   (3) $\frac{5}{8} = \frac{x}{2.88}$
   (4) $\frac{3}{8} = \frac{x}{2.88}$
   (5) $\frac{3}{8} = \frac{2.88}{x}$

5. The Clemsons' real estate agent agreed to 4 percent commission. If the selling price was $110,000, how much did the agent collect?

   (1) $400
   (2) $4,000
   (3) $4,400
   (4) $6,600
   (5) $27,500

6. 30 factory employees belong to a union. If the factory employs 250 people, what percent of the employees belong to the union?

   (1) 83%
   (2) 12%
   (3) 75%
   (4) 120%
   (5) 7,500%

7. A cleanser calls for $1\frac{1}{2}$ cups of ammonia for every $\frac{1}{4}$ cup of detergent. How much detergent is needed for 12 cups of ammonia?

   (1) 48 cups
   (2) 8 cups
   (3) 6 cups
   (4) 4 cups
   (5) 2 cups

• LESSON 23 • Percent II

Mental Math Exercises

1. 25% of 40 = x
2. 50% of 20 = k
3. 20% of 35 = n
4. 10% of 75 = m
5. 200% of 25 = p
6. $33\frac{1}{3}$% of 90 = k

• Estimating with Easy Percents . . . .

You may have found the answers in the Mental Math Exercises by using fractions for the percents and dividing into the compatible numbers. You can estimate percentages mentally by finding compatible numbers that are close to the ones given.

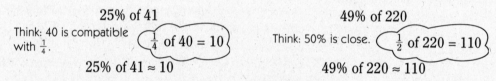

25% of 41

Think: 40 is compatible with $\frac{1}{4}$. $\frac{1}{4}$ of 40 = 10

25% of 41 ≈ 10

49% of 220

Think: 50% is close. $\frac{1}{2}$ of 220 = 110

49% of 220 ≈ 110

PROBLEM 1 Write an estimate of each problem, then **estimate** the answer. (Your estimates may be different from the ones on the answer pages.)

a) 11% of 90 = p f) 9% of 1,099 = n
b) 27% of 120 = m g) 48% of 64 = w
c) 20% of 37 = b h) 32% of 66 = v
d) 98% of 67 = x i) 0.8% of 400 = d
e) 296% of 500 = k j) 25% of 45 = c

PROBLEM 2 Using your calculator, find the precise answers to the equations in problem 1. Discuss everyday situations when your estimates for percents would have been adequate.

Tipping

You can estimate when you leave a tip at a restaurant. It is common for people to leave at least a 15% tip if they are satisfied with the service. Here is an easy way to figure an estimate of 15%.

Example A:
The total bill of
$8.13 ≈ $8.00

Step 1: Round the total to the nearest dollar.

Example B:
The total of
$24.67 ≈ $25.00

10% is $.80

Step 2: Find 10% by moving the decimal point 1 place to the left.

10% is $2.50

5% is + .40

Step 3: Find 5% by taking half of 10%.

5% is + 1.25

15% is $1.20

Step 4: Add the two amounts to find 15%.

15% is $3.75

PROBLEM 3   Estimate the 15% tip for each of the following totals.

   a) $4.88   b) $11.31   c) $17.65   d) $24.05   e) $31.72

PROBLEM 4   A group of 6 friends shared pizzas and pitchers of drinks. The total bill was $31.45. Estimate a tip to leave and the amount that each person should contribute if they share the bill equally.

Estimating the Rate

When the number that is missing from a percent equation is the **rate** (the number with the % sign), both the **proportion** and the **equation** method lead to the same ratio:

Example: Find the percent in $66 = x\%$ of 88.

using proportions		**using equation solving**
$\dfrac{x}{100} = \dfrac{66}{88}$	Simplify the fraction before you divide.	$x\% = \dfrac{66}{88}$

$$\tfrac{66}{88} = \tfrac{3}{4} = 75\%$$

This was easy because you know that $\tfrac{3}{4} = 75\%$.

You already know the percent equivalents of many fractions:

$$\tfrac{1}{2} = 50\% \quad \tfrac{1}{3} = 33\tfrac{1}{3}\% \quad \tfrac{1}{4} = 25\% \quad \tfrac{1}{5} = 20\% \quad \tfrac{1}{10} = 10\% \quad \tfrac{1}{100} = 1\%$$

When estimating, make the numbers compatible so that you have an easy fraction to simplify.

Examples: $29 = x\%$ of 90 $78 = x\%$ of 20

$$\frac{x}{100} = \frac{29}{90} \qquad\qquad x\% = \frac{78}{20}$$

How can this be changed to be an easy fraction?   What number is compatible with 20?

$$\tfrac{78}{20} \approx \tfrac{80}{20} = 4 = 400\%$$

$$\tfrac{29}{90} \approx \tfrac{30}{90} = \tfrac{1}{3} = 33\tfrac{1}{3}\%$$

PROBLEM 5   **Estimate** the missing rate using the methods shown above. Your estimates may differ from those on the answer pages.

   a) $102 = x\%$ of 400   f) $398 = x\%$ of 500
   b) $30 = x\%$ of 147   g) $52 = x\%$ of 75
   c) $95 = x\%$ of 50   h) $1.00 = x\%$ of $9.95
   d) $8 = x\%$ of 83   i) $1.50 = x\%$ of $3.09
   e) $0.9 = x\%$ of 100   j) $19 = x\%$ of $98.59

PROBLEM 6   Walter left a $4.00 tip for the server when the bill was $19.45. His tip was <u>about</u> what percent of the bill?

PROBLEM 7   Joe completed 24 passes out of 35 attempts. <u>About</u> what percent did he complete?

• Simple Interest . . . .

While arranging financing to buy a car, Ruth was informed that for a loan of $6,000, she would end up paying $8,160 back to the finance company over the 3 years. She will pay $2,160 in <u>interest</u>.

After leaving $1,000 in a savings account for one year, Raul now has $1,096 in the account. He was paid $96 in <u>interest</u>.

Interest is a fee paid for the use of money. (Think of it as rent for money used.) If you use the bank's money, you pay interest to the bank. If the bank uses your money, the bank pays you and you earn interest.

The amount of **interest** paid is usually a percentage **(rate)** of the amount borrowed. The amount borrowed is called the principal of the loan.

$$\text{interest} = \underline{\quad}\% \text{ of principal}$$

The **length of time** the money is used is also a factor.

If Raul had left his money in the bank for only 6 months ($\frac{1}{2}$ year), he would have earned only half the interest. If he had left it in there for 2 years, he would have earned twice as much.

The formula for calculating interest is on the formulas page (page 246). It says:

$$\text{simple interest is } i = prt, \text{ where } p = \text{principal}, r = \text{rate}, \text{ and } t = \text{time}$$

The formula says, to find interest, multiply the principal by the rate of time (in years). The equation-solving method of finding percentages works well for this type of problem.

PROBLEM 8 Complete the following table, finding the interest for 1 year.
Example:

Principal ($) Rate	500	1,000	1,500	2,000
6%	$30			
12%				

$$i = prt$$
$$i = \$500 \times \frac{6}{100} \times 1$$
$$i = \frac{\overset{5}{\$500} \times 6}{100_1} = \$30$$

PROBLEM 9 Complete the table again using a time of 6 months ($t = \frac{1}{2}$).

Interest rates often involve fractional or decimal parts of a percent. You will see rates such as these:

$$5.5\% \qquad 6\frac{1}{2}\% \qquad 8.75\% \qquad 10\frac{1}{4}\%$$

To solve problems with these rates, you must write them as decimals. Remember that the % sign is replaced by a decimal point <u>2</u> places to the left.

3% = 0.03	So:	
3.5% = 0.035	$3\frac{1}{2}\% = 0.035$	
4% = 0.04		

8% = 0.08	So:
8.75% = 0.0875	$8\frac{3}{4}\% = 0.0875$
9% = 0.09	

PROBLEM 10 Write these percents as decimals. Then find how much interest $100 deposited for 1 year would earn at each rate.
a) 6.5%   b) $7\frac{1}{2}\%$ c) 10.25%   d) $8\frac{1}{4}\%$ e) 6.6%

• The Total Is 100%—How Much Is Left? . . . .

Example:

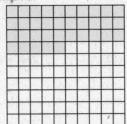

35 of the 100 squares in the big square are shaded. 35% are shaded.

How many are not shaded? 65, or 100 − 35
What % are not shaded? 65%

The whole circle in a circle graph represents 100%.

Example:

A marketing survey showed that 43% of the households in a county did *not* have a videocassette recorder. What % of the households <u>do</u> have one?

$$100\% - 43\% = 57\%$$

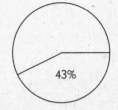

Example:

Inventory
Sale
40% OFF

What percent is the discount?   40%
What percent is the sale price?   60%

What price would you pay for a sweater marked $45?

$$60\% \text{ of } 45 = x$$

$$\frac{3}{5} \times 45 = \$27$$

PROBLEM 11

a) Ground beef marked "80% lean" must contain at least 80% lean (no fat) beef. What is the greatest percentage of fat that can be present in this ground beef?

b) Rhonda got 70% of the problems correct on a test. What percentage did she get wrong?

c) When a weather forecaster says that there is a 40% chance of rain, what is the chance of it *not* raining?

d) What is the missing percent in this circle graph?

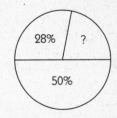

e) Deductions take 19% of Jerry's gross pay. What percentage of his gross pay is take-home pay?

f) George attended 95% of the classes this term. If there were 40 classes, how many classes did he <u>miss</u>?

g) At a 25%-off sale, what would you pay for an electric heater marked $28?

• Percent of Decrease ....

Discount and Sale Price

PROBLEM 12 Elmer's Electric Emporium is having a 30%-off sale. Complete the table below.

Marked Price ($)	Discount ($)	Sale Price ($)
50	$0.30 \times 50 = 15$	$50 - 15 = 35$
60		
70		
80		
p		

The last row of the table should be $0.30p$ for discount and $p - 0.30p$ for sale price. However, from doing the problems on the previous page, you know that the sale price is 70% of the marked price, or $0.70p$.

$$p - 0.30p = 0.70p \quad (\text{price} - 30\% \times \text{price} = 70\% \times \text{price})$$

This means that you have two choices for finding the sale price.

Example: Say that the marked price was $90.

You can find the discount first:
$$0.30 \times \$90 = \$27$$
Then subtract the discount from the marked price to get the sale price:
$$\$90 - \$27 = \$63$$

In a single equation:
$$\$90 - 0.30(\$90) = s$$

Or you can subtract first:
$$100\% - 30\% = 70\%$$
Then multiply to find the sale price.
$$0.70 \times \$90 = \$63$$

In a single equation:
$$(1 - 0.30)\$90 = s$$

For the problems on the GED Test that ask how to set up an equation, you must recognize that both forms are correct.

PROBLEM 13 For some automobiles, the value **depreciates** (value is lost) 20% in the first year of ownership.

Complete this table in the manner shown.

Original Value ($)	Depreciation ($)	Value After 1 year ($)
8,000	$0.20 \times 8,000 = 1,600$	$8,000 - 1,600 = 6,400$
9,000		
10,000		
v		

PROBLEM 14 The value of the cars after 1 year is what % of the original value? Find the values in the last column of the table in problem 13 by using this rate directly instead of subtracting.

PROBLEM 15 The population of a city is expected to drop 6% in the next year. If the present population is 30,000, what is the expected population at the end of next year?

• Percent of Increase . . . .

Eileen's salary is $22,000 per year. She has been promised a raise of 20% when she is promoted. What will her new annual salary be?

Picture Eileen's old salary as this rectangle.

A 20% raise is $\frac{1}{5}$ of the old salary.

But the $\frac{1}{5}$ must be *added* to the old salary.

Her new salary is 120% of the old salary.

Again, look at the two possible ways to solve this problem.

You can find the raise first:	**Or you can add first:**
$0.20 \times \$22,000 = \$4,400$	$100\% + 20\% = 120\%$
Then add the raise to the old salary:	Then find the new salary directly:
$\$22,000 + \$4,400 = \$26,400$	$1.20 \times \$22,000 = \$26,400$
As a single equation:	As a single equation:
$\$22,000 + 0.20(\$22,000) = n$	$1.20(\$22,000) = n$

PROBLEM 16 The sales tax rate in a county is 7%. Complete the following table.

Price ($)	Sales Tax ($)	Total ($)
40.00	$0.07 \times 40.00 = 2.80$	$40.00 + 2.80 = 42.80$
60.00		
100.00		
1,000.00		
p		

PROBLEM 17 Find each of the totals in the last column directly. (total = 107% of price)

PROBLEM 18 If the rate of inflation is 4% per year, what would you expect to pay for a washing machine next year if it costs $350 this year?

PROBLEM 19 Because of the construction of a new factory, the population of the city is expected to increase by 75% in the next 5 years. If the present population is 40,000, what is the expected population in 5 years?

PROBLEM 20 To make a profit and to pay overhead costs, a furniture store sells furniture at a price that is 100% more than the store paid the manufacturer. What price would the store charge for a chair for which it paid $180?

• Finding the Rate of Increase and Decrease......

To find the amount of increase or decrease in the problems on the last two pages, you used this percent equation:

$$\text{amount of increase or decrease} = \text{rate} \times \text{original number}$$
$$(\text{percentage} = \text{rate} \times \text{base})$$
$$(\text{rate} = x\%)$$

using proportions

$$\frac{x}{100} = \frac{\text{amount of increase or decrease}}{\text{original number}}$$

using equation solving

$$\text{rate} = \frac{\text{amount of increase or decrease}}{\text{original number}}$$

Notice that the **base** in both cases is the **original number**.

Example:

Theo paid $856 (total, including tax) for a stereo system that was marked $800. What is the sales tax rate that he paid?

marked price   [   ] $800

total paid   [   ] $856

Be careful! The 2 numbers given in the problem are *not* the 2 numbers in the ratio. You must subtract first to find the tax.

First find the amount of tax (increase). $856 − $800 = $56   new number found by subtraction

Now set up the ratio and solve.

$$\text{rate} = \frac{\text{amount of tax}}{\text{original number}} = \frac{56}{800} = \frac{7}{100}$$

$$\text{rate} = 7\%$$

PROBLEM 21   Find the following amounts. You may want to use your calculator.

a) Karen put $500 into a savings account. At the end of 1 year, the amount in the account was $540. What rate of interest was she paid on her money?

b) Theresa bought a new car for $7,000. After owning it for a year, she sold it for $5,250. What was the rate of depreciation on her car?

c) Pat received a raise in his salary. Before the raise, he was earning $320 a week. After the raise, he earned $360 a week. The raise was what percent of his salary?

d) Laurinda bought a recliner that had a marked price of $440 and a sale price of $330. The discount was what percent of the original price?

e) A parking lot near the airport raised its daily rates from $4 per day to $5 per day. By what percent were the rates raised?

f) According to the census, a city's population went from 69,717 in 1980 to 76,838 in 1990. **Estimate** the percent of increase.

You may use your calculator on any problem for which it seems appropriate.

1. **Estimate** the following answers by finding compatible numbers. Any reasonable estimate is correct; yours does not have to be exactly the same as the one on the answer page.

   a) 48% of 32 = n

   b) 25% of 811 = p

   c) 98 = x% of 200

   d) 98 = x% of 498

   e) 19% of 75 = m

   f) 8.9% of 480 = c

   g) $2.99 = x% of $4.99

   h) $19.75 = x% of $58.67

   i) 6% of $47.50 = t

   j) 35 = x% of 600

2. Write the decimal equivalents of each percent.

   a) 3% = _____

   b) $3\frac{1}{2}$% = _____

   c) 30% = _____

   d) 35% = _____

   e) 350% = _____

   f) 1% = _____

   g) 0.5% = _____

   h) $\frac{1}{2}$% = _____

   i) 0.75% = _____

   j) $\frac{3}{4}$% = _____

3. On a recent trash-collecting day, 54% of the households of a city had separated their newspapers and glass from the rest of the trash for pickup. What percent of the households did <u>not</u> participate in the recycling efforts?

4. The sales tax for a county was $6\frac{1}{4}$% before a vote to raise the tax by $\frac{1}{2}$%. What was the sales tax rate after the vote?

5. Many credit card companies charge $1\frac{1}{2}$% interest <u>per month</u> on the unpaid balance. What is the annual (yearly) rate of interest that they charge?

6. **Estimate** the sale price of a $188.88 camera when it is discounted 25%.

7. A living room furniture set is discounted from $800 to $560 during a sale. What is the rate of discount?

8. A T-shirt shop sells T-shirts at twice the price that it pays the supplier for them. Is this markup a percent increase of 50%, 100%, or 200%?

9. Terry's salary is $1,500 a month. If 21% of his pay is taken out in deductions, what is his take-home pay?

10. If you are charged $360 interest per year on a $3,000 loan, what rate of interest are you paying?

GED Practice

11. Walter's promotion results in a 10% raise in his salary. If he was earning a salary of $21,000 a year before the promotion, which of the following expressions shows his new salary?

    (1) 0.10 ($21,000)
    (2) 0.90 ($21,000)
    (3) $21,000 − 0.10 ($21,000)
    (4) $21,000 + 0.10 ($21,000)
    (5) 2.10 ($21,000)

• LESSON 24 • Relating Rates and Slopes to Graphs

Mental Math Exercises

1. $3 - 5 = x$	**6.** $7 - 0 = u$
2. $-3 - 5 = y$	**7.** $-7 - 0 = v$
3. $4 - 7 = r$	**8.** $2 - 6 = m$
4. $-4 - 7 = s$	**9.** $-2 - 6 = n$
5. $0 - 7 = t$	**10.** $6 - 2 = k$

To find the answers to the Mental Math Exercises, just picture the first number on the number line, then move to the left when you subtract a number. You will learn more about negative numbers in this lesson.

• More About Slopes . . . .

On page 163, you learned that the **slope** of a line is defined by the ratio $\frac{rise}{run}$.

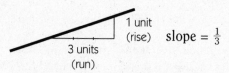

slope = $\frac{1}{3}$

The right triangle beneath the line shows how far up the line rises as you move from left to right. When a line is drawn on grid lines, you must picture or draw the slope triangle and find the number of units in the rise and the run.

If a line leans upward from left to right, it has a positive slope

Example: To find the slope of a line:

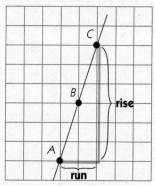

Step 1: Find any two points on the line where there is an **intersection** of the grid lines. In the sketch, you could pick any two of the lettered points. To illustrate, pick points A and C.

Step 2: Following the grid lines, draw a triangle.

Step 3: Count the number of units in the rise (6) and in the run (2).

Step 4: Set up the ratio $\frac{rise}{run}$, and write it in simplest terms.

$$\frac{rise}{run} = \frac{6}{2} = \frac{3}{1} = 3$$

PROBLEM 1 Slopes of straight lines are the same regardless of which two points you choose. Using point B and point C in the example above, find the slope.

PROBLEM 2 Find the slopes of the lines drawn on the grid below. You may choose any two points and draw a rise and run. The first one is started for you.

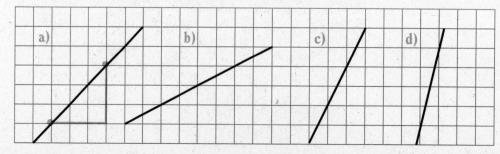

a)   b)   c)   d)

If a line leans downward from left to right, it has a negative slope

Slopes of lines are not always **positive** numbers. If a line leans **downward** as you move *from left to right*, it has a **negative** slope.

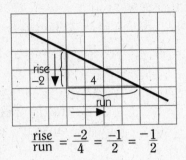

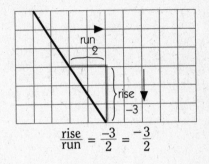

$$\frac{\text{rise}}{\text{run}} = \frac{-2}{4} = \frac{-1}{2} = -\frac{1}{2}$$

$$\frac{\text{rise}}{\text{run}} = \frac{-3}{2} = -\frac{3}{2}$$

The slope of a horizontal line is 0.

The slope of a vertical line is **undefined**. Remember about dividing by zero.

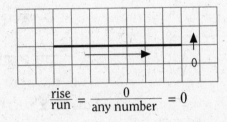

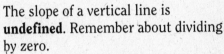

$$\frac{\text{rise}}{\text{run}} = \frac{0}{\text{any number}} = 0$$

$$\frac{\text{rise}}{\text{run}} = \frac{\text{any number}}{0} = \text{undefined}$$

PROBLEM 3 Find the slopes of the following lines. Choose two points, and draw the rise and run as in 3a.

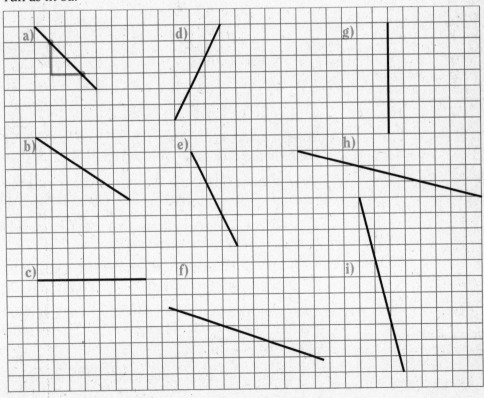

• Finding Slopes from Coordinates . . . .

You should also be able to find the slope of a line if you are given 2 specific points on the line. Before you go on, you may need to review pages 40–41 of Lesson 5 to be clear on the (x, y) coordinates.

Example: Find the slope of the line between points A (6, 3), and B (1, 2).

Step 1:
Draw the x and y axes.

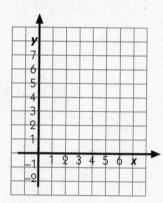

Step 2:
Locate points A (6, 3) and B (1, 2). The first number tells how far to the left or right to move; the second tells how far up or down.

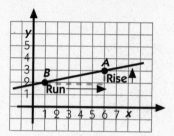

Step 3:
Proceed as before.
$$\frac{\text{rise}}{\text{run}} = \frac{1 \text{ unit}}{5 \text{ units}} = \frac{1}{5}$$

You could also find the slope without the sketch. Use the sketch above only to follow the logic of the steps below.

Step 1: To find the **rise**, subtract the y-values of the points $(x, \boldsymbol{y})$ from (6, **3**) and (1, **2**).

$$\text{rise: } 3 - 2 = 1$$

Step 2: To find the **run**, subtract the x-values of the points $(\boldsymbol{x}, y)$ from (**6**, 3) and (**1**, 2).

$$\text{run: } 6 - 1 = 5$$

Step 3: Set up the ratio for slope, $\dfrac{\text{rise}}{\text{run}} = \dfrac{1}{5}$

The second method corresponds to the formula for the slope of a line as given on the formulas page (page 246) and on the GED Test:

slope of a line (m) $m = \dfrac{y_2 - y_1}{x_2 - x_1}$, where (x_1, y_1) and (x_2, y_2) are two points on a plane.

The subscripts (small numbers) make this formula look a lot more difficult than it actually is. There are two points:

P_1, (x_1, y_1) in this case is (1, 2). So x_1 is 1, and y_1 is 2.
P_2, (x_2, y_2) in this case is (6, 3). So x_2 is 6, and y_2 is 3.

You subtracted the y-values to find the rise and subtracted the x-values to find the run, then you set up the ratio $\frac{\text{rise}}{\text{run}}$. Using the formula, you do exactly the same thing:

$$m = \frac{y_2 - y_1}{x_2 - x_1} = \frac{3 - 2}{6 - 1} = \frac{1}{5}$$

Subscripts are used in the formula to make sure that you keep the *order* of subtraction the same for both the rise and the run. If you don't, you may get a slope with the *opposite* sign of what it should be.

When you divide with the same sign, the answer is **positive**.

$$\frac{1}{3} = \frac{1}{3} \text{ and } \frac{-1}{-3} = \frac{1}{3}$$

When you divide with a different sign, the answer is **negative**.

$$\frac{-1}{3} = -\frac{1}{3} \text{ and } \frac{1}{-3} = -\frac{1}{3}$$

To find slopes, you can choose the method that best suits you and the problem. Either draw a sketch or use the formula. If you have time to do both when taking a test, use one method as a check of the other.

Examples:

Find the slope of the line between (9, 1) and (5, 3).

Let (9, 1) be point 2 and (5, 3) be point 1.

$$m = \frac{1 - 3}{9 - 5} = \frac{-2}{4} = \frac{-1}{2} \text{ OR } -\frac{1}{2}$$

Since one number in the ratio is negative, the ratio is negative. It could also be written as $-\frac{1}{2}$.

Find the slope of the line between (2, –2) and (7, 0).

Let (2, –2) be point 2 and (7, 0) be point 1.

$$m = \frac{-2 - 0}{2 - 7} = \frac{-2}{-5} = \frac{2}{5}$$

When 2 negatives are divided, the answer is positive.

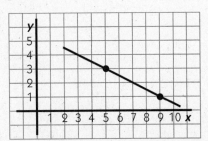

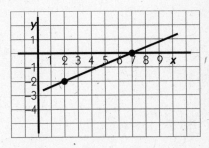

PROBLEM 4 Switch the order of the points in the first example above. That is, let (5, 3) be point 2 and (9, 1) be point 1. Is the slope the same?

PROBLEM 5 Find the coordinates of each point on this graph.

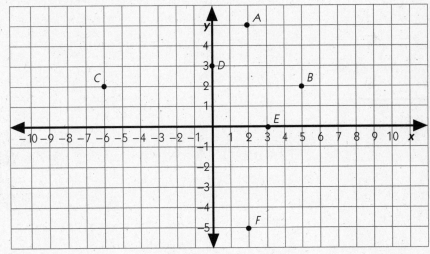

PROBLEM 6 Use either the formula or the graph (or both) to find the slope of the line between the following points. If you are using the formula, keep the points in the same order on the top and bottom.

a) points A and B

b) points C and B

c) points D and E

d) points A and F

e) points D and B

Graphs That Are Pictures of Equations ....

Slopes of lines have more meaning when they represent something real. Since a slope is a ratio, it can represent a **rate**—any common rate that defines the relationship between two quantities. In the following examples and problems, relationships between variables are shown in three ways: (1) by a table of values, (2) by a graph, and (3) by an equation.

Example: According to the nutrition information on a package, 1 serving ($\frac{1}{2}$ oz.) of White Cheddar Popcorn has 90 calories. The package contains $4\frac{1}{4}$ oz.

First, consider the relationship between the *servings* and the *ounces*. Each serving is $\frac{1}{2}$ oz. (or 0.5 oz.).

PROBLEM 7 Complete the table below.

# of Servings	1	2	4	6	8	10
# of Ounces	0.5					

The numbers 2, 4, 6, 8, and 10 were chosen for two reasons. First, they are small enough to fit easily on a graph. Second, they result in "nice" numbers to graph. Since they are even numbers, they produce whole numbers for the number of servings.

To make a graph from this table, treat each <u>pair</u> of numbers in the table as a **point** on a graph. For example, 1 serving and 0.5 oz. could be thought of as (1, 0.5).

Position this point on the graph below by finding the 1 on the axis that represents servings and the 0.5 on the axis for ounces. (0.5 is halfway between 0 and 1.) Follow the grid marks until they intersect. This is point A (1, 0.5).

The other points, B (2, 1), C (4, 2), D (6, 3), E (8, 4), and F (10, 5), can be located in the same way.

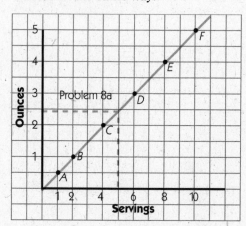

Now connect the points with a straight line.

The line is the graph of the equation:
ounces = 0.5 times servings
$$o = 0.5\,s$$

Any and all points on this line also satisfy the relationship between servings and ounces; they all will make the equation true.

PROBLEM 8 Analyze the graph for the following information. Problem 8a is started for you on the graph.

a) How many ounces are there in 5 servings?

b) How many ounces are there in 9 servings?

c) Approximately how many servings are there in the entire $4\frac{1}{4}$ oz. package?

PROBLEM 9 Use the equation for this line to find how many ounces there are in 50 servings.

What is the **slope** of the line on the graph? It is best to use the formula here.

Since the horizontal and vertical units are different, it would be too confusing to count squares.

If you use the formula, you could choose the two points, such as (8, 4) and (2, 1).

Example: $m = \dfrac{4 - 1}{8 - 2} = \dfrac{3}{6} = \dfrac{1}{2}$ (Notice that $\frac{1}{2}$ is also the rate of ounces per serving.)

Next, consider the relationship between the number of servings and the number of calories.

PROBLEM 10 Complete this table of values:

Servings	1	2	4	6	8
Calories	90				

PROBLEM 11 Plot the points from the table on the graph below, and connect them with a straight line. Extend the line past the points you have plotted. The point for 1 serving (90 calories) has been plotted for you.

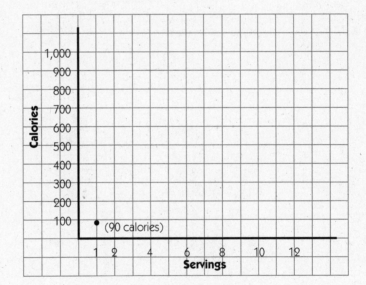

PROBLEM 12 Use your graph to answer the following questions.

a) How many calories are there in 3 servings?

b) How many servings would total 450 calories?

c) Approximately how many servings would total 1,000 calories?

PROBLEM 13 Complete this equation so that it defines the relationship between servings (*s*) of popcorn and calories (*c*): $c =$ _____.

PROBLEM 14 Use your equation to find the number of calories there are in one entire package of this popcorn. (One pkg. contains 8.5 servings.) Does this correspond to the graph?

PROBLEM 15 Determine the slope of this line. (Use any two points.) How does it correspond to the **rate** of calories per serving?

• Comparing Graphed Equations . . . .

When more than one equation is graphed on a pair of axes, you can make interesting comparisons.

Example:

During an auto race, the distance traveled was noted every 20 minutes. The tables below contain this information for the winner and for the last-place finisher.

Blue Car

Minutes	20	40	60	80	100
Miles	50	100	150		

Red Car

Minutes	20	40	60	80	100
Miles	40	80	120	160	

The figures in the tables show that both cars kept a constant pace. Therefore, each graph should be a straight line.

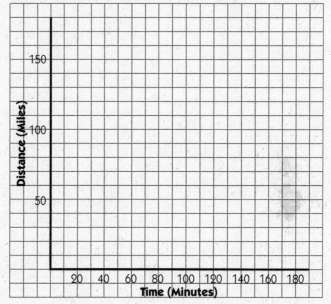

PROBLEM 16 Plot the points from the blue car's information. Connect the points with a blue line (or a solid line), being sure to extend the line past the given points.

PROBLEM 17 Plot the points from the red car's information. Connect these points with a red line (or a dotted line ----), extending it beyond the points given.

PROBLEM 18 The race course is 175 miles long. If both cars kept their pace, how many minutes after the start would each finish?

PROBLEM 19 What is the slope of each line? (You can use any two points on the line to determine slope.) Which line is steeper?

PROBLEM 20 The slopes you found in problem 19 represent the rate of each car in miles per minute.

a) How fast was each going in miles per hour?

b) Using this mph number as the rate, d for distance, and t for time, complete the distance equation for each line of the graph:

$$d = _____$$

Check Your Understanding

You may use your calculator on any problem for which it seems appropriate.

To solve problems 1–2, use the graph in problem 1.

1. Label each of the points with its coordinates. (Remember that the first number tells how far right or left of the origin the point is, and the second number tells how far up or down it is.)

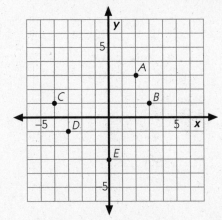

A = (____, ____)

B = (____, ____)

C = (____, ____)

D = (____, ____)

E = (____, ____)

2. Find the slope of each of the following lines:

   a) point A to point B

   b) point B to point A

   c) point B to point C

   d) point A to point C

   e) point D to point B

   _____

3. 1 inch in English measurement equals approximately 2.5 cm in metric measure. Complete this table:

Inches	1	2	4	6	8
Centimeters	2.5				

4. On this graph, plot the points from the table in problem 3. Connect the dots with a straight line.

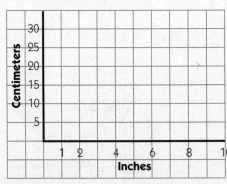

5. Jerry and his mother both drove to the mall, which is 50 highway miles away. Jerry broke the speed limit and drove 70 mph, while his mother drove at 55 mph. The graph shows their progress.

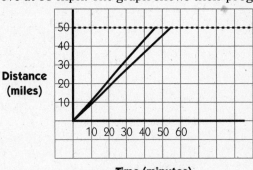

   a) Which line (top or bottom) pictures Jerry's trip?

   b) How much time did he cut off the trip by speeding?

   c) What is the slope of each of the lines?

6. The following graph tells the story of a fabled race between 2 competitors. Each line represents the way one character in the fable ran the race.

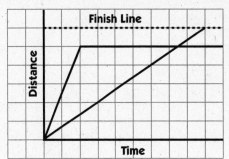

Who are the famous competitors?

GED Practice

7. Find the slope of the line between (0, 5) and (5, 0).

   (1) −5
   (2) −1
   (3) 0
   (4) 1
   (5) 5

Checkpoint IV

In this section, you used your knowledge of fractions and equations to solve proportion and percent problems. Since so many of the problems on the GED Test can be solved using proportion, you now have a powerful tool. Remember to read problems carefully, looking for clues that will tell you that a proportional relationship is present.

• Test-Taking Tips . . . .

You now know that the answers on multiple-choice tests reflect common mistakes that many students make. Often students have the correct digits in an answer but they are wrong because they have placed the decimal point incorrectly.

Where Does the Decimal Point Go?

You have already learned that decimal points need to be lined up so that the digits you add or subtract have the same place value.

However, it is easy to forget the rules when you are taking a test. What can you do? You already know the answer: use estimation to determine the range, then choose from the alternatives.

Example:

While running errands, Rick paid $5.75 to have a shoe repaired, $.50 for stamps, $20.13 for groceries, and $8 for gas. How much did he spend in all?

  (1) $3.44
  (2) $26.46
  (3) $34.38
  (4) $207.63
  (5) $343.80

You may have estimated this way:

Groceries, stamps, and gas come to under $30. So when the $5.75 is added, the total is between $30 and $35. Only one choice is in this range: **(3)** $34.38.

The other answer choices come from mistakes in placing the decimal point. Try to find the errors that lead to choices **(2)** and **(4)**.

When multiplying or dividing, it is even more common to make mistakes because of the decimal point. Often the answer choices on tests reflect these mistakes. You will be able to choose the right answer by estimating, remembering how to handle trailing 0s, and using your number sense.

Example:

To keep fit, Troy does 40 push-ups a day, 5 days a week. How many push-ups will he do in a year (52 weeks)?

  (1) 104
  (2) 200
  (3) 1,040
  (4) 2,080
  (5) 10,400

Mathematically, the problem is:

$$t = 5(40)(52)$$

Mentally, 5×40 is 200. Then estimating the rest, $200 \times 50 = 10$ with 3 0s after it, or 10,000.

Now you can choose the only answer that is in this range: **(5)** 10,400.

Example:

The sales tax rate in a county is 5%. What is the total, including tax, that one would pay for 3 shirts, each costing $20?

   (1) $60
   (2) $60.30
   (3) $63
   (4) $65
   (5) $90

Since the 3 shirts will cost $60, this is the amount that will be taxed.

Will the amount of tax be
    $.30   answer choice (**2**),
    $3.00   answer choice (**3**),
or $30.00   answer choice (**5**)?

Remembering that 5% means 5 out of a hundred, you know that the tax on $100 would be $5, so on $60 it would be $3: (**3**) $63.

Example:

How many pieces of wire 0.25 m long can be cut from a coil containing 10 m of wire?

   (1) 2.5
   (2) 4
   (3) 25
   (4) 40
   (5) 400

After understanding this problem, you realize that the words ask "How many 0.25s are there in 10?" The mathematical problem is $10 \div 0.25 = x$.

Answer choices (**1**) and (**3**) are given for those who thought they should multiply. The other 3 choices contain the correct digit (4) but have the decimal point in different places. Should the answer be 4, 40, or 400?

Someone with number sense would say, "There are four $\frac{1}{4}$s in 1 m, so there must be 10 times that in 10 m." Choose (**4**) 40.

Use Your Number Sense

By this time, you have developed a strong ability to find many answers mentally, a fine sense of numbers, and estimation skills to find the answers to most problems. These are the most important skills for enabling you to be in control of the numbers in your life. By using these and a calculator for the complicated problems, you can be the master of every numerical situation.

You can also be the master of the GED Math Test with these skills. Try this experiment to prove that this statement is true.

Optional Approach:

Complete the checkup on the following pages without using scratch paper. Use your pencil to record your answers. Force yourself to *think* of other ways to find the answer.

This optional approach exercise is not meant to suggest that you should not use scratch paper when you take the actual GED Test. At that time, you will want to have all possibilities available to you. The purpose of this experiment is to show you two things. First, the test questions are not the kind of problems that are complicated—the numbers used are "nice" numbers. Secondly, you may not be aware of the mental skills and number sense that you have acquired. You may be surprised by the good results and your own ability.

To simulate actual test conditions, you should spend no more than 45 minutes on these questions. You may use the formulas (page 246) as a reference during the test, but the use of calculators is not allowed.

1. The label on a dairy dessert states that it is 93% fat-free. What percent of the weight of a 64 oz. package would you expect to consist of fat?

   (1) 7%
   (2) 36%
   (3) 45.8%
   (4) 59.52%
   (5) 64%

2. On average, the high temperature of the day is 18° higher than the low temperature of that day. Using this as a rule, what would you expect the high temperature to be on a day when the low is −11°?

   (1) −29°
   (2) −7°
   (3) 7°
   (4) 9°
   (5) 29°

3. The value of $\sqrt{45.7}$ is between

   (1) 4 and 5
   (2) 6 and 7
   (3) 7 and 8
   (4) 8 and 9
   (5) 9 and 10

4. Which of the following expressions indicates how much change Rhonda should receive from a $20 bill after buying 8 gallons of gas at $1.37 per gallon?

   (1) 20(8)(1.37)
   (2) 20 − (8 + 1.37)
   (3) 20 − 8 − 1.37
   (4) 8(1.37) − 20
   (5) 20 − 8(1.37)

Problems 5–7 refer to the following diagram.

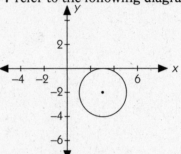

5. What are the coordinates of the center of the circle?

   (1) (2, 3)
   (2) (−2, 3)
   (3) (3, 2)
   (4) (−3, 2)
   (5) (3, −2)

6. How many units long is the <u>diameter</u> of the circle?

   (1) 2
   (2) 3
   (3) 4
   (4) 6
   (5) 8

7. Approximately how many units are there in the <u>circumference</u> of the circle?

   (1) 9.42
   (2) 12.56
   (3) 18.86
   (4) 25.12
   (5) Not enough information is given.

8. During an open house at the local airport, 20-minute airplane rides were being offered to the public for the price of 10¢ per pound. What would it cost Lynda, who weighs 116 pounds, to go on a ride?

    (1) $116.00
    (2) $23.20
    (3) $11.60
    (4) $2.32
    (5) $1.60

9. Roy borrowed $20,000 from his uncle at an <u>annual</u> interest rate of 9%. How much <u>total</u> <u>interest</u> will he have to pay if he keeps the money for 5 years?

    (1) $180
    (2) $900
    (3) $1,800
    (4) $9,000
    (5) $90,000

10. In a 20-day period, it rained on 16 days. Which expression below tells what percentage of the days in this period that it was *not* raining?

    (1) $\frac{20 - 16}{20}$
    (2) $\frac{16}{20}$
    (3) $\frac{20}{16}$
    (4) $\frac{20 - 16}{16}$
    (5) $20 - 16$

11. As a general rule, a person's skin (s) weighs $\frac{1}{16}$ of his or her entire body weight (w). Which formula expresses this relationship?

    (1) $w = s + 16$
    (2) $s = \frac{w}{16}$
    (3) $s = \frac{1}{16} + w$
    (4) $s = w \div \frac{1}{16}$
    (5) $w = \frac{s}{16}$

Problems 12–13 refer to the following diagram.

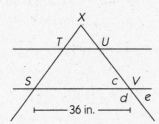

This is a side view of a display shelving unit. The shelves are parallel to the floor.

12. The assembly instructions for the unit say that $\angle d$ should measure 135°. How many degrees should be in the measure of $\angle e$?

    (1) 35°
    (2) 45°
    (3) 65°
    (4) 180°
    (5) Not enough information is given.

13. $\triangle SXV$ is similar to $\triangle TXU$. What is the length of the shelf from point T to point U?

    (1) 6 in.
    (2) 9 in.
    (3) 12 in.
    (4) 18 in.
    (5) Not enough information is given.

14. During the year-end sale, all merchandise in the small-appliances section of a store was discounted 20%. On which of the following items would the savings be more than $10?

a. a waffle iron marked $29.99

b. a wet-dry vacuum marked $48.88

c. a food processor marked $149.99

(1) a only
(2) b only
(3) c only
(4) b and c only
(5) Not enough information is given.

15. During the first part of the 1990 season, Pooh Richardson of the Minnesota Timberwolves was the NBA player playing the most minutes per game. He played an average of 42 of the 48 minutes of every game. What percentage of the game did he play?

(1) $\frac{7}{8}$%
(2) $\frac{6}{7}$%
(3) $62\frac{1}{2}$%
(4) $87\frac{1}{2}$%
(5) $112\frac{1}{2}$%

16. The slope ($\frac{\text{rise}}{\text{run}}$) of a roof is to be $\frac{2}{5}$.

How long does the brace pictured need to be?

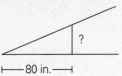

(1) 10 in.
(2) 32 in.
(3) 64 in.
(4) 200 in.
(5) Not enough information is given.

17. The instructions for roasting a turkey say to roast it 20 minutes per pound. According to these instructions, how long should you roast a $10\frac{1}{2}$-pound turkey?

(1) 2,000 minutes
(2) 20 minutes
(3) 2 hours
(4) $3\frac{1}{2}$ hours
(5) $4\frac{1}{5}$ hours

18. What is the price one would pay for a $400 bedroom set during a sale where everything is marked 25% off and the sales tax is $7\frac{1}{2}$%?

(1) $107.50
(2) $307.50
(3) $322.50
(4) $382.50
(5) $537.50

Problems 19–20 refer to the following information.

The unit by which electricity is measured is the kilowatt-hour (kWh). It equals the use of 1,000 watts for 1 hour.

For example, a 100-watt lamp bulb would use 1 kWh if left burning for 10 hours, and 2 kWh for 20 hours.

The following table shows the length of time some common household appliances would take to use 1 kWh of electricity.

radio	80 hr.
color TV	9 hr.
iron	45 min.
room heater	20 min.

19. <u>Approximately</u> how many times more electricity does a color TV set use than a radio?

   (1) $\frac{1}{12}$
   (2) $\frac{1}{9}$
   (3) 9
   (4) 12
   (5) 20

20. How many kWh of electricity would be used by a room heater that was on for 8 hours?

   (1) 24
   (2) 12
   (3) 9
   (4) 6
   (5) $2\frac{2}{3}$

21. A modern expressway is typically constructed with 3 12-ft.-wide traffic lanes in each direction and a dividing median strip that is 16.4 ft. wide. Which expression represents the total width of such an expressway?

   (1) 3(12)
   (2) 3(12) + 16.4
   (3) 3(12) − 16.4
   (4) 6(12) + 16.4
   (5) 6(12) − 16.4

22. A blueprint has a scale of 1 in. = $1\frac{1}{2}$ ft. This represents a ratio of

   (1) 1:24
   (2) 1:18
   (3) 1:15
   (4) 1:12
   (5) 2:3

Problem 23 refers to the following diagram.

23. Which expression indicates the <u>perimeter</u> of the rectangle?

   (1) $3n^2$
   (2) $4n$
   (3) $4n^2$
   (4) $8n^2$
   (5) $8n$

Problems 24–26 refer to the following information.

The table and the graph both show the price of various amounts of candy that is sold in bulk.

Weight (oz.)	4	8	12	16
Cost ($)	0.80	1.60		

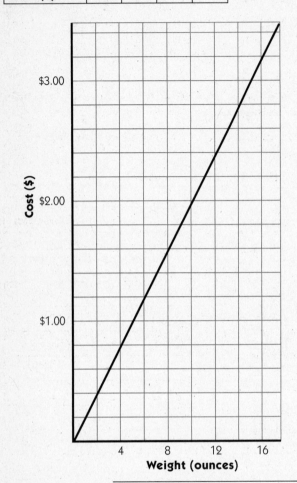

24. How many ounces of candy could you buy for $2.00?

   (1) 1
   (2) 6
   (3) 10
   (4) 15
   (5) 20

25. Which proportion could be used to find the cost (*c*) of 12 ounces of the candy?

   (1) $\frac{4}{12} = \frac{c}{0.80}$
   (2) $\frac{4}{12} = \frac{0.80}{c}$
   (3) $\frac{4}{0.80} = \frac{c}{12}$
   (4) $\frac{4}{c} = \frac{12}{0.80}$
   (5) $\frac{4}{12} = \frac{0.20}{c}$

26. What is the cost of 2 pounds of candy? (1 pound = 16 ounces)

   (1) $ .40
   (2) $ 1.60
   (3) $ 3.20
   (4) $ 4.80
   (5) $ 6.40

27. The entrance to a banquet room is a doorway that is 6 feet across and 8 feet high. Workers carry circular tabletops through this doorway. What is the diameter of the largest tabletop that they can fit through this doorway at an angle?

   (1) 6 ft.
   (2) 8 ft.
   (3) 10 ft.
   (4) 12 ft.
   (5) 14 ft.

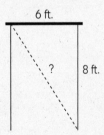

6 ft.

? 8 ft.

28. Each year since 1980, U.S. traffic deaths have occurred at the rate of about 20 per 100,000 population. This rate, expressed as a percent is

   (1) 20%
   (2) 2%
   (3) 0.2%
   (4) 0.02%
   (5) 0.002%

Self-Evaluation

Although this set of problems did contain many review problems, it concentrated on the concepts of rate, ratio, proportion, and percent. Since these are the topics that you have studied most recently, they were fresh in your memory.

1) If you tried to complete the checkup without using scratch paper, evaluate this strategy by answering the following questions.

   a) How many items were you *not* able to complete?

   b) If you had used scratch paper, could you have successfully completed these items?

   c) Are you pleased with your progress toward being an estimator and having a greater sense of number relationships?

2) If you had been able to use your calculator during this checkup, for which problems would you have used it?

3) Identify the areas that you need to review before the final checkup.

Problems	Skills	Lessons
1, 10, 18	Percent	23
2	Negative numbers	5
3	Estimating square roots	11
4, 21	Multi-step problems/Order of operations	10
5	Coordinate graph	5
6	Coordinate graph/Circles	5 & 12
7	Circles	12
8, 17, 25	Proportions	21
9	Simple interest	23
11, 20	Multiplying fractions	17
12	Complementary and supplementary angles	4
13	Not enough information/Similar triangles	14 & 21
14	Estimating with easy percents	23
15, 28	Solving percent problems with proportions	22
16	Slopes/Proportions	20 & 21
19	Compatible numbers	7
22	Equal ratios	20
23	Grouping with variables	2
24, 26	Equivalent equations/Equal ratios	9 & 20
27	Pythagorean theorem/Circles	11 & 12

• LESSON 26 • Data Analysis

This lesson and the next are about data analysis—collecting, organizing, presenting, and interpreting information.

• Collecting Information . . . .

- How much trash does the average household throw away each week?

- How much long-distance calling does a household do each month?

- Which city services are most critical to residents?

- How much does the average household spend for food each week?

- For what reason do most people work to pass the GED Test?

Accurate answers to questions like these are important to businesses, governments, and individuals. In some cases, the answers can be found in business records or other documents. However, up-to-the-minute information on many subjects can be found only by conducting a survey of the population.

Which cars do people want?

The answer would be interesting to auto manufacturers and dealers. However, for the answer to be useful, the question needs to be more specific.

Revise the question, considering these issues: What make (brand name) and model (convertible, 4-wheel-drive, etc.) do you prefer? Why do you prefer it? Is this a dream car, or one that you might actually buy? The following questionnaire has been designed to gather more accurate information.

Questionnaire
Male/Female_____   Age: 15–20__ 21–30__ 31–40__ 41+__
What car (make, model) do you <u>dream</u> of owning? _____   Price estimate _____   ☐ foreign ☐ domestic
Why this car? Choose <u>two</u> of the following: a. styling (looks nice)   b. cost (to buy or to operate)   c. power   d. comfort   e. quality construction   f. carries a lot
More realistically, what car (make, model) would you <u>probably purchase</u> in the next few years? _____ Price estimate_____   ☐ foreign ☐ domestic
Why this car? Choose <u>two</u> of the following: a. styling (looks nice)   b. cost (to buy or to operate)   c. power   d. comfort   e. quality construction   f. carries a lot

Although it would be best to know how every person in the community (the **population**) would answer these questions, that is not practical. We will have to be satisfied with the information gathered from a small group (a sample). From the sample, we make inferences about the whole population.

PROBLEM 1   Using the questionnaire above and the 3 on the next page, interview 4 people. (You may include yourself.) Try to include at least 2 age groups and both sexes in your sample. Accept the price estimate that each interviewee provides.

```
┌─────────────────────────────────────────────────────────────┐
│                        Questionnaire                          │
│                                                               │
│  Male/Female_____        Age: 15–20__ 21–30__ 31–40__ 41+__ │
│                                                               │
│  What car (make, model) do you dream of owning? _____  │
│  Price estimate _____   ☐ foreign  ☐ domestic          │
│                                                               │
│  Why this car? Choose two of the following:                   │
│  a. styling (looks nice)    b. cost (to buy or to operate)  c. power │
│  d. comfort                 e. quality construction         f. carries a lot │
│                                                               │
│  More realistically, what car (make, model) would you probably purchase in the next │
│  few years? _____ Price estimate_____ │
│  ☐ foreign  ☐ domestic                                        │
│                                                               │
│  Why this car? Choose two of the following:                   │
│  a. styling (looks nice)    b. cost (to buy or to operate)  c. power │
│  d. comfort                 e. quality construction         f. carries a lot │
└─────────────────────────────────────────────────────────────┘

┌─────────────────────────────────────────────────────────────┐
│                        Questionnaire                          │
│                                                               │
│  Male/Female_____        Age: 15–20__ 21–30__ 31–40__ 41+__ │
│                                                               │
│  What car (make, model) do you dream of owning? _____  │
│  Price estimate _____   ☐ foreign  ☐ domestic          │
│                                                               │
│  Why this car? Choose two of the following:                   │
│  a. styling (looks nice)    b. cost (to buy or to operate)  c. power │
│  d. comfort                 e. quality construction         f. carries a lot │
│                                                               │
│  More realistically, what car (make, model) would you probably purchase in the next │
│  few years? _____ Price estimate_____ │
│  ☐ foreign  ☐ domestic                                        │
│                                                               │
│  Why this car? Choose two of the following:                   │
│  a. styling (looks nice)    b. cost (to buy or to operate)  c. power │
│  d. comfort                 e. quality construction         f. carries a lot │
└─────────────────────────────────────────────────────────────┘

┌─────────────────────────────────────────────────────────────┐
│                        Questionnaire                          │
│                                                               │
│  Male/Female_____        Age: 15–20__ 21–30__ 31–40__ 41+__ │
│                                                               │
│  What car (make, model) do you dream of owning? _____  │
│  Price estimate _____   ☐ foreign  ☐ domestic          │
│                                                               │
│  Why this car? Choose two of the following:                   │
│  a. styling (looks nice)    b. cost (to buy or to operate)  c. power │
│  d. comfort                 e. quality construction         f. carries a lot │
│                                                               │
│  More realistically, what car (make, model) would you probably purchase in the next │
│  few years? _____ Price estimate_____ │
│  ☐ foreign  ☐ domestic                                        │
│                                                               │
│  Why this car? Choose two of the following:                   │
│  a. styling (looks nice)    b. cost (to buy or to operate)  c. power │
│  d. comfort                 e. quality construction         f. carries a lot │
└─────────────────────────────────────────────────────────────┘
```

Organizing Information . . . .

To solve problems 2 and 3 below, you will use the data from the questionnaires on pages 250–254 in the appendix and your own data (pages 210 and 211). Carefully tear out the questionnaires at the end of the book.

The questionnaires offer answers to many different questions. First, consider this issue:

"Compare the cost of the cars people want according to age groups."

Notice that each dot on the following scatter plots corresponds to a value from the questionnaires on pages 250–254. They provide an overview of the information gathered.

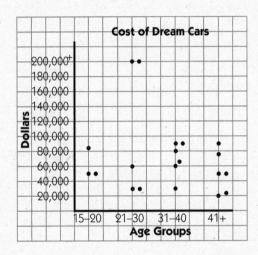
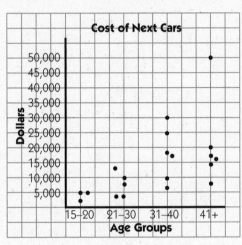

PROBLEM 2   Plot the additional data that you collected (pages 210–211) on the graphs above.

PROBLEM 3   On the graphs below, plot the data comparing the costs of men's and women's car preferences. Use the data from the book's questionnaires plus your own data. (You can remove the questionnaires from the back of the book to make this easier.)

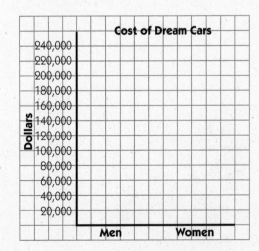
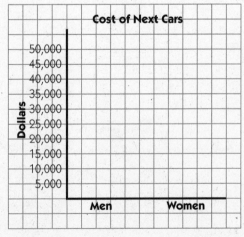

Making a Table

You will need to use the data from the questionnaires to answer questions in this lesson and the next. To quickly find the information you need, you can organize the data into a table.

A table is organized into columns (up and down) and into rows (across). The table below compares, by age, responses about the cost of <u>dream cars</u> and <u>next cars</u>. Also note that (M) stands for male respondents and (F) stands for female respondents.

The table below summarizes the data from the questionnaires on pages 250–254.

Comparison of Cost of Cars, by Age of Respondent				
	15–20	21–30	31–40	41+
Dream Car	$50,000 (M)*	$200,000 (M)	$65,000 (F)	$25,000 (M)
	85,000 (F)**	250,000 (M)	80,000 (M)	90,000 (M)
	50,000 (F)	60,000 (F)	30,000 (M)	50,000 (F)
		30,000 (M)	60,000 (F)	20,000 (F)
		30,000 (F)	90,000 (F)	75,000 (M)
			90,000 (M)	50,000 (M)

*(M) male   **(F) female

	15–20	21–30	31–40	41+
Next Car	$5,000 (M)	$4,000 (M)	$17,000 (F)	$8,000 (M)
	2,500 (F)	13,000 (M)	30,000 (M)	16,000 (M)
	5,000 (F)	4,000 (F)	18,000 (M)	20,000 (F)
		10,000 (M)	25,000 (F)	14,000 (F)
		8,000 (F)	7,000 (F)	17,000 (M)
			10,000 (M)	50,000 (M)

Analyzing Numerical Data . . . .

The data that you organized on the scatter plots and in the tables involves numerical values. In cases like these, it is important to have one number to represent all the others in the group. A single value helps to understand the meaning of the data.

Examine the 5 values on the table on page 213 for the cost of <u>dream cars</u> for the age group 21–30. What would be a number that would represent all of them? The values were:

$30,000; $30,000; $60,000; $200,000; and $250,000 _____

The number you chose should be a number somewhere in the middle of the group. There are three established ways to find such an average number. Each is a measure of central tendency

Four Key Numbers

The following terms are important in data analysis:

mode   median   mean   range

The mode is the value that occurs most often.

1) Find the mode. The mode is the value that occurs the <u>most often</u>.

Example:
Find the <u>mode</u> of the values for the cost of the dream cars for the age group 21–30. Look at the box above.

The only value that occurs more than once is $30,000, so $30,000 is the <u>mode</u>.

The median is the middle value.

2) Find the median. The median is the middle number of the group.

Arrange the values from least to greatest, then find the middle value. This works easily when the number of values is <u>odd</u>—there is a single middle value as in Example A below. However, when the number of values is <u>even</u>, the median is the average of the two middle values as shown by Example B.

Example A:
Find the <u>median</u> of the values for the cost of the dream cars for the age group 21–30.

Arrange the values in order:

median

$30,000 $30,000 $60,000 $200,000 $250,000

Choose the number in the middle:

The <u>median</u> is $60,000.

Example B:
Find the <u>median</u> of the values for the cost of the dream cars for the age group 31–40.

Arrange the values in order:

median

$30,000 $60,000 $65,000 $80,000 $90,000 $90,000

Here the middle is halfway between 65,000 and 80,000.

$$\text{The } \underline{\text{median}} = \frac{65,000 + 80,000}{2} = \frac{145,000}{2} = \$72,500$$

3) Find the mean. The mean is what is often referred to as the average.

Recall from Lesson 10 that finding an average is a two-step problem. First, you add the values. Then you divide this sum by the number of values. As a single equation:

$$\text{mean} = \frac{\text{sum of values}}{\text{number of values}}$$

Example:

Find the mean of the values for the cost of dream cars for the age group 21–30.

$$\text{mean} = \frac{\$200{,}000 + \$250{,}000 + \$60{,}000 + \$30{,}000 + \$30{,}000}{5}$$

$$\text{mean} = \frac{\$570{,}000}{5} = \$114{,}000$$

PROBLEM 4 Examine the 3 different single values that are meant to describe the cost of a dream car for the age group 21–30. They are:

mode—$30,000; median—$60,000; and mean—$114,000

a) Which of these numbers is closest to the value you chose at the top of the previous page?

b) Which value do *you* think is the most representative of this group? Which value is the least representative?

PROBLEM 5 Find the mode, mean, and median of the costs of the "next" car for the age group 21–30. The values are $4,000; $4,000; $8,000; $10,000; and 13,000.

PROBLEM 6 For the dream cars, the values $200,000 and $250,000 are called outliers because they are so far away from most of the values in the group. Their presence explains why the *mean* (average) for the dream cars did not seem as representative as the *median* (middle value). Notice that these measures (median and mean) were much closer for the "next" car category. Explain why they were closer.

PROBLEM 7 In their publications, U.S. government statisticians use the *median* price of homes and the *median* household income. Explain why in these cases the median might be the most representative type of "average."

The **range** is the
difference between the
highest and lowest values.

4) Find the range. The range is the difference between the highest and lowest values in the group. It is often not sufficient to describe a group of data points by merely using one number to represent the central tendency. We also have to be concerned with how the data varies from this single value. The range helps us to do that.

Example:

What is the range of the cost of next cars for the age group 15–20 (as shown in the box below)?

$2,500 $5,000 $5,000

The range is the difference between the highest and lowest values.

$$\text{range} = \$5{,}000 - \$2{,}500 = \$2{,}500$$

highest   lowest

Use this table, repeated from page 213, to solve problems 8–11.

Comparison of Cost of Cars, by Age of Respondent				
	15–20	**21–30**	**31–40**	**41+**
Dream Car	$50,000 (M)*	$200,000 (M)	$65,000 (F)	$25,000 (M)
	85,000 (F)**	250,000 (M)	80,000 (M)	90,000 (M)
	50,000 (F)	60,000 (F)	30,000 (M)	50,000 (F)
		30,000 (M)	60,000 (F)	20,000 (F)
		30,000 (F)	90,000 (F)	75,000 (M)
			90,000 (M)	50,000 (M)

*(M) male   **(F) female

	15–20	**21–30**	**31–40**	**41+**
Next Car	$5,000 (M)	$4,000 (M)	$17,000 (F)	$8,000 (M)
	2,500 (F)	13,000 (M)	30,000 (M)	16,000 (M)
	5,000 (F)	4,000 (F)	18,000 (M)	20,000 (F)
		10,000 (M)	25,000 (F)	14,000 (F)
		8,000 (F)	7,000 (F)	17,000 (M)
			10,000 (M)	50,000 (M)

PROBLEM 8   For the age group 21–30, what is the <u>range</u> . . .

a) for the costs of the dream cars?

b) for the costs of the next cars?

PROBLEM 9   For the age group 41+, what is the <u>range</u> . . .

a) for the costs of the dream cars?

b) for the costs of the next cars?

PROBLEM 10   Look at the costs of *dream cars* for the entire group of 20 respondents. Find the range of the data and the three measures of central tendencies—the mean, the mode, and the median.

PROBLEM 11   Look at the costs of *next cars* for all 20 people. Find the range, mean, mode, and median.

The Sample

Generally speaking, the results of any survey can be made more dependable by increasing the number of people surveyed. The results of a survey can be made more dependable if the people surveyed represent a random sampling of the population meant to be studied.

PROBLEM 12   The *Los Angeles Times* reports that the median cost of a new car in 1990 is $15,000. This is based on an exhaustive search of all available automobiles. Compare this to the <u>medians</u> you found in problems 10 (dream car) and 11 (next car). In addition to the fact that our sample was only 20 people, how can you explain the differences?

PROBLEM 13   In your opinion, how would the mean and median have been affected by . . .

a) interviewing only the subscribers to an automotive magazine?

b) interviewing people as they left an auto show?

c) interviewing only nurses, teachers, and social workers?

The Mean

Generally speaking, the *mean* is the most widely used of what are called the "averages," so it needs further discussion. In many situations, when you are asked for the average, you are looking for the mean. As you do the following problems, remember that the mean is the answer to a division problem:

$$\text{mean} = \frac{\text{sum of values}}{\text{number of values}}$$

PROBLEM 14 a) Consider the original set of values for dream cars in the age group 21–30: $30,000; $30,000; $60,000; $200,000; $250,000. (Its mean is $114,000.) Add one more value—$150,000. Find the mean of this <u>new</u> group.

b) Next consider the <u>original</u> set of values (not including $150,000) plus <u>this one new value</u>—$100,000. Find the mean of this new group.

c) Compare the mean found in part a to the original mean of $114,000. Then compare the mean found in part b to the original mean. Explain the difference.

PROBLEM 15 a) Consider the following group of values for the dream car: $30,000; $30,000; $60,000; $100,000; $100,000; $100,000; $150,000. The sum of these values is $570,000, the same as the sum on the top of page 215. What is the <u>mean</u> of this group of values?

b) Generalize from your discovery: if the sum remains the same, but the number of values is greater, how is the mean affected?

Use what you know about equivalent equations to answer problems 16 and 17 below.

PROBLEM 16 The mean of a group of numbers is 12, and the sum of their values is 96. How many values are in this group?

PROBLEM 17 The mean of a group of 20 values is 5. What is the sum of this group of values?

Example:

To get a *B* in his class, Angel must have an average (mean) of 80 on the 5 tests during the semester. He already has scores of 90, 85, 78, and 76. What score does he need to get on the fifth test in order to earn a *B*?

Step 1: Determine what the *sum* of the values would be if the mean were 80.

$$80 = \frac{sum}{5} \qquad\qquad sum = 5(80) = 400$$

Step 2: Find the value necessary to achieve that sum.

$$90 + 85 + 78 + 76 = 329 \qquad\qquad 400 - 329 = 71$$

PROBLEM 18 A basketball player scored 25, 13, and 17 points in the first three games of a 4-game tournament. How many points does she have to score in the last game to maintain her season average of 19 points per game?

PROBLEM 19 Average attendance at a play must be 200 per night to stay open. For 4 of the 5 performances last week, attendance figures were 185, 150, 230, and 183. How many need to attend the last performance of the week in order to attain the average required?

Presenting and Interpreting Data: Bar Graphs ...

"Pictures speak louder than words."

A graph is the best way to tell others of the results of the research you have done. Consider the first questions of this lesson.

How much do people's dream cars cost?

Example:
First find the means (rounded to the nearest thousand) of each of the age groups as shown below.

Dream Cars

15–20 ....$62,000

21–30 ....$114,000

31–40 ....$69,000

41+ $52,000

This kind of information can be shown most clearly on a bar graph. First, decide on the scale values on the left-hand side (vertical axis), so that the graph can fit in the space available and show the entire range of values.

Example:
For the dream cars graph, the largest value to be shown is $114,000. The intervals (spaces between values) must be equal, so the value of each interval is $25,000.

Cost of Dream Cars

The height of the bars corresponds to the mean of each age group.

Notice that each graph has a title and that the axes are labeled.

How much will people's next car cost?

PROBLEM 20
Find the means for the following age groups. Refer to the table on page 213. Round each answer to the nearest thousand.

Next Cars

15–20 ....$_____

21–30 ....$_____

31–40 ....$_____

41+ ....$_____

Example:
For the next cars graph, the largest value is $21,000. (Let $25,000 be the top value on the graph.)

PROBLEM 21
Determine the size of the intervals, and label the marks on this graph.

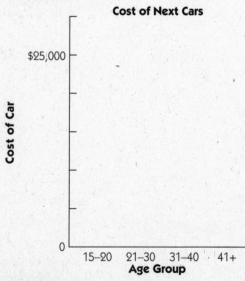

PROBLEM 22
Draw bars to show the means of the age groups. Use the values from problem 20.

As a final refinement, combine these two graphs into one by using **double bars**. Here you can compare the costs of the dream cars and the next cars for each age group.

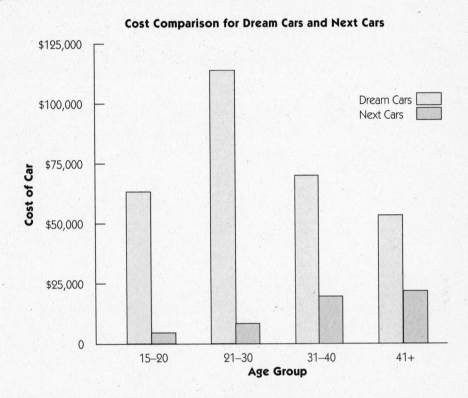

Cost Comparison for Dream Cars and Next Cars

Finally, with all the pertinent information on one graph, you can *see* the trends and the comparisons. You are now ready to **interpret** the data.

"Just the Facts, Ma'am"

PROBLEM 23 In which age group do people dream of the most expensive cars?

PROBLEM 24 In which age group are people able to buy the most expensive cars?

PROBLEM 25 In which age group is the difference the <u>least</u> between the cost of the dream car and the cost of the next car?

PROBLEM 26 For the following statements, tell whether the conclusion is true, false, or could be true.

a) As people grow older, the trend is to buy more expensive cars.

b) As people grow older, they dream of more expensive cars.

c) The cars young people (under 30) dream of owning are over 10 times more expensive than what they can afford.

d) Teenagers are not sophisticated enough to be aware of the most expensive cars.

e) As people grow older, they grow wiser.

"Numbers Don't Lie"

While it is true that numbers do not lend themselves to much interpretation, the methods of reporting those numbers can be altered to tell different stories.

Example:

Both of these graphs show the same information.

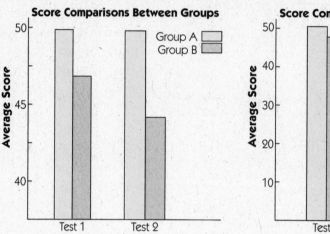 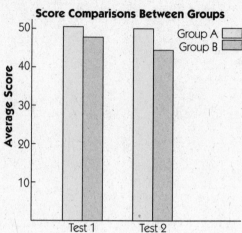

Both graphs are "correct" in the sense that both have titles and legends, and the axes are labeled. Notice the differences between the graphs. For instance, the vertical scale of the graph on the left <u>does not</u> begin at 0. What are some other differences?

PROBLEM 27   On the first graph, the length of the bar for Group A on Test 2 is about twice that of the bar for Group B on that test. Is this **proportional** (in proportion) to the scores that they represent? In other words, was Group A's score twice as big as Group B's?

PROBLEM 28   Which graph would you choose to use if your message is to encourage the members of Group B?

PROBLEM 29   Which graph would you choose to use if you wanted your audience to be aware of the precise differences between the groups?

PROBLEM 30   It is a fact that the typical graph reader does not look carefully at the scales on the sides and bottoms of graphs. With this in mind, which graph gives a <u>truer picture</u> of the situation?

You may use your calculator on any problem for which it seems appropriate.

1. The following listing shows the salaries of all the employees in a small company.

President	$250,000
Manager	$ 60,000
Secretary	$ 22,000
Shipping clerk	$ 20,000
Machinist (2)	$ 18,000 each
Assembler (2)	$ 18,000 each

a) Find the mean, mode, and median for this group of 8 numbers.

b) Which of the three measures of central tendency (mean, mode, or median) would you suggest that the president use if he were trying to convince stockholders that he was running a cost-conscious ("lean and mean") business?

c) Which of these measures of central tendency would the president use on a report if he wanted the company to look as if it paid a high average salary?

2. Nationwide public opinion polls (those published by the TV networks and major newspapers as well as the Nielsen ratings) are scientifically designed to reflect the opinions of the entire nation of 200 million people. Yet they typically interview only 1,500 people. What do you think is the secret of their success?

3. A trucker must make a trip of 2,600 miles. How many miles per day must he average to make the trip in 4 days?

4. Using the axes in 4b, make a graph that shows the comparison between the cost of *men's* and *women's dream cars* and *next cars*. (You will have four bars.) Follow these steps:

a) Find the mean cost for each category. Use these data points, and **round to the nearest thousand**.

Comparison of Cars Preferred by Men and Women				
Dream Cars	**Men**		**Women**	
	$ 50,000	$ 30,000	$ 85,000	$ 60,000
	200,000	90,000	50,000	90,000
	250,000	25,000	60,000	50,000
	30,000	90,000	30,000	20,000
	80,000	75,000	65,000	
		50,000		
Next Cars	$ 5,000	$ 10,000	$ 2,500	$ 7,000
	4,000	30,000	5,000	20,000
	13,000	18,000	4,000	14,000
		10,000	8,000	
		8,000	17,000	
		16,000	25,000	
		17,000		
		50,000		

Mean Cost

	Dream Cars	Next Cars
Men	_____	_____
Women	_____	_____

b) Complete the following graph by using double bars to show the comparison.

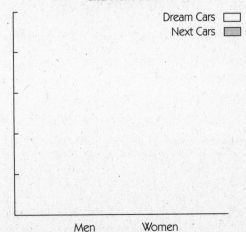

Cost Comparison for Dream Cars and Next Cars

Circle Graphs and Probability

In the previous lesson, a survey was taken about automobiles, and the numerical data points were organized and graphed. In this lesson, you will study the data from the survey that gives information about how opinion is divided among the group. Again, the data points will be organized, graphed, and interpreted.

• Organizing Data . . . .

"Why do people choose the cars that they do?"

The people in the survey had a choice of 6 reasons for preferring the cars they named. We are looking for the statistics showing how often they chose each reason. Our final step will be to make 2 circle graphs showing the reasons—one for the "dream cars" and one for the "next cars." The circles will be divided into wedges whose different sizes will show how often the different answers were chosen. To organize this kind of data, a tally sheet or frequency distribution chart works well.

The following tally sheet shows the count for the various responses. It was divided among the age groups on the 20 questionnaires. (There is a total of 40 responses to the question above.)

Reason	Age				Total	Fractional Part	Percent
	15–20	21–30	31–40	41+			
Dream Cars							
1. styling	//	////	////	//////	16	$\frac{2}{5}$	40%
2. cost					0	_____	_____
3. power	///	///	/	//	9	_____	_____
4. comfort			//	/	3	_____	_____
5. quality	/	//	////	///	10	_____	_____
6. capacity		/	/		2	_____	_____
Next Cars							
1. styling	//	/	//	//	7	_____	_____
2. cost	///	////	///	///	13	_____	_____
3. power		//	/	/	4	_____	_____
4. comfort			/	//	3	_____	_____
5. quality	/	/	//	////	8	_____	_____
6. capacity		//	///		5	_____	_____

Note: You will need to use the questionnaires from pages 250–254 in the appendix. A protractor will help you with some problems, marked **.

Problems 1–2 are based on the chart on page 222.

PROBLEM 1 Which answer was given most often as the reason for choosing a particular . . .

a) dream car?   b) next car?

PROBLEM 2 Often, the structure of a questionnaire or the phrasing of a question can influence people's choices. In what way was the questionnaire structured so that it could have influenced the respondents to select <u>cost</u> most often as a reason for choosing their next car?

"Do people want foreign or domestic makes of cars?"

PROBLEM 3 Complete the first part of the following chart to show the **frequency** of the choices. Use the questionnaires on pages 250–254. Note: Since it is difficult to trace just where a car is made today (some Hondas are made in the United States, and some Chevrolets are made in Japan), look at the boxes marked foreign or domestic.

	Age				Fractional Part	Percent
	15–20	21–30	31–40	41+		
Dream Cars						
Foreign	___	___	___	___	$\frac{15}{20} = \frac{3}{4}$	75%
Domestic	___	___	___	___	$\frac{}{20} =$	___
Next Cars						
Foreign	___	___	___	___	$\frac{}{20} =$	___
Domestic	___	___	___	___	$\frac{}{20} =$	___

• Graphing the Data: Circle Graphs . . . .

In a circle graph, the entire circle represents the total. The size of each wedge (part of the circle) corresponds to the part of the total that it represents.

Styling
$\frac{2}{5}$ of the circle

For example, for the dream cars, the wedge representing "styling" should be $\frac{2}{5}$ of the total circle.

The first step in finding the size of the various wedges is to <u>find the fractional part of the total</u>.

. . .
The size of the wedges should be **proportional** to the portion of the response that they represent.
. . .

PROBLEM 4 Complete the Fractional Part column of the chart on page 222. Remember that each section (dream car and next car) has a total of 40 responses.

Example: 16 out of 40 is $\frac{16}{40} = \frac{16 \div 8}{40 \div 8} = \frac{2}{5}$

PROBLEM 5 Complete the Percent column on the chart. (**You will use the percentages to label your graph**.)

Example: $\frac{2}{5} = \frac{p}{100}$ $5 \times p = 2 \times 100$ OR   Looking across

$p = \frac{2 \times \overset{20}{100}}{\underset{1}{5}} = 40\%$ $5 \times 20 = 100$

$2 \times 20 = 40$

Next, use the fractions to determine the size of the wedges of the circle.

The key thing to remember is that the entire circle contains 360°.

The size of a wedge is determined by the measure of its central angle.

Here are two methods that you can use to find the number of degrees in each wedge.

You can set up a proportion and solve it.

$$\frac{2}{5} = \frac{s}{360}$$

$$5s = 720$$

$$s = 144°$$

Or you can find a fraction of the total degrees.

$$\frac{2}{5} \text{ of } 360°$$

$$\frac{2}{5} \times \frac{\overset{72}{360}}{1} = 144°$$

PROBLEM 6 Complete the Next Cars column of the following table, which shows the size of the central angles of the wedges to be used in the two circle graphs. Use the fractional parts from page 222. (You may want to use your calculator.)

Reason	Dream Cars	Next Cars
styling	144°	__63°__ (Hint: $\frac{7}{40} \times 360°$)
cost	0°	___
power	81°	___
comfort	27°	___
quality	90°	___
capacity	18°	___

Now, divide the circle into wedges.

Since the angle measures above are not easy to "eyeball," use a protractor to measure them. If you don't have a protractor, just read the steps below. Start by drawing any radius of the circle (fig. 1). This will be the base line for the first angle.

Using the protractor, mark off the number of degrees in the first wedge. Since the order is not important and 90° is the easiest to measure, start with the wedge for <u>quality</u>. (fig. 2).

Either radius can now be the base for the second wedge measurement—144° for styling (fig. 3).

Continue around the circle, repeating the process for the 81° wedge and the 27° wedge (fig. 4). Measure the remaining angle to be sure that it is equal to the remaining wedge measurement—18° (fig. 4).

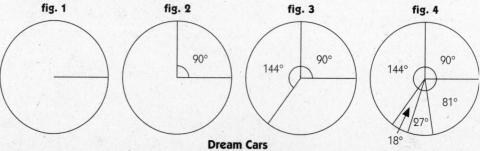

fig. 1   fig. 2   fig. 3   fig. 4

Dream Cars

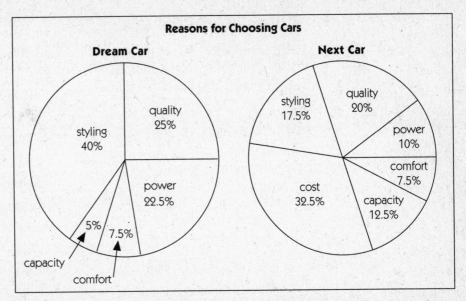

Reasons for Choosing Cars

The graph above is the final version, in percentages, showing the comparison between the reasons for choosing a dream car and the reasons for choosing a next car.

**PROBLEM 7   If you have a protractor, measure to check that the central angles of the wedges in the Next Car graph correspond to the values you found in problem 6.

PROBLEM 8   Check that the total of the percentages in each circle graph is 100%.

PROBLEM 9   "People dream of owning cars that . . ." Complete the sentence using the top three reasons as determined by the survey. Do the same for a typical next car. "People intend to *buy* cars that . . ."

**PROBLEM 10   Complete the rest of the table in problem 3. Then, if you have a protractor, follow the steps to construct circle graphs <u>comparing the preference for foreign and domestic brands</u> of cars.

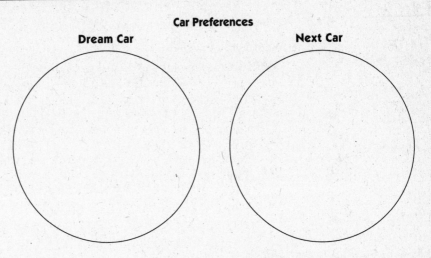

Car Preferences

What Are the Chances? . . . .

When surveys are carried out scientifically, the results can be used to predict the results over a large population. Before beginning that important phase, you should know some basic principles of probability.

Probability is the branch of mathematics that is concerned with the likelihood of events happening.

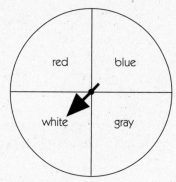

The circle is divided into 4 equal parts.

The spinner is just as likely to stop in one section as another.

The probability (P) that the spinner will stop in the red section is "one out of four," or $\frac{1}{4}$.

$$P(\text{red}) = \frac{\text{red area}}{\text{total area}} = \frac{1}{4}$$

There are 6 sides to a die. On a fair die, each side is equally likely to be turned up after the die is tossed.

The probability that the side with 3 dots lands up is $\frac{1}{6}$.

$$P(3) = \frac{\text{number of sides with 3 dots}}{\text{total number of sides}} = \frac{1}{6}$$

die

Generally speaking,

$$\text{probability of an event happening} = \frac{\text{number of favorable ways}}{\text{total number of ways}}$$

Probabilities can be expressed as fractions, decimals, or percents, and these values are always between 0 and 1.

Example:
What is the probability of rolling an odd number with a die?

There are 3 faces of the die with odd numbers: 1, 3, and 5.

$$P(\text{odd number}) = \tfrac{3}{6} = \tfrac{1}{2} = 0.5 \text{ or } 50\%$$

Example:
What is the probability of the spinner above landing in a yellow area?

There is no yellow area in the circle above, so there is no way that this could happen.

$$P(\text{yellow}) = 0$$

If an event is *impossible*, the probability of that event happening is 0.

Example:
What is the probability of rolling a die and getting a number whose value is less than 7?

All possible faces of the die have values less than 7, so there are 6 ways that are favorable.

$$P(\text{less than 7}) = \tfrac{6}{6} = 1$$

If an event is *certain*, the probability of that event happening is 1.

In most cases, something either happens or it doesn't. The probabilities of the two are related. They are said to be complementary

$$P(\text{rolling a 3}) + P(\text{not rolling a 3}) = 1$$

with $\frac{1}{6}$ labeled above "P(rolling a 3)", "?" labeled above "P(not rolling a 3)", and "total ways" labeled above "1".

Using an equivalent equation,

$$P(\text{not rolling a 3}) = 1 - P(\text{rolling a 3}) = 1 - \tfrac{1}{6} = \tfrac{5}{6}$$

with "?" labeled below "P(not rolling a 3)", "total ways" labeled above "1", "$\frac{1}{6}$" labeled above "P(rolling a 3)", and (5 in 6 chances of not rolling a 3.)

Example:

If the letters of the word *CHEER* were placed in a container and one letter was picked at random, what is the probability that it would *not* be an *E*?

Method 1: Two of the 5 letters are *E*s.

$$P(E) = \tfrac{2}{5} \qquad P(\text{not } E) = 1 - \tfrac{2}{5} = \tfrac{3}{5}$$

Method 2: Three of the 5 letters are not *E*s.

$$P(\text{not } E) = \tfrac{3}{5}$$

When expressed as a fraction, probability is an example of a <u>ratio</u>. When stated probabilities are used to predict results, <u>proportions</u> also are used.

Example:

If you roll a die 60 times, how many times would you expect a 6 to appear?

$P(6) = \tfrac{1}{6}$. Using the proportion $\tfrac{1}{6} = \tfrac{n}{60}$, you can see that *n* is 10.

PROBLEM 11 When rolling a die, what is the probability of getting . . .

a) a 2?

b) a 0?

c) a number less than 3?

d) an even number?

PROBLEM 12 In a standard deck of 52 cards, there are 13 cards per suit. Two suits are black (spades and clubs), and two are red (hearts and diamonds). There are 3 face cards in each suit—the king, queen, and jack. When picking a card, what is the probability of picking . . .

a) a card from one of the black suits?

b) a 10?

c) the king of hearts?

d) a face card?

PROBLEM 13 If you spin the spinner on the previous page 20 times, how many times would you expect that it will land in the red area?

PROBLEM 14 If you roll a die 100 times, how many times would you expect that you will roll a number less than 4?

PROBLEM 15 When picking a card from a standard deck of 52 cards, what is the probability of <u>not</u> getting . . .

a) an ace?

b) the jack of clubs?

PROBLEM 16 Probability is sometimes discussed in terms of "odds."

The odds for an event happening is the ratio $\dfrac{\text{number of favorable ways}}{\text{number of unfavorable ways}}$.

The odds <u>for</u> rolling a 3 on a die are $\tfrac{1}{5}$. The odds <u>against</u> rolling a 3 are $\tfrac{5}{1}$.

What are the odds . . .

a) <u>for</u> rolling an even number?

b) <u>for</u> the spinner landing in red?

c) <u>for</u> picking an ace from the deck?

d) <u>against</u> rolling a number greater than 4?

e) <u>against</u> the spinner landing in red?

f) <u>against</u> picking the 5 of diamonds?

The principles of probability are easy to see in games of chance. However, these ideas have more serious applications in today's world. Let's take another look at the results of the survey from the previous chapter.

To tell the truth, these survey results are not of much value except that they are interesting to us. No car manufacturer would pay to know the results, and no advertiser would base an ad campaign on the findings. Why not? We did not interview enough people, and the methods we used in constructing the questionnaire and choosing the people to be interviewed were not scientific. However, for the sake of learning the ideas, we will go ahead as if the results of our survey really did represent the opinion of the general population.

Example:

Next Car Preferences

What is the probability that someone will choose a foreign car as his or her next car?

The graph shows that the two choices are <u>not</u> "equally likely" for the people we surveyed. Assuming that this holds for the entire population,

P(foreign) = 60% or $\frac{3}{5}$ will choose a foreign car

PROBLEM 17   Based on the circle graph above, what is the probability that someone will choose a domestic car for his or her next car?

PROBLEM 18   To see how valid the survey results are in your community, investigate the parking lot at work or school. Note the frequency of foreign as opposed to domestic brands of cars found in the lot. Are your results close to those of the book's survey for next cars?

PROBLEM 19   Imagine that you are thinking of opening an auto dealership in your town. Based on your survey of the parking lot and assuming all other factors are equal, would you open one dealing in foreign cars or domestic brands?

Problems 20–22 are based on the circle chart to the left.

Next Car

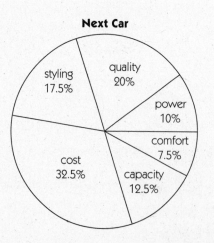

PROBLEM 20
What is the <u>probability</u> that someone would consider the quality of construction in choosing his or her next car?

PROBLEM 21
What are <u>the odds</u> that someone will consider the car's power when deciding on his or her next car?

PROBLEM 22
What is the <u>probability</u> that someone is *not* looking for a car that can carry a lot (capacity)?

PROBLEM 23   According to the graph, no one buys a car because it is the kind that lends status to its owner. Would it be correct to assume that this is a true statement for the population? What error might have led to this incorrect conclusion?

Probability of Independent and Dependent Events

To find the probability of two events happening in succession (one after another), multiply together the probabilities of each.

Example:

When throwing a die, what is the probability of throwing 2 sixes in a row?

Since each throw of the die is **independent** of another, this would be $\frac{1}{6} \times \frac{1}{6} = \frac{1}{36}$.

Example:

What is the probability of drawing 2 aces in a row from a deck of cards?

This is an example of **dependent** events. After drawing 1 ace from the deck of 52, there are only 3 left among the remaining 51 cards.

$P(\text{1st ace}) = \frac{4}{52}$

$P(\text{2nd ace}) = \frac{3}{51}$

$P(\text{2 in a row}) = \frac{4}{52} \times \frac{3}{51}$
$= \frac{12}{2,652} = \frac{1}{221}$

In sports, probabilities are based on past records. These are dependent events.

Example:

Scottie Pippen of the Chicago Bulls pulled down 104 of the team's 412 rebounds during the 1991 NBA playoffs. Based on this record,

- What was the probability of his getting the team's first rebound during the final series?

- What was the probability of his getting the team's first two rebounds?

$P(\text{Pippen rebound}) = \frac{104}{412} \approx \frac{1}{4}$

$P(\text{2 Pippen rebounds in a row}) =$
$\frac{1}{4} \times \frac{1}{4} = \frac{1}{16}$

PROBLEM 24 What is the probability of getting 3 heads in a row when flipping coins?

PROBLEM 25 If a fair coin has been tossed 9 times, and each time it has landed on heads, what is the probability of the tenth toss coming up tails? Why?

PROBLEM 26 Pat has established a free-throw percentage of 60%. What is the probability that she will make both of her next two free throws?

Did You Know?

You have a better chance of getting hit by lightning than of winning the lottery.

- The odds against winning in a lottery game where you pick 6 numbers out of 49 are 14 million to 1.

- The odds against being struck by lightning this year are 701,537 to 1.

You are 20 times more likely to get hit by lightning this year than you are to win the lottery on any one draw.

In 1986, $12.5 billion was spent on state-run lotteries.

Check Your Understanding

You may use your calculator on any problem for which it seems appropriate.

In 1990, the GED Testing Service published findings that profiled the people who take the GED Test. The following information and problems 1–5 are taken from that study.

> In 1989, nearly 54% of the adults who took the tests said that they did so because they wanted to go on for further study.

1. What percent of the adults taking the test were <u>not</u> interested in pursuing further education?

2. Is this finding also valid in your GED class? Survey your fellow class members to determine whether this is accurate for the class population.

> In 1980, adults reported having studied for the GED Test an average of 20.0 hours. In 1989, the average number of hours of study was reported to be 30.5.

3. Since the report does not state differently, we assume that this average is the *mean*. Is it necessarily true that 50% of the adults reporting in 1989 studied fewer than 30.5 hours for the tests?

4. Approximately what is the percent of increase in hours reportedly studied from 1980 to 1989?

5. 24.2% of the adults in 1989 said that they studied over 100 hours, and 16.2% said that they didn't study at all. What percent of the adults in 1989 studied between 1 and 100 hours?

Problems 6–8 refer to the following graphs.

Stone Age People's Diet   **Modern American Diet**

6. What percent of Stone Age people's diet was protein?

7. What percent of the modern American diet is complex carbohydrates?

8. The fat content of the modern diet is approximately how many times the fat content of the Stone Age diet?

GED Practice

9. A survey showed that of 1,000 automobiles that passed by, 300 were gray or silver, 250 were blue, 200 were red, 180 were white, and 70 were other colors. Based on this information, what is the probability that the next car passing by will be red?

   (1) $\frac{3}{10}$

   (2) $\frac{1}{10}$

   (3) $\frac{1}{4}$

   (4) $\frac{2}{5}$

   (5) $\frac{1}{5}$

• LESSON 28 • GED Practice Test

Throughout this book, you have studied the topics that are the most likely to come up on the GED Test. All that remains is for you to practice your skills by trying a full-length, simulated GED math test.

Keep in mind the test-taking tips mentioned in the checkpoints.

Estimate

This is the most important advice for you to follow. Whenever you can estimate the answer, you shouldn't waste valuable test time working out the problem. This will save you time to work on the problems that are not as easy for you.

Ask Yourself Whether the Answer You Have Chosen Makes Sense

Step back and see the problem as a whole, relating the answer to the numbers in the problem.

* Should the answer be larger or smaller than the numbers given?
  For example, the amount of interest a person pays per year is usually much less than the amount borrowed.

* Does the answer choice fit your estimate?
  Check to be sure that you correctly handled any trailing zeros.

* Does the answer seem to be a logical choice for the situation?
  Trees are not usually 400 feet tall, and people do not normally pay $5 for a car.

Use a Variety of Strategies with Unfamiliar Problems

It is nearly impossible to predict all of the kinds of problems that will appear on the test. So expect to see some that are unfamiliar to you. Since the path to the solution may not be immediately obvious, you will need time to study each problem. What should you look for?

* You need to find the relationships between the numbers or values in the problem.
  Can you see a "for each" relation? (multiplication)
  Is the problem asking how many of one thing fit into another? (division)
  Are the values proportional?

* Try to translate the words of the problem into the language of mathematics.
  On your scratch paper, write the parts of the problem that you know—for example, apples = 5 × number of trees.

* Draw pictures of the relationships.
  For example, the following picture would indicate that you need to subtract to find a missing number.

450	?

818

* Substitute simpler numbers than the ones given in the problem so that you are comfortable setting up the relationship.
  For example, $\frac{422}{82}$ could be estimated as $\frac{400}{80}$.

Use the Formulas Page in the Test Booklet

Look for a formula on the formulas page that connects the values given in the problem.

Example:

A train that travels d miles in 45 minutes travels how many <u>miles per hour</u>?

(1) $\frac{d}{45}$

(2) $\frac{3}{4}d$

(3) $\frac{4}{3}d$

(4) $45d$

(5) $\frac{1}{4}d$

The formula that applies here is distance = rate × time ($d = rt$). The problem gives distance as d and time as 45 minutes or $\frac{3}{4}$ of an hour. It asks for miles per hour (the <u>rate</u>).

Put these values into the formula:

$$d = r \times \tfrac{3}{4}$$

Since the problem asks for the rate, reorganize this equation so that the variable r is alone on its side of the equation.

$$r = d \div \tfrac{3}{4}$$

How do you divide by a fraction? Multiply by its reciprocal:

$$r = \tfrac{4}{3}d, \text{ choice } \textbf{(3)}.$$

Use the Answer Choices

When all else fails, use the given answer choices. Substitute them, one by one, into the problem, and see which one is correct.

Example:

What value of x makes the following equation true?

$$5x - 3 = 2x + 6$$

(1) 1

(2) 2

(3) 3

(4) 4

(5) 5

You know that x is merely holding the place for a number. The question asks which number, used in place of x, will make a true statement. Try each one:

$x = 1;\quad 5(1) - 3 \neq 2(1) + 6$

$x = 2;\quad 5(2) - 3 \neq 2(2) + 6$

$x = 3;\quad 5(3) - 3 = 2(3) + 6$ ⠀⠀Choice (3) is correct.

$x = 4;\quad 5(4) - 3 \neq 2(4) + 6$

$x = 5;\quad 5(5) - 3 \neq 2(5) + 6$

Final Test-Taking Hints

- Don't spend too much time on any one problem if you haven't finished the others. Be sure to be careful with your answer sheet if you skip a problem.

- Come back to the difficult problems after you are satisfied that you have done your best on the ones you understand.

- When time is running out, guess the answers to the problems you haven't finished. At least you will have a chance with those problems.

Final Checkpoint

To simulate actual test conditions, you should spend no more than 90 minutes on these questions. You may use the formulas page (page 246) as a reference during the test, but the use of calculators is not allowed.

1. In the 1990 football season, Joe Montana completed 62% of his passes. Which fraction is closest to this percentage?

   (1) $\frac{1}{2}$
   (2) $\frac{3}{4}$
   (3) $\frac{3}{8}$
   (4) $\frac{5}{8}$
   (5) $\frac{7}{8}$

2. What value does the point p represent on this number line?

   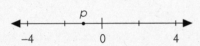

   (1) $-\frac{1}{2}$
   (2) $\frac{1}{2}$
   (3) -1
   (4) 1
   (5) Not enough information is given.

3. A commuter bus has 16 benches that seat 2 passengers and 5 benches that hold 4 passengers. How many seated passengers can this bus carry?

   (1) 27
   (2) 38
   (3) 41
   (4) 52
   (5) 71

4. When Ricardo buys 12 gallons of gasoline priced at $1.09 per gallon, how much change should he receive from a $20 bill?

   (1) $13.08
   (2) $11.01
   (3) $ 8.99
   (4) $ 6.92
   (5) Not enough information is given.

Problem 5 refers to the following diagram.

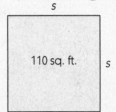

5. The floor area of a square platform is 110 square feet. Which is the best estimate of the length of each side?

   (1) between 11 and 12 feet
   (2) between 10 and 11 feet
   (3) between 9 and 10 feet
   (4) between 8 and 9 feet
   (5) between 7 and 8 feet

_____

6. After fertilizing, a farmer expects a harvest of 100 bushels of corn per acre. If he has planted 3 20-acre fields in corn, what is the total number of bushels of corn that he can expect?

   (1)   300
   (2)   600
   (3)   3,000
   (4)   6,000
   (5) 60,000

Item 7 refers to the following diagram.

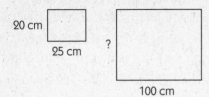

20 cm

25 cm

?

100 cm

7. A rectangular drawing that originally measured 20 cm × 25 cm was enlarged so that its longer side was 100 cm long. What is the length of the shorter side of the enlarged drawing?

(1) 40 cm
(2) 50 cm
(3) 80 cm
(4) 90 cm
(5) 120 cm

_____

8. The following kinds of milk are available.

> Whole milk—3.3% fat
> Low-fat milk—2% fat
> Extra-light milk—1% fat

How many grams of fat are in a glass of low-fat milk?

(1) 1
(2) 2
(3) 3.3
(4) 98
(5) Not enough information is given.

9. Debra received a $500 bonus at the end of the year. She bought a pair of roller skates for $169 and a leather chair for $283. Which expression shows how many dollars of the bonus she has left?

(1) (169 + 283) − 500
(2) 169 + 283 − 500
(3) 500 − 169 + 283
(4) 500 − (169 + 283)
(5) 500 − (169 − 283)

10. A record store counted the number of customers who came into the store during a 3-day holiday weekend. The store counted 310 on Saturday, 150 on Sunday, and 260 on Monday. On the average, how many customers came in each day?

(1) 205
(2) 240
(3) 305
(4) 720
(5) Not enough information is given.

11. After a game, Shawnelle collected 130 aluminum cans. The recycling center pays 5¢ for 2 cans. How much can she earn for these cans?

(1) $32.50
(2) $6.50
(3) $5.20
(4) $3.25
(5) $.65

Items 12 and 13 refer to the following graph.

Pete's Monthly Budget

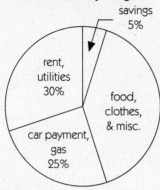

savings 5%

rent, utilities 30%

food, clothes, & misc.

car payment, gas 25%

12. What percent of Pete's money is budgeted for food, clothes, and miscellaneous expenses?

   (1) 25%
   (2) 30%
   (3) 40%
   (4) 60%
   (5) Not enough information is given.

13. If Pete's total monthly income is $2,500, how much money has he budgeted to save?

   (1) $50
   (2) $75
   (3) $125
   (4) $500
   (5) $1,250

14. A survey reported that 3 out of 5 people in the county oppose raising the sales tax. Assuming this is true, how many from a neighborhood of 250 people are likely to oppose raising the tax?

   (1) 50
   (2) 60
   (3) 80
   (4) 100
   (5) 150

15. After writing a check for $85, Steve had a balance of $308 in his account. Which of the following equations could be used to find d, the number of dollars in his account before he wrote the check?

   (1) $d - 85 = 308$
   (2) $308 - 85 = d$
   (3) $d + 85 = 308$
   (4) $308 - d = 85$
   (5) $\frac{308}{85} = d$

16. During a sale where everything is discounted 25%, on which of the following items would you <u>save</u> more than $50?

   a. a student desk marked $129.97

   b. a microwave oven marked $288.96

   c. a color TV marked $209.92

   (1) a only
   (2) b only
   (3) c only
   (4) a and b only
   (5) b and c only

Items 17–19 refer to the following table and graph.

The following high and low temperatures (°F) were recorded one day in January in these northern U.S. cities.

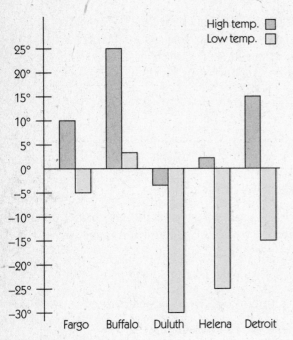

	Fargo	Buffalo	Duluth	Helena	Detroit
High	10°	25°	–3°	2°	15°
Low	–5°	3°	–30°	–25°	–15°

High temp. ▢
Low temp. ▢

17. In which city was the lowest low for the day recorded?

(1) Fargo
(2) Buffalo
(3) Duluth
(4) Helena
(5) Detroit

18. Which city had the greatest <u>range</u> of temperatures that day?

(1) Fargo
(2) Buffalo
(3) Duluth
(4) Helena
(5) Detroit

19. What is the difference between the high temperatures in Duluth and Detroit that day?

(1) 18°
(2) 12°
(3) 10°
(4) 8°
(5) 2°

Item 20 refers to the following diagram.

The diagram shows the position of several men's homes with respect to the ballpark where they meet to play every week.

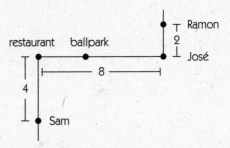

20. If Ramon must travel 7 miles on the route shown to get from his house to the ballpark, how many miles is it from the restaurant to the ballpark?

(1) 2
(2) 3
(3) 5
(4) 8
(5) Not enough information is given.

21. Vivian, a letter carrier, walks 9.7 miles on her postal route each working day. During one month of 31 days, there were 5 Sundays and 2 holidays on which she did not deliver the mail. How many miles did she walk on her route that month?

    (1) 23.28
    (2) 232.8
    (3) 300.7
    (4) 2,328
    (5) Not enough information is given.

22. A mail-order catalog charges $7 for shipping and handling on all orders. Jesse ordered 3 T-shirts at $12 each and 2 pairs of shorts at $24 each. Which of the following expressions equals the number of dollars she must pay for this order?

    (1) 5(12 + 24) + 7
    (2) 12(36)
    (3) (3 + 12)(2 + 24)(7)
    (4) 3(12) + 2(24) − 7
    (5) 3(12) + 2(24) + 7

Items 23 and 24 refer to the following information.

At one of its printing speeds, a computer printer can print $2\frac{1}{4}$ lines per second. The following graph pictures this information.

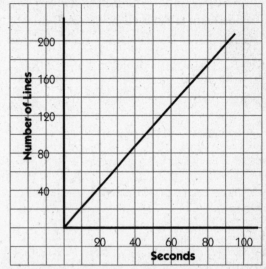

23. At this rate, how many lines can the printer print in one minute?

    (1) 26.7
    (2)   60
    (3) 135
    (4) 200
    (5) 225

24. How many seconds will it take the printer to print a page that contains 50 lines?

    (1) 22
    (2) 46
    (3) 56
    (4) 112
    (5) Not enough information is given.

25. A parking lot near the airport charges $1.00 per hour for parking but not more than $7.00 for any 24-hour period. The business also offers free shuttle service to the airport. What additional information would you need to know to figure the cost of parking for a two-day trip?

(1) the distance from the lot to the airport
(2) the total number of hours you parked in the lot
(3) the number of spaces that are available
(4) whether these are weekend days
(5) what time of day you arrived

26. A cookie recipe that yields 50 cookies calls for $1\frac{3}{4}$ cups flour. To make 100 cookies of the same size, how much flour would be needed?

(1) $\frac{7}{8}$ cup
(2) $\frac{7}{4}$ cup
(3) $2\frac{3}{8}$ cups
(4) $2\frac{3}{4}$ cups
(5) $3\frac{1}{2}$ cups

27. The organizers of a picnic plan to provide 3 cans of soda for each of the 64 people who will be there. Which expression below will determine the number of <u>cases</u> the organizers should buy if each case contains 24 cans of soda?

(1) $\frac{64}{3 \times 24}$
(2) $\frac{3 \times 24}{64}$
(3) $\frac{64 \times 3}{24}$
(4) $\frac{24 \times 8}{64 \times 3}$
(5) $\frac{64 + 3}{24}$

Items 28–30 refer to the following diagram.

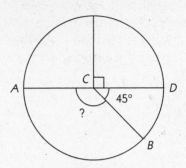

C is the center of this circle.

28. The measure of $\angle ACB$ is

(1) 55°
(2) 90°
(3) 135°
(4) 155°
(5) Not enough information is given.

29. If the distance between point A and point D is 20 cm, the area of the circle would be represented by

(1) $2(20)\pi$
(2) $10^2\pi$
(3) 20π
(4) $20\pi^2$
(5) 10π

30. Which line segment is a diameter of the circle?

(1) AB
(2) AC
(3) AD
(4) BC
(5) BD

31. The specifications for the manufacture of a 3-inch bolt say that the actual length of every bolt must be within 0.1 of an inch of the standard, 3 inches. Which of the following measurements is within the specifications?

    (1) 3.02 in.
    (2) 3.12 in.
    (3) 2.88 in.
    (4) 2.75 in.
    (5) 3.2 in.

32. In preparation for her new job, Dorene bought 3 skirts and 5 tops, each of which coordinated with all of the skirts. How many different combinations of skirt and top are possible with her new purchases?

    (1) 2
    (2) 8
    (3) 15
    (4) 30
    (5) Not enough information is given.

33. One plan to curb the use of water is to limit each household to 300 gallons per day. Under this plan, how many gallons would a 5-member household be allowed during a 30-day month?

    (1) 45,000
    (2) 9,000
    (3) 1,800
    (4) 900
    (5) 10

34. An observer who watched a fast-food counter for 30 minutes during a lunch period reported that the restaurant served an average of 2.7 people per minute. What was the total number of people served during the observed time?

    (1) 9
    (2) 81
    (3) 90
    (4) 810
    (5) Not enough information is given.

Problems 35 and 36 refer to the following diagram:

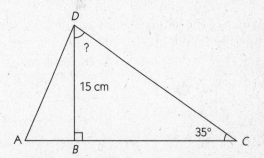

35. If $\angle BCD = 35°$, which expression shows the measure of $\angle BDC$?

    (1) 360° − 35°
    (2) 180° − 35°
    (3) 180° + 35°
    (4) 180° − (90° + 35°)
    (5) 180° − (90° − 35°)

36. If the length of the line from point A to point C is 20 cm, what is the area of $\triangle ACD$?

    (1) 600 cm²
    (2) 300 cm²
    (3) 150 cm²
    (4) 75 cm²
    (5) Not enough information is given.

Item 37 refers to the following diagram.

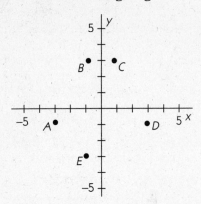

37. Which of the lettered points on the graph above has coordinates of (–3, –1) ?

   (1) *A*
   (2) *B*
   (3) *C*
   (4) *D*
   (5) *E*

38. It took Tom 15 minutes to pedal his bike up a 2-mile uphill stretch of the highway. What was his rate of speed on this portion of the trip?

   (1) 30 mph
   (2) 8 mph
   (3) 7.5 mph
   (4) 4 mph
   (5) Not enough information is given.

39. Which expression below shows the number of postage stamps that you can buy with $5.00 if each stamp costs *x* ¢?

   (1) $\frac{5}{x}$
   (2) 5*x*
   (3) $\frac{500}{x}$
   (4) $\frac{x}{500}$
   (5) 500*x*

Item 40 refers to the following diagram.

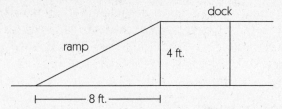

40. A ramp leads to a loading dock that is 4 ft. above the ground. The ramp begins 8 ft. from the end of the dock. What is the slope ($\frac{\text{rise}}{\text{run}}$) of the ramp?

   (1) 8
   (2) 4
   (3) 2
   (4) $\frac{1}{2}$
   (5) $\frac{1}{4}$

41. At the beginning of a business trip, the odometer on Sarah's car read 55,433, and at the end, it read 55,900. She is reimbursed $.25 per mile by her employer. Which expression below shows the amount she would be reimbursed for this trip?

   (1) $\frac{55,900 - 55,433}{.25}$
   (2) $\frac{55,433 - 55,900}{4}$
   (3) 4(55,900 + 55,433)
   (4) 0.25(55,900 – 55,433)
   (5) 0.25(55,433 – 55,900)

Items 42 and 43 refer to the following information:

As a fund-raising project, the Booster Club members sold raffle tickets for a new car whose selling price was $12,000. They sold a total of 6,000 tickets for $5 apiece. One ticket was chosen at a drawing to determine the winner of the car.

42. The car dealer charged the Booster Club only $9,850 for the car. Disregarding miscellaneous expenses, what was the net amount of funds that the club raised by this project?

    (1) $30,000
    (2) $22,000
    (3) $20,150
    (4) $18,000
    (5) $2,150

43. Theo bought 10 tickets. What is the probability that one of his tickets will be the winning ticket?

    (1) $\frac{1}{10}$
    (2) $\frac{1}{12}$
    (3) $\frac{1}{60}$
    (4) $\frac{1}{100}$
    (5) $\frac{1}{600}$

Items 44 and 45 refer to the following diagram.

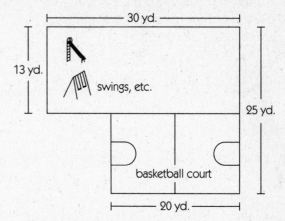

These are the plans for a playground to be built on vacant land.

44. How many yards of fencing will be needed to enclose the basketball court?

    (1) 200
    (2) 64
    (3) 32
    (4) 30
    (5) Not enough information is given.

45. How many square yards of surface are contained in the <u>entire</u> playground?

    (1) 120
    (2) 380
    (3) 500
    (4) 630
    (5) Not enough information is given.

46. A necklace is made of round beads that are $\frac{5}{8}$-inch in diameter. If there is no space between the beads, how many of them are needed to make a 20-inch necklace?

    (1) 12
    (2) 15
    (3) 20
    (4) 32
    (5) 48

47. What is the value of the expression $a^2 - b$ if $a = 5$ and $b = 4$?

    (1) 25
    (2) 21
    (3) 11
    (4) 6
    (5) 3

Item 48 refers to the following diagram.

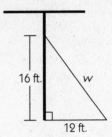

48. To keep a telephone pole erect, a wire is attached to it 16 ft. above the ground. If the wire is anchored 12 ft. from the base of the pole, which equation will determine the length of wire (w) needed?

    (1) $w = \frac{1}{2}(16)(12)$
    (2) $12^2 = 16^2 + w^2$
    (3) $16^2 = 12^2 + w^2$
    (4) $w^2 = 16^2 + 12^2$
    (5) $w = 2(16) + 2(12)$

49. A bulk food warehouse advertises that people can <u>save</u> 56% on their monthly food bills by buying in bulk. The Powers spend about $450 a month on food at the supermarket. If they switch and buy in bulk, how much should they expect to pay each month for food?

    (1) $702
    (2) $648
    (3) $394
    (4) $252
    (5) $198

50. For 3 years, Scott has been paying 12% interest on a loan of $5,000. Which of the expressions below shows how many dollars he has paid in interest over that time?

    (1) $5,000 \times .12 \times 3$
    (2) $\dfrac{5,000 \times 12}{3}$
    (3) $5,000 \times 12 \times 3$
    (4) $\dfrac{5,000 \times 3}{0.12}$
    (5) $\dfrac{5,000 \times 3}{12}$

Item 51 refers to the following diagram.

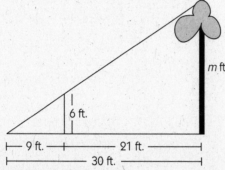

51. Which of the following proportions is the correct one for finding the height of the tree (*m*)?

    (1) $\dfrac{6}{m} = \dfrac{9}{30}$
    (2) $\dfrac{6}{m} = \dfrac{9}{21}$
    (3) $\dfrac{6}{9} = \dfrac{m}{21}$
    (4) $\dfrac{6}{9} = \dfrac{30}{m}$
    (5) $\dfrac{6}{30} = \dfrac{9}{m}$

52. After its price was discounted by 20%, a sewing machine cost $240. What was the original price of the machine?

    (1) $192
    (2) $220
    (3) $288
    (4) $300
    (5) $360

53. A bank was charging its customers an interest rate of 9.85% on loans. If the bank lowered this interest rate by $\frac{1}{4}$%, what would the new rate be?

    (1) 9.35%
    (2) 9.6%
    (3) 9.9%
    (4) 10.1%
    (5) 10.35%

Item 54 refers to the following diagram.

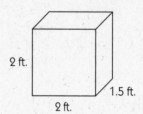

54. Which expression shows how many <u>cubic feet</u> of material can be packed in a shipping carton that is 2 ft. long, 1.5 ft. wide, and 2 ft. high?

    (1) $(2 + 1.5)\,2$
    (2) $2 + 1.5 + 2$
    (3) $24 \times 18 \times 24$
    (4) $2 \times 1.5 \times 2$
    (5) $2^2 + 1.5^2 + 2^2$

55. A bakery has eggs delivered 5 days a week. On Monday through Thursday, it has a standing order of n dozen eggs, and on Friday, it gets double that amount. Which of the following expressions shows the number of dozens of eggs the bakery gets each week?

(1) $5n$
(2) $5 + n$
(3) $6n$
(4) $6 + n$
(5) $6(12n)$

56. Phil's hourly rate of pay is $12 for the first 40 hours each week and <u>double</u> that rate for any overtime he works. How many hours of overtime did he work in a week when his pay (before deductions) was $576 ?

(1) 4
(2) 8
(3) 12
(4) 48
(5) Not enough information is given.

• Determine Your Readiness to Take the GED Test . . . .

You can use the results from this practice test to determine your readiness to take the actual test.

Step 1: Use the answer key on pages 304–307 to check your answers.

Step 2: Fill out the Practice Test Evaluation Chart on page 245.

- Put an X next to the items you answered correctly.

- Put a check mark (✓) next to the items you answered incorrectly.

Step 3: Determine whether you are ready to take the actual test.

- Add up the total number of X marks. On the Practice Test Scoring Chart, circle the number under the heading **Number Correct** that comes closest to the number of items you answered correctly.

- Look across from that number to the number under **Score**. If your score is 45 or above, you may wish to try the actual test. Of course the higher your score, the more ready you are.

- If your score is lower than 45, read Step 4 below.

Step 4: Decide what material you need to review.

- Look at the check marks (✓) on your evaluation chart. You may see particular lessons that you need to review, or you may see a pattern that corresponds to particular sections of this book. (The table of contents divides this book into four sections.)

Practice Test Evaluation Chart

Item	Lesson	Item	Lesson	Item	Lesson
1 _____	18	20 _____	1	39 _____	9
2 _____	5	21 _____	10	40 _____	24
3 _____	10	22 _____	10	41 _____	10
4 _____	10	23 _____	24, 9	42 _____	10
5 _____	11	24 _____	24, 9	43 _____	27
6 _____	8	25 _____	*	44 _____	8
7 _____	21	26 _____	21	45 _____	10
8 _____	22	27 _____	10	46 _____	17
9 _____	10	28 _____	4	47 _____	11
10 _____	10, 26	29 _____	12	48 _____	11
11 _____	21	30 _____	12	49 _____	22
12 _____	26	31 _____	2	50 _____	23
13 _____	22	32 _____	*	51 _____	21
14 _____	21	33 _____	7	52 _____	23
15 _____	3	34 _____	26	53 _____	*
16 _____	*	35 _____	4	54 _____	8
17 _____	5	36 _____	8	55 _____	7, 10
18 _____	5 or 26	37 _____	5	56 _____	10
19 _____	5	38 _____	9		

* Some of the problems are not discussed in the book, and others are not easy to correlate to specific lessons. The GED Math Test will have items that you have not directly prepared for. That is why you have been building your "number sense" throughout this book.

Practice Test Scoring Chart

Although this test is not designed to be an absolutely accurate prediction of your success on the GED Math Test, it can give you a good idea of whether you are ready to take the actual test. To feel confident to take the GED Math Test, you should have a **score** of **45 or above** (30 or more correct answers).

Number Correct	Score	Number Correct	Score
6	less than 20	30	45
9	25	37	50
11	30	43	55
16	35	46	60
22	40	48 or more	65

Appendix

● Formulas

Description	Formula
AREA (A) of a:	
square	$A = s^2$; where s = side
rectangle	$A = lw$; where l = length, w = width
parallelogram	$A = bh$; where b = base, h = height
triangle	$A = \frac{1}{2}bh$; where b = base, h = height
circle	$A = \pi r^2$; where π = 3.14, r = radius
PERIMETER (P) of a :	
square	$P = 4s$; where s = side
rectangle	$P = 2l + 2w$; where l = length, w = width
triangle	$P = a + b + c$; where a, b, and c are the sides
circumference (C) of a circle	$C = \pi d$; where π = 3.14, d = diameter
VOLUME (V) of a:	
cube	$V = s^3$; where s = side
rectangular container	$V = lwh$; where l = length, w = width, h = height
cylinder	$V = \pi r^2 h$; where π = 3.14, r = radius, h = height
Pythagorean relationship	$c^2 = a^2 + b^2$; where c = hypotenuse, a and b are legs of a right triangle
distance (d) between two points in a plane	$d = \sqrt{(x_2 - x_1)^2 + (y_2 - y_1)^2}$; where (x_1, y_1) and (x_2, y_2) are two points in a plane
slope of a line (m)	$m = \dfrac{y_2 - y_1}{x_2 - x_1}$; where (x_1, y_1) and (x_2, y_2) are two points in a plane
mean	mean $= \dfrac{x_1 + x_2 + \cdots + x_n}{n}$; where the x's are the values for which a mean is desired, and n = number of values in the series.
median	median = the point in an ordered set of numbers at which half of the numbers are above and half of the numbers are below this value
simple interest (i)	$i = prt$; where p = principal, r = rate, t = time
distance (d) as function of rate and time	$d = rt$; where r = rate, t = time
total cost (c)	$c = nr$; where n = number of units, r = cost per unit

Source: GED Testing Service of the American Council on Education, © 1987

• Other Ways to Compute ....

Some Other Ways to Add: Adding Without Carrying

Front-end addition $46 + 38$ $34 + 57$

Start from the left. Think: 40 + 30 is 70   Think: 30 + 50 is 80
                                6 + 8 is 14   4 + 7 is 11
                                70 + 14 is 84   80 + 11 is 91

Balancing with addition $18 + 35$ $49 + 56$

Make it an easier problem: 18 + 35 = 53   49 + 56 = 105

Subtract the same thing that you add. plus 2   minus 2   same   plus 1   minus 1   same

                                  20 + 33 = 53   50 + 55 = 105

Try these without paper and pencil.

1. 23 + 18   4. 25 + 37   7. 57 + 27   10. 44 + 37
2. 34 + 27   5. 78 + 16   8. 27 + 18   11. 51 + 79
3. 69 + 24   6. 33 + 49   9. 35 + 56   12. 65 + 85

Another Way to Subtract: Subtracting Without Borrowing

Balancing with subtraction $83 - 28$

Make it an easier problem:

1. Add to *make the second number an even 10.*   83 - 28 = 55

2. Add the same amount to the first number.   plus 2   plus 2   same

   The difference between the numbers   85 - 30 = 55
   remains the same.

   $73 - 47$ $65 - 39$

The difference 73 – 47 is the same as   What number should you
the difference 76 – 50, which is easy   add to both?
to see as 26.   66 – 40 = 26 The same difference!

Change these to problems you can do in your head.

1. 44 – 18   4. 76 – 39   7. 55 – 38   10. 96 – 58
2. 35 – 16   5. 63 – 15   8. 60 – 24   11. 104 – 69
3. 51 – 33   6. 77 – 29   9. 52 – 26   12. 120 – 47

Another Way to Multiply: The Front-End Method

$$\boxed{46 \times 7}$$

```
 46    (40 + 6)
×  7    Start by multiplying 7 by 40 (the front end of the number).
280 ← 7 × 40
+ 42    Next, multiply 7 by 6.
322    Add the two partial products.
```

Picture this problem as finding the area of two adjoining rectangles.

The same problem can be written as an exercise in using the distributive property.

$7(46) = 7(40 + 6)$ Expand 46 into its place values.

$= 7 \cdot 40 + 7 \cdot 6$ Write in expanded form.

$= 280 + 42$ Multiply first.

$= 322$ Then add.

	40	6
7	280	42

One advantage of using this method is that the first partial product you find is a good estimate of the total answer.

Example:

When you are finding the answer to 762×8, the first partial product ($700 \times 8 = 5,600$) gives you an idea of how big the answer will be. Look at the sketch of the rectangles involved.

	700	60	2
8	5,600	480	←16

The first partial product (5,600) told you the most about the answer. In some situations (including the GED Test), the first front-end product may be all you need.

This method can also be used to multiply one 2-digit number by another. Just as in the traditional method, each digit of one number must be multiplied by each digit of the other. However, when you are using the front-end method, the order in which you multiply doesn't matter.

$$\boxed{64 \times 35}$$

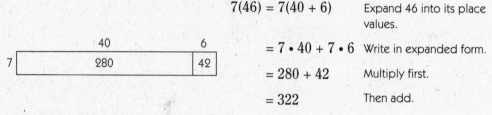

METHOD 1 (traditional)

```
   64
 × 35
  320
 1920
2,240
```

METHOD 2 (front-end)

```
   64    (60 + 4)
 × 35    (30 + 5)
 1800 ← (60 × 30)
  120 ← (4 × 30)
  300 ← (60 × 5)
+  20 ← (4 × 5)
 2,240
```

	60	4
30	1,800	120
5	300	20

Use the front-end method to multiply the following.

1. 37×8
2. 29×6
3. 108×7
4. 431×9
5. $2,008 \times 4$
6. 32×45
7. 72×91
8. 56×33

Another Way to Divide

Do you need to find the exact answer to a division problem, and you don't have a calculator? This method for long division is easy to remember because there are not a lot of rules involved. Just remember that division is repeated subtraction.

Example A:
The problem $\frac{385}{35}$ asks, "How many times can you subtract 35 from 385?"

First, estimate the number *of times you can subtract 35 from 385*. This estimate <u>must be less</u> than the actual answer, but does not necessarily have to be close.

To keep this easy, think about the multiples of 35 that you know mentally. Ask, "Can I subtract 100 35s? (3,500)." No. "Can I subtract 10 35s? (350)." Yes.

```
35)385
   350  | 10   Subtract 10 35s from 385 and keep track of the 10 off to the side.
    35  |      How many 35s can you subtract from the number remaining?
    35  | +1   Again, subtract and then keep track of the number.
     0  | 11   When you cannot subtract any more 35s, add the numbers on
        |         the side for the answer.
```

Example B:
The problem $\frac{2,382}{22}$ asks, "How many times can you subtract 22 from 2,382?"

Estimate the number of times by thinking about multiplying 22 by powers of 10. You can subtract 22×100 (2,200).

```
22)2,382
   2200  | 100    Subtract 100 22s from 2,382. Write the number on the side.
    182  |        Can you subtract 10 × 22 (220) from this? No.
     88  | 4      Estimate how many and multiply.
     94  |        Subtract and keep track of the number.
         |          (Your estimates may differ—see below.)
     88  | +4     You can subtract 4 22s again from the number remaining.
      6  | 108 r 6  You cannot subtract any more 22s. The number left is the
         |          remainder.
```

Example C:
Three solutions are shown. The steps are different, yet the answer is the same. You may use different estimates from these, but your answer should be the same.

```
53)13,455           53)13,455              53)13,455
   5300  | 100        10600  | 200           10600  | 200
   8155  |             2855  |                2855  |
   5300  | 100         1590  | 30            2650  | 50
   2855  |             1265  |                205  |
   1060  | 20          1060  | 20            159  | + 3
   1795  |              205  |                46  | 253 r 46
   1060  | 20          159  | + 3
    735  |              46  | 253 r 46
    530  | 10
    205  |
    159  | + 3
     46  | 253 r 46
```

Find the exact answer by using the method shown above.

a) $\frac{288}{24}$ b) $\frac{1,453}{45}$ c) $\frac{4,680}{72}$ d) $\frac{5,955}{29}$

Questionnaire
Person A

Male/Female __M__   Age: 15–20 _x_ 21–30__ 31–40__ 41+__

What car (make, model) do you <u>dream</u> of owning? __BMW 735__

Price estimate __$50,000__   ☒ foreign ☐ domestic

Why this car? Choose <u>two</u> of the following:
a. styling (looks nice)   b. cost (to buy or to operate)   (c.) power
d. comfort   (e.) quality construction   f. carries a lot

More realistically, what car (make, model) would you <u>probably purchase</u> in the next few years? __used Honda Accord__   Price estimate __$5,000__

☒ foreign ☐ domestic

Why this car? Choose <u>two</u> of the following:
a. styling (looks nice)   (b.) cost (to buy or to operate)   c. power
d. comfort   (e.) quality construction   f. carries a lot

Questionnaire
Person B

Male/Female __F__   Age: 15–20 _x_ 21–30__ 31–40__ 41+__

What car (make, model) do you <u>dream</u> of owning? __Porsche 911__

Price estimate __$85,000__   ☒ foreign ☐ domestic

Why this car? Choose <u>two</u> of the following:
(a.) styling (looks nice)   b. cost (to buy or to operate)   (c.) power
d. comfort   e. quality construction   f. carries a lot

More realistically, what car (make, model) would you <u>probably purchase</u> in the next few years? __used Honda Civic__   Price estimate __$2,500__

☒ foreign ☐ domestic

Why this car? Choose <u>two</u> of the following:
(a.) styling (looks nice)   (b.) cost (to buy or to operate)   c. power
d. comfort   e. quality construction   f. carries a lot

Questionnaire
Person C

Male/Female __F__   Age: 15–20 _x_ 21–30__ 31–40__ 41+__

What car (make, model) do you <u>dream</u> of owning? __Corvette__

Price estimate __$50,000__   ☐ foreign ☒ domestic

Why this car? Choose <u>two</u> of the following:
(a.) styling (looks nice)   b. cost (to buy or to operate)   (c.) power
d. comfort   e. quality construction   f. carries a lot

More realistically, what car (make, model) would you <u>probably purchase</u> in the next few years? __used VW Rabbit__   Price estimate __$5,000__

☒ foreign ☐ domestic

Why this car? Choose <u>two</u> of the following:
(a.) styling (looks nice)   (b.) cost (to buy or to operate)   c. power
d. comfort   e. quality construction   f. carries a lot

Questionnaire
Person D

Male/Female __M__   Age: 15–20__ 21–30 _x_ 31–40__ 41+__

What car (make, model) do you <u>dream</u> of owning? __Ferrari Testarossa__

Price estimate __$200,000__   ☒ foreign ☐ domestic

Why this car? Choose <u>two</u> of the following:
(a.) styling (looks nice)   b. cost (to buy or to operate)   (c.) power
d. comfort   e. quality construction   f. carries a lot

More realistically, what car (make, model) would you <u>probably purchase</u> in the next few years? __used Chevy Camaro__   Price estimate __$4,000__

☐ foreign ☒ domestic

Why this car? Choose <u>two</u> of the following:
a. styling (looks nice)   (b.) cost (to buy or to operate)   (c.) power
d. comfort   e. quality construction   f. carries a lot

Questionnaire
Person E

Male/Female __M__   Age: 15–20__ 21–30 x 31–40__ 41+__

What car (make, model) do you <u>dream</u> of owning? ___Lamborghini___

Price estimate __$250,000___   ☒ foreign ☐ domestic

Why this car? Choose <u>two</u> of the following:
- (a) styling (looks nice)   b. cost (to buy or to operate)   (c) power
- d. comfort   e. quality construction   f. carries a lot

More realistically, what car (make, model) would you <u>probably purchase</u> in the next
few years? ___VW Scirocco___   Price estimate ___$13,000___
☒ foreign ☐ domestic

Why this car? Choose <u>two</u> of the following:
- (a) styling (looks nice)   b. cost (to buy or to operate)   (c) power
- d. comfort   e. quality construction   f. carries a lot

Questionnaire
Person F

Male/Female __F__   Age: 15–20__ 21–30 x 31–40__ 41+__

What car (make, model) do you <u>dream</u> of owning? ___Mercedes 500 SEL___

Price estimate __$60,000___   ☒ foreign ☐ domestic

Why this car? Choose <u>two</u> of the following:
- (a) styling (looks nice)   b. cost (to buy or to operate)   c. power
- d. comfort   (e) quality construction   f. carries a lot

More realistically, what car (make, model) would you <u>probably purchase</u> in the next
few years? ___used Ford Escort___   Price estimate ___$4,000___
☐ foreign ☒ domestic

Why this car? Choose <u>two</u> of the following:
- a. styling (looks nice)   (b) cost (to buy or to operate)   c. power
- d. comfort   (e) quality construction   f. carries a lot

Questionnaire
Person G

Male/Female __M__   Age: 15–20__ 21–30 x 31–40__ 41+__

What car (make, model) do you <u>dream</u> of owning? ___Ford Bronco XLT___

Price estimate __$30,000___   ☐ foreign ☒ domestic

Why this car? Choose <u>two</u> of the following:
- a. styling (looks nice)   b. cost (to buy or to operate)   (c) power
- d. comfort   e. quality construction   (f) carries a lot

More realistically, what car (make, model) would you <u>probably purchase</u> in the next
few years? ___Toyota pick-up truck___   Price estimate ___$10,000___
☒ foreign ☐ domestic

Why this car? Choose <u>two</u> of the following:
- a. styling (looks nice)   (b) cost (to buy or to operate)   c. power
- d. comfort   e. quality construction   (f) carries a lot

Questionnaire
Person H

Male/Female __F__   Age: 15–20__ 21–30 x 31–40__ 41+__

What car (make, model) do you <u>dream</u> of owning? ___BMW 318 convertible___

Price estimate __$30,000___   ☒ foreign ☐ domestic

Why this car? Choose <u>two</u> of the following:
- (a) styling (looks nice)   b. cost (to buy or to operate)   c. power
- d. comfort   (e) quality construction   f. carries a lot

More realistically, what car (make, model) would you <u>probably purchase</u> in the next
few years? ___Toyota Tercel hatchback___   Price estimate ___$8,000___
☒ foreign ☐ domestic

Why this car? Choose <u>two</u> of the following:
- a. styling (looks nice)   (b) cost (to buy or to operate)   c. power
- d. comfort   e. quality construction   (f) carries a lot

Questionnaire
Person I

Male/Female___F___   Age: 15–20___ 21–30___ 31–40_x_ 41+___

What car (make, model) do you <u>dream</u> of owning? ___Mercedes___

Price estimate ___$65,000___   ☒ foreign   ☐ domestic

Why this car? Choose <u>two</u> of the following:
a. styling (looks nice)   b. cost (to buy or to operate)   c. power
d. comfort   (e.) quality construction   (f.) carries a lot

More realistically, what car (make, model) would you <u>probably purchase</u> in the next
few years? ___Jeep Cherokee___   Price estimate ___$17,000___
☐ foreign   ☒ domestic

Why this car? Choose <u>two</u> of the following:
a. styling (looks nice)   b. cost (to buy or to operate)   c. power
d. comfort   (e.) quality construction   (f.) carries a lot

Questionnaire
Person J

Male/Female___M___   Age: 15–20___ 21–30___ 31–40_x_ 41+___

What car (make, model) do you <u>dream</u> of owning? ___Porsche 911SC Cabriolet___

Price estimate ___$80,000___   ☒ foreign   ☐ domestic

Why this car? Choose <u>two</u> of the following:
(a.) styling (looks nice)   b. cost (to buy or to operate)   (c.) power
d. comfort   e. quality construction   f. carries a lot

More realistically, what car (make, model) would you <u>probably purchase</u> in the next
few years? ___Nissan 300ZX___   Price estimate ___$30,000___
☒ foreign   ☐ domestic

Why this car? Choose <u>two</u> of the following:
(a.) styling (looks nice)   b. cost (to buy or to operate)   (c.) power
d. comfort   e. quality construction   f. carries a lot

Questionnaire
Person K

Male/Female___M___   Age: 15–20___ 21–30___ 31–40_x_ 41+___

What car (make, model) do you <u>dream</u> of owning? ___Cadillac Seville___

Price estimate ___$30,000___   ☐ foreign   ☒ domestic

Why this car? Choose <u>two</u> of the following:
(a.) styling (looks nice)   b. cost (to buy or to operate)   c. power
(d.) comfort   e. quality construction   f. carries a lot

More realistically, what car (make, model) would you <u>probably purchase</u> in the next
few years? ___Ford Taurus___   Price estimate ___$18,000___
☐ foreign   ☒ domestic

Why this car? Choose <u>two</u> of the following:
a. styling (looks nice)   (b.) cost (to buy or to operate)   c. power
(d.) comfort   e. quality construction   f. carries a lot

Questionnaire
Person L

Male/Female___F___   Age: 15–20___ 21–30___ 31–40_x_ 41+___

What car (make, model) do you <u>dream</u> of owning? ___Mercedes SEl___

Price estimate ___$60,000___   ☒ foreign   ☐ domestic

Why this car? Choose <u>two</u> of the following:
(a.) styling (looks nice)   b. cost (to buy or to operate)   c. power
d. comfort   (e.) quality construction   f. carries a lot

More realistically, what car (make, model) would you <u>probably purchase</u> in the next
few years? ___Volvo 740 Wagon___   Price estimate ___$25,000___
☒ foreign   ☐ domestic

Why this car? Choose <u>two</u> of the following:
a. styling (looks nice)   b. cost (to buy or to operate)   c. power
d. comfort   (e.) quality construction   (f.) carries a lot

Questionnaire
Person M

Male/Female___F___   Age: 15–20___ 21–30___ 31–40_X_ 41+___

What car (make, model) do you <u>dream</u> of owning? ___BMW 850___

Price estimate ___$90,000___   ☒ foreign   ☐ domestic

Why this car? Choose <u>two</u> of the following:
- (a) styling (looks nice)   b. cost (to buy or to operate)   c. power
- d. comfort   (e) quality construction   f. carries a lot

More realistically, what car (make, model) would you <u>probably purchase</u> in the next few years? ___used Dodge Caravan___ Price estimate ___$7,000___

☐ foreign   ☒ domestic

Why this car? Choose <u>two</u> of the following:
- a. styling (looks nice)   (b) cost (to buy or to operate)   c. power
- d. comfort   e. quality construction   (f) carries a lot

Questionnaire
Person N

Male/Female___M___   Age: 15–20___ 21–30___ 31–40_X_ 41+___

What car (make, model) do you <u>dream</u> of owning? ___BMW 850___

Price estimate ___$90,000___   ☒ foreign   ☐ domestic

Why this car? Choose <u>two</u> of the following:
- a. styling (looks nice)   b. cost (to buy or to operate)   c. power
- (d) comfort   (e) quality construction   f. carries a lot

More realistically, what car (make, model) would you <u>probably purchase</u> in the next few years? ___used Honda Accord___ Price estimate ___$10,000___

☒ foreign   ☐ domestic

Why this car? Choose <u>two</u> of the following:
- (a) styling (looks nice)   (b) cost (to buy or to operate)   c. power
- d. comfort   e. quality construction   f. carries a lot

Questionnaire
Person O

Male/Female___M___   Age: 15–20___ 21–30___ 31–40___ 41+_X_

What car (make, model) do you <u>dream</u> of owning? ___Cadillac___

Price estimate ___$25,000___   ☐ foreign   ☒ domestic

Why this car? Choose <u>two</u> of the following:
- (a) styling (looks nice)   b. cost (to buy or to operate)   c. power
- (d) comfort   e. quality construction   f. carries a lot

More realistically, what car (make, model) would you <u>probably purchase</u> in the next few years? ___Ford Escort___ Price estimate ___$8,000___

☐ foreign   ☒ domestic

Why this car? Choose <u>two</u> of the following:
- a. styling (looks nice)   (b) cost (to buy or to operate)   c. power
- d. comfort   (e) quality construction   f. carries a lot

Questionnaire
Person P

Male/Female___M___   Age: 15–20___ 21–30___ 31–40___ 41+_X_

What car (make, model) do you <u>dream</u> of owning? ___'58 Porsche Speedster___

Price estimate ___$90,000___   ☒ foreign   ☐ domestic

Why this car? Choose <u>two</u> of the following:
- (a) styling (looks nice)   b. cost (to buy or to operate)   c. power
- d. comfort   (e) quality construction   f. carries a lot

More realistically, what car (make, model) would you <u>probably purchase</u> in the next few years? ___Honda Accord___ Price estimate ___$16,000___

☒ foreign   ☐ domestic

Why this car? Choose <u>two</u> of the following:
- a. styling (looks nice)   (b) cost (to buy or to operate)   c. power
- d. comfort   (e) quality construction   f. carries a lot

Questionnaire
Person Q

Male/Female __F__   Age: 15–20___ 21–30___ 31–40___ 41+_X_
What car (make, model) do you <u>dream</u> of owning? ___new Mercedes___
Price estimate __$50,000__   ☒ foreign ☐ domestic

Why this car? Choose <u>two</u> of the following:
(a.) styling (looks nice)   b. cost (to buy or to operate)   c. power
d. comfort   (e.) quality construction   f. carries a lot

More realistically, what car (make, model) would you <u>probably purchase</u> in the next
few years? ___used Mercedes_____ Price estimate ___$20,000___
☒ foreign ☐ domestic

Why this car? Choose <u>two</u> of the following:
a. styling (looks nice)   b. cost (to buy or to operate)   c. power
(d.) comfort   (e.) quality construction   f. carries a lot

Questionnaire
Person R

Male/Female __F__   Age: 15–20___ 21–30___ 31–40___ 41+_X_
What car (make, model) do you <u>dream</u> of owning? ___restored Mustang convert.___
Price estimate __$20,000__   ☐ foreign ☒ domestic

Why this car? Choose <u>two</u> of the following:
(a.) styling (looks nice)   b. cost (to buy or to operate)   (c.) power
d. comfort   e. quality construction   f. carries a lot

More realistically, what car (make, model) would you <u>probably purchase</u> in the next
few years? ___Ford Taurus_____ Price estimate ___$14,000___
☐ foreign ☒ domestic

Why this car? Choose <u>two</u> of the following:
(a.) styling (looks nice)   b. cost (to buy or to operate)   c. power
(d.) comfort   e. quality construction   f. carries a lot

Questionnaire
Person S

Male/Female __M__   Age: 15–20___ 21–30___ 31–40___ 41+_X_
What car (make, model) do you <u>dream</u> of owning? ___Acura NSX___
Price estimate __$75,000__   ☒ foreign ☐ domestic

Why this car? Choose <u>two</u> of the following:
(a.) styling (looks nice)   b. cost (to buy or to operate)   (c.) power
d. comfort   e. quality construction   f. carries a lot

More realistically, what car (make, model) would you <u>probably purchase</u> in the next
few years? ___Chrysler Le Baron convertible___ Price estimate ___$17,000___
☐ foreign ☒ domestic

Why this car? Choose <u>two</u> of the following:
(a.) styling (looks nice)   (b.) cost (to buy or to operate)   c. power
d. comfort   e. quality construction   f. carries a lot

Questionnaire
Person T

Male/Female __M__   Age: 15–20___ 21–30___ 31–40___ 41+_X_
What car (make, model) do you <u>dream</u> of owning? ___BMW 735___
Price estimate __$50,000__   ☒ foreign ☐ domestic

Why this car? Choose <u>two</u> of the following:
(a.) styling (looks nice)   b. cost (to buy or to operate)   c. power
d. comfort   (e.) quality construction   f. carries a lot

More realistically, what car (make, model) would you <u>probably purchase</u> in the next
few years? ___BMW 735_____ Price estimate ___$50,000___
☒ foreign ☐ domestic

Why this car? Choose <u>two</u> of the following:
a. styling (looks nice)   b. cost (to buy or to operate)   (c.) power
d. comfort   (e.) quality construction   f. carries a lot

Answer Key

......
Lesson 1
"Seeing" Addition and Subtraction

Pages 2–9
Lesson

1. Pictures will vary.

2. Pictures will vary.

3. **a)** $10 + 7$ or $7 + 10$

   b) $130 + 205$ or $205 + 130$

4. **a)** $15 - 4$ **b)** $450 - 250$

5. **a)** $12 - 5$ **d)** $11 - 2$

   b) $10 + 3$ or $3 + 10$ **e)** $4 + 5$ or $5 + 4$

   c) $6 + 4$ or $4 + 6$ **f)** $37 - 19$

6. **a)** $3 + 8$ or $8 + 3$ **g)** $18 - 10$

   b) $n + 8$ or $8 + n$ **h)** $12 - 4$

   c) $9 + 2$ or $2 + 9$ **i)** $t - 4$

   d) $b + 2$ or $2 + b$ **j)** $15 - 7$

   e) $12 - 4$ **k)** $b - 7$

   f) $12 - x$

7. **a)** $5,000$

   b) $150; 1,500; 15,000$

   c) $40; 400; 4,000$

   d) $30; 300; 3,000$

8. **a)** 540 **e)** 120

   b) 40 **f)** $1,010$

   c) 730 **g)** $2,500$

   d) $1,020$ **h)** $8,100$

9. **a)** 134 **c)** $33, 83, 103, 243$

   b) $54, 84, 94$ **d)** $49, 69, 99, 549$

10. **b)** $600 - 300 = 300$

    c) $100 + 600 = 700$

    d) $800 + 1100 = 1900$

    e) $1100 - 900 = 200$

    f) $700 - 700 = 0$

11. **a)** $60 + 30 = 90$

    b) $70 + 20 = 90$

    c) $80 + 40 = 120$

    d) $120 - 40 = 80$

    e) $100 - 60 = 40$

    f) $60 - 30 = 30$

12. **(3)** $1,584$ miles

    Estimate: $671 + 913 \approx$

    $700 + 900 = 1,600$

    Choice **(3)** $1,584$ is closest to the estimate.

Check Your Understanding

1. $5 + 6$ OR $6 + 5$

2. $8 + b$ OR $b + 8$

3. $7 - 3$

4. $14 - 8$

5. $3 + 6$ OR $6 + 3$

6. $x + 6$ OR $6 + x$

7. $18 - 9$

8. $18 - x$

9. $54 - 10$

10. $x - 10$

11. $r + 0.3$ OR $0.3 + r$

12. $l + 15$ OR $15 + l$

13. $h - 8$

14. $b + 75$ or $75 + b$

15. $b - 25$

16. $7 + a$ or $a + 7$

17. $a - 7$

18. $b + 25$ or $25 + b$

19. $p - 25$

20. $1,300$

21. 600

22. $7,500$

23. $5,800$

24. 61

25. 91

26. 101

27. 241

28. 65

29. 85

30. 95

31. 445

32. $37 + 78 \approx 40 + 80 = 120$

33. $188 + 521 \approx 200 + 500 = 700$

34. $79 - 43 \approx 80 - 40 = 40$

35. $98 - 33 \approx 100 - 30 = 70$

36. $188 + 703 \approx 200 + 700 = 900$

37. $1,102 - 444 \approx 1,100 - 400 = 700$

38. $976 - 622 \approx 1,000 - 600 = 400$

39. $5,987 + 3,421 \approx 6,000 + 3,000 = 9,000$

40. **(2)** $520

$$\$815 - \$295 \approx$$
$$\$800 - \$300 = \$500$$

$500 is closest to choice **(2)** $520.

• • • • • •

Lesson 2

Grouping to Add More than Two Numbers

Pages 10–17
Mental Math Exercises

1. 40

2. 60

3. 80

4. 90

5. 70

6. 40

Lesson

1. **a)** $37 + (27 + 3)$
   $37 + 30 = 67$

   b) $(11 + 19) + 24$
   $30 + 24 = 54$

   c) $(6 + 14) + (13 + 7) + 56$
   $(20 + 20) + 56 = 96$

2. **a)** $56 + (99 + 1) =$
   $56 + 100 = 156$

   b) $(56 + 4) + 37 =$
   $60 + 37 = 97$

   c) $(17 + 3) + 24 =$

$20 + 24 = 44$

   d) $15 + (9 + 21) =$
   $15 + 30 = 45$

   e) $(15 + 5) + (26 + 4) + 32 =$
   $20 + 30 + 32 =$
   $50 + 32 = 82$

   f) $(22 + 8) + (3 + 37) + 24 =$
   $30 + 40 + 24 =$
   $70 + 24 = 94$

3. **a)** $(23 + 7) + (9 + 11) + 42 =$
   $30 + 20 + 42 =$
   $50 + 42 = 92$

   b) $(46 + 4) + (21 + 9) + 17 =$
   $50 + 30 + 17 =$
   $80 + 17 = 97$

   c) $(12 + 18) + (4 + 26) + 53 =$
   $30 + 30 + 53 =$
   $60 + 53 = 113$

   d) $(35 + 5) + (17 + 3) + 16 =$
   $40 + 20 + 16 =$
   $60 + 16 = 76$

*4. **a)** $(6 + 4) + (5 + 9) =$
   $10 + 14 = 24$

   b) $(7 + 3) + (5 + 4) =$
   $10 + 9 = 19$

   c) $(8 + 12) + 4 + x =$
   $20 + 4 + x = 24 + x$

   d) $(7 + 3) + 13 + x =$
   $10 + 13 + x = 23 + x$

5. **a)** $(14 + 6) + 13 = 33$

   b) $(14 + 6) + 18 = 38$

6. **Figure A**

   a) $(12 + 13) + (6 + 6) =$
   $25 + 12 = 37$

   b) $(12 + 13) + (8 + 8) =$
   $25 + 16 = 41$

   c) $(12 + 13) + (11 + 11) =$
   $25 + 22 = 47$

*Note: You can use parentheses to group compatible pairs for easy adding.

Figure B

a) $(6 + 6) + (6 + 6) + 6 =$

$12 + 12 + 6 = 30$

b) $(8 + 8) + (8 + 8) + 8 =$

$16 + 16 + 8 = 40$

c) $(11 + 11) + (11 + 11) + 11 =$

$22 + 22 + 11 = 55$

7. a) $x + y + 8$

b) $(4 + 6) + 8 =$

$10 + 8 = 18$

c) $5 + (7 + 8) =$

$5 + 15 = 20$

8.

	Front End	Second Look	Calculator Answer
a)	$\$2 + 4 + 1 = \$7$	$\$2 + 4 + 1 = \$7$	$\$7.83$
b)	$\$7 + 11 + 0 = \$18$	$\$7 + 12 + 1 = \$20$	$\$20.14$
c)	$\$6 + 1 + 1 = \$8$	$\$6 + 2 + 2 = \$10$	$\$10.27$

9. a) about $5   **b) about $10**   **c) about $15**

$\$4.21 + .84$	$\$9.15 + .84$	$\$9.15 + 5.89$
$\$2.65 + 2.12$	$\$4.21 + 5.89$	$\$12.30 + 2.65$
	$\$7.39 + 2.65$	$\$7.68 + 7.39$
	$\$7.68 + 2.12$	$\$11.09 + 4.21$

10.

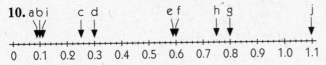

11. a) 0.6

0.6**0** or 0.07? 60 is larger than 7.

b) 0.7

0.677 or 0.**700**? 700 is larger than 677.

c) 0.2

0.04 or 0.**20**? 20 is larger than 4.

d) 3.9

3.**90** or 3.09? 390 is larger than 309.

e) 1.3

1.**30** or 0.13? 130 is larger than 13.

f) 1.005

1.005 or 1.**000**? 1,005 is larger than 1,000.

g) 2

2.0 or 0.50? 200 is larger than 50.

h) 70.8

70.**80** or 7.08? 7,080 is larger than 708.

12. a) 8 is greater than 6.

b) 6 is less than 8.

c) 40 is greater than 10.

d) 10 is less than 40.

e) 1.6 is greater than .67.

f) 7.2 is less than 10.

13. a) $<$ **e)** $=$

b) $=$ **f)** $<$

c) $<$ **g)** $<$

d) $>$ **h)** $>$

14. (4) .06, .2, .26, .6

.06; .20; .26; .60

15. a) Marcus

b) 25 miles

c)

Ben	Marcus
2	12
8	18
9	19
13	23
20	30

16. b, c, e

17. Diagram A

Check Your Understanding

1. $(45 + 5) + (8 + 12) = 50 + 20 = 70$

2. $(21 + 9) + (3 + 17) + 16 = 30 + 20 + 16 = 66$

3. $(36 + 4) + (15 + 15) + 29 = 40 + 30 + 29 = 99$

4. $(19 + 11) + (8 + 32) + 56 = 30 + 40 + 56 = 126$

5. $(7 + 13) + 17 = 20 + 17 = 37$

6. $(4.5 + 4.5) + (3.1 + 6.9) = 9 + 10 = 19$

7. $(27 + 23) + 35 + x = 50 + 35 + x = 85 + x$

8. $(4.8 + 5.2) + 1.7 + x = 10 + 1.7 + x = 11.7 + x$

9. $22 + 18 + x = 40 + x$

10. a) $(22 + 18) + 16 =$

$40 + 16 = 56$

Lesson 2 continued

b) $(22 + 18) + 13 =$

$40 + 13 = 53$

c) $(22 + 18) + 17.7 =$

$40 + 17.7 = 57.7$

11. $x + 3$

12. a) $24 + 3 = 27$ inches

b) $32 + 3 = 35$ inches

c) $18 + 3 = 21$ inches

13. All of the following estimates used rounding. You could also use front-end estimates.

a) Estimate: $\approx \$12.00$

$\$4 + 2 + 6 = \$12$

Exact: $\$12.50$

b) Estimate: $\approx \$43.00$

$\$15 + 23 + 5 = \$43$

Exact: $\$42.99$

c) Estimate: $\approx \$25.00$

$\$12 + 5 + 6 + 2 = \$25$

Exact: $\$24.99$

d) Estimate: $\approx \$24.00$

$\$3 + 13 + 7 + 1 = \$24$

Exact: $\$24.14$

14. a) ≈ 40 km (using rounding)

$8 + 10 + 4 + 12 + 6 = 40$

b) 39.85 km

15. a) $>$ **e)** $>$

b) $<$ **f)** $>$

c) $>$ **g)** $<$

d) $=$ **h)** $>$

16. (5) $\$1.54$

$\$1.47 + .03 + .04 = \$1.54$

• • • • • •

Lesson 3

Equivalent Equations: Addition and Subtraction

Pages 18–25

Mental Math Exercises

1. 59

2. 46

3. 39

4. 67

5. 93

Lesson

1. a) $8 + 7 = 15, 15 - 7 = 8, 15 - 8 = 7$

b) $3 + 9 = 12, 12 - 3 = 9, 12 - 9 = 3$

c) $7 + 6 = 13, 13 - 6 = 7, 13 - 7 = 6$

d) $9 + 7 = 16, 16 - 7 = 9, 16 - 9 = 7$

2. a) $x + 9 = 17, 17 - 9 = x, 17 - x = 9$

b) $x + 7 = 12, 12 - x = 7, 12 - 7 = x$

c) $8 + x = 13, 13 - x = 8, 13 - 8 = x$

d) $6 + x = 14, 14 - x = 6, 14 - 6 = x$

3. a) $20 - 9 = 11, 20 - 11 = 9$

b) $7 - x = 6, 7 - 6 = x$

c) $14 - 8 = x, 14 - x = 8$

d) $12 - x = 8, 12 - 8 = x$

e) $17 - x = 9, 17 - 9 = x$

f) $15 - x = 12, 15 - 12 = x$

g) $100 - x = 45, 100 - 45 = x$

h) $30 - x = 29.9, 30 - 29.9 = x$

i) $100 - x = 81, 100 - 81 = x$

4. a) $13 - 6 = 7, 6 + 7 = 13$

b) $x = 15 - 13, 13 + x = 15$

c) $28 - 20 = x, 20 + x = 28$

d) $17 - 9 = x, 9 + x = 17$

e) $x = 20 - 15, 15 + x = 20$

f) $x - 20 = 15, 20 + 15 = x$

g) $x - 6 = 8, 8 + 6 = x$

h) $x - 32 = 8, 32 + 8 = x$

i) $75 - 40 = x, 40 + x = 75$

5. a) $\$500 + x = \$1,125$ ($x = $ what Andy needs to save)

b) $\$100 - x = \$12$ ($x = $ what LaTonya spent)

For 6 and 7, your equation does not have to be exactly the same as those given, but it must be equivalent.

6. a) $p = $ profit, $\$8 + p = \$49$

b) $m = $ miles of trip, $11,031.8 + m = 11,988.2$

c) $w = $ original weight, $w - 32 = 185$

d) $p = $ profit, $\$850 + p = \$1,099$

7. a) $100 + 80 + x = 230$

b) $567 = 121 + x$

8. a) $x = 6$

b) $x = 60$

c) $x = 5$

d) $x = 75$

e) $x = 8$

f) $n = 20$

g) $x = 11$

h) $p = 70$

9. a) $100 + x = 125$

$125 - 100 = x$

$25 = x$

b) $100 - x = 70$

$100 - 70 = x$

$30 = x$

c) $x + 100 = 225$

$225 - 100 = x$

$125 = x$

d) $x - 100 = 225$

$225 + 100 = x$

$325 = x$

e) $p + 30 = 56$

$56 - 30 = p$

$26 = p$

f) $56 - p = 30$

$56 - 30 = p$

$26 = p$

10. These are solutions for problem 6.

a) $p = \$49 - 8$

$p = \$41$

b) $m = 11{,}988.2 - 11{,}031.8$

$m = 956.4$ miles

c) $w = 185 + 32$

$w = 217$ pounds

d) $p = \$1{,}099 - 850$

$p = \$249$

These are solutions for problem 7.

a) $x = 230 - 180$

$x = 50$ feet

b) $x = 567 - 121$

$x = 446$ grams

11. a) $23 - 8$

$25 - 10 = 15$

b) $35 - 7$

$38 - 10 = 28$

c) $62 - 38$

$64 - 40 = 24$

d) $33 - 15$

$38 - 20 = 18$

e) $51 - 19$

$52 - 20 = 32$

f) $46 - 29$

$47 - 30 = 17$

g) $75 - 48$

$77 - 50 = 27$

h) $143 - 96$

$147 - 100 = 47$

12. (4) $\$109 - \$78 = p$

13. (2) $15 = 5 + 7 + m$

Check Your Understanding

1. a) $14.7 + 8 + x$

b) $14.7 + 8 + x = 30$

OR $22.7 + x = 30$

c) $x = 30 - 22.7$

d) $x = 7.3$ inches

2. a) $106 + w = 125$

b) $w = 125 - 106$

c) $w = 19$ pounds

3. a) $x - 41 = 299$

b) $299 + 41 = x$

c) 340 pounds $= x$

4. a) $\$46{,}500 + p = \$90{,}000$

b) $\$90{,}000 - 46{,}500 = p$

c) $\$43{,}500 = p$

5. a) $x = 15 - 4$

b) $y = 20 - 9$

c) $x = 45 - 15$

d) $n = 35 - 30.5$

6. a) $23 - 15 = a$ (Think: $28 - 20$)

$8 = a$

b) $x = 75 - 54$

$x = 21$

c) $s = 68 - 39$ (Think: $69 - 40$)

$s = 29$

Lesson 3 continued

d) $t = 61 + 49$

   $t = 110$

e) $104 - 85 = p$ (Think: $109 - 90$)

   $19 = p$

7. (4) $855 = 327 + x + 288$

Skill Maintenance
Lessons 1–3
Pages 26–27
Part One

1. a) $6 - 3$ **d)** $m + 1{,}250$

   b) $s + 23$ **e)** $f + 9$

   c) $p - 10$ **f)** $17 + n$

2. a) $(125 + 75) + (130 + 100)$

   b) $(12 + 8) + (10 + 6)$

   c) $26 + 26 + 26$

3. a) $1{,}000 - 650 = x$

   b) $470 - 99 = y$

   c) $430 - 300 = x$

4. a) 675 miles $+ 300$ miles $= 975$ miles

   b) $\$925 - 200 = \$725$

   c) $\$78 + 7 = \$85$

Part Two

1. (2) $.15$

   $.20; .15; .17; 1.10; 1.20$

     ↑
   lightest

2. (4) $\$13$

   Estimate: $\$10 + 2 + 1 = \$13$

3. (4) $2{,}716$

   Estimate: $1{,}215 + 672 + 829 \approx$

          $1{,}200 + 700 + 800 = 2{,}700$

   Choice **(4)** $2{,}716$ is the closest.

4. (4) 505

   Estimate: $1{,}200 - 700 = 500$

   Choice **(4)** 505 is closest to the estimate.

5. (1) 6

   $14 - 8 = 6$

6. (5) $855 = 190 + 475 + x$

---

7. (2) 7

   $12 = x + 5$

   $12 - 5 = x$

   $7 = x$

8. (3) 557

   Estimate: $(150 + 150) + (150 + 100)$

          $300 + 250 = 550$

   Choice **(3)** 557 is the closest to the estimate.

· · · · · ·
Lesson 4
Geometry Topics
Pages 28–35
Mental Math Exercises

1. $n = 140$ **4.** $n = 56$

2. $x = 145$ **5.** $c = 22$

3. $p = 95$

Lesson

1. a) right   **d)** straight

   b) obtuse   **e)** acute

   c) obtuse   **f)** acute

2. acute

3. right

4. a) $20° + c = 90°$ $20° + s = 180°$

      $c = 90° - 20°$ $s = 180° - 20°$

      $c = 70°$ $s = 160°$

   b) $75° + c = 90°$ $75° + s = 180°$

      $c = 90° - 75°$ $s = 180° - 75°$

      $c = 15°$ $s = 105°$

   c) $42° + c = 90°$ $42° + s = 180°$

      $c = 90° - 42°$ $s = 180° - 42°$

      $c = 48°$ $s = 138°$

   d) $115° + s = 180°$

        $s = 180° - 115°$

        $s = 65°$

5. $60°$

6. $180° - m°$

7. $x + 90° + 30° = 180°$

   $x = 180° - 120°$

   $x = 60°$

8. a) $m + 80° + 35° = 180°$

    $m = 180° - 115°$

    $m = 65°$

    b) $m + 110° + 22° = 180°$

    $m = 180° - 132°$

    $m = 48°$

    c) $m + 90° + 37° = 180°$

    $m = 180° - 127°$

    $m = 53°$

9. **(3)** $180° - (90° + x°)$

10. Answers will vary. One possible answer is railroad tracks.

11. Answers will vary. One possible answer is a window frame.

12. a) $\angle 1 = \angle 3$

    $\angle 2 = \angle 4$

    b) $\angle 1 + \angle 2$

    $\angle 2 + \angle 3$

    $\angle 3 + \angle 4$

    $\angle 4 + \angle 1$

13. a) $\angle 2$ and $\angle 6$

    b) $\angle 3$ and $\angle 7$

    c) $\angle 4$ and $\angle 8$

14. a) $140°$

    b) $40°$

    $180° - 140° = 40°$

    c) $40°$

    $180° - 140° = 40°$

    d) $140°$

15. **(2)** $180° - 140°$

Check Your Understanding

1. $\angle MNO, \angle ONM, \angle N$

2. $\angle Q + \angle R = 180°$

    and

    $\angle P + \angle O = 180°$

3. a) $180° - 95° - 51° = \angle F$

    b) $34° = \angle F$

    c) $180° - 95° - x = \angle F$

    d) $180° - 90° - 27° = \angle E$

    $63° = \angle E$

    e) Both angles must be acute angles, and their measures must total $90°$.

4. corner $2 = 180° - 45° = 135°$

5. a) $90° - 47° = x$

    $43° = x$

    b) $180° - 47° = x$

    $133° = x$

6. a) $\angle 3 = 90°$

    b) $\angle 2 = 180° - 130° = 50°$

    c) The sum of the angles in a triangle $= 180°$.

    d) Together $\angle 4 + \angle 5 + \angle 6$ make a straight angle.

7. **(2)** $67°$

    The angles are supplementary angles.

• • • • • •
Lesson 5
The Number Line and the Coordinate Graph
Pages 36–43
Mental Math Exercises

1. less

2. less

3. more

4. more

5. more

6. less

Lesson

1. a) 8

    b) 0

    c) -25

    d) -5.6

2. a) $-9 < -8$

    b) $5 < 6$

    c) $5 > -6$

    d) $-5 > -6$

    e) $2 > -2$

    f) $5.4 < 5.5$

    g) $-5.4 > -5.5$

    h) $-2 < -1.2$

3. a) $6 + 9 = 15$

    b) $15 - 9 = 6$

    c) $11 - 17 = -6$

    d) $(-6) - 9 = -15$

4. a) $17°$

    b) $22°$

    c) $23°$

    d) $-3° - 13° = x$

    $-16° = x$

5. a) $15 - 27 = x$

    $-12 = x$

    b) $47 + (-67) = x$

    $-20 = x$

c) $-9 + 27 = m$

$18 = m$

d) $-32 + 16 = b$

$-16 = b$

e) $(-34) + (-44) = n$

$-78 = n$

f) $(-22) - 33 = k$

$-55 = k$

6. A $(3, 6)$ I $(-3, -4)$

B $(1, 9)$ J $(3, -4)$

C $(9, 1)$ K $(4, -3)$

D $(6, 2)$ L $(0, 5)$

E $(-3, 6)$ M $(4, 0)$

F $(-5, 6)$ N $(-6, 0)$

G $(-6, 5)$ P $(0, -7)$

H $(-1, 3)$

Check Your Understanding

1. a) $7 > 2$ **e)** $0 > -9$

b) $-7 < -2$ **f)** $7 > 6.5$

c) $-3 > -4$ **g)** $-7 < -6.5$

d) $0 < 9$ **h)** $-7 < 6.5$

2. a) $15° - 18° = x$ **d)** $-4° + 31° = x$

$-3° = x$ $x = 27°$

b) $16°$ **e)** $(-2°) - n°$

c) $11°$

3. a) $25 - 34 = k$ **d)** $-39 + 13 = x$

$-9 = k$ $-26 = x$

b) $57 + (-45) = m$ **e)** $-48 + (-48) = n$

$12 = m$ $-96 = n$

c) $-7 + 21 = n$ **f)** $(-72) - 28 = p$

$14 = n$ $-100 = p$

4. A $(3, 4)$ F $(-3, -4)$

B $(0, 5)$ G $(0, -5)$

C $(-3, 4)$ H $(4, -3)$

D $(-4, 3)$ I $(5, 0)$

E $(-5, 0)$

5. (5) $-4 > -14$

6. (3) $-3°$

$10°F$ is $13°$ higher than $-3°F$.

Checkpoint I

Pages 44–49
Mental Math Exercises

1. 1,300   **6.** -100

2. 78   **7.** 96

3. 84   **8.** -35

4. 140   **9.** 540

5. 296   **10.** -20

Check Your Skills

1. (4) 0.9, 0.95, 1.01, 1.11, 1.2

Step 1: Give the numbers the same number of decimal places.

1.01, 0.**90**, 1.**20**, 0.95, 1.11

Step 2: Order from smallest to largest.

0.90, 0.95, 1.01, 1.11, 1.20

2. (2) $233.12 + 1,180.00 - 980.12$
↑ ↑ ↑
beginning   deposits   checks
balance   written

3. (2) 100

$(29 + 11) + (25 + 35) =$

$40 + 60 = 100$

4. (4) $x - 35$
↑ ↑
present   weight
weight   to lose

5. (3) 368 ft.   Picture the situation:

Estimate:

Step 1: $331 + 37 \approx$

$330 + 40 = 370$ ft.

331 ft.
37 ft.

Step 2: 370 is closest to answer choice **(3)** 368 ft.

6. (2) $\$9,782 - \$7,990$
↑ ↑
retail price   purchase price after discounts

7. (3) $82°$

$$180° - 45° - 53° = x$$

↑
straight
angle

Estimate: $45° + 53° \approx 100°$

$$180° - 100° = 80°$$

Answer choice **(3)** $82°$ is the closest.

Or solve the equation:

$$180° - 98° = x$$
$$82° = x$$

8. (3) $74°$

$$\angle 2 + \angle 4 + \angle 5 = 180°$$

$$53° + 53° + x = 180°$$

Estimate: $53° + 53° \approx 100°$

$$180° - 100° = 80°$$

Answer choice **(3)** $74°$ is the closest.

Or solve the equation:

$$106° + x = 180°$$
$$x = 180° - 106° = 74°$$

• • • • • •
Lesson 7
"Seeing" Multiplication and Division

Pages 50–59
Mental Math Exercises

1. 8   4. 28

2. 15   5. 50

3. 20

Lesson

1. Answers will vary.

2. Answers will vary.

3. $6\overline{)54}$ OR $54 \div 6$ OR $\frac{54}{6}$

4. These pairs had different answers:

   c, d, g, and h

5. **Equivalent Forms**   **Numbers and Words**

   a) $\frac{21}{7}$ OR $7\overline{)21}$ 21 divided by 7

   b) $21 - 7$ 21 minus 7

   c) $20 \times x$ OR $20(x)$ 20 times x

        OR $20 \cdot x$

d) $3\overline{)m}$ OR $m \div 3$ m divided by 3

e) $4 + 15$ OR $15 + 4$ 4 plus 15

f) $36 \div 6$ OR $\frac{36}{6}$ 36 divided by 6

6. a) $32 \div 8$ OR $\frac{32}{8}$ OR $8\overline{)32}$

     b) $8 \div 32$ OR $\frac{8}{32}$ OR $32\overline{)8}$

     c) $32 \div b$ OR $\frac{32}{b}$ OR $b\overline{)32}$

     d) $8 \div x$ OR $\frac{8}{x}$ OR $x\overline{)8}$

     e) 6×3 OR $6(3)$

     f) $6 + 3$ OR $3 + 6$

     g) $6 \div 3$ OR $\frac{6}{3}$ OR $3\overline{)6}$

     h) $6 - 3$

7. Expression   **Reason**

     a) 5×10 combining

     b) $20 \div 5$ OR $\frac{20}{5}$ separating

     c) $36 \div 12$ OR $\frac{36}{12}$ separating

     d) $3y$ combining

     e) $2 \cdot 12$ combining

     f) $12 \cdot x$ combining

     g) $\frac{100}{25}$ separating

     h) $\frac{125}{25}$ separating

8. a) 10,000   **i)** 0.0001

     b) 0   **j)** 0

     c) 10,000   **k)** 0

     d) 9,999   **l)** 10,000

     e) undefined   **m)** n

     f) 10,001   **n)** n

     g) 10,000   **o)** 0

     h) 10,000   **p)** 0

9. a) 1,200   **h)** 30,000

     b) 420   **i)** 720,000

     c) 630   **j)** 1,700

     d) 5,400   **k)** 300

     e) 3,200   **l)** 7

     f) 80   **m)** 400,000

     g) 300   **n)** 500

10. Your estimated answers do not have to be exactly the same as those listed.

  a) $3 \times 49 \approx 3 \times 50 = 150$

  b) $8 \times 411 \approx 8 \times 400 = 3,200$

  c) $769 \times 7 \approx 800 \times 7 = 5,600$

  d) $53 \times 78 \approx 50 \times 80 = 4,000$

  e) $92 \times 39 \approx 90 \times 40 = 3,600$

  f) $27 \times 63 \approx 30 \times 60 = 1,800$

  g) $\$6.18 \times 43 \approx \$6 \times 40 = \$240$

  h) $\$24.75 \times 105 \approx \$25 \times 100 = \$2,500$

11. (4) 2,160

  Estimate: $20 \times 100 = 2,000$

  Choice (4) is the only close answer.

12.
Easier	Solution
a) $\frac{200}{4}$	50
b) $\frac{880}{8}$	110
c) $\frac{1,200}{60}$	20
d) $\frac{1,600}{40}$	40

13. a) $\frac{418}{7} \approx \frac{420}{7} = 60$

  b) $\frac{1,823}{3} \approx \frac{1,800}{3} = 600$

  c) $\frac{537}{9} \approx \frac{540}{9} = 60$

  d) $\frac{779}{4} \approx \frac{800}{4} = 200$

  e) $\frac{1,486}{50} \approx \frac{1,500}{50} = 30$

  f) $\frac{1,486}{500} \approx \frac{1,500}{500} = 3$

  g) $\frac{1,221}{40} \approx \frac{1,200}{40} = 30$

  h) $\frac{1,221}{400} \approx \frac{1,200}{400} = 3$

  i) $\frac{12,211}{4,000} \approx \frac{12,000}{4,000} = 3$

14.
Problem	Fact
a) $\frac{230}{3} \approx \frac{240}{3} = 80$	$24 \div 3 = 8$
b) $\frac{621}{8} \approx \frac{640}{8} = 80$	$64 \div 8 = 8$
c) $\frac{1,823}{3} \approx \frac{1,800}{3} = 600$	$18 \div 3 = 6$
d) $\frac{2,234}{3} \approx \frac{2,100}{3} = 700$	$21 \div 3 = 7$
e) $\frac{3,816}{6} \approx \frac{3,600}{6} = 600$	$36 \div 6 = 6$

15. a) $\frac{91}{4} \approx \frac{80}{4}$ is better because 91 is closer to 80.

  b) $\frac{662}{8} \approx \frac{640}{8}$ is better because 662 is closer to 640.

  c) $\frac{1,399}{6} \approx \frac{1,200}{6}$ is better because 1,399 is closer to 1200.

16. (3) $1,254

  Estimate: $\frac{\$6,270}{5} \approx \frac{\$6,000}{5} = \$1,200$

  Choice (3) $1,254 is closest to the estimate.

Check Your Understanding

1. a) $2(12)$ OR 2×12 OR $2 \cdot 12$

  b) $\frac{42}{3}$ OR $42 \div 3$

  c) 7×21 OR $7 \cdot 21$ OR $7(21)$

  d) $\frac{104}{52}$ OR $104 \div 52$

  e) $\frac{72}{6}$ OR $72 \div 6$

  f) $100y$ OR $100 \times y$ OR $100(y)$ OR $100 \cdot y$

  g) $2p$ OR $2 \times p$ OR $2(p)$ OR $2 \cdot p$

2. a) $\frac{2,600,000}{10}$

  b) $260,000

3. a) 500×8

  b) 4,000 sheets

4. a) $450 + 350$

  b) 800 calories

5. a) $\frac{1000}{200}$

  b) $\frac{1000}{200} = 5$ payments

6. $30n$

7.
a) 420	h) 30
b) 4,200	i) 30
c) 42,000	j) 30
d) 420,000	k) 3,000
e) 1,300	l) 1,600
f) 60	m) 3,000
g) 600	n) 30,000

8. Your estimated answers do not have to be exactly the same as those listed.

  a) $7(683) \approx 7(700) = 4,900$

  b) $3(926) \approx 3(900) = 2,700$

  c) $43 \times 68 \approx 40 \times 70 = 2,800$

  d) $92(79) \approx 90(80) = 7,200$

  e) $98 \times 438 \approx 100 \times 400 = 40,000$

  f) $\frac{566}{3} \approx \frac{600}{3} = 200$

  g) $4,188 \div 6 \approx 4,200 \div 6 = 700$

  h) $733 + 319 \approx 700 + 320 = 1,020$

  i) $1,010 - 397 \approx 1,000 - 400 = 600$

9. (3) 1,296 miles

Estimate: 27 miles per gallon × 48 gallons ≈
$$30 \times 50 = 1,500$$

1,500 miles is closest to the answer choice **(3)** 1,296.

10. (4) $\dfrac{2,000}{40}$

$$\dfrac{2,000 \text{ pounds}}{40 \text{ pounds per carton}} = \text{cartons}$$

Lesson 8
Measurement: Multiplying More than Two Numbers
Pages 60–67
Mental Math Exercises

1. 589

2. 589

3. 589

4. 589

5. undefined

6. 1

Lesson

1. Answers will vary.

2. a) miles

   b) feet or yards

   c) square yards

   d) cubic feet

3. a) 44 m^2 or 44 square meters

   b) 480 sq. in.

   c) 27 cm^2 or 27 square centimeters

   d) 40 sq. ft.

4. Yes. You have been multiplying the length (l) by the width (w) to find the area (A).

5. a) 2.9 ft. × 19.5 ft. ≈

     3 ft. × 20 ft. = 60 sq. ft.

   b) 2.9 ft. × 19.5 ft. = 56.55 sq. ft.

   c) In this case, you would probably use the estimate so you wouldn't take the chance of being short of tiles.

6. (4) $A = 2 \times 5$

This expression represents multiplying the length by the width.

7. a) 9 ft. × 7 ft. = 63 sq. ft.

   b) 6 mm × 11 mm = 66 mm^2

   c) 7 m × 4 m = 28 m^2

   d) 5 in. × 8 in. = 40 sq. in.

8. Yes. You have been multiplying the base (b) by the height (h) to get the area (A).

9. (5) $(10 \times 7) - (10 \times 4)$

This represents subtracting to find the difference between the areas.

$$(l \times w) - (b \times h)$$
$$(10 \times 7) - (10 \times 4)$$

10. a) $A = \frac{1}{2}bh$

     $A = \frac{1}{2} \times 25 \times 12$

     $A = (\frac{1}{2} \times 12) \times 25$

     $A = 6 \times 25$

     $A = 150$ sq. in.

   b) $A = \frac{1}{2}bh$

     $A = (\frac{1}{2} \times 20) \times 33$

     $A = 10 \times 33$

     $A = 330$ m^2

   c) $A = \frac{1}{2}bh$

     $A = \frac{1}{2} \times 12 \times n$

     $A = 6n$ sq. ft.

11. (2) 12 sq. ft.

$$A = \frac{1}{2} \times (6 \times 4)$$
$$A = \frac{1}{2} \times 24 = 12$$

12. a) A of rectangle = lw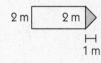

     $A = 5 \times 2 = 10$ m^2

     A of triangle = $\frac{1}{2}bh$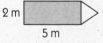

     $A = \frac{1}{2}(2 \times 1)$

     $A = \frac{1}{2}(2) = 1$ m^2

     Total area:

     10 m^2 + 1 m^2 = 11 m^2

   b) A of rectangle = lw

     $A = 11 \times 4 = 44$ sq. in.

     A of triangle = $\frac{1}{2}bh$

     $A = \frac{1}{2}(11 \times 2) = 11$ sq. in.

     Shaded area: 44 sq. in. − 11 sq. in. = 33 sq. in.

   c) A of first rectangle = lw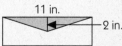

     $A = 12 \times 2 = 24$ sq. in.

A of second rectangle $= lw$

$A = 10 \times 3 = 30$ sq. in.

Add: 24 sq. in. + 30 sq. in. = 54 sq. in.

13. **a)** $11 \times (2 \times 4) = 88$ m^3

 b) $x \times (9 \times 5) = 45x$ cu. ft.

 c) $9 \times (10 \times 3) = 270$ cm^3

 d) $(24 \times 10) \times n = 240n$ cu. in.

14. **(3)** 48 cu. ft.

 $6 \times (4 \times 2)$

 $6 \times 8 = 48$ cu. ft.

15. **a)** $(2 \times 5) \times 57 = 570$

 b) $(5 \times 6) \times 13 = 390$

 c) $(4 \times 25) \times 89 = 8{,}900$

 d) $(2 \times 50) \times 44 = 4{,}400$

 e) $(4 \times 5) \times 41 = 820$

 f) $(2 \times 15) \times 22 = 660$

16. **a)** $6 \times (4 \times 25) = 600$

 b) $8 \times (2 \times 50) = 800$

 c) $(15 \times 2) \times 9 = 270$

 d) $14 \times (2 \times 500) = 14{,}000$

 e) $8 \times (4 \times 25) = 800$

 f) $(9 \times 9) \times (5 \times 2) = 810$

17. **a)** $58 \times 2 = 116$

 double 50 = 100

 double 8 = + 16

 116

 b) $\frac{58}{2} = 29$

 half of 50 = 25

 half of 8 = + 4

 29

 c) $127 \times 2 = 254$

 double 100 = 200

 double 20 = 40

 double 7 = + 14

 254

d) $\frac{284}{2} = 142$

 half of 200 = 100

 half of 80 = 40

 half of 4 = + 2

 142

e) $177 \times 2 = 354$

 double 100 = 200

 double 70 = 140

 double 7 = + 14

 354

f) $\frac{76}{2} = 38$

 half of 60 = 30

 half of 16 = + 8

 38

Check Your Understanding

1. **a)** 1 yd. = 3×12 in. = 36 in.

 b) 1 mi. = 5,280 ft. ÷ 3 = 1,760 yd.

 c) 1 sq. ft. = 12 in. $\times$ 12 in. = 144 sq. in.

 d) 1 sq. yd. = 3 ft. $\times$ 3 ft. = 9 sq. ft.

 e) 1 cu. ft. = 12 in. $\times$ 12 in. $\times$ 12 in. = 1,728 cu. in.

2. **a)** $A = lw$

 $A = 12 \cdot 7 = 84$ cm^2

 b) $A = \frac{1}{2}bh$

 $A = (\frac{1}{2} \times 8) \times 15$

 $A = 4 \times 15 = 60$ sq. in.

 c) $A = \frac{1}{2}bh$

 $A = \frac{1}{2}(11 \times 11)$

 $A = \frac{1}{2}(121)$

 half of 120 = 60.0

 half of 1 = + .5

 60.5 m^2

 d) Total Area = Area of $\boxed{1}$ + Area of $\boxed{2}$

 $= (15 \times 7) + (4 \times 5)$

 $= 105 + 20$

 $A = 125$ m^2

 e) $A = bh$

 $A = 25 \times 28$

 $A = (25 \times 4) \times 7 = 100$ m $\times$ 7 m

 $A = 700$ m^2

f) $A = bh$

$A = 50 \times n$ or $50n$ sq. ft.

g) $A = bh$

$A = 9 \times 16$

$A = 144$ mm^2

h) Total Area = Area of $\square$ + Area of $\triangle$

$= (20 \times 25) + (\frac{1}{2} \times 10 \times 25)$

$= 500 + 125$

$= 625$ sq. ft.

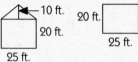

3. $A = lw - lw$

$A = (9 \times 5) - (3 \times 2) = 39$ sq. yd.

4. a) $3 + 3 + 1 = 7$ yd.

b) $A = \frac{1}{2}bh$

$A = \frac{1}{2} \cdot 1 \cdot 2.5 = 1.25$ sq. yd.

5. a) $24 + 10 + 24 + 10 = 68$ cm

b) $24 \times 10 = 240$ cm^2

c) $V = lwh$

$V = (24 \times 10) \times 30$

$V = 240 \times 30$

$V = 7,200$ cm^3

6. (3) $V = 9 \times 5 \times 2$

$V = lwh$

$V = (9 \text{ in.}) \times (5 \text{ in.}) \times (2 \text{ in.})$

Lesson 9
Equivalent Equations: Multiplication and Division
Pages 68–75
Mental Math Exercises

1. 108	**4.** 800	
2. 342	**5.** 700	
3. 360	**6.** 2,900	

Lesson

1. a) $5 \times \$14 = \$70$

b) $10 \times \$14 = \$140$

c) multiply $14 by *the number of discs*.

d) $70 \times \$14 = \$980$

2. a) About $112 (a little above $110)

b) 7 CDs

c) Since the problem asks how many 14s there are in $100, you would divide: $\frac{100}{14}$.

d) divide the *total cost* by 14

3. a) $5 \times 250 = 1,250$ miles

b) $10 \times 250 = 2,500$ miles

c) multiply 250 by the *number of hours*

d) $250n$

4. a) 2,000 miles (move up from 8, then over to 2,000)

b) Since 1,500 falls between 1,400 and 1,600, start between those lines. Move over to the diagonal line, then down to 6 hours.

c) Since the problem asks how many 250s there are in 1,500, you would divide: $\frac{1,500}{250}$.

d) divide *the distance* by 250, $t = \frac{d}{r}$

5. a) $\frac{72}{8} = 9$, $\frac{72}{9} = 8$

b) $\frac{72}{8} = b$, $\frac{72}{b} = 8$

c) $\frac{100}{5} = 20$, $\frac{100}{20} = 5$

d) $\frac{100}{5} = m$, $\frac{100}{m} = 5$

e) $\frac{1,200}{50} = 24$, $\frac{1,200}{24} = 50$

f) $\frac{d}{24} = 50$, $\frac{d}{50} = 24$

6. a) $6 \times 9 = 54$, $\frac{54}{6} = 9$

b) $6 \times n = 54$, $\frac{54}{6} = n$

c) $2 \times 64 = 128$, $\frac{128}{64} = 2$

d) $2t = 128$, $\frac{128}{t} = 2$

e) $5(600) = 3,000$; $\frac{3,000}{600} = 5$

f) $5(600) = p$, $\frac{p}{600} = 5$

7. a) $w = \frac{45}{9}$ **f)** $n = \frac{75}{15}$

b) $k = \frac{96}{8}$ **g)** $m = 125(10)$

c) $p = \frac{39}{13}$ **h)** $b = \frac{105}{21}$

d) $x = \frac{95}{5}$ **i)** $w = 6(9)$

e) $t = \frac{99}{11}$

8. a) time

b) $d = rt$ OR $t = \frac{d}{r}$

$90 = 20t$ $t = \frac{90}{20}$

$t = \frac{90}{20}$ $t = 4.5$ hours

$t = 4.5$ hours

9. Not enough information is given. You could have figured how much time had passed, but not what time it was when he finished.

10. **a)** price per nail

    b) $c = nr$ OR $r = \frac{c}{n}$

        $69 = 25r$ OR $r = \frac{69}{25}$

        $r = \frac{69}{25}$ $r = 2.8¢$

         $r = 2.8¢$ OR $.028$

11. $d = rt$

    $d = 8.5(1.4)$

    $d = 11.9$ km

12.

r	c
$.50	$6.00
.75	9.00
.85	10.20
.99	11.88
1.00	12.00
1.50	18.00
2.00	24.00
3.00	36.00

13. **a)** It increases.

    b) $12

    c) $12

    d) less, more

14. **a)** greater   **d)** greater

    b) less   **e)** greater

    c) less

15. **a)** 97   **c)** 23

    b) 522   **d)** 103

16.

r	n
$.50	24
.75	16
1.00	12
4.00	3
6.00	2
12.00	1
24.00	0.5

17. **a)** decreases

    b) more

    c) less

    d) 1

    e) greater, less, one

18. **a)** more   **c)** less than

    b) less than   **d)** more

19. **a)** 152   **c)** 1

    b) 71   **d)** 1

20. **(1)** $t = \frac{350}{54}$ ← distance
                   ← miles per hour

21. **a)** less than 7 hours

    b) At 50 mph, it would take 7 hours to travel 350 miles. Therefore, traveling a little faster (54 mph) would take Hazel less than 7 hours.

22. **(5)** Not enough information is given. You would need to know how many miles Hazel's car gets to the gallon.

23. **(5)** $31.60

    To find the cost of 40 pounds, multiply:

    $40 \times \$.79$

    $40 \times \$.79 \approx 40 \times \$.80 = \$32.00$

    $32.00 is closest to choice **(5)** $31.60.

24. **(2)** $60 - 30$

    ↑

    distance to Chicago   distance to Gary

25. **(1)** less than an hour

    If you are traveling 65 miles an hour you will travel more than 60 miles if you drive for an hour. Therefore, you will get to Chicago (60 miles away) before you have driven for an hour.

Check Your Understanding

1. $\frac{40}{8} = 5$

   $\frac{40}{5} = 8$

2. **a)** $c = (6)(24.99)$

   b) $c = \$149.94$

3. **a)** $r = \frac{186}{6}$

   b) $r = \$31$

4. **a)** $A = lw$

       $84 = 7w$

   b) $\frac{84}{7} = w$

   c) 12 ft. $= w$

5. **a)** total savings = number of weeks $\times$ weekly savings

       $\$1,000 = w \times \$50$

   b) $\frac{1,000}{50} = w$

       20 weeks $= w$

6. **a)** $c = 1.2(\$2.45)$

   b) The cost will be more because the package weighs more than 1 pound.

7. **a)** $d = rt$

   $d = 50k$

   b) $c = nr$

   $\frac{c}{r} = n$

   $\frac{12}{\$b} = n$

   c) $c = nr$

   $\frac{c}{n} = r$

   $\frac{\$n}{12} = r$

8. $\$19.95 \times 5 = \$99.75$

9. **(2)** 7 hours

   Estimate: $3{,}640 \div 520 \approx 3{,}500 \div 500 = 7$ hours

10. **(4)** $\frac{49.95}{x}$ ◄— total cost
   ◄— number of items

11. **(2)** $(.8)(2)(5)$

   Tracy walks 0.8 of a mile each way, 5 times a week.

· · · · · · ·
Lesson 10
Multi-Step Problems
Pages 76–85
Mental Math Exercises

1. no   **4.** no

2. yes   **5.** yes

3. yes

Lesson

1. **a)** 5, 11, 21, 2

   b) 13, 13, 4, 30

   c) 260, 36, 15, 49

2. **a)** $12 - 6 \div 2$

   $12 - 3 = 9$

   b) $(12 - 6) \div 2$

   $6 \div 2 = 3$

   c) $3 + 12 \times 2$

   $3 + 24 = 27$

   d) $(3 + 12) \times 2$

   $15 \times 2 = 30$

   e) $6 \times 3 + 2$

   $18 + 2 = 20$

   f) $6 \times (3 + 2)$

   $6 \times 5 = 30$

   g) $\frac{12 - 7}{5} = \frac{5}{5} = 1$

   h) $\frac{21 - 7}{7 - 5} = \frac{14}{2} = 7$

   i) $15 \div (6 - 4 + 1)$

   $15 \div 3 = 5$

3. **a)** $8(2) + 8(5)$ **d)** $5(4) + 5(3) + 5(8)$

   b) $34(21) + 34(19)$ **e)** $13x + 13(3)$

   c) $12(10) - 12(5)$ **f)** $8k - 3k$

4. **a)** $6(8 + 2)$ **d)** $11(17 - 7)$

   b) $12(7 + 3)$ **e)** $x(7 + 6)$ OR $13x$

   c) $22(10 - 4)$ **f)** $n(13 - 9)$ OR $4n$

5. **(4)** $4x$

*6. **a)** $\boxed{2}\,\boxed{5}\,\boxed{6}\,\boxed{\div}\,\boxed{3}\,\boxed{2}$

   $\boxed{\times}\,\boxed{4}\,\boxed{=}\ \boxed{\ \ 32.}$

   b) $\boxed{4}\,\boxed{3}\,\boxed{7}\,\boxed{+}\,\boxed{7}\,\boxed{8}\,\boxed{=}$

   $\boxed{515.}\,\boxed{\times}\,\boxed{3}\,\boxed{1}\,\boxed{=}\ \boxed{15965.}$

   c) $\boxed{4}\,\boxed{5}\,\boxed{\times}\,\boxed{3}\,\boxed{2}\,\boxed{=}\ \boxed{1440.}$

   $\boxed{2}\,\boxed{6}\,\boxed{0}\,\boxed{4}\,\boxed{-}\,\boxed{1}\,\boxed{4}\,\boxed{4}\,\boxed{0}\,\boxed{=}\ \boxed{1164.}$

   d) $\boxed{6}\,\boxed{5}\,\boxed{0}\,\boxed{+}\,\boxed{3}\,\boxed{7}\,\boxed{6}\,\boxed{=}$

   $\boxed{1026.}\,\boxed{\div}\,\boxed{3}\,\boxed{=}\ \boxed{\ \ 342.}$

   e) $\boxed{3}\,\boxed{0}\,\boxed{\times}\,\boxed{7}\,\boxed{2}\,\boxed{=}\ \boxed{2160.}$

   $\boxed{2}\,\boxed{5}\,\boxed{\times}\,\boxed{4}\,\boxed{3}\,\boxed{=}$

   $\boxed{\ \ 1075.}\,\boxed{+}\,\boxed{2}\,\boxed{1}\,\boxed{6}\,\boxed{0}\,\boxed{=}\ \boxed{3235.}$

   f) $\boxed{4}\,\boxed{5}\,\boxed{+}\,\boxed{7}\,\boxed{9}\,\boxed{=}\ \boxed{\ \ 124.}$

   $\boxed{1}\,\boxed{3}\,\boxed{6}\,\boxed{4}\,\boxed{\div}\,\boxed{1}\,\boxed{2}\,\boxed{4}\,\boxed{=}\ \boxed{\ \ 11.}$

7. **a)** $2(5.1) + 2(3.9)$

   b) $2(5.1 + 3.9)$

   c) $2(9) = 18$ m

8. **a)** average $= \dfrac{85 + 90 + 70 + 80 + 85}{5}$

   b) average $= 82°$

9. **(1)** $\dfrac{4 + 5 + 6 + 3 + 4}{5}$

10. **a)** $3 + 4 \times 12$

   b) $5 - (3 \times .25)$

   c) $5(2) + 3(4)$

   d) $5(2) + 8(2)$

11. **a)** $6 + 3 \times 7$

   b) $10(15 - 7)$

   c) $6(5 + 8)$

   d) $\dfrac{35 - 25}{2}$

   e) $\dfrac{98.99}{4 + 3}$

*Remember, calculators may differ.

f) 5($.25) + 7($.15)

g) 8($8) + 3($12)

12. a) 50 − 12(3) = r

  14 ft. = r

b) $p = \dfrac{283 + 165}{4} = \dfrac{448}{4} = \$112$

c) 3(2.05 + .70 + .85) = t

  t = 3(3.60) = $10.80

13. (1) $.72

  2(14.95) + 7.50 + 1.88 ≈ 2(15) + 8 + 2 = $40
  (a little less than $40, so the change from $40
  should be less than a dollar)

14. a) Equation: $2,000 − ($17.95 × 50) ≈

  Estimate: $2,000 − ($20 × 50) = $1,000

  Exact: $1,102.50

b) Equation: $\dfrac{\$23{,}245 + \$10{,}755}{12} \approx$

  Estimate: $\dfrac{\$24{,}000 + 12{,}000}{12} = \dfrac{36{,}000}{12} = \$3{,}000$

  Exact: $2,833.33

c) Equation: 55 (3 + 4) ≈

  Estimate: 60(7) = 420 miles

  Exact: 385 miles

d) Equation: (8 × $6.25) + (3.5 × $10) ≈

  Estimate: (8 × $6) + (4 × $10) = $48 + $40 = $88

  Exact: $85

15. (4) $\dfrac{154 \times 22}{400}$

Check Your Understanding

1. a) no (21,11)   **f)** no (50, 98)

b) yes (8 + k)   **g)** yes (38)

c) yes (8)   **h)** yes (150)

d) yes (4m + 2)   **i)** yes (9x)

e) yes (35)

2. a) 18   **d)** 3

b) 31   **e)** 4

c) 16   **f)** 152

3. a) 145   **d)** 32

b) 288   **e)** 139

c) 946

4. a) 5(9) − 3   **c)** 4b + 6

b) 10(30 + 8)   **d)** $\dfrac{12 + m}{15}$

5. P = 2(l + w)

  = 2(7 + 13)

  = 40 in.

  A = lw = 7 • 13 = 91 sq. in.

6. a) x = $10 − 5($.35)

b) Estimate: x = 10 − 2 = 8

c) x = $8.25

7. a) p = 40($7.20) + 5(1.5)($7.20)

b) Estimate: $280 + 10($7) =
      $280 + $70 = $350

c) p = $342

8. a) r = 2($24) + 200($.15)

b) Estimate: $50 + $30 = $80

c) r = $78

9. a) $m = \dfrac{23 + 20 + 27 + 21}{4}$

b) Estimate: pick a number in the middle—23

c) m = 22.75 mpg

10. a) c = 2(26) + 3(43)

b) Estimate: 50 + 120 = 170

c) c = 181 mg

11. (2) 5(3.95 + 0.50)

12. (4) 2(1.5 + 2.5)

Skill Maintenance

Lessons 7–10
Pages 86–87
Part One
1. a) A = bh

  A = 25 × 18

b) P = 2l + 2w

  P = 2(8) + 2(5)

    OR

  P = 2(l + w)

  P = 2(8 + 5)

c) V = lwh

  V = 10 × 5 × 6

2. a) 3×52

$3 \times 52 = (3 \times 50) + (3 \times 2) =$

$150 + 6 = 156$ weeks

b) $\frac{344}{4}$ OR $\$344 \div 4$ OR $4\overline{)344}$

$\frac{344}{4} = \$86$

c) $\$.43$ (2×12) OR $\$.43 \times 2 \times 12$

$\$.43 \times 24 = \$10.32$

d) $50 \times y$ seats

$50y$ seats

3. Your estimates should be *similar* to the ones below. All *reasonable estimates* are acceptable.

a) $\frac{2,073}{500} \approx \frac{2,000}{500} = 4$

b) $8 \times 189 \approx 8 \times 200 = 1,600$

c) $99(12) \approx 100(12) = 1,200$

d) $\frac{187}{90} \approx \frac{180}{90} = 2$

e) $\frac{403}{7} \approx \frac{420}{7} = 60$

4. $A = lw - lw$

$A = (25 \times 12) - (3 \times 3)$

$A = (25 \times 4 \times 3) - 9$

$A = (100 \times 3) - 9$

$A = 300 - 9 = 291$ m^2

5. This problem could be solved several different ways. You could use 6×1 cu. ft., 3×2 cu. ft., or 2×3 cu. ft. because the pattern is *$22.50 for each cubic foot.* (Always check a chart to see if the pattern stays the same.)

Use 3×2 cu. ft. (for easiest multiplication):

3×2 cu. ft. $=$

$3 \times \$45 = (3 \times 40) + (3 \times 5) = 120 + 15 = \$135$

6. a) $20 - 14 \div 2 =$

$20 - \underbrace{7} = 13$

b) $(12 + 20) \div 4 + 102 =$

$32 \div 4 + 102 =$

$8 + 102 = 110$

c) $\frac{74 - 50}{8} = \frac{24}{8} = 3$

7. $\frac{d}{r} = t$

$\frac{45 \text{ miles}}{15 \text{ miles per hour}} = t$

$\frac{45}{15} = 3$ hours

Part Two

1. (3) $4(1,119 + 689)$

2. (3) $\$11.72$

Equation: $\$5.00 + (.07 \times 96)$

Estimate: $\$5.00 + (.07 \times 96) \approx$

$5.00 + (.07 \times 100)$

$\$5.00 + 7.00 = \$12.00$

The estimate $12 is closest to choice **(3)** $11.72.

3. (2) $\frac{720}{h}$

$r = \frac{d}{t}$

$r = \frac{720}{h}$

4. (5) 260

$V = lwh$

$V = 13 \times (10 \times 2)$

$V = 13 \times 20 = 260$ cu. ft.

5. (5) $2(22 + 45)$

$P = 2l + 2w$ OR $P = 2(l + w)$

$P = 2(22) + 2(45)$ OR $P = 2(22 + 45)$

6. (2) 20

$\frac{3,000}{150} = \frac{3000}{150} = \frac{20}{1} = 20$ lb.

7. (2) $\$.69$

$\frac{\$2.76}{4} \approx \frac{2.80}{4} = \$.70$

Estimate: The estimate $.70 is closest to choice **(2)** $.69.

8. (4) 110

$A \boxed{1} - A \boxed{2}$

$A = lw - lw$

$A = (15 \times 10) - (5 \times 8)$

$A = 150 - 40 = 110$ sq. ft.

- - - - - - -

Lesson 11
Powers and Roots
Pages 88–95
Mental Math Exercises

1. 64

2. 6

3. 16

4. 10

5. 144

Lesson

1. **d)** 8×8 "8 squared" OR "8 to the second power"

  e) $2 \cdot 2 \cdot 2 \cdot 2 \cdot 2$ 2^5

  f) 5^2 "5 squared" OR "5 to the second power"

  g) $4 \cdot 4 \cdot 4$ 4^3

  h) $8 \cdot 8 \cdot 8 \cdot 8$ "8 to the 4th power"

  i) $4 \cdot 4 \cdot 4 \cdot 4 \cdot 4 \cdot 4 \cdot 4 \cdot 4$ 4^8

  j) m^2 "m squared" OR "m to the second power"

2. **a)** $A = s^2 = 15^2 = 225 \text{ mm}^2$

  b) $A = 36^2 = 1{,}296 \text{ sq. in.}$

  c) $A = \dfrac{16 \times 18}{144} = \dfrac{288}{144} = 2 \text{ sq. ft.}$

  d) $A = 10^2 = 100 \text{ mm}^2$

  e) $A = 250 \times 300 = 75{,}000 \text{ mm}^2$

3. **a)** 4   **c)** 10

  b) 5   **d)** 12

4. $A = s^2$

  $81 = s^2$

  $s = \sqrt{81} = 9 \text{ ft.}$

5. **a)** $5 + 3^2$ $(5 + 3)^2$ $5 + 3(2)$

      $5 + 9 = 14$ $8^2 = 64$ $5 + 6 = 11$

  b) $2(3)^2$ $(2 \times 3)^2$ $2 \times 3(2)$

      $2(9) = 18$ $6^2 = 36$ $2 \times 6 = 12$

  c) $5(6) + 4^2$ $5^2 - \sqrt{4}$ $\sqrt{16} + \sqrt{4}$

      $30 + 16 = 46$ $25 - 2 = 23$ $4 + 2 = 6$

6. **a)** no

     $4^2 + 5^2 \neq 6^2$

     $16 + 25 \neq 36$

     $41 \neq 36$

  b) yes

     $8^2 + 15^2 = 17^2$

     $64 + 225 = 289$

     $289 = 289$

  c) yes

     $9^2 + 12^2 = 15^2$

     $81 + 144 = 225$

     $225 = 225$

  d) yes

     $30^2 + 40^2 = 50^2$

     $900 + 1{,}600 = 2{,}500$

     $2{,}500 = 2{,}500$

  e) no

     $6^2 + 11^2 \neq 12^2$

     $36 + 121 \neq 144$

     $157 \neq 144$

  f) yes

     $12^2 + 16^2 = 20^2$

     $144 + 256 = 400$

     $400 = 400$

  g) yes

     $5^2 + 12^2 = 13^2$

     $25 + 144 = 169$

     $169 = 169$

  h) yes

     $7^2 + 24^2 = 25^2$

     $49 + 576 = 625$

     $625 = 625$

  i) yes

     $15^2 + 20^2 = 25^2$

     $225 + 400 = 625$

     $625 = 625$

7. **(1)** 5 mi.

     $c^2 = a^2 + b^2$

     $13^2 = 12^2 + b^2$

     $13^2 - 12^2 = b^2$

     $169 - 144 = b^2$

     $25 = b^2$

     $\sqrt{25} = b$

     $5 = b$

8. **(4)** 50 ft.

     $c^2 = a^2 + b^2$

     $c^2 = 30^2 + 40^2$

     $c^2 = 900 + 1{,}600 = 2{,}500$

     $c = \sqrt{2500} = 50 \text{ ft.}$

9. **(2)** $30^2 - 10^2 = b^2$

     This equation represents $c^2 - a^2 = b^2$.

10. **a)** 7 (a little more than 7)

   b) between 8 and 9

   c) between 20 and 25

   d) between 30 and 40; closer to 30

   e) between 40 and 50; a good estimate is 45

   f) between 5 and 6; a good estimate is 5.5

   g) between 11 and 12; closer to 11

   h) between 8 and 9; a good estimate is 8.5

11. $169 = s^2$

     $s = \sqrt{169} = 13 \text{ cm}$

12. $25 + 144 = c^2$

     $c^2 = 169$

     $c = \sqrt{169} = 13 \text{ in.}$

13. $144 + b^2 = 400$

$b^2 = 400 - 144 = 256$

$b = \sqrt{256} = 16$ ft.

Check Your Understanding

1. a) 49   g) 36

   b) 8   h) 144

   c) 5   i) 48

   d) 11   j) 1,700

   e) 7   k) 76

   f) 2   l) 300

2. a) $9^2 = 81$

   b) $19^2 = 361$

   c) $45^2 = 2,025$

3. a) no $3^2 + 5^2 \neq 8^2$

   b) yes $600^2 + 800^2 = 1,000^2$

   c) yes $16^2 + 30^2 = 34^2$

   d) yes $10^2 + 24^2 = 26^2$

4. a) between 3 and 4

   b) between 6 and 7

   c) between 12 and 13

5. $196 = s^2$

   $s = \sqrt{196} = 14$ ft.

6. $a^2 + b^2 = c^2$

   $3^2 + 4^2 = c^2$

   $25 = c^2$

   $c = \sqrt{25} = 5$ blocks

7. (5) between 8 and 9 ft.

   $8^2 + 4^2 = c^2$

   $64 + 16 = c^2$

   $c = \sqrt{80}$ = just less than 9 ft.

8. (2) $600

   15 ft. × 18 ft. =

   (15 ft. ÷ 3) × (18 ft. ÷ 3) =

   5 yd. × 6 yd. = 30 sq. yd.

   30 × $20 = $600

9. (2) $500^2 - 400^2 = a^2$

   $c^2 = a^2 + b^2$

$500^2 = a^2 + 400^2$

$500^2 - 400^2 = a^2$

Lesson 12
Circles
Pages 96–101
Mental Math Exercises

1. 10   4. 7

2. 100   5. 6.5

3. 6

Lesson

1. a) 5 m

   b) $d = 2r$

      $d = 2(1) = 2$ cm

   c) 9 ft.

   d) $d = 2r$

      $d = 2(3) = 6$ in.

2. a) $r = \frac{1}{2}d$

      $r = \frac{1}{2}(2) = 1$ ft.

   b) 2 ft.

   c) $r = \frac{1}{2}d$

      $r = \frac{1}{2}(8) = 4$ m

   d) 7 in.

3. a) Estimate: $C = \pi d$

            $C \approx (3)(12) = 36$ m

      Using 3.14: $(3.14)(12) = 37.68$ m

   b) Estimate: $C = \pi d$

            $C \approx (3)(5) = 15$ in.

      Using 3.14: $C = (3.14)(5) = 15.7$ in.

   c) Estimate: $C = \pi d$ $r = 2d$

            $C \approx (3)(4.5)(2)$

            $C \approx 3(9) = 27$ ft.

      Using 3.14: $C = (3.14)(4.5)(2) = 28.26$ ft.

   d) Estimate: $C \approx (3)(10)(2)$

            $C \approx (30)(2) = 60$ in.

      Using 3.14: $C = (3.14)(10)(2) = 62.8$ in.

4. a) 37.699112   c) 28.274334

   b) 15.707963   d) 62.831853

5. When you find how far the bicycle travels when the wheel goes around once—you are finding the circumference of the wheel.

    a) Using 3: $3(2.25) = 6.75$ ft.

    Using 3.14: $3.14(2.25) = 7.065$ ft.

    Using $\boxed{\pi}$:   7.0685835 ft.

    b) If you had a calculator handy, using the $\boxed{\pi}$ key is easiest. Without a calculator, using 3 is easiest and will give an accurate enough answer.

6. a) $C = \pi d$

    $\frac{C}{\pi} = d$

    $\frac{6.28}{3.14} = 2$ m

    b) $r = \frac{1}{2}d$

    $r = \frac{1}{2}(2) = 1$ m

7. a) $C = \pi d$

    $C = (3.14)(9.5)$

    Estimate: $C \approx (3)(10) = 30$ in.

    b) Using 3.14: $(3.14)(9.5) = 29.83$ in.

    You would need to *round* up to 30 inches.

8. (4) $2 \times 8 \times 3.14$

    radius = 8; diameter = $2 \cdot 8 = 16$

    $C = \pi d$

    $C = 2 \times 8 \times 3.14$

9. (4) 157

    $C = \pi d$

    Estimate: $3 \times 50 = 150$

    This is closest to answer choice **(4)** 157.

    Exact: $C = 3.14 \times 50 = 157$

10. a) $A = \pi r^2$

    $A = (3.14)(10)^2$

    $A = (3.14)(100) = 314$ sq. in.

    b) $A = \pi r^2$

    $A = (3.14)(5)^2$

    $A = (3.14)(25) = 78.5$ cm^2

    c) $A = \pi r^2$

    $A = (3.14)(50)^2$

    $A = (3.14)(2,500) = 7,850$ sq. ft.

    d) $A = \pi r^2$

    $A = (3.14)(25)^2$

    $A = (3.14)(625) = 1,962.5$ m^2

11. (1) 7.85

    $C = \pi d$

    $C = 3.14(2.5)$

    Estimate: $3(2.5) = 7.5$ is closest to **(1)** 7.85.

    Exact: $3.14(2.5) = 7.85$

12. (4) 52.56

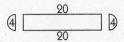

    This diagram shows two figures.

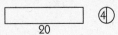

    $P = 2l + \pi d$

    $P = (2 \bullet 20) + (3.14 \bullet 4)$

    $P \approx 40 + 12 = 52$ ft.

    This is the closest to choice **(4)** 52.56.

13. (4) $\dfrac{\pi \times 4 \times 4}{3}$

    $A = \dfrac{\pi r^2}{3}$

    $A = \dfrac{\pi \times 4 \times 4}{3}$

14. (4) $3.14(7.5)(7.5)$

    diameter = 15

    $r = \frac{1}{2}d = 7.5$

    $A = \pi r^2 = (3.14)(7.5)(7.5)$

Check Your Understanding

1. a) Estimate: $C = \pi d$

                    $C \approx (3)(10) = 30$ cm

    Using 3.14: $C = (3.14)(9.8) = 30.77$ cm

    b) Estimate: $C = \pi d$

                    $C \approx (3)(50) = 150$ ft.

    Using 3.14: $C = (3.14)(47) = 147.58$ ft.

    c) Estimate: $C = \pi d$

                    $C \approx (3)(3 \times 2) = 18$ m

    Using 3.14: $C = (3.14)(3.1)(2) = 19.47$ m

    d) Estimate: $C = \pi d$

                    $C \approx (3)(50 \times 2) = 300$ ft.

    Using 3.14: $C = (3.14)(47)(2) = 295.16$ ft.

2. $d = \frac{C}{\pi}$

    $d = \frac{25,000}{\pi} \approx \frac{24,000}{3} \approx 8,000$ miles

3. $A = \pi r^2$

   $A = (3.14)(3)^2 = (3.14)(9)$

   $A = 28.26 \text{ m}^2$

4. Large Pizza:

   $A = \pi r^2 = 3.14 \cdot 8^2 = 200.96 \text{ sq. in.}$

   Medium Pizza:

   $A = \pi r^2 = 3.14 \cdot 6^2 = 113.04 \text{ sq. in.}$

   Difference:

   $200.96 - 113.04 = 87.92 \text{ sq. in.}$

5. (2) 31.4

   $d = 2r = 2 \cdot 5 = 10 \text{ inches}$

   Estimate: $C = \pi d$

   $\qquad\qquad C = (3)(10) = 30 \text{ inches}$

   Exact: $\quad C = (3.14)(10) = 31.4 \text{ inches}$

6. (2) *AD*

   A diameter must pass through the center of the circle.

7. (4) $(20)(20)\pi$

   The formula says Area $= \pi r^2$

   AC is a radius.

   $\pi \cdot (20)(20)$ is the same as $(20)(20)\pi$

8. (2) 100

   The circumference is about 3 times the diameter of any circle. 315 is about 3 times 100.

   $\frac{315}{3.14} \approx \frac{300}{3} = 100$

Lesson 13

More Powers—Powers of 10

Pages 102–111

Mental Math Exercises

1. 350   **4.** 42,000

2. 600   **5.** 691,000

3. 9,250

Lesson

1. a) 8 tens (80)   **d)** 8 ten millions (80,000,000)

   b) 8 tenths (.8)   **e)** 8 hundredths (.08)

   c) 8 thousands (8,000)

2. a) $3(100) + 8(10)$

   b) $5(1,000) + 2(.01)$

   c) $6(10,000) + 4(100)$

   d) $2(10^7) + 9(10^6)$

   e) $1(100) + 4(\frac{1}{1,000})$

3. a) 5×10^1 **f)** 9×10^3

   b) 5×10^{-1} **g)** 6×10^8

   c) 8×10^4 **h)** 6×10^{-3}

   d) 8×10^2 **i)** 3×10^4

   e) 9×10^{-2} **j)** 3×10^7

4. a) 7,302; 0.7302; 730,200

   b) 21.05; 0.002105; 2,105

   c) 450; 0.045; 45,000

   d) 0.8; 0.00008; 80

5. a) 7×10^4 **e)** 8×10^{-3}

   b) 3×10^5 **f)** 3×10^{-5}

   c) 8×10^8 **g)** 9×10^{-6}

   d) 9×10^9 **h)** 2×10^{-7}

6. 5.4×10^6

7. $12,500,000,000

8. $4 \times 10^{-4} \text{ m}$

9. 0.00000001 cm

10. Your answers may vary from these estimates. Check that your answers are reasonable.

   a) $7(400 + 70)$

   $\qquad = 2,800 + 490 = 3,290$

   b) $10 \times 744 = 7,440$

   c) $50 \times 8 = 400$

   d) $1,000 \times 0.055 = 55$

   e) $50 \times 66 = 3,300$

   f) $25 \times 88 = (25 \times 4) \times 22 = 2,200$

   g) $100 \times 64.2 = 6,420$

   h) $3 \times 6 = 18$

   i) $80 \times 20 = 1,600$

   j) $100 \times 537 = 53,700$

   k) $60 \times 40 = 2,400$

   l) $100 \times 13.5 = 1,350$

11. Your answers may vary from these estimates. Check that your answers are reasonable.

   a) $6 \times 8,000 = 48,000$

b) $100 \times 72 = \$7,200$

c) $300 \times 50 = 15,000$

d) $7 \times 70 = 490$

e) $(12 \times 1{,}000) + \frac{1}{2}(12 \times 1{,}000) =$

$12{,}000 + \frac{1}{2}(12{,}000) = 18{,}000$

f) $365 \times \$100 = \$36{,}500$

12. (4) 9,096

Estimate: $\$189.50 \times 48 \approx$

$\$200 \times 50 = \$10{,}000^{-}$

(The answer is a little less than $10,000.)

Choice **(4)** is the closest to less than $10,000.

13. (5) $10,500

Estimate: $\$875 \times 10 = \$8{,}750^{+}$

The only answer more than $8,750 is choice **(5)**.

14. a) $\frac{350}{7} = 50$; exact is 50^{+} (more than 50)

b) $\frac{360}{12} = 30$; exact is 30^{+} (more than 30)

c) $\frac{630}{9} = 70$; exact is 70^{-} (less than 70)

d) $\frac{880}{11} = 80$; exact is 80^{-} (less than 80)

e) $\frac{800}{4} = 200$; exact is 200^{+} (more than 200)

f) $\frac{50{,}000}{25} = 2{,}000$; exact is $2{,}000^{-}$ (less than 2,000)

15. a) $\frac{922}{105} \approx \frac{900}{100} = 9$

b) $\frac{3{,}525}{69} \approx \frac{3{,}500}{70} = 50$

c) $\frac{3.99}{19} \approx \frac{4.00}{20} = 0.20$

d) $\frac{4.50}{75} \approx \frac{4.80}{80} = 0.06$

16. Your estimates may vary. Check that your answers are reasonable.

a) $\frac{1{,}011}{31} \approx \frac{900}{30} = 30$

b) $\frac{976}{52} \approx \frac{1{,}000}{50} = 20$

c) $\frac{1{,}252}{19} \approx \frac{1{,}200}{20} = 60$

d) $\frac{5.64}{3} \approx \frac{6}{3} = 2$

e) $\frac{4.78}{25} \approx \frac{5.00}{25} = 0.20$

f) $\frac{87.35}{4} \approx \frac{88.00}{4} = 22.00$

17. Your estimates may vary. Check that your answers are reasonable.

a) $\frac{62}{11} \approx \frac{60}{10} = 6$

b) $\frac{8.88}{3} \approx \frac{9}{3} = 3$

c) $\frac{177}{16} \approx \frac{160}{16} = 10$

d) $\frac{3{,}165}{78} \approx \frac{3{,}200}{80} = 40$

e) $\frac{8.14}{97} \approx \frac{8.00}{100} = 0.08$

f) $\frac{7{,}633}{26} \approx \frac{7{,}500}{25} = 300$

18. (1) 7

28 pieces ÷ 4 people = ?

$28 \div 4 = 7$ pieces

19. (2) 8×120

    servings   calories

20. (5) 50

total = $(6 \times 5) + (10 \times 2)$

hr.   days   hr.   days

$30 + 20 = 50$ hours

21. (4) $\frac{522}{9}$ ← miles / ← gallons

22. (1) $8.35

$\$20 - 1.189(9.8) = $ (change)

Estimate: $\$20 - (1.20 \times 10) = \$20 - 12 = \$8$

The estimate $8 is closest to choice **(1)** $8.35.

23. (5) $40 \times \$9.60 \times 52$

hours   pay   weeks

Check Your Understanding

1. a) 6 tens (60)

b) 6 tenths

c) 6 thousands

d) 6 ten thousands (60 thousand)

e) 6 hundredths

2. a) $7(10) + 8(1)$

b) $4(1) + 7(\frac{1}{10}) + 3(\frac{1}{100})$

c) $5(1{,}000) + 3(1) + 9(\frac{1}{10})$

d) $6(10{,}000) + 2(1{,}000)$

e) $9(10^{7}) + 3(10^{6})$ ← Use exponents for larger numbers.

3. a) 9×10^{4}

b) 7×10^{-3}

c) 4.5×10^6

d) 2.9×10^{-5}

e) 8.8×10^7

4. $\$5 \times 10^{11}$

5. $\$3,500,000$

6. 5.88×10^{12}

7. 7×10^{100}

8. a) $g = \frac{550}{8}$

b) Estimate: $\frac{560}{8} = 70$ gal.

c) $g = 68.75$ gal.

9. a) $c = 4(\$1.49)$

b) Estimate: $4(\$1.50) = \$6.00$

c) $c = \$5.96$

10. a) $p = \frac{\$2.95}{24}$

b) Estimate: $\frac{\$2.40}{24} = \$.10$

c) $p = \$.12$

11. a) $p = \frac{\$4.39}{6}$

b) Estimate: $\frac{\$4.20}{6} = \$.70$

c) $p = \$.73$

12. a) $g = \frac{100}{16}$

b) Estimate: $\frac{100}{20} = 5$ gallons

c) $g = 6.25$ gallons

13. a) $t = \frac{41}{2}$

b) Estimate: $= \frac{40}{2} = 20$ seconds

c) $t = 20.5$ seconds

14. (4) $\$18,000$

Estimate: *more* than $\$1,500 \times 10 = \$15,000$.

Choice **(4)** $\$18,000$ is more.

15. (3) $\$481$

$\$18.50 \times (\frac{1}{2} \bullet 52)$ weeks =

Estimate: $\$20 \times 26 = \$520$ is closest to **(3)** $\$481$.

Lesson 14
Checkpoint II
Pages 112–117
Check Your Skills

1. (3) 8 and 9

$8^2 = 64$, $9^2 = 81$; 72 is between these.

Estimate: $\sqrt{72}$ is between 8 and 9.

2. (4) 150

$d = rt$

$375 = 2.5\,r$

Estimate: $r = \frac{375}{2.5} \approx$ more than 100 but less than 200

This is closest to **(4)** 150.

3. (4) 6

area of large rectangle – area of cutout

$(55 \times 50) - (40 \times 15)$

$2,750 - 600 = 2,150$ sq. ft.

$\frac{2,150}{400} =$ more than 5 gallons. Choice **(4)** 6 gallons is closest.

4. (2) $\frac{48}{7}$

1,050 is extra information.

5. (1) $\$20$

$V = lwh$

$(5 \times 5 \times 8) \times \$.10 = 200 \times \$.10 = \$20$

6. (3) 3.14×10

$C = \pi d$; 10 is the diameter.

7. (3) $65°$

$180° - 115° = 65°$

The measure of angle COD is extra information.

8. (2) $\$.60$

total spent for coffee $= \$4.95 - 3(\$1.25)$

$c = \dfrac{\$4.95 - 3(\$1.25)}{2} = \dfrac{\$1.20}{2} = \$.60$

9. (4) $15 + 2n$

10. (5) *Not enough information is given.*

To average over 5 days, you need to know temperatures for each day.

11. (5) $(1, -3)$

$(1, -3)$ is located 1 unit to the right of the origin and 3 units down.

12. (4) $\$19,080$

$y = (\$1,950 - \$360) \times 12$

Estimate: $y \approx 1,600 \times 10 = 16,000^{+}$

Choice **(4)** is higher than but close to $\$16,000$.

13. (2) 15

$a^2 + b^2 = c^2$

$$9^2 + 12^2 = c^2$$
$$81 + 144 = c^2$$
$$225 = c^2$$
$$\sqrt{225} = c$$
$$15 = c$$

14. (4) 12

$$h = 3^2 + 3 = 9 + 3 = 12$$

15. (1) $100(6 + 3 + 7)$

16. (3) 12 cm

$$A = \tfrac{1}{2}bh$$
$$30 = \tfrac{1}{2} \times 5 \times h$$
$$\tfrac{30}{5} = \tfrac{1}{2}h$$
$$6 = \tfrac{1}{2}h$$
$$12 = h$$

Lesson 15
Size of Fractions
Pages 118–125
Mental Math Exercises

1. 1
2. 2
3. 3
4. 4
5. 6
6. 12

Lesson
1. **a)** 0.25
   b) 0.2
   c) 0.125
   d) 2
   e) 0.25
   f) 0.2
   g) 2.4
   h) 1.5
   i) 0.8

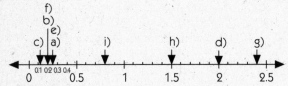

2. less or smaller

3. less than 1: a, e, f, h

   more than 1: b, c, d

   equal to 1: g, i

4. Your answers can match exactly or be close to these answers.

   a) $\frac{11}{12}$ **d)** $\frac{3}{4}$
   b) $\frac{5}{6}$ **e)** $\frac{13}{14}$
   c) $\frac{19}{20}$ **f)** $\frac{9}{10}$

5. **a)** $\frac{4}{3} = \frac{3}{3} + \frac{1}{3} = 1\frac{1}{3}$
   b) $\frac{5}{2} = \frac{4}{2} + \frac{1}{2} = 2\frac{1}{2}$
   c) $\frac{7}{4} = \frac{4}{4} + \frac{3}{4} = 1\frac{3}{4}$
   d) $\frac{10}{7} = \frac{7}{7} + \frac{3}{7} = 1\frac{3}{7}$
   e) $\frac{7}{3} = \frac{6}{3} + \frac{1}{3} = 2\frac{1}{3}$
   f) $\frac{11}{5} = \frac{10}{5} + \frac{1}{5} = 2\frac{1}{5}$
   g) $\frac{17}{6} = \frac{12}{6} + \frac{5}{6} = 2\frac{5}{6}$
   h) $\frac{20}{3} = \frac{18}{3} + \frac{2}{3} = 6\frac{2}{3}$

6. exactly $\frac{1}{2}$: b, c, g

   greater than $\frac{1}{2}$: a, d, e, f, h, i

7. **a)** about $\frac{1}{2}$: $\frac{3}{7}$, $\frac{5}{11}$, $\frac{9}{19}$
   b) about 1: $\frac{8}{9}$, $\frac{11}{12}$, $\frac{14}{15}$
   c) almost 0: $\frac{1}{10}$, $\frac{1}{15}$, $\frac{1}{20}$

8. **(3)** $\frac{9}{16}$ yd. The only answer close to $\frac{1}{2}$ is $\frac{9}{16}$.

9. **a)** $\frac{4}{5}$ (same numerator, smaller denominator)
   b) $\frac{8}{11}$ (higher numerator)
   c) $\frac{5}{6}$ (same numerator, smaller denominator)
   d) $\frac{5}{8}$ ($\frac{5}{8}$ is greater than $\frac{1}{2}$; $\frac{4}{9}$ is less than $\frac{1}{2}$)
   e) $\frac{10}{9}$ ($\frac{10}{9}$ is greater than 1; $\frac{9}{10}$ is less than 1)
   f) $\frac{13}{5}$ (same numerator, smaller denominator)
   g) $\frac{6}{11}$ (higher numerator)
   h) $\frac{5}{9}$ ($\frac{5}{9}$ is greater than $\frac{1}{2}$; $\frac{8}{17}$ is less than $\frac{1}{2}$)

10. **a)** $.30, 0.3
    b) $.70, 0.7
    c) $.90, 0.9
    d) $.40, 0.4
    e) $.60, 0.6
    f) $.80, 0.8
    g) $.50, 0.5
    h) $.50, 0.5

11. **a)** 0.8   **i)** $\frac{1}{10}$
    b) 0.33••• OR $0.\overline{3}$ **j)** $\frac{4}{10} = \frac{2}{5}$
    c) 0.3   **k)** $\frac{2}{3}$
    d) 0.75   **l)** $\frac{6}{10} = \frac{3}{5}$
    e) 0.5   **m)** 0.9
    f) $\frac{2}{10} = \frac{1}{5}$ **n)** 1
    g) $\frac{1}{4}$ **o)** 1.1
    h) $\frac{7}{10}$

12. (1) $\frac{1}{2} + \frac{1}{4}$

$\frac{1}{2} + \frac{1}{4} = .50 + .25 = .75$

13. a) $\frac{2}{8}$ g) $\frac{8}{16}$

     b) $\frac{6}{8}$ h) $\frac{3}{8}$

     c) $\frac{5}{4}$ i) $\frac{10}{16}$

     d) $\frac{12}{8}$ j) $\frac{10}{4}$

     e) $\frac{9}{8}$ k) $\frac{20}{16}$

     f) $\frac{2}{16}$ l) $\frac{8}{4}$

14. a) >   d) <

     b) >   e) <

     c) >   f) <

Check Your Understanding

1. a) $\frac{1}{2}$ ($\frac{5}{9}$ is a little more than $\frac{1}{2}$.)

     b) $\frac{1}{3}$ ($\frac{11}{30} \approx \frac{10}{30}$ or $\frac{1}{3}$)

     c) $\frac{3}{4}$ ($\frac{15}{21} \approx \frac{15}{20}$ or $\frac{3}{4}$)

     d) $\frac{1}{3}$ ($\frac{9}{28} \approx \frac{9}{27}$ or $\frac{1}{3}$)

     e) $\frac{1}{5}$ ($\frac{4}{25} \approx \frac{5}{25}$ or $\frac{1}{5}$)

     f) $\frac{1}{4}$ ($\frac{12}{49} \approx \frac{12}{48}$ or $\frac{1}{4}$)

     g) $\frac{1}{3}$ ($\frac{7}{20} \approx \frac{7}{21}$ or $\frac{1}{3}$)

     h) $\frac{1}{2}$ ($\frac{15}{31} \approx \frac{15}{30}$ or $\frac{1}{2}$)

     i) $\frac{1}{5}$ ($\frac{11}{53} \approx \frac{11}{55}$ or $\frac{1}{5}$)

2. $0.2, \frac{1}{2}, 0.6, \frac{5}{8}$

Compare first as decimals from smaller to larger:

0.200; 0.500; 0.600; 0.625

Now, rename in their orginal form:

$0.2; \frac{1}{2}; 0.6; \frac{5}{8}$

3. $\frac{1}{2}$ yd. is longer because $\frac{3}{8}$ is less than $\frac{1}{2}$ ($\frac{4}{8}$).

4. a) $\frac{1}{4}$ d) $\frac{7}{8}$

     b) $\frac{5}{8}$ e) $\frac{13}{16}$

     c) $\frac{5}{16}$ f) $\frac{9}{16}$

5. a) $\frac{5}{10}$ d) $\frac{10}{100}$

     b) $\frac{4}{16}$ e) $\frac{12}{16}$

     c) $\frac{4}{10}$ f) $\frac{60}{100}$

6. $2\frac{3}{8}$ in.

7. (3) $\frac{1}{4}$ in.

     $.25 = \frac{25}{100} = \frac{1}{4}$

8. (2) $\frac{1}{4}$ and $\frac{1}{2}$

$\frac{1}{4} = \frac{2}{8}$ and $\frac{1}{2} = \frac{4}{8}$

$\frac{3}{8}$ is halfway between $\frac{2}{8}$ and $\frac{4}{8}$.

Lesson 16

Adding and Subtracting Fractions

Pages 126–135

Mental Math Exercises

1. $\frac{1}{3}$ **3.** $\frac{1}{4}$

2. $\frac{5}{7}$ **4.** $\frac{1}{2}$

Lesson

1. a) $\frac{1}{2} = \frac{2}{4}, \frac{4}{8}, \frac{3}{6}, \frac{5}{10}$

     b) $\frac{2}{3} = \frac{4}{6}$

     c) $1 = \frac{2}{2}, \frac{4}{4}, \frac{8}{8}, \frac{3}{3}, \frac{6}{6}, \frac{5}{5}, \frac{10}{10}$

The top number is the same as the bottom number.

2. a) $\frac{1}{4} > \frac{1}{5}$ e) $\frac{1}{6} < \frac{1}{3}$

     b) $\frac{5}{6} < \frac{7}{8}$ f) $1 < \frac{11}{10}$

     c) $\frac{1}{4} > \frac{1}{10}$ g) $\frac{1}{2} < \frac{3}{5}$

     d) $\frac{7}{8} < \frac{9}{10}$ h) $\frac{15}{10} > \frac{10}{8}$

3. a) $\frac{5}{4} = 1\frac{1}{4}$ d) $\frac{19}{10} = 1\frac{9}{10}$

     b) $\frac{5}{3} = 1\frac{2}{3}$ e) $\frac{15}{8} = 1\frac{7}{8}$

     c) $\frac{13}{8} = 1\frac{5}{8}$

4. a) $\frac{2 \times 2}{3 \times 2} = \frac{4}{6}$ d) $\frac{1 \times 8}{4 \times 8} = \frac{8}{32}$

     b) $\frac{5 \times 3}{6 \times 3} = \frac{15}{18}$ e) $\frac{5 \times 2}{8 \times 2} = \frac{10}{16}$

     c) $\frac{3 \times 4}{5 \times 4} = \frac{12}{20}$ f) $\frac{3 \times 2}{16 \times 2} = \frac{6}{32}$

5. a) $\frac{4 \div 2}{6 \div 2} = \frac{2}{3}$ d) $\frac{16 \div 16}{32 \div 16} = \frac{1}{2}$

     b) $\frac{4 \div 4}{12 \div 4} = \frac{1}{3}$ e) $\frac{5 \div 5}{10 \div 5} = \frac{1}{2}$

     c) $\frac{12 \div 4}{16 \div 4} = \frac{3}{4}$ f) $\frac{5 \div 5}{20 \div 5} = \frac{1}{4}$

6. No, because 7 is not a multiple of 4.

7. a) $\frac{1}{2}$ f) $\frac{7}{8}$

     b) $\frac{3}{4}$ g) $\frac{9}{16}$

     c) $\frac{3}{8}$ h) $\frac{5}{16}$

     d) $\frac{1}{2}$ i) $\frac{11}{16}$

     e) $\frac{3}{4}$ j) $\frac{7}{16}$

8. a) $\frac{4}{8} = \frac{1}{2}$ g) $\frac{7}{10}$

   b) $\frac{3}{4}$ h) $\frac{7}{10}$

   c) $\frac{5}{16}$ i) $\frac{13}{20}$

   d) $\frac{7}{16}$ j) $\frac{11}{12}$

   e) $\frac{11}{16}$

   f) $\frac{9}{16}$

9. (4) $\frac{5}{6}$ hour

$$\frac{1}{2} + \frac{1}{3} = \frac{3}{6} + \frac{2}{6} = \frac{5}{6}$$

10. (3) $\frac{5}{8}$

$$\frac{3}{8} + \frac{2}{8} = \frac{5}{8}$$

11. a) $\frac{1}{4}$ f) $\frac{1}{8}$

   b) $\frac{2}{8} = \frac{1}{4}$ g) $\frac{3}{8}$

   c) $\frac{1}{8}$ h) $\frac{1}{16}$

   d) $\frac{1}{8}$ i) $\frac{4}{8} = \frac{1}{2}$

   e) $\frac{1}{4}$ j) $\frac{4}{16} = \frac{1}{4}$

12. a) $\frac{3}{8}$ f) $\frac{2}{10} = \frac{1}{5}$

   b) $\frac{7}{16}$ g) $\frac{1}{20}$

   c) $\frac{9}{16}$ h) $\frac{1}{12}$

   d) $\frac{5}{16}$ i) $\frac{1}{6}$

   e) $\frac{3}{8}$ j) $\frac{1}{15}$

13. a) $\frac{2}{5}$ d) $\frac{1}{12}$

   b) $\frac{5}{8}$ e) $\frac{7}{20}$

   c) $\frac{5}{11}$

14. a) $1\frac{1}{2}$

$$\frac{3}{4} + \frac{3}{4} = \frac{6}{4} = 1\frac{2}{4} = 1\frac{1}{2}$$

   b) $\frac{3}{8}$

$$1\frac{1}{4} - \frac{7}{8} = \frac{5}{4} - \frac{7}{8} = \frac{10}{8} - \frac{7}{8} = \frac{3}{8}$$

   c) $4\frac{3}{4}$

$$5\frac{1}{2} - \frac{3}{4} = 5\frac{2}{4} - \frac{3}{4} =$$
$$4\frac{4}{4} + \frac{2}{4} - \frac{3}{4} = 4\frac{6}{4} - \frac{3}{4} = 4\frac{3}{4}$$

   d) $8\frac{7}{8}$

$$3\frac{1}{8} + 5\frac{3}{4} = (3 + 5) + (\frac{1}{8} + \frac{6}{8}) = 8\frac{7}{8}$$

   e) $2\frac{1}{16}$

$$4\frac{5}{16} - 2\frac{1}{4} = 4\frac{5}{16} - 2\frac{4}{16} = 2\frac{1}{16}$$

   f) $18\frac{9}{20}$

$$8\frac{1}{5} + 10\frac{1}{4} =$$
$$(8 + 10) + (\frac{4}{20} + \frac{5}{20}) = 18\frac{9}{20}$$

g) $11\frac{7}{10}$

$$7\frac{1}{10} + 4\frac{3}{5} =$$
$$(7 + 4) + (\frac{1}{10} + \frac{6}{10}) = 11\frac{7}{10}$$

h) $6\frac{7}{8}$ OR   First, subtract the 2.

$$9 - 2\frac{1}{8}$$ $9 - 2 = 7$
Then subtract $\frac{1}{8}$: $7 - \frac{1}{8} = 6\frac{7}{8}$

$$8\frac{8}{8} - 2\frac{1}{8} = 6\frac{7}{8}$$

i) $12\frac{1}{8}$

$$3\frac{7}{8} + 8\frac{1}{4} =$$
$$(3 + 8) + (\frac{7}{8} + \frac{2}{8}) = 11\frac{9}{8} = 12\frac{1}{8}$$

j) $4\frac{1}{4}$ OR   First, subtract the 5.

$$10 - 5\frac{3}{4} =$$ $10 - 5 = 5$
Then subtract $\frac{3}{4}$: $5 - \frac{3}{4} = 4\frac{1}{4}$

$$9\frac{4}{4} - 5\frac{3}{4} = 4\frac{1}{4}$$

k) $79\frac{1}{6}$

$$66\frac{2}{3} + 12\frac{1}{2} =$$
$$(66 + 12) + (\frac{4}{6} + \frac{3}{6}) = 78\frac{7}{6} = 79\frac{1}{6}$$

l) $20\frac{5}{6}$

$$37\frac{1}{2} - 16\frac{2}{3} =$$
$$37\frac{3}{6} - 16\frac{4}{6} =$$
$$36\frac{6}{6} + \frac{3}{6} - 16\frac{4}{6} =$$
$$36\frac{9}{6} - 16\frac{4}{6} = 20\frac{5}{6}$$

15. a) $1 + 0 = 1$

   b) $1 - 1 = 0$

   c) $\frac{1}{2} + \frac{1}{2} = 1$

   d) $\frac{1}{2} + 0 = \frac{1}{2}$

   e) $1 - \frac{1}{2} = \frac{1}{2}$

   f) $1 + 1 = 2$

   g) $\frac{1}{2} - 0 = \frac{1}{2}$

   h) $1 + \frac{1}{2} = 1\frac{1}{2}$

16. Compare to:

   a) $\frac{1}{3} + \frac{2}{3}$ (since $\frac{1}{4}$ is less than $\frac{1}{3}$): less than 1

   b) $\frac{3}{4} + \frac{1}{4}$ (since $\frac{1}{5}$ is less than $\frac{1}{4}$): less than 1

   c) $\frac{1}{4} + \frac{1}{4}$ (since both are less than $\frac{1}{4}$):

     less than $\frac{1}{2}$

   d) $\frac{5}{8} - \frac{1}{8}$ (since $\frac{1}{10}$ is less than $\frac{1}{8}$):

     more than $\frac{1}{2}$

   e) $1 - \frac{1}{2}$ (since $\frac{13}{15}$ is less than 1):

     less than $\frac{1}{2}$

f) $\frac{3}{16} - \frac{1}{16}$ (since $\frac{1}{10}$ is more than $\frac{1}{16}$):

less than $\frac{1}{4}$

17. Compare to:

a) Estimate: $\frac{8}{17} + \frac{1}{4} \approx$

$\frac{8}{16} + \frac{1}{4} = \frac{1}{2} + \frac{1}{4} = \frac{3}{4}$

Exact: less than $\frac{3}{4}$

because $\frac{8}{17}$ is less than $\frac{1}{2}$

b) Estimate: $\frac{9}{10} + \frac{1}{16} \approx$

$\frac{9}{10} + \frac{1}{10} \approx 1$

Exact: less than 1

because $\frac{1}{16}$ is less than $\frac{1}{10}$

c) Estimate: $\frac{5}{6} + \frac{1}{5} \approx$

$\frac{5}{6} + \frac{1}{6} = 1$

Exact: more than 1

because $\frac{1}{5}$ is larger than $\frac{1}{6}$

d) Estimate: $\frac{1}{2} - \frac{11}{40} \approx$

$\frac{1}{2} - \frac{1}{4} = \frac{1}{4}$

Exact: less than $\frac{1}{4}$

because $\frac{11}{40}$ is more than $\frac{1}{4}$

e) Estimate: $\frac{19}{20} - \frac{2}{5} \approx$

$1 - \frac{2}{5} = \frac{3}{5}$

Exact: less than $\frac{3}{5}$

because $\frac{19}{20}$ is less than 1

18. Your estimates should be close to the answers given.

a) $(3 + 9) + (1 + 1) = 14$

b) $(6 + 3) + (\frac{1}{4} + \frac{1}{4}) = 9\frac{1}{2}$

c) $(10 + 3) + (\frac{1}{2} + 1) = 14\frac{1}{2}$

d) $(40 + 16) + (\frac{1}{2} + 1) = 57\frac{1}{2}$

e) $18\frac{1}{3} - 6 = 12\frac{1}{3}$

f) $20\frac{3}{5} - 9 = 11\frac{3}{5}$

g) $9\frac{11}{12} - 3 = 6\frac{11}{12}$

h) $11\frac{1}{4} - 8 = 3\frac{1}{4}$

19. Your answers should be close to the answers given.

a) $0 + \frac{1}{2} + 0 = \frac{1}{2}$

b) $0 + 4 + 4\frac{1}{2} = 8\frac{1}{2}$

c) $1 + 6\frac{1}{2} + 0 = 7\frac{1}{2}$

d) $3 + 5 + 2 = 10$

e) $8\frac{1}{2} + 7 + 7 = 22\frac{1}{2}$

f) $15 + 3 + 2\frac{1}{2} = 20\frac{1}{2}$

20. An estimate of $1\frac{1}{2}$ cups is probably adequate.

21. An estimate would be appropriate but since these are "nice" numbers, find the exact answer.

$5\frac{5}{8} - 1\frac{2}{8} = 4\frac{3}{8}$ lb.

22. (1) $1\frac{1}{2}$ in.

$5 - (1\frac{3}{4} + 1\frac{3}{4}) \approx$

$5 - (2 + 2) = 1$

The estimate of 1 is closest to choice **(1)** $1\frac{1}{2}$ in.

23. (4) $7\frac{3}{8}$

$2\frac{1}{2} + 1\frac{3}{4} + 3\frac{1}{8} \approx$

$2\frac{1}{2} + 2 + 3 = 7\frac{1}{2}$ mi.

The estimate is closest to choice **(4)** $7\frac{3}{8}$ mi.

Check Your Understanding

1. a) $\frac{7}{8}$

b) $1\frac{1}{4}$

c) $\frac{3}{8}$

d) $\frac{23}{16} = 1\frac{7}{16}$

e) $\frac{23}{16} = 1\frac{7}{16}$

f) $\frac{2}{10} = \frac{1}{5}$

g) $\frac{11}{10} = 1\frac{1}{10}$

h) $\frac{5}{12}$

i) $\frac{14}{15}$

2. a) Estimate: $1\frac{1}{2}$

$\frac{3}{7} + \frac{4}{5} \approx \frac{1}{2} + 1 = 1\frac{1}{2}$

The exact answer would be less than $1\frac{1}{2}$ since both fractions are less than their estimates.

b) Estimate: 2

$\frac{11}{12} + \frac{13}{15} \approx 1 + 1 = 2$

The exact answer would be less than 2 since both fractions are less than their estimates.

c) Estimate: $\frac{1}{2}$

$\frac{1}{5} + \frac{1}{4} \approx \frac{1}{4} + \frac{1}{4} = \frac{1}{2}$

The exact answer would be less than $\frac{1}{2}$ since $\frac{1}{5}$ is less than $\frac{1}{4}$.

d) Estimate: 1

$\frac{15}{16} - \frac{1}{20} \approx 1 - 0 = 1$

The exact answer would be less than 1 since $\frac{15}{16}$ is less than 1.

e) Estimate: $\frac{3}{5}$

$\frac{15}{16} - \frac{2}{5} \approx 1 - \frac{2}{5} = \frac{3}{5}$

The exact answer would be less than $\frac{3}{5}$ since $\frac{15}{16}$ is less than 1.

3. $50 - 4\frac{1}{3} = 45\frac{2}{3}$ ft.

4. $6\frac{1}{3} + 1\frac{1}{2} + 1\frac{1}{2} = 9\frac{1}{3}$ ft.

5. Your estimates should be close to the answers shown.

   a) $(7+4) + (\frac{1}{4} + \frac{1}{4}) = 11\frac{1}{2}$

   b) $10\frac{1}{3} - 6 = 4\frac{1}{3}$

   c) $5 + 2\frac{1}{2} = 7\frac{1}{2}$

   d) $6\frac{2}{3} + \frac{1}{3} = 7$

   e) $30\frac{1}{2} - 10\frac{1}{2} = 20$

6. **(4)** $10\frac{1}{4}$ ft.

   $(7+2) + (\frac{3}{4} + \frac{1}{2}) = 9 + 1\frac{1}{4} = 10\frac{1}{4}$

7. **(4)** $6\frac{1}{2}$ in.

   $(1 + 2 + 2) + (\frac{3}{8} + \frac{7}{8} + \frac{2}{8})$

   $5 + \frac{12}{8} = 5 + \frac{8}{8} + \frac{4}{8} = 6\frac{1}{2}$

Skill Maintenance
Lessons 15–16
Pages 136–137
Part One

1. **a)** $\frac{3}{8}$ **d)** $1\frac{1}{8}$

   b) $\frac{13}{16}$ **e)** $\frac{7}{12}$

   c) $\frac{3}{3} = 1$ **f)** $\frac{2}{10} = \frac{1}{5}$

2. Your estimates should be close to the answers given.

   a) $1 - \frac{1}{2} = \frac{1}{2}$ **d)** $\frac{1}{2} + 0 = \frac{1}{2}$

   b) $0 + 1 = 1$ **e)** $1 - \frac{1}{2} = \frac{1}{2}$

   c) $\frac{3}{4} - \frac{1}{4} = \frac{2}{4} = \frac{1}{2}$ **f)** $1 + 1 = 2$

3. **a)** $0.1; \frac{1}{3}; \frac{3}{5}; 0.8; \frac{14}{15}$

   b) $\frac{3}{10}; 0.5; \frac{4}{5}; 0.9; 1.0$

4. **a)** $\frac{1}{2}$ **d)** $\frac{7}{8}$

   b) $\frac{9}{10}$ **e)** $\frac{5}{6}$

   c) $\frac{1}{4}$

5. the rod

6. $65\frac{1}{2}$

   $21\frac{3}{4} \approx 22$

   $19\frac{1}{16} \approx 19$

   $12\frac{7}{8} \approx 13$

   $11\frac{2}{5} \approx \underline{+ 11\frac{1}{2}}$

            $65\frac{1}{2}$

Part Two

1. **(3)** $1\frac{1}{2}$ in.

   $1.48 \approx 1.50 = 1\frac{1}{2}$

2. **(2)** $5.89

   $10.00 - (\$3.89 + \$.22) = \$5.89$

3. **(3)** $\frac{1}{3}$

   $\frac{11}{31} \approx \frac{11}{33} = \frac{1}{3}$

4. **(1)** $9\frac{5}{8}$

   $20 - 10\frac{3}{8} \approx 20 - 10\frac{1}{2} = 9\frac{1}{2}$

   This is closest to choice **(1)** $9\frac{5}{8}$.

5. **(4)** D, B, C, A

   Change to decimals with the same place value.

   A. 0.2 mile $= 0.200$ ④

   B. $\frac{3}{8}$ mile $= 0.375$ ②

   C. $\frac{1}{4}$ mile $= 0.250$ ③

   D. 0.5 mile $= 0.500$ ①

6. **(3)** $73\frac{1}{4}$

   $25\frac{1}{2} + 13\frac{1}{8} + 22\frac{3}{8} + 12\frac{1}{4}$

   Step 1: Rearrange and add the whole numbers.

   $25 + 25 + 22 = 72$

   Step 2: The answer choices are too close to estimate. Add the fractions.

   $\frac{1}{2} + \frac{1}{8} + \frac{3}{8} + \frac{1}{4}$

   $\frac{4}{8} + \frac{1}{8} + \frac{3}{8} + \frac{2}{8} = \frac{10}{8}$

   Step 3: Combine.

   $72 + \frac{10}{8} = 72 + 1\frac{2}{8} = 73\frac{1}{4}$

Lesson 17
Multiplying and Dividing Fractions
Pages 138–145
Mental Math Exercises

1. more   **3.** less

2. less   **4.** less

Lesson

1. **a)** $\frac{3}{8}$ **e)** $\frac{2}{6} = \frac{1}{3}$

   b) $\frac{5}{24}$ **f)** $\frac{3}{20}$

   c) $\frac{3}{32}$ **g)** $\frac{3}{24} = \frac{1}{8}$

   d) $\frac{8}{15}$ **h)** $\frac{4}{40} = \frac{1}{10}$

2. a) $\frac{1}{\underset{1}{\cancel{2}}} \times \frac{\overset{24}{\cancel{48}}}{1} = 24$ **g)** $\frac{1}{\underset{1}{\cancel{8}}} \times \frac{\overset{7}{\cancel{56}}}{1} = 7$

b) $\frac{1}{\underset{1}{\cancel{4}}} \times \frac{\overset{12}{\cancel{48}}}{1} = 12$ **h)** $\frac{3}{\underset{1}{\cancel{8}}} \times \frac{\overset{7}{\cancel{56}}}{1} = 21$

c) $\frac{1}{\underset{1}{\cancel{3}}} \times \frac{\overset{16}{\cancel{48}}}{1} = 16$ **i)** $\frac{5}{\underset{1}{\cancel{8}}} \times \frac{\overset{7}{\cancel{56}}}{1} = 35$

d) $\frac{2}{\underset{1}{\cancel{3}}} \times \frac{\overset{4}{\cancel{12}}}{1} = 8$ **j)** $\frac{1}{\underset{1}{\cancel{5}}} \times \frac{\overset{12}{\cancel{60}}}{1} = 12$

e) $\frac{2}{\underset{1}{\cancel{3}}} \times \frac{\overset{8}{\cancel{24}}}{1} = 16$ **k)** $\frac{1}{\underset{1}{\cancel{10}}} \times \frac{\overset{6}{\cancel{60}}}{1} = 6$

f) $\frac{2}{\underset{1}{\cancel{3}}} \times \frac{\overset{16}{\cancel{48}}}{1} = 32$ **l)** $\frac{3}{\underset{1}{\cancel{5}}} \times \frac{\overset{12}{\cancel{60}}}{1} = 36$

3. 8 oz.

$$\frac{1}{\underset{1}{\cancel{4}}} \times \frac{\overset{8}{\cancel{32}}}{1} = 8 \text{ oz.}$$

4. $24

$$\frac{2}{\underset{1}{\cancel{5}}} \times \frac{\overset{12}{\cancel{60}}}{1} = 24$$

5. a) $\frac{\overset{1}{\cancel{3}}}{5} \times \frac{1}{\underset{2}{\cancel{6}}} = \frac{1}{10}$ **e)** $\frac{\overset{1}{\cancel{3}}}{\underset{1}{\cancel{4}}} \times \frac{\overset{2}{\cancel{8}}}{\underset{3}{\cancel{9}}} = \frac{2}{3}$

b) $\frac{\overset{1}{\cancel{2}}}{3} \times \frac{1}{\underset{2}{\cancel{4}}} = \frac{1}{6}$ **f)** $\frac{\overset{1}{\cancel{5}}}{\underset{2}{\cancel{6}}} \times \frac{\overset{3}{\cancel{9}}}{\underset{2}{\cancel{10}}} = \frac{3}{4}$

c) $\frac{1}{\underset{1}{\cancel{2}}} \times \frac{\overset{2}{\cancel{4}}}{5} = \frac{2}{5}$ **g)** $\frac{\overset{1}{\cancel{2}}}{5} \times \frac{3}{\underset{4}{\cancel{8}}} = \frac{3}{20}$

d) $\frac{1}{\underset{1}{\cancel{3}}} \times \frac{\overset{1}{\cancel{3}}}{4} = \frac{1}{4}$ **h)** $\frac{\overset{1}{\cancel{2}}}{\underset{1}{\cancel{3}}} \times \frac{\overset{1}{\cancel{3}}}{\underset{4}{\cancel{8}}} = \frac{1}{4}$

6. Notice that all of the estimated numbers below are evenly divisible by 3.

a) $\frac{1}{3} \times \$24 = \$8$

b) $\frac{1}{3} \times \$9 = \$3$

c) $\frac{1}{3} \times \$18 = \$6$

d) $\frac{1}{3} \times \$120 = \$40$

e) $\frac{1}{3} \times \$210 = \$70$

7. The estimates below show one possible way to estimate.

a) Estimate: $\frac{3}{1} \times \frac{3}{4} = \frac{9}{4} = 2\frac{1}{4}^{+}$ (The exact answer is more.)

Exact: $2\frac{1}{2}$

b) Estimate: $\frac{7}{8} \times \frac{3}{1} = \frac{21}{8} = 2\frac{5}{8}^{+}$ (The exact answer is more.)

Exact: $2\frac{4}{5}$

c) Estimate: $2 \times 3\frac{1}{3} = 6\frac{2}{3}^{-}$ (The exact answer is less.)

Exact: 6

d) Estimate: $12 \times 5\frac{1}{4} = 60 + 3 = 63$

e) Estimate: $10 \times 17 = 170$

f) Estimate: $8 \times 6\frac{1}{2} = 48 + 4 = 52$

8. (3) 465

$$30 \times 15\frac{1}{2} = 450 + 15 = 465$$

9. a) $\frac{7}{8} \div \frac{1}{8} = \frac{7}{\underset{1}{\cancel{8}}} \times \frac{\cancel{8}}{1} = 7$

b) $8 \div \frac{1}{3} = \frac{8}{1} \times \frac{3}{1} = 24$

c) $8 \div \frac{2}{3} = \frac{\overset{4}{\cancel{8}}}{1} \times \frac{3}{\underset{1}{\cancel{2}}} = 12$

d) $\frac{3}{4} \div \frac{1}{2} = \frac{3}{\underset{2}{\cancel{4}}} \times \frac{\overset{1}{\cancel{2}}}{1} = \frac{3}{2} = 1\frac{1}{2}$

e) $\frac{3}{4} \div \frac{1}{8} = \frac{3}{\underset{1}{\cancel{4}}} \times \frac{\overset{2}{\cancel{8}}}{1} = 6$

f) $\frac{3}{4} \div \frac{7}{8} = \frac{3}{\underset{1}{\cancel{4}}} \times \frac{\overset{2}{\cancel{8}}}{7} = \frac{6}{7}$

g) $10 \div \frac{5}{6} = \frac{\overset{2}{\cancel{10}}}{1} \times \frac{6}{\underset{1}{\cancel{5}}} = 12$

h) $3 \div \frac{3}{4} = \frac{\overset{1}{\cancel{3}}}{1} \times \frac{4}{\underset{1}{\cancel{3}}} = 4$

i) $20 \div \frac{2}{3} = \frac{\overset{10}{\cancel{20}}}{1} \times \frac{3}{\underset{1}{\cancel{2}}} = 30$

10. 225 miles

$d = rt$

$d = (60)\left(3\frac{3}{4}\right)$

$d = (60 \times 3) + \left(60 \times \frac{3}{4}\right)$

$d = 180 + 45 = 225$

11. 40 sheets

You are asking, "How many $\frac{5}{8}$s in 25?"

$$25 \div \frac{5}{8} = \frac{\overset{5}{\cancel{25}}}{1} \times \frac{8}{\underset{1}{\cancel{5}}} = 40 \text{ sheets}$$

12. $8\frac{1}{4}$ gallons

You are asking, "What is $\frac{1}{2}$ of $16\frac{1}{2}$?"

$16\frac{1}{2} \times \frac{1}{2} = \left(16 \times \frac{1}{2}\right) + \left(\frac{1}{2} \times \frac{1}{2}\right) =$

$8 + \frac{1}{4} = 8\frac{1}{4}$

13. (1) $2\frac{1}{4}$ in.

You are asked to separate $20\frac{1}{4}$ into 9 equal pieces. This means dividing by 9.

$20\frac{1}{4} \div 9 =$

$20\frac{1}{4} \times \frac{1}{9}$

$\frac{^9\cancel{81}}{4} \times \frac{1}{\cancel{9}_1} = \frac{9}{4} = 2\frac{1}{4}$ in.

OR

An estimate of $20 \div 10 = 2$ would provide enough information to choose **(1)** $2\frac{1}{4}$ inches.

Check Your Understanding

1. **a)** 24   **d)** 55

   b) 12   **e)** 72

   c) 30   **f)** 45

2. **a)** $\frac{1}{4}$ of $2.00 = \$.50$

   b) $\frac{1}{4}$ of $5.60 = \$1.40$

   c) $\frac{1}{4}$ of $10.00 = \$2.50$

   d) $\frac{1}{4}$ of $12.00 = \$3.00$

   e) $\frac{1}{4}$ of $20.00 = \$5.00$

3. **a)** $\frac{1}{3}$ cup $(1 \times \frac{1}{3} = \frac{1}{3})$

   b) $\frac{1}{2}$ cup $(1\frac{1}{2} \times \frac{1}{3} = \frac{^1\cancel{3}}{2} \times \frac{1}{\cancel{3}_1} = \frac{1}{2})$

   c) $\frac{2}{3}$ cup $(2 \times \frac{1}{3} = \frac{2}{3})$

   d) $\frac{1}{6}$ cup $(\frac{1}{2} \times \frac{1}{3} = \frac{1}{6})$

   e) $\frac{1}{4}$ lb. each $(\frac{^1\cancel{3}}{4} \times \frac{1}{\cancel{3}_1} = \frac{1}{4})$

4. **a)** Estimate: $4\frac{1}{10} + 6\frac{4}{7} \approx 4 + 6\frac{1}{2} = 10\frac{1}{2}$

   b) Estimate: $7\frac{1}{2} \times 4\frac{5}{6} \approx 7\frac{1}{2} \times 5 =$

   $(7 \times 5) + (\frac{1}{2} \times 5) =$

   $35 + 2\frac{1}{2} = 37\frac{1}{2}$

   c) Estimate: $33\frac{1}{3} - 12\frac{1}{2} \approx$

   $33 - 12\frac{1}{2} = 20\frac{1}{2}$

   d) Estimate: $15\frac{3}{4} \div \frac{1}{2} \approx$

   $\frac{16}{1} \times \frac{2}{1} = 32$

   e) Estimate: $9\frac{7}{8} \times 12\frac{1}{5} \approx$

   $10 \times 12 = 120$

5. $7\frac{3}{8}$ points

   $58\frac{7}{8} - 51\frac{1}{2} = 58\frac{7}{8} - 51\frac{4}{8} = 7\frac{3}{8}$

6. **(4)** 48

   You are asking, "How many $\frac{3}{4}$s in 36?"

   $36 \div \frac{3}{4} = \frac{^{12}\cancel{36} \times \frac{4}{\cancel{3}_1}} = 48$

   Since you divided by a number less than 1, your answer would be greater than 36.

7. **(4)** $\frac{7}{20}$

   $\frac{7}{\cancel{8}4} \times \frac{2\frac{1}{}}{5} = \frac{7}{20}$

   interest portion of mortgage   fraction of income going to mortgage   fraction of income going to interest

Lesson 18
Making Connections
Pages 146–153
Mental Math Exercises

1. $\frac{1}{8}$ 4. $\frac{3}{10}$

2. $\frac{1}{16}$ 5. $\frac{3}{20}$

3. $\frac{1}{6}$ 6. $\frac{2}{12} = \frac{1}{6}$

Lesson

1. **a)** $13\frac{3}{4} + 9\frac{1}{2} = 22 + 1\frac{1}{4} = 23\frac{1}{4}$ in.

   $13.75 + 9.5 = 23.25$ in.

   b) $3\frac{1}{2} - 2\frac{3}{8} = 1\frac{1}{8}$ in.

   $3.5 - 2.375 = 1.125$

   c) $50 \div \frac{9}{2} = \frac{100}{9} = 11\frac{1}{9} \approx 11$ pieces

   $50 \div 4.5 = 11.1\bullet\bullet\bullet \approx 11$ pieces

   d) $\frac{5}{8} \times \$64 = \$40$

   $.625 \times \$64 = \$40$

   $(\frac{5}{8} = .625)$

   e) $\frac{7}{8} \times \$2.35 \approx \frac{7}{8} \times \$2.40 = \$2.10$

   $.875 \times \$2.35 = \$2.056 \approx \$2.06$

   $(\frac{7}{8} = .875)$

2. **a)** $14 \times \frac{22}{7} = 44$ m

   $14 \times 3.14 = 43.96$ m

   b) It is easier to use the fraction form $(\frac{22}{7})$ because 14 is a multiple of 7, and you can cancel.

3. **a)** $\frac{5}{8}$ is more.

   $.6 = .600$

   $\frac{5}{8} = .625$

   b) $1.88

   $5.00 - \$3.12 = \$1.88$

   c) 7.9 m

   15 m $- 7.1$ m $= 7.9$ m

d) 0.36 m^2

$A = s^2$

$A = (0.6 \text{ m})^2$

$A = 0.36 \text{ m}^2$

4. a) 50 stamps

$\frac{\$12.50}{.25} = 50$

b) 125 cans

$\frac{5.00}{.04} = 125$

c) \$2.10

$\frac{\$7.35}{3.5} = \$2.10$

d) 640 nails

$\frac{16.000}{.025} = 640$

5. a) $\$119.97 \times \frac{3}{4} \approx \$120 \times \frac{3}{4} = \$90$

b) $\$18.88 \times \frac{3}{4} \approx \$20 \times \frac{3}{4} = \$15$

c) $\$47.88 \times \frac{3}{4} \approx \$48 \times \frac{3}{4} = \$36$

d) $\$31.99 \times \frac{3}{4} \approx \$32 \times \frac{3}{4} = \$24$

e) $\$14.94 \times \frac{3}{4} \approx \$16 \times \frac{3}{4} = \$12$

Notice that the rounded numbers were chosen to be divisible by the 4 in $\frac{3}{4}$.

6. a) \$89.98   **d)** \$24.00

b) \$14.16   **e)** \$11.21

c) \$35.91

7. **(3)** $s = 400 - \frac{1}{4}(400)$

8. a) $10 - (\frac{3}{2} \times 5.60) = c$

$10 - (\frac{3}{2} \times \frac{5.6}{1}) = c$

$\$1.60 = c$

b) $180° - (50\frac{1}{4}° + 51\frac{3}{4}°) = a$

$180° - 102° = a$

$78° = a$

c) $g = (1 - \frac{1}{8})\, 15.2$

$g = \frac{7}{8} \times \frac{15.2}{1} = 13.3$ gal. (Divide 15.2 by 8 on your calculator.)

d) $\frac{d}{t} = r$

$144 \div 2\frac{1}{4} = r$

$144 \div \frac{9}{4} = 144 \times \frac{4}{9} = r$ (Divide 144 by 9.)

$64 \text{ mph} = r$

e) $C = \$1.69\,(\pi d) =$

$\$1.69\,(\frac{22}{7} \times 7)$

$C = 1.69\,(\frac{22}{7} \times \frac{7}{1})$

$C = 1.69\,(22)$

$C = \$37.18$

Check Your Understanding

1. lower

.357 (*average*)

.333 (*last game—1 out of 3*)

2. $\frac{3}{4} = .750$

$\frac{9}{16} = .563$

3. Rijo

Rijo: $\frac{1}{3} = (.333)$

Davis: $\frac{4}{14} = \frac{2}{7} = (.286)$

$\frac{1}{3}$ is greater than $\frac{2}{7}$.

4. $A = \frac{1}{2}bh$

$A = \frac{1}{2}\,(5 \times 3\frac{1}{4})$

$A = \frac{1}{2} \times \frac{5}{1} \times \frac{13}{4} = \frac{65}{8} = 8\frac{1}{8}$ sq. ft.

5. $A = lw$

$A = 5 \times 2\frac{1}{3}\ (\frac{4}{12} = \frac{1}{3} \text{ foot})$

$A = (5 \times 2) + (5 \times \frac{1}{3})$

$A = 10 + \frac{5}{3} = 10 + 1\frac{2}{3} = 11\frac{2}{3}$ sq. ft.

6. $\frac{1}{2}$ of $\frac{1}{3} = \frac{1}{6}$

7. In each case, you could first find $1 - \frac{1}{3} = \frac{2}{3}$.

a) $\frac{\$6}{1} \times \frac{2}{3} = \$4.00$

b) $\frac{\$4.50}{1} \times \frac{2}{3} = \$3.00$

c) $\frac{\$3}{1} \times \frac{2}{3} = \$2.00$

8. 110 stitches

$10 \div \frac{1}{11} = \frac{10}{1} \times \frac{11}{1} = 110$

9. **(4)** $\frac{1}{3}$

$\frac{2}{6} = \frac{1}{3}$

10. **(3)** \$17.24

Estimate: $\$.69 \times 4 \approx \$.70 \times 4 = \$2.80$

$\$20.00 - \$2.80 \approx \$20.00 - \$3.00 = \$17.00$

This estimate of \$17.00 is closest to choice **(3)** \$17.24.

Lesson 19
Checkpoint III
Pages 154–159
Check Your Skills

1. **(4)** $6.55

   Estimate: $10 − (5 × $.70) =

   $10 − $3.50 = $6.50

2. **(2)** $\frac{1}{8}$ in.

   Remember: $\frac{1}{8} = \frac{1}{2} \times \frac{1}{4}$

   $\frac{1}{2} \times .25 = .12\frac{1}{2}$ OR .125

3. **(4)** $9m$

   Each yard has 3 ft., so the length is $3m$ ft.

   $A = lw$ or $A = 3 \cdot 3m = 9m$ sq. ft.

4. **(5)** Not enough information is given. You need the total seating capacity to find the answer.

5. **(4)** $6\frac{1}{4}$ yd.

   $5 \times 1\frac{1}{4} = (5 \times 1) + 5(\frac{1}{4}) =$

   $5 + \frac{5}{4} = 5 + 1\frac{1}{4} = 6\frac{1}{4}$

6. **(4)** 8

   $(3 \times 8) − 7 = 17$

7. **(3)** 75°

   $\frac{180° − 30°}{2} = 75°$

8. **(2)** .750

   $\frac{9}{12} = \frac{3}{4} = .750$

9. **(2)** 5.35 km

   one-tenth = .1

   $5.25 + .1 = 5.25 + .10 = 5.35$

10. **(4)** 8.89×10^8

    889 million is 889,000,000

    8 places

11. **(3)** $9

    Look at the dot above 12 pounds. It is between 8 and 10 dollars.

12. **(4)** $13\frac{1}{3}$

    Look across from 10 dollars. The value lies between 12 and 14 pounds. $13\frac{1}{3}$ pounds is the closest answer choice.

13. **(3)** $7\frac{7}{8}$%

    Putting all the rates in decimal form, you are comparing 7.75%, 7.46%, 7.875%, 7.77%, and 7.5%. The highest is 7.875%, or $7\frac{7}{8}$%.

14. **(1)** 20

    $2\frac{1}{2} \div \frac{1}{8} =$

    $\frac{5}{\underset{1}{2}} \times \frac{\overset{4}{8}}{1} = 20$

15. **(5)** 42

    $(40 − 12) \div \frac{2}{3} =$

    $\frac{28}{1} \div \frac{2}{3} = \frac{\overset{14}{28}}{1} \times \frac{3}{\underset{1}{2}} = 42$

16. **(4)** 135°

    $180° − 45° = 135°$

17. **(2)** right

18. **(3)** $\frac{4}{5}$

    $\frac{100}{127} \approx \frac{100 \div 25}{125 \div 25} = \frac{4}{5}$

19. **(2)** 9(8.50)

    ↑ ↑
    total hourly
    hours pay

20. **(5)** 35 km

    $d = rt = 30\ (1\ \text{hr. } 10\ \text{min.})$

    1 hr. 10 min. $= 1\frac{10}{60}$ hr., so

    $d = 30 \times 1\frac{1}{6}$

    $= (30 \times 1) + (30 \times \frac{1}{6}) = 30 + 5 = 35$

Lesson 20
Comparisons: Fractions as Ratios
Pages 160–167
Mental Math Exercises

1. yes
2. no
3. yes
4. no
5. no
6. yes

Lesson

1. a) $\frac{\text{cans}}{\text{cents}} = \frac{2}{5}$

   b) $\frac{\text{miles}}{\text{hours}} = \frac{25}{3}$

   c) $\frac{\text{miles}}{\text{days}} = \frac{3,300}{5}$

   d) $\frac{\text{width}}{\text{length}} = \frac{7}{10}$

   e) $\frac{\text{gallons}}{\text{square feet}} = \frac{1}{400}$

   f) $\frac{\text{pounds}}{\text{dollars}} = \frac{3}{4}$

2. a) $25 per day

   b) 4 glasses per quart

   c) 65 miles per hour

   d) $9.50 per hour

   e) 320 miles per hour

f) $3 per month

g) $32 per ticket

h) $.75 per can

3. a) no

b) yes, $\dfrac{\text{miles}}{\text{hour}} = \dfrac{40}{1}$

c) yes, $\dfrac{\text{height}}{\text{base}} = \dfrac{5}{1}$

d) no

e) yes, $\dfrac{\text{red}}{\text{yellow}} = \dfrac{3}{2}$

f) no

g) no

h) yes, $\dfrac{\text{Thomas}}{\text{Ted}} = \dfrac{5}{1}$

i) yes, $\dfrac{9}{10}$

j) This information can be represented both ways:

   (1) 9 more people voted for the measure than against (no ratio).

   (2) The ratio $\dfrac{\text{for}}{\text{against}} = \dfrac{19}{10}$.

4. a) 9   **d)** 14

b) 13   **e)** 6, 18, 60

c) 7

5. a) $\dfrac{2}{1}$ **c)** $\dfrac{1}{3}$

b) $\dfrac{4}{3}$ **d)** $\dfrac{1}{10}$

6. 6 yd.

7. a) $\dfrac{360 \div 3}{3 \div 3} = \dfrac{120}{1}$

b) $\dfrac{250 \div 250}{1,000 \div 250} = \dfrac{1}{4}$

c) $\dfrac{80 \div 8}{8 \div 8} = \dfrac{10}{1}$

d) $\dfrac{100 \div 5}{5 \div 5} = \dfrac{20}{1}$

e) $\dfrac{14 \div 7}{7 \div 7} = \dfrac{2}{1}$

f) $\dfrac{80 \div 4}{12 \div 4} = \dfrac{20}{3}$

8.

$	2	4	6	8	10	12
Rolls	3	6	9	12	15	18

9.

Length	5	10	15	20	25	30
Width	3	6	9	12	15	18

10. a) 18   **d)** 100

b) 5   **e)** 60

c) 500   **f)** 60

11. a) no   **g)** no

b) yes   **h)** yes

c) yes   **i)** no

d) no   **j)** yes

e) no   **k)** yes

f) yes   **l)** no

12. a) yes

b) $\dfrac{\text{shots made}}{\text{attempted shots}}$ $\dfrac{9}{12} = \dfrac{x}{16}$

13. a) no, because only two values are given

14. (a) $\dfrac{4}{5} = \dfrac{d}{200}$ **(c)** $\dfrac{5}{4} = \dfrac{200}{d}$ and **(e)** $\dfrac{4}{d} = \dfrac{5}{200}$

Both proportions keep the ratios in the same order.

(a) $\dfrac{\text{doctors recommend Brand Y}}{\text{total doctors surveyed}}$ OR

(c) $\dfrac{\text{total doctors surveyed}}{\text{doctors recommend Brand Y}}$

Check Your Understanding

1. a) $\dfrac{8}{1}$ **d)** $\dfrac{5}{8}$

b) $\dfrac{3}{5}$ **e)** $\dfrac{4}{5}$

c) $\dfrac{3}{8}$

2. $\dfrac{250}{10} = \dfrac{25}{1}$ (or 25 miles per gallon)

3. $\dfrac{2}{12} = \dfrac{1}{6}$

4.

Speed (mph)	20	30	40	50	60
Car Lengths	2	3	4	5	6

5. $\dfrac{11}{100} = 11$ would drop out

6. $\dfrac{2}{5}$

7.

c	22	44	66	88	
d	7	14	21	28	

8. a) 100   **d)** 110

b) 72   **e)** 22

c) 55   **f)** 7

9. **a)** yes   **d)** yes

    b) no   **e)** no

    c) no

10. **(2)** 7:40

$$\frac{35}{200} = \frac{7}{40}$$

Lesson 21
Proportions
Pages 168–175
Mental Math Exercises

1. no   **4.** no

2. yes   **5.** no

3. no   **6.** no

Lesson

1. **a)** True: $\frac{\text{miles}}{\text{hours}}$: $\frac{165}{3} = \frac{55}{1}$

      $165 = 55 \times 3$

   b) False: $\frac{\text{oranges}}{\text{cents}}$: $\frac{2}{35} \neq \frac{8}{150}$

      $2 \times 150 \neq 35 \times 8$

   c) False: $\frac{\text{tables}}{\text{people}}$: $\frac{1}{6} \neq \frac{16}{64}$

      $1 \times 64 \neq 6 \times 16$

   d) False: $\frac{\text{cans}}{\text{cents}}$: $\frac{2}{5} \neq \frac{200}{1,000}$ (1,000 cents = \$10.00)

      $2 \times 1,000 \neq 5 \times 200$

   e) False: $\frac{\text{oil}}{\text{gas}}$: $\frac{1}{10} \neq \frac{2}{5}$

      $1 \times 5 \neq 10 \times 2$

   f) True: $\frac{\text{beef}}{\text{people}}$: $\frac{2}{6} = \frac{8}{24}$

      $2 \times 24 = 6 \times 8$

   g) True: $\frac{\text{tax}}{\text{price}}$: $\frac{6}{100} = \frac{30}{500}$

      $6 \times 500 = 30 \times 100$

   h) True: $\frac{\text{women}}{\text{total}}$: $\frac{3}{5} = \frac{12}{20}$

      $3 \times 20 = 12 \times 5$

   i) True: $\frac{\text{men}}{\text{total}}$: $\frac{2}{5} = \frac{8}{20}$

      $2 \times 20 = 8 \times 5$

2. **a)** $b = \frac{40}{4} = 10$ **d)** $d = \frac{75}{10} = 7.5$

   b) $t = \frac{100}{5} = 20$ **e)** $s = \frac{450}{25} = 18$

   c) $x = \frac{140}{7} = 20$ **f)** $y = \frac{143}{11} = 13$

3. **a)** $c = 4$

$$\frac{c}{5} = \frac{24}{30}$$

$$30c = 24 \times 5$$

$$c = \frac{24 \times \overset{1}{5}}{\underset{6}{30}} = \frac{24}{6} = 4$$

   b) $m = 12$

$$\frac{8}{m} = \frac{20}{30}$$

$$20 \times m = 8 \times 30$$

$$m = \frac{8 \times \overset{3}{30}}{\underset{2}{20}} = \frac{24}{2} = 12$$

   c) $p = 55$

$$\frac{5}{8} = \frac{p}{88}$$

$$8 \times p = 5 \times 88$$

$$p = \frac{5 \times \overset{11}{88}}{\underset{1}{8}} = 55$$

   d) $b = 75$

$$\frac{4}{15} = \frac{20}{b}$$

$$4 \times b = 20 \times 15$$

$$b = \frac{\overset{5}{20} \times 15}{\underset{1}{4}} = 75$$

   e) $t = 15$

$$\frac{t}{9} = \frac{10}{6}$$

$$t \times 6 = 10 \times 9$$

$$t = \frac{10 \times \overset{3}{9}}{\underset{2}{6}} = \frac{30}{2} = 15$$

   f) $c = 40$

$$\frac{10}{c} = \frac{25}{100}$$

$$25 \times c = 100 \times 10$$

$$c = \frac{\overset{4}{100} \times 10}{\underset{1}{25}} = 40$$

   g) $w = 25$

$$\frac{6}{15} = \frac{10}{w}$$

$$6 \times w = 15 \times 10$$

$$w = \frac{\overset{5}{15} \times 10}{\underset{2}{6}} = \frac{50}{2} = 25$$

   h) $k = 33$

$$\frac{3}{11} = \frac{k}{121}$$

$$11 \times k = 3 \times 121$$

$$k = \frac{3 \times \overset{11}{121}}{\underset{1}{11}} = 33$$

4. **a)** $b = 15$ OR   Looking across:

$$\frac{4}{5} = \frac{12}{b}$$ $4 \times 3 = 12$

$$4b = 5 \times 12$$ So, $5 \times 3 = 15$

$$b = \frac{5 \times \overset{3}{12}}{\underset{1}{4}} = 15$$

b) $k = 9$　　　　OR　　Simplify first:

$$\frac{k}{12} = \frac{6}{8}$$

$$8k = 12 \times 6$$

$$k = \frac{\overset{3}{12} \times 6}{8_2} = \frac{18}{2} = 9$$

$$\frac{6}{8} = \frac{3}{4}$$

Looking across:

$$\frac{k}{12} = \frac{3}{4}$$

$$4 \times 3 = 12$$

So, $3 \times 3 = 9$

c) $r = 24$　　　　OR　　Looking across:

$$\frac{3}{8} = \frac{r}{64}$$

$$8r = 3 \times 64$$

$$r = \frac{3 \times \overset{8}{64}}{8_1} = 24$$

$$8 \times 8 = 64$$

So, $3 \times 8 = 24$

d) $v = 12$　　　　OR　　Looking from top to bottom:

$$\frac{3}{v} = \frac{7}{28}$$

$$7v = 3 \times 28$$

$$v = \frac{3 \times \overset{4}{28}}{7_1} = 12$$

$$7 \times 4 = 28$$

$$3 \times 4 = 12$$

e) $n = 25$　　　　OR　　Looking from top to bottom:

$$\frac{8}{32} = \frac{n}{100}$$

$$32n = 8 \times 100$$

$$n = \frac{\overset{1}{8} \times 100}{32_4} =$$

$$\frac{100}{4} = 25$$

$$32 \div 4 = 8$$

So, $100 \div 4 = 25$

f) $d = 12$　　　　OR　　Looking across:

$$\frac{3}{7} = \frac{d}{28}$$

$$7d = 3 \times 28$$

$$d = \frac{3 \times \overset{4}{28}}{7_1} = 12$$

$$7 \times 4 = 28$$

$$3 \times 4 = 12$$

g) $n = 12$　　　　OR　　Looking across:

$$\frac{n}{25} = \frac{48}{100}$$

$$100n = 48 \times 25$$

$$n = \frac{48 \times \overset{1}{25}}{100_4} =$$

$$\frac{48}{4} = 12$$

$$100 \div 4 = 25$$

$$48 \div 4 = 12$$

h) $r = 4\frac{2}{7}$

$$\frac{3}{7} = \frac{r}{10}$$

$$7r = 3 \times 10$$

$$r = \frac{3 \times 10}{7} = \frac{30}{7} = 4\frac{2}{7}$$

i) $d = 121$　　　OR　　Looking from top to bottom:

$$\frac{44}{4} = \frac{d}{11}$$

$$4d = 44 \times 11$$

$$d = \frac{\overset{11}{44} \times 11}{4_1} = 121$$

$$44 = 4 \times 11$$

So, $121 = 11 \times 11$

j) $n = 62\frac{1}{2}$

$$\frac{5}{8} = \frac{n}{100}$$

$$8n = 5 \times 100$$

$$n = \frac{5 \times \overset{25}{100}}{8_2} = \frac{125}{2} = 62\frac{1}{2}$$

k) $z = 2$

$$\frac{1.2}{z} = \frac{4.8}{8}$$

$$4.8z = 1.2 \times 8$$

$$z = \frac{\overset{1}{1.2} \times 8}{4.8_4} = \frac{8}{4} = 2$$

l) $s = 2$

$$\frac{1.5}{9} = \frac{s}{12}$$

$$9s = 1.5 \times 12$$

$$s = \frac{1.5 \times \overset{4}{12}}{9_3} = \frac{6.0}{3} = 2$$

m) $n = 3$

$$\frac{\frac{1}{4}}{6} = \frac{\frac{1}{8}}{n}$$

$$\frac{1}{4}n = 6 \times \frac{1}{8}$$

$$n = \left(6 \times \frac{1}{8}\right) \times 4 = \frac{3}{4} \times 4 = 3$$

n) $c = \frac{1}{25}$

$$\frac{\frac{1}{5}}{20} = \frac{c}{4}$$

$$20c = \frac{1}{5} \times 4$$

$$c = \frac{\frac{1}{5} \times 4}{20} = \frac{\frac{4}{5}}{20} = \frac{\overset{1}{4}}{5} \times \frac{1}{20_5} = \frac{1}{25}$$

o) $a = 200$　　　OR　Looking from top to bottom:

$$\frac{2\frac{1}{2}}{5} = \frac{100}{a}$$

$$2\frac{1}{2}a = 5 \times 100$$

$$\frac{5}{2}a = 5 \times 100$$

$$a = (5 \times 100) \times \frac{2}{5} = \frac{\overset{100}{500}}{1} \times \frac{2}{5_1} = 200$$

$2\frac{1}{2}$ is $\frac{1}{2}$ of 5

100 is $\frac{1}{2}$ of 200

$a = 200$

5. a) $w = 56$ women

$$\frac{\text{women}}{\text{total}} : \frac{7}{12} = \frac{w}{96}$$

$$12w = 7 \times 96$$

$$w = \frac{7 \times \cancel{96}^{8}}{\cancel{12}_{1}} = 56$$

b) $c = 210$¢ or $2.10

$$\frac{\text{oranges}}{\text{cents}} : \frac{2}{35} = \frac{12}{c}$$

$$2c = 35 \times 12$$

$$c = \frac{35 \times \cancel{12}^{6}}{\cancel{2}_{1}} = 210$$

c) $s = \frac{5}{4} = 1\frac{1}{4}$ cups

$$\frac{\text{sugar}}{\text{servings}} : \frac{\frac{1}{2}}{4} = \frac{s}{10}$$

$$4s = \frac{1}{2} \times 10$$

$$s = \frac{\frac{1}{2} \times 10}{4} = \frac{5}{4} = 1\frac{1}{4}$$

d) $t = \$14$

$$\frac{\text{tax}}{\text{dollars}} : \frac{7}{100} = \frac{t}{200}$$

$$100t = 7 \times 200$$

$$t = \frac{7 \times \cancel{200}^{2}}{\cancel{100}_{1}} = 14$$

e) $x = \$108$

$$\frac{\$}{\text{days}} : \frac{540}{5} = \frac{x}{1}$$

$$5x = 540 \times 1$$

$$x = \frac{540}{5} = 108$$

f) $g = 11.75$ gal.

$$\frac{\text{miles}}{\text{gallon}} : \frac{52}{1} = \frac{611}{g}$$

$$52g = 1 \times 611$$

$$g = \frac{611}{52} = 11.75$$

6. a) 4 m

$$\frac{5}{x} = \frac{15}{12}$$

$$15x = 5 \times 12$$

$$x = \frac{\cancel{5}^{1} \times 12}{\cancel{15}_{3}} = \frac{12}{3} = 4$$

b) $70°$

$$180° - (35° + 75°)$$

$$180° - 110° = 70°$$

7. $x = 40$ ft.

$$\frac{40}{100} = \frac{16}{x}$$

$$40x = 100 \times 16$$

$$x = \frac{100 \times 16}{40} = 40$$

8. $n = 12$ in. OR Looking across:

$$\frac{3}{4} = \frac{9}{n}$$

$3 \times 3 = 9$

$$3n = 4 \times 9$$

So, $4 \times 3 = 12$

$$n = \frac{4 \times \cancel{9}^{3}}{\cancel{3}_{1}} = 12$$

9. $f = 6$ ft.

$$\frac{\text{in.}}{\text{ft.}} = \frac{1}{\frac{3}{2}} = \frac{4}{f}$$

$$f = \frac{3}{2} \times 4 = 6$$

10. $n = 350$ ft.

$$\frac{\text{in.}}{\text{ft.}} = \frac{1}{100} = \frac{3\frac{1}{2}}{n}$$

$$n = 100 \times 3\frac{1}{2}$$

$$n = 100 \times \frac{7}{2} = 350$$

11. $p \approx 1.5$ in.

$$\frac{\text{in.}}{\text{mi.}} = \frac{1}{135} = \frac{p}{208}$$

$$135p = 208$$

$$p = \frac{208}{135} \approx 1.5$$

12. a) $\frac{279}{24} \approx \frac{240}{24} = 10$¢ apiece

$\frac{649}{100} \approx \frac{650}{100} = 6.5$¢ apiece (better buy)

b) $\frac{159}{22} \approx \frac{160}{20} = 8$¢ per oz.

$\frac{249}{32} \approx \frac{240}{30} = 8$¢ per oz.

With a calculator, $\frac{159}{22} = 7.227$¢ per oz. (better buy), and $\frac{249}{32} = 7.78$¢ per oz.

c) $\frac{1099}{30} \approx \frac{1200}{30} = 40$¢ per diaper

$\frac{1999}{64} \approx \frac{2000}{60} = 33$¢ per diaper (better buy)

d) $\frac{63}{8} \approx \frac{64}{8} = 8$¢ per oz.

$\frac{179}{32} \approx \frac{180}{30} = 6$¢ per oz. (better buy)

e) $6 \times 1\frac{1}{2}$ oz. = 9 oz. for $.88

This is cheaper than $1.09 for a regular-price 9-ounce box.

Check Your Understanding

1. $x = 4$ hr.

$$\frac{320}{1} = \frac{1{,}280}{x}$$
$$320x = 1{,}280 \times 1$$
$$x = \frac{1{,}280}{320} = 4$$

2. $d = 250¢$ or $\$2.50$

$$\frac{100}{4} = \frac{d}{10}$$
$$4d = 100 \times 10$$
$$d = \frac{\overset{25}{100} \times 10}{\underset{1}{4}} = 250$$

3. $y = 56$ oz.

$$\frac{1}{16} = \frac{3\frac{1}{2}}{y}$$
$$y = 16 \times 3\frac{1}{2}$$
$$y = \frac{\overset{8}{16}}{1} \times \frac{7}{\underset{1}{2}} = 56$$

4. $t = 150$ shots

$$\frac{6}{9} = \frac{100}{t}$$
$$6t = 9 \times 100$$
$$t = \frac{\overset{3}{9} \times 100}{\underset{2}{6}} = 150$$

5. $d = 86$ ft.

$$\frac{3}{21\frac{1}{2}} = \frac{12}{d}$$
$$3d = 12 \times 21\frac{1}{2}$$
$$d = \frac{\overset{4}{12} \times 21\frac{1}{2}}{\underset{1}{3}}$$
$$d = (4 \times 21) + (4 \times \tfrac{1}{2})$$
$$d = 84 + 2 = 86$$

6. $w = \frac{16}{3} = 5\frac{1}{3}$ tsp.

$$\frac{2}{3} = \frac{w}{8}$$
$$3w = 2 \times 8$$
$$w = \frac{16}{3} = 5\frac{1}{3}$$

7. $m = 8$ mph

$$\frac{26}{3\frac{1}{4}} = \frac{m}{1}$$
$$3\tfrac{1}{4}m = 26 \times 1$$
$$m = 26 \div 3\tfrac{1}{4} = \frac{\overset{2}{26} \times 4}{\underset{1}{13}} = \frac{8}{1}$$

8. $r = 2\frac{1}{2}$ ft.

$$\frac{1}{20} = \frac{r}{50}$$
$$20r = 1 \times 50$$
$$r = \frac{50}{20} = \frac{5}{2} = 2\frac{1}{2}$$

9. $20 - 6 = 14$ passes

10. $n = 475$ parts

$$\frac{19}{20} = \frac{n}{500}$$
$$20n = 19 \times 500$$
$$n = \frac{19 \times \overset{25}{500}}{\underset{1}{20}} = 19 \times 25 = 475$$

11. $\frac{55}{11} = \frac{5}{1}$

12. $\frac{5}{7} \neq \frac{8}{10}$, no

13. The package of 3 rolls is a better buy.

$$\frac{199}{2} \approx \frac{200}{2} = 100¢ \text{ or } \$1.00 \text{ per roll}$$
$$\frac{267}{3} \approx \frac{270}{3} = 90¢ \text{ per roll}$$

14. $z = 3\frac{1}{3}$ hr.

$$\frac{1}{60} = \frac{z}{200}$$
$$60z = 1 \times 200$$
$$z = \frac{200}{60} = \frac{20}{6} = 3\frac{1}{3}$$

15. $\frac{99}{2} \approx \frac{100}{2} = 50¢$ each

$\$.59 - \$.50 = \$.09$ savings per taco

16. (2) 375 mi.

$$\frac{2}{75} = \frac{10}{m}$$
$$2m = 75 \times 10$$
$$m = \frac{75 \times \overset{5}{10}}{\underset{1}{2}} = 375$$

Lesson 22
Percent I
Pages 176–183
Mental Math Exercises

1. $\frac{1}{2}$		**5.** $\frac{3}{5}$
2. $\frac{3}{4}$		**6.** $\frac{2}{5}$
3. $\frac{1}{5}$		**7.** $\frac{1}{3}$
4. $\frac{1}{10}$		**8.** $\frac{1}{8}$

Lesson

1. a) 40; 4; 0.4   d) 300; 300; 300

b) 100; 10; 1   e) 2,000; 200; 20

c) 500; 50; 5   f) 1,500; 10; 15

2. a) $x = 9$ f) $k = 0.69$

b) $g = 9.1$ g) $x\% = 10\%$

c) $p = 8.9$ h) $n\% = 100\%$

d) $n = 0.7$ i) $p\% = 1\%$

e) $h = 0.71$

Lesson 22 continued

3. a) 20, 10, 5

   b) 120, 50%, 30

   c) 80, 80, 80

4. a) $x = 4$

   b) $b = 8$

   c) $n = 6$

   d) $c = 8$

   e) $t = 40$

   f) $w = 60$

   g) $x\% = 50\%$

   h) $n\% = 25\%$

   i) $p\% = 20\%$

5. a) 30, 60, 90

   b) 9, 18, 300%

   c) 150, 200%, 300%

6. a) $c = 16, d = 8, n = 24, t = 64, x = 128$

   b) $m = 2, b = 4, p = 22, s = 24$

   c) 10%, 20%, 30%

   50%, 25%, 75%

   d) 100; 200; 900; 1,800

7. a) $\frac{90}{100} = \frac{9}{10}$; true

   b) $\frac{75}{100} \neq \frac{70}{96}$; false

   c) $\frac{15}{100} = \frac{6}{40}$; true

   d) $\frac{40}{100} = \frac{30}{75}$; true

   e) $\frac{2}{100} \neq \frac{18}{90}$; false

   f) $\frac{110}{100} \neq \frac{50}{40}$; false

   g) $\frac{200}{100} \neq \frac{20}{40}$; false

   h) $\frac{300}{100} = \frac{36}{12}$; true

8. a) $\frac{65}{100} = \frac{n}{120}$

   $100 \times n = 65 \times 120$

   $n = \frac{65 \times 120}{100}$

   $n = 78$

   b) $\frac{x}{100} = \frac{70}{105}$

   $105 \times x = 70 \times 100$

   $x = \frac{70 \times 100}{105}$

   $x\% = 66\frac{2}{3}\%$

   c) $\frac{75}{100} = \frac{45}{p}$

   Simplify: $\frac{3}{4} = \frac{45}{p}$ OR Looking across:

   $3 \times p = 45 \times 4$ $3 \times 15 = 45$
   So, $4 \times 15 = 60$

   $p = \frac{45 \times 4}{3}$

   $p = 60$

d) $\frac{35}{100} = \frac{s}{80}$

   Simplify: $\frac{7}{20} = \frac{s}{80}$ OR Looking across:

   $20 \times s = 7 \times 80$ $20 \times 4 = 80$
   So, $7 \times 4 = 28$

   $s = \frac{7 \times 80}{20}$

   $s = 28$

e) $\frac{105}{100} = \frac{42}{b}$

   Simplify: $\frac{21}{20} = \frac{42}{b}$ OR Looking across:

   $21 \times b = 42 \times 20$ $21 \times 2 = 42$
   So, $20 \times 2 = 40$

   $b = \frac{{}^2\!\cancel{42} \times 20}{\cancel{21}_1}$

   $b = 40$

f) $\frac{t}{100} = \frac{9}{72}$

   $72 \times t = 9 \times 100$

   $t = \frac{{}^1\!\cancel{9} \times 100}{\cancel{72}_8}$

   $t\% = 12\frac{1}{2}\%$

g) $\frac{52}{100} = \frac{f}{150}$

   $100 \times f = 52 \times 150$

   $f = \frac{52 \times \cancel{150}^3}{\cancel{100}_2} = \frac{156}{2}$

   $f = 78$

h) $\frac{250}{100} = \frac{10}{d}$

   Simplify: $\frac{5}{2} = \frac{10}{d}$ OR Looking across:

   $5 \times d = 2 \times 10$ $5 \times 2 = 10$
   So, $2 \times 2 = 4$

   $d = \frac{2 \times \cancel{10}^2}{\cancel{5}_1}$

   $d = 4$

i) $\frac{36}{100} = \frac{252}{n}$

   $36 \times n = 252 \times 100$

   $n = \frac{{}^7\cancel{252} \times 100}{\cancel{36}_1}$

   $n = 700$

j) $\frac{m}{100} = \frac{200}{125}$

   Simplify: $\frac{m}{100} = \frac{8}{5}$ OR Looking across:

   $5 \times m = 8 \times 100$ $5 \times 20 = 100$
   So, $8 \times 20 = 160$

   $m = \frac{8 \times \cancel{100}^{20}}{\cancel{5}_1}$

   $m\% = 160\%$

9. a) 10% of $46 = m$

   b) $1.47 = x\%$ of $21.00

   c) 11% of $c = 2,200$

d) $12,000 = n\%$ of $80,000

e) 20% of $85 = p

f) $12 = p\%$ of 30

10. a) $c = 135$

$$90\% \times 150 = c$$

$$.90 \times 150 = 135$$

b) $x = 60$

$$125\% \times 48 = x$$

$$1\tfrac{1}{4} \times 48 = (48 \times 1) + (48 \times \tfrac{1}{4}) = x$$

$$x = 48 + 12 = 60$$

c) $x\% = 62\tfrac{1}{2}\%$

$$55 = x\% \times 88$$

$$\frac{55}{88} = x\%$$

$$\frac{55 \div 11}{88 \div 11} = \frac{5}{8} = 62\tfrac{1}{2}\%$$

d) $n\% = 125\%$

$$2,000 = n\% \times 1,600$$

$$\frac{2,000}{1,600} = n\%$$

$$\frac{5}{4} = n\%$$

$$\frac{5}{4} = 125\%$$

e) $y = 240$

$$80 = 33\tfrac{1}{3}\% \times y$$

$$\frac{80}{\tfrac{1}{3}} = 80 \div \tfrac{1}{3} = y$$

$$\frac{80}{1} \times \frac{3}{1} = 240$$

f) $b = 20$

$$250\% \times b = 50$$

$$b = \frac{50}{2\tfrac{1}{2}} = 50 \div 2\tfrac{1}{2}$$

$$b = 50 \div \frac{5}{2}$$

$$b = 50 \times \frac{2}{5} = 20$$

11. a) 4.6 ounces

$$10\% \times 46 = m$$

〔1〕〔0〕〔×〕〔4〕〔6〕〔%〕〔 4.6 〕

b) 7%

$$\$1.47 = x\% \times \$21$$

$$\$1.47 \div \$21 = x\%$$

〔1〕〔·〕〔4〕〔7〕〔÷〕〔2〕〔1〕〔%〕〔 7 〕

c) 20,000 people

$$11\% \times c = 2,200$$

$$c = 2,200 \div 11\%$$

〔2〕〔2〕〔0〕〔0〕〔÷〕〔1〕〔1〕〔%〕〔 20000 〕

d) 15%

$$\$12,000 = n\% \times \$80,000$$

$$12,000 \div 80,000 = n\%$$

〔1〕〔2〕〔0〕〔0〕〔0〕〔÷〕〔8〕〔0〕〔0〕〔0〕〔0〕〔%〕〔15〕

e) $17

$$20\% \times \$85 = p$$

〔2〕〔0〕〔×〕〔8〕〔5〕〔%〕〔 17 〕

f) 40%

$$12 = p\% \times 30$$

$$12 \div 30 = p\%$$

〔1〕〔2〕〔÷〕〔3〕〔0〕〔%〕〔 40 〕

Check Your Understanding

1. a) 35   **f)** 125

b) 12   **g)** 4.5

c) 75   **h)** 45

d) 20   **i)** 80

e) 0   **j)** 12

2. a) $\frac{20}{100} = \frac{4}{20}$; true   **f)** $\frac{250}{100} = \frac{30}{12}$; true

b) $\frac{30}{100} = \frac{9}{30}$; true   **g)** $\frac{1}{100} \neq \frac{3}{3,000}$; false

c) $\frac{40}{100} = \frac{16}{40}$; true   **h)** $\frac{110}{100} \neq \frac{95}{85}$; false

d) $\frac{80}{100} \neq \frac{35}{45}$; false   **i)** $\frac{75}{100} \neq \frac{8}{12}$; false

e) $\frac{10}{100} \neq \frac{2.15}{215}$; false

3. 6% of $90,000 = c

$$c = \$5,400$$

4. 25% of $78.00 = d

$$d = \$19.50$$

5. $20 = 80\%$ of t

$$t = 25$$

6. 5% of $s = 200$

$$s = \$4,000$$

7. $175 = x\%$ of 250

$$x\% = 70\%$$

8. $88 = p\%$ of 400

$p\% = 22\%$

9. 40% of $900 = c$

$c = \$360$

10. $36 = 90\%$ of d

$d = 40$

11. **(3)** 10%

$50 = x\%$ of 500

$x\% = 10\%$

Skill Maintenance

Lessons 20–22

Pages 184–185

Part One

1. $\dfrac{\text{women}}{\text{men}} = \dfrac{45}{75} = \dfrac{3}{5}$

2. $\dfrac{\text{women}}{\text{total employees}} = \dfrac{45}{120}$ OR $\dfrac{3}{8}$

3. minorities $= 30\%$ of 120

$10\% = 12$, so $30\% = 36$ minority employees

4. executives $= 20\%$ of 120

$10\% = 12$, so $20\% = 24$ executive employees

5. $\dfrac{\text{executives}}{\text{total employees}} = \dfrac{24}{120}$ OR $\dfrac{1}{5}$ which is 20%

6. $\dfrac{\text{favor health plan}}{\text{total employees}} = \dfrac{x}{120} = \dfrac{2}{3}$

$3x = 120 \times 2$ OR Looking across:
$120 = 3 \times 40$
$x = \dfrac{\overset{40}{120} \times 2}{\underset{1}{3}} = 80$ $x = 2 \times 40$
$x = 80$
80 favor health plan

7.

gallons paint	3	$4\frac{1}{2}$	6	$7\frac{1}{2}$	9	$10\frac{1}{2}$
# rooms	2	3	4	5	6	7

8.
a) 12 ounces
b) $1\frac{1}{2}$ pints
c) $2\frac{1}{2}$ pounds
d) $4\frac{1}{2}$ cups
e) 4 cups

9.
a) T
b) T
c) F
d) T

10. 345 labels

10% of $1{,}150 = 115$

30% of $1{,}150 = 3 \times 115 = 345$

Part Two

1. **(5)** 4

$\dfrac{\frac{3}{4}}{1} = \dfrac{3}{x}$

3 in. $\div \dfrac{3}{4} = \dfrac{\overset{1}{3}}{1} \times \dfrac{4}{\underset{1}{3}} = 4$ ft.

2. **(2)** 5:1

$\dfrac{\text{enlisted}}{\text{officers}} = \dfrac{120 - 20}{20} = \dfrac{100}{20} = 5{:}1$

3. **(4)** 200

$\dfrac{1}{35} = \dfrac{x}{7{,}000}$

$35x = 1 \times 7{,}000$

$x = \boxed{\dfrac{7{,}000}{35}} = 200$

4. **(2)** $\dfrac{3}{5} = \dfrac{2.88}{x}$

5. **(3)** $\$4{,}400$

4% of $110{,}000 = x$

$1\% = \$1{,}100$

$4\% = \$4{,}400$

6. **(2)** 12%

$\dfrac{\text{union members}}{\text{total employees}} = \dfrac{30}{250} = \dfrac{x}{100}$

$250x = 30 \times 100$

$x = \dfrac{30 \times 100}{250} = \dfrac{3000}{250} = 12\%$

7. **(5)** 2 cups

$\dfrac{\text{ammonia}}{\text{detergent}} = \dfrac{1\frac{1}{2}}{\frac{1}{4}} = \dfrac{12}{x}$

$1\frac{1}{2}x = 12 \times \dfrac{1}{4}$

$1\frac{1}{2}x = 3$

$x = 3 \div 1\frac{1}{2} = 3 \div \dfrac{3}{2}$

$x = \overset{1}{3} \times \dfrac{2}{\underset{1}{3}} = 2$

Lesson 23

Percent II

Pages 186–193

Mental Math Exercises

1. $x = 10$

2. $k = 10$

3. $n = 7$

4. $m = 7.5$

5. $p = 50$

6. $k = 30$

Lesson

1. Your estimates should be close to these.

   a) $p \approx 9$

   11% of 90 $\approx$ 10% $\times$ 90 = 9

   b) $m \approx 30$

   27% of 120 $\approx$ 25% $\times$ 120 = 30

   c) $b \approx 8$

   20% of 37 $\approx$ 20% $\times$ 40 = 8

   d) $x \approx 67$

   98% of 67 $\approx$ 100% $\times$ 67 = 67

   e) $k \approx 1,500$

   296% of 500 $\approx$ 300% $\times$ 500 = 1,500

   f) $n \approx 110$

   9% of 1,099 $\approx$ 10% $\times$ 1,100 = 110

   g) $w \approx 32$

   48% of 64 $\approx$ 50% $\times$ 64 = 32

   h) $v \approx 22$

   32% of 66 $\approx$ 33$\frac{1}{3}$% $\times$ 66 = $\frac{1}{3}$ $\times$ 66 = 22

   i) $d \approx 4$

   0.8% of 400 $\approx$ 1% $\times$ 400 = 4

   j) $c \approx 11$

   25% of 45 $\approx$ 25% $\times$ 44 = $\frac{1}{4}$ $\times$ 44 = 11

2. a) 9.9   f) 98.91

   b) 32.4   g) 30.72

   c) 7.4   h) 21.12

   d) 65.66   i) 3.2

   e) 1,480   j) 11.25

3. Your estimates should be close to these.

   a) $.75

   $4.88 \approx $5.00

   $.50 + $.25 = $.75

   b) $1.65

   $11.31 \approx $11.00

   $1.10 + $.55 = $1.65

   c) $2.70

   $17.65 \approx $18.00

   $1.80 + $.90 = $2.70

   d) $3.60

   $24.05 \approx $24.00

   $2.40 + $1.20 = $3.60

   e) $4.80

   $31.72 \approx $32

   $3.20 + $1.60 = $4.80

4. Estimate:

   $31 \approx $30

   $30 $\times$ 15% = $4.50

   $31 + $4.50 \approx $35.50

   $35.50 \approx $36 $\div$ 6 = $6

   Each person should pay $6.

5. Your estimates may vary from these. Make sure they are reasonable.

   a) $\frac{102}{400} \approx \frac{100}{400} = \frac{1}{4} = 25\%$

   b) $\frac{30}{147} \approx \frac{30}{150} = \frac{1}{5} = 20\%$

   c) $\frac{95}{50} \approx \frac{100}{50} = \frac{2}{1} = 200\%$

   d) $\frac{8}{83} \approx \frac{8}{80} = \frac{1}{10} = 10\%$

   e) $\frac{0.9}{100} \approx \frac{1}{100} = 1\%$

   f) $\frac{398}{500} \approx \frac{400}{500} = \frac{4}{5} = 80\%$

   g) $\frac{52}{75} \approx \frac{50}{75} = \frac{2}{3} = 66\frac{2}{3}\%$

   h) $\frac{1.00}{9.95} \approx \frac{1}{10} = 10\%$

   i) $\frac{1.50}{3.09} \approx \frac{1.50}{3.00} = \frac{1}{2} = 50\%$

   j) $\frac{19.00}{98.59} \approx \frac{20.00}{100.00} = \frac{1}{5} = 20\%$

6. $\frac{4.00}{19.45} \approx \frac{4}{20} = \frac{1}{5} = 20\%$

7. $\frac{24}{35} \approx \frac{24}{36} = \frac{2}{3} = 66\frac{2}{3}\%$

8. Use $i = prt$; $t = 1$.

	500	1,000	1,500	2,000
6%	$30	$60	$90	$120
12%	$60	$120	$180	$240

9. Use $i = prt$; t = $\frac{1}{2}$.

	500	1,000	1,500	2,000
6%	$15	$30	$45	$60
12%	$30	$60	$90	$120

10. a) 0.065

   $100 $\times$ .065 = $6.50

b) 0.075

$100 \times .075 = \$7.50$

c) 0.1025

$100 \times .1025 = \$10.25$

d) 0.0825

$100 \times .0825 = \$8.25$

e) 0.066

$100 \times .066 = \$6.60$

11. a) $100\% - 80\% = 20\%$

b) $100\% - 70\% = 30\%$

c) $100\% - 40\% = 60\%$

d) $100\% - 50\% - 28\% = 22\%$

e) $100\% - 19\% = 81\%$

f) $100\% - 95\% = 5\%$

5% of $40 = \frac{1}{20} \times 40 = 2$

g) $100\% - 25\% = 75\%$

75% of $28 = \frac{3}{4} \times 28 = \$21$

12.

Marked Price ($)	Discount ($)	Sale Price ($)
50	$0.30 \times 50 = 15$	$50 - 15 = 35$
60	$0.30 \times 60 = 18$	$60 - 18 = 42$
70	$0.30 \times 70 = 21$	$70 - 21 = 49$
80	$0.30 \times 80 = 24$	$80 - 24 = 56$
p	$0.30p$	$p - 0.30p$

13.

Depreciation ($)	Value After 1 year ($)
$0.20 \times 8,000 = 1,600$	$8,000 - 1,600 = 6,400$
$0.20 \times 9,000 = 1,800$	$9,000 - 1,800 = 7,200$
$0.20 \times 10,000 = 2,000$	$10,000 - 2,000 = 8,000$
$0.20v$	$v - 0.20v$

14. $100\% - 20\% = 80\%$

80% of $\$8,000 = \$6,400$

80% of $\$9,000 = \$7,200$

80% of $\$10,000 = \$8,000$

80% of $v = 0.80v$

15. $100\% - 6\% = 94\%$

94% of $30,000 = 28,200$

OR

6% of $30,000 = 1,800$

$30,000 - 1,800 = 28,200$

16.

Sales Tax ($)	Total ($)
$0.07 \times 40.00 = 2.80$	$40.00 + 2.80 = 42.80$
$0.07 \times 60.00 = 4.20$	$60.00 + 4.20 = 64.20$
$0.07 \times 100.00 = 7$	$100.00 + 7.00 = 107.00$
$0.07 \times 1,000.00 = 70$	$1,000.00 + 70.00 = 1,070.00$
$0.07p$	$p + 0.07p = 1.07p$

17. $107\% \times \$40 = \$42.80$

$107\% \times \$60 = \$64.20$

$107\% \times \$100 = \$107$

$107\% \times \$1,000 = \$1,070$

$107\% \times p = 1.07p$

18. 104% of $\$350 = \$364$

19. 175% of $40,000 = 70,000$

20. 200% of $\$180 = \$360$

21. a) $40 = x\%$ of 500

$\frac{40 \div 5}{500 \div 5} = \frac{8}{100} = 8\%$

b) $7,000 - 5,250 = 1,750$

$1,750 = x\%$ of $7,000$

$\frac{1,750 \div 70}{7,000 \div 70} = \frac{25}{100} = \frac{1}{4} = 25\%$

c) $360 - 320 = 40$

$40 = x\%$ of 320

$\frac{40 \div 40}{320 \div 40} = \frac{1}{8} = 12\frac{1}{2}\%$

d) $440 - 330 = 110$

$110 = x\%$ of 440

$\frac{110}{440} = \frac{1}{4} = 25\%$

e) $5 - 4 = 1$

$1 = x\%$ of 4

$\frac{1}{4} = 25\%$

f) Estimate: $76,838 - 69,717 \approx$

$77,000 - 70,000 = 7,000$

$7,000 = x\%$ of $70,000$

$\frac{7,000}{70,000} = \frac{1}{10} = 10\%$

Check Your Understanding

1. Your estimates may vary from these, but they should be reasonable.

a) $n = 48\%$ of $32 \approx 50\% \times 32 = \underline{16}$

b) $p = 25\%$ of $811 \approx 25\% \times 800 = \underline{200}$

c) $98 = x\%$ of $200 \approx 100 = \underline{50\%} \times 200$

d) $98 = x\%$ of $498 \approx 100 = \underline{20}\% \times 500$

e) $m = 19\%$ of $75 \approx 20\% \times 75 = \underline{15}$

f) $c = 8.9\%$ of $480 \approx 10\% \times 480 = \underline{48}$

g) $\$2.99 = x\%$ of $\$4.99 \approx \$3 = \underline{60}\% \times \$5$

h) $\$19.75 = x\%$ of $58.67 \approx \$20 = \underline{33\tfrac{1}{3}}\% \times \$60$

i) $t = 6\%$ of $\$47.50 \approx 6\%$ of $\$50 = \$\underline{3}$

j) $35 = x\%$ of $600 \approx 36 = \underline{6}\%$ of 600

2. a) 0.03   **f)** 0.01

   b) 0.035   **g)** 0.005

   c) 0.30   **h)** 0.005

   d) 0.35   **i)** 0.0075

   e) 3.50   **j)** 0.0075

3. $100\% - 54\% = 46\%$

4. $6\tfrac{1}{4}\% + \tfrac{1}{2}\% = 6\tfrac{1}{4}\% + \tfrac{2}{4}\% = 6\tfrac{3}{4}\%$

5. $12 \times 1\tfrac{1}{2}\% = 18\%$

6. Estimate: $75\% \times \$188.88 \approx$

$75\% \times 200 = \$150$

7. $\$800 - \$560 = \$240$

$\$240 = x\%$ of $\$800$

$\dfrac{240}{800} = x\%$

$\dfrac{240 \div 8}{800 \div 8} = \dfrac{30}{100} = 30\%$

8. 200%

9. $100\% - 21\% = 79\%$

79% of $\$1,500 = \$1,185$

10. $\dfrac{\$360 \div 30}{\$3,000 \div 30} = \dfrac{12}{100} = 12\%$

11. (4) $\$21,000 + 0.10(\$21,000)$

Lesson 24
Relating Rates and Slopes to Graphs
Pages 194–201
Mental Math Exercises

1. $-2 = x$ **6.** $7 = u$

2. $-8 = y$ **7.** $-7 = v$

3. $-3 = r$ **8.** $-4 = m$

4. $-11 = s$ **9.** $-8 = n$

5. $-7 = t$ **10.** $4 = k$

Lesson

1. $\dfrac{\text{rise}}{\text{run}} = \dfrac{3}{1} = 3$

2. You may have chosen any two points. The slope would be the same.

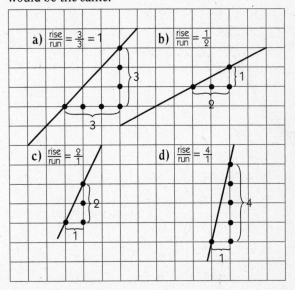

3. You may have chosen any two points. The slope would be the same.

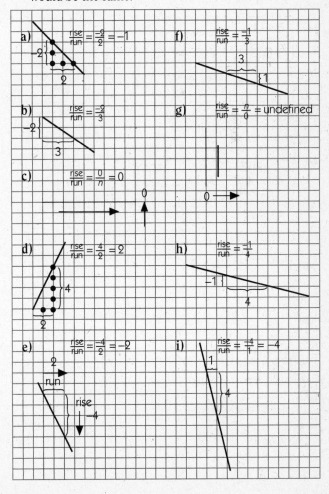

4. Yes. The slopes are the same.

$$m = \frac{3 - 1}{5 - 9} = \frac{2}{-4} = \frac{1}{-2} = -\frac{1}{2}$$

5.

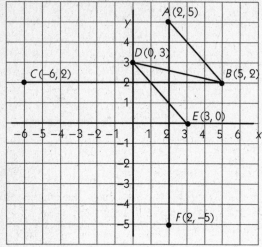

6. a) $m = \dfrac{5 - 2}{2 - 5} = -1$

b) You can see that this line is horizontal, so the slope is 0.

$$m = \frac{2 - 2}{-6 - 5} = \frac{0}{-11} = 0$$

c) $m = \dfrac{3 - 0}{0 - 3} = \dfrac{3}{-3} = -1$

d) You can see that this line is vertical, so the slope is undefined.

$$m = \frac{-5 - 5}{2 - 2} = \frac{-10}{0} = \text{undefined}$$

e) $m = \dfrac{3 - 2}{0 - 5} = \dfrac{1}{-5}$ OR $-\dfrac{1}{5}$

7.

# of Servings	1	2	4	6	8	10
# of Ounces	0.5	1	2	3	4	5

8. a) 2.5 (between the 2 oz. and 3 oz. marks)

b) 4.5 (between the 4 oz. and 5 oz. marks)

c) about 8.5

9. $o = 0.5s$

$o = 0.5(50)$

$o = 25$ oz.

10.

Servings	1	2	4	6	8
Calories	90	180	360	540	720

11.

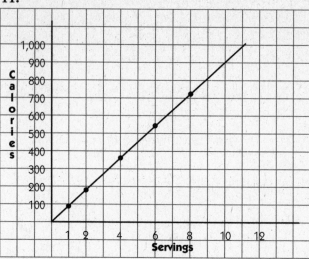

12. a) about 270

b) 5

c) about 11

13. $c = 90s$

14. $c = 90 (8.5)$

$c = 765$ calories; yes, this answer corresponds to the graph in problem 11.

15. Using (4, 360) and (2, 180):

$$m = \frac{360 - 180}{4 - 2} = \frac{180}{2} = 90$$

The slope of the line (90) is the same as the number of calories per serving.

16. and **17.**

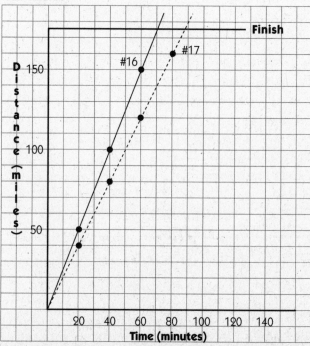

18. Estimating from the graph,

blue: 70 min.; red: 85 min.

19. blue: $m = \dfrac{100 - 50}{40 - 20} = \dfrac{50}{20} = 2.5$

red: $m = \dfrac{80 - 40}{40 - 20} = \dfrac{40}{20} = 2$

The blue car's line is steeper.

20. a) blue: 2.5 miles per min. × 60 min. = 150 miles per hour

red: 2 miles per min. × 60 min. = 120 miles per hour

b) blue: $d = 150t$

red: $d = 120t$

Check Your Understanding
1.

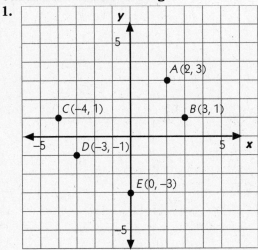

2. For these, you could use either the graph or the formula, $m = \dfrac{y_2 - y_1}{x_2 - x_1}$

a) $m = \dfrac{3 - 1}{2 - 3} = \dfrac{2}{-1} = -2$

b) $m = \dfrac{1 - 3}{3 - 2} = \dfrac{-2}{1} = -2$

c) horizontal line: $m = 0$

d) $m = \dfrac{1 - 3}{-4 - 2} = \dfrac{-2}{-6} = \dfrac{1}{3}$

e) $m = \dfrac{-1 - 1}{-3 - 3} = \dfrac{-2}{-6} = \dfrac{1}{3}$

3.

Inches	1	2	4	6	8
Centimeters	2.5	5.0	10.0	15.0	20.0

4.

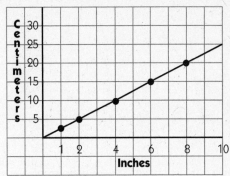

5. a) The steeper (top) line shows Jerry's trip.

b) about 10 minutes

c) Recognizing that the slope of the line is the same as the rate, the slope of Jerry's line is 70, and his mother's is 55.

6. the tortoise and the hare

7. (2) −1

$m = \dfrac{5 - 0}{0 - 5} = \dfrac{5}{-5} = -1$

Lesson 25
Checkpoint IV
Pages 202–209

1. (1) 7%

100% − 93% = 7%

2. (3) 7°

−11° + 18° = 7°

3. (2) 6 and 7

$\sqrt{36} = 6$ and $\sqrt{49} = 7$

4. (5) 20 − 8(1.37)

5. (5) (3, −2)

From the origin, go 3 to the right and 2 down.

6. (3) 4

The diameter is the entire distance across the circle.

7. (2) 12.56

$C = \pi d$

$C = 3.14 \times 4 \approx 3 \times 4 = 12$

12 is closest to choice **(2)** 12.56.

8. (3) $11.60

116 × .10 = $11.60

9. (4) $9,000

$i = prt$

$i = \$20,000 \times .09 \times 5 = \$9,000$

10. (1) $\dfrac{20 - 16}{20}$

11. (2) $s = \dfrac{w}{16}$

12. (2) 45°

$180° - 135° = 45°$

13. (5) Not enough information is given. To set up a ratio to solve this problem, you would need to know the length of one of the other sides of each triangle.

14. (3) c only

20% of $50 = $10, so the savings would have to be on an item priced at more than $50.

15. (4) $87\frac{1}{2}\%$

$\dfrac{42}{48} \div \dfrac{6}{6} = \dfrac{7}{8} = 87\frac{1}{2}\%$

16. (2) 32 in.

$\dfrac{2}{5} = \dfrac{x}{80}$

$5x = 80 \times 2$

$x = \dfrac{\overset{16}{\cancel{80}} \times 2}{\underset{1}{\cancel{5}}} = 32$

17. (4) $3\frac{1}{2}$ hours

Step 1: $10\frac{1}{2} \times 20 = (10 \times 20) + \frac{1}{2}(20)$

$200 + 10 = 210$ min.

Step 2: $\dfrac{210}{60} = 3\frac{1}{2}$ hr.

18. (3) $322.50

Step 1: Find the sale price.

$\$400 - .25(\$400) =$

$\$400 - \frac{1}{4}(\$400) =$ OR $\frac{3}{4}(\$400) = \$300$

$\$400 - \$100 = \$300$

Step 2: Add the sales tax.

$\$300 \times 7\frac{1}{2}\% \approx$

$\$300 \times .07 = \$21$

$\$300 + \$21 = \$321$

This answer is closest to choice **(3)** $322.50.

19. (3) 9

$\dfrac{80 \text{ hr.}}{9 \text{ hr.}} \approx \dfrac{81}{9} = 9$

20. (1) 24

$\dfrac{1 \text{ kWh}}{20 \text{ min.}} = \dfrac{x \text{ hr.}}{8 \text{ hr.}}$

20 min. $= \frac{1}{3}$ hr., so

$\dfrac{1}{\frac{1}{3}} = \dfrac{x}{8}$

$\frac{1}{3}x = 8$

$x = 8 \times 3 = 24$

21. (4) $6(12) + 16.4$

22. (2) 1:18

$1\frac{1}{2}$ ft. = 18 inches

23. (5) $8n$

24. (3) 10

Start at $2.00 on the vertical axis. Go to the right, to the line, then drop down to the bottom axis. You are at the value halfway between 8 and 12, or 10.

25. (2) $\dfrac{4}{12} = \dfrac{0.80}{c}$

26. (5) $6.40

There are many ways to solve this problem. One is:

Step 1: 2 lb. = 32 oz.

Step 2: $\dfrac{4 \text{ oz.}}{\$.80} = \dfrac{32 \text{ oz.}}{x}$

$4x = 32 \times .80$

$x = \dfrac{\overset{8}{\cancel{32}} \times .80}{\underset{1}{\cancel{4}}} = 6.40$

27. (3) 10 ft.

$6^2 + 8^2 = c^2$

$36 + 64 = c^2$

$\sqrt{100} = c$

$10 = c$

28. (4) 0.02%

Lesson 26

Data Analysis

Pages 210–221

Lesson

1. Questionnaire responses will vary.

2. Answers will vary depending on responses to questionnaires.

3. These graphs show only the information from the book's questionnaires.

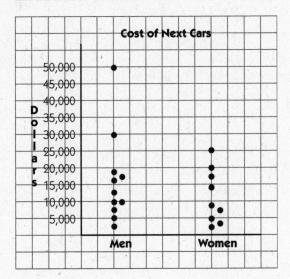

4. **a)** Answers will vary.

   b) The median, the middle number, would seem the most representative. Either the mode or the mean could be the least representative.

5. mode = $4,000

   mean $= \dfrac{\$4,000 + \$13,000 + \$4,000 + \$10,000 + \$8,000}{5} = \$7,800$

   median = $8,000

6. All of the responses given for the "next" car category were relatively close in value. There are no outliers, so both the median and mean are representative.

7. A few very high prices or very high incomes would have an undue effect on the *mean*. The median value indicates that it is in the middle; there are just as many values higher than the median as lower.

8. **a)** dream car: $250,000 − $30,000 = $220,000

   b) next car: $13,000 − $4,000 = $9,000

9. **a)** dream car: $90,000 − $20,000 = $70,000

   b) next car: $50,000 − $8,000 = $42,000

10. range = $250,000 − $20,000 = $230,000

    mean $= \dfrac{\$1,480,000}{20} = \$74,000$

    mode = $50,000 (occurs 4 times)

    median = $60,000

11. range = $50,000 − $2,500 = $47,500

    mean $= \dfrac{\$283,500}{20} = \$14,175$

    mode: No mode exists because many values occur 2 times at most.

    median $= \dfrac{\$10,000 + \$13,000}{2} = \$11,500$

12. The *dream car* median was $60,000, much higher than $15,000. This could be explained by the fact that dream cars are generally more expensive than the average car that is sold. The *next car* median was $11,500, lower than $15,000. This difference could be explained by the fact that many respondents said they would buy a used car next.

13. Your answers may vary from these.

    a) Automotive magazine subscribers are interested in cars and are so well informed that the mean and median for their choices of a dream car would be higher than the averages in the example. They would also probably spend more money on their next car than the typical person would.

    b) People leaving an auto show would be exposed to the newest and best models and might be excited by the prospect of owning one. Therefore, the mean and median would probably be higher for this group.

    c) Nurses, teachers, and social workers are not known for their interest in flashy cars, nor do their salaries allow them to own one. Therefore, the mean and median for dream cars and next cars would probably be lower.

14. a) mean = $120,000

b) mean = $111,667

c) $120,000 is greater than $114,000. The mean rose because you added a value that was higher than the original mean of $114,000. $111,667 is less than $114,000. The mean decreased because you added a value that was less than the original mean of $114,000.

15. a) mean = $81,429

b) Increasing the number of values (the number you are dividing by) decreases the mean. Refer to "What happens when you divide?" in Lesson 9.

16. $\text{mean} = \dfrac{\text{sum of values}}{\text{number of values}}$

$12 = \dfrac{96}{n}$

$n = \dfrac{96}{12}$

$n = 8$

17. $5 = \dfrac{\text{sum}}{20}$

$\text{sum} = 5 \times 20$

$\text{sum} = 100$

18. Step 1: Find the sum if the average is 19.

$\dfrac{\text{sum}}{4} = 19$

$\text{sum} = 19 \times 4 = 76$

Step 2: Find the value needed to achieve that sum.

$76 - (25 + 13 + 17) = x$

$76 - 55 = x$

$21 = x$

19. Step 1: Find the sum if the average is 200.

$\dfrac{\text{sum}}{5} = 200$

$\text{sum} = 200 \times 5 = 1{,}000$

Step 2: Find the values needed to achieve that sum.

$1{,}000 - (185 + 150 + 230 + 183) = x$

$1{,}000 - 748 = x$

$252 = x$

20. 15–20: $\dfrac{12{,}500}{3} = 4{,}166.67 \approx \$4{,}000$

21–30: $\dfrac{39{,}000}{5} = 7{,}800 \approx \$8{,}000$

31–40: $\dfrac{107{,}000}{6} = 17{,}833.33 \approx \$18{,}000$

41+: $\dfrac{125{,}000}{6} = 20{,}833.33 \approx \$21{,}000$

21. Each interval represents $5,000.

22.

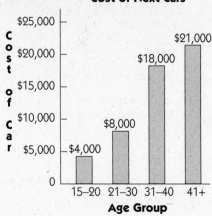

Cost of Next Cars

23. 21–30

24. 41+

25. 41+

26. a) true   **d)** could be true

b) false   **e)** could be true

c) true

27. no

28. the one on the right

29. the one on the left

30. the one on the right

Check Your Understanding

1. a) mean: $\dfrac{\$424{,}000}{8} = \$53{,}000$

mode: $18,000

median: $\dfrac{\$18{,}000 + \$20{,}000}{2} = \$19{,}000$

b) Use either the mode or the median. These are both smaller than the mean of $53,000.

c) The mean of $53,000 would imply that most salaries were around that amount.

2. They choose a sample that is representative of the entire population of TV viewers.

3. $\dfrac{2{,}600 \text{ miles}}{4 \text{ days}} = 650$ miles per day

4.
a) men—dream cars: $\dfrac{\$970,000}{11} \approx \$88,000$

next cars: $\dfrac{\$181,000}{11} \approx \$16,000$

women—dream cars: $\dfrac{\$510,000}{9} \approx \$57,000$

next cars: $\dfrac{\$102,500}{9} \approx \$11,000$

b)

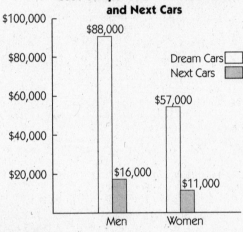

Cost Comparison for Dream Cars and Next Cars

4. and 5.

Reason	Age				Total	Fractional Part	Percent
	15–20	21–30	31–40	41+			
Dream Cars							
1. styling	//	////	////	//////	16	$\frac{2}{5}$	40%
2. cost					0	0	0
3. power	///	///	/	//	9	$\frac{9}{40}$	22.5%
4. comfort			//	/	3	$\frac{3}{40}$	7.5%
5. quality	/	//	////	///	10	$\frac{1}{4}$	25%
6. capacity		/		/	2	$\frac{1}{20}$	5%
Next Cars							
1. styling	//	/	//	//	7	$\frac{7}{40}$	17.5%
2. cost	///	////	///	///	13	$\frac{13}{40}$	32.5%
3. power		//	/	/	4	$\frac{1}{10}$	10%
4. comfort			/	//	3	$\frac{3}{40}$	7.5%
5. quality	/	/	//	////	8	$\frac{1}{5}$	20%
6. capacity		//	///		5	$\frac{1}{8}$	12.5%

Lesson 27
Circle Graphs and Probability
Pages 222–230
Lesson

1. a) dream car: styling

b) next car: cost

2. By asking them to choose their next car immediately after choosing their dream car, the questionnaire made the people focus on why they couldn't have the car they dreamed of—the cost.

3.

	Age				Fractional Part	Percent
	15–20	21–30	31–40	41+		
Dream Cars						
Foreign	2	4	5	4	$\frac{15}{20} = \frac{3}{4}$	75%
Domestic	1	1	1	2	$\frac{5}{20} = \frac{1}{4}$	25%
Next Cars						
Foreign	3	3	3	3	$\frac{12}{20} = \frac{3}{5}$	60%
Domestic	0	2	3	3	$\frac{8}{20} = \frac{2}{5}$	40%

6.

Reason	Dream Cars	Next Cars
styling	144°	63°
cost	0°	117°
power	81°	36°
comfort	27°	27°
quality	90°	72°
capacity	18°	45°

7. Check all angles based on problem 6.

8. dream cars: 40% + 25% + 22.5% + 7.5% + 5% = 100%

next cars: 32.5 % + 17.5%+ 12.5% + 20% + 7.5% + 10% = 100%

9. "People dream of owning cars that look nice, are well-built, and are powerful."

"People intend to buy cars that are economical, well-built, and look nice."

10.

Car Preferences

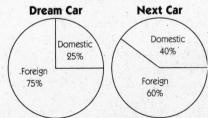

11. **a)** $\frac{1}{6}$ **c)** $\frac{2}{6}$ or $\frac{1}{3}$

    b) 0   **d)** $\frac{3}{6}$ or $\frac{1}{2}$

12. **a)** $\frac{1}{2}$ **c)** $\frac{1}{52}$

    b) $\frac{4}{52} = \frac{1}{13}$ **d)** $\frac{12}{52} = \frac{3}{13}$

13. $\frac{1}{4}$ of 20 = 5 times

14. $\frac{1}{2}$ of 100 = 50 times

15. **a)** $1 - \frac{1}{13} = \frac{12}{13}$ (4 cards $= \frac{4}{52} = \frac{1}{13}$)

    b) $1 - \frac{1}{52} = \frac{51}{52}$ (1 card)

16. **a)** $\frac{3}{3}$ or $\frac{1}{1}$ = even odds   **d)** $\frac{4}{2}$ or $\frac{2}{1}$

    b) $\frac{1}{3}$ **e)** $\frac{3}{1}$

    c) $\frac{4}{48}$ or $\frac{1}{12}$ **f)** $\frac{51}{1}$

17. $\frac{5}{5} - \frac{3}{5} = \frac{2}{5}$, or 40%

18. Answers will vary.

19. Answers will vary.

20. 20% or $\frac{1}{5}$

21. $\frac{10}{90} = \frac{1}{9}$

22. $\frac{7}{8}$ or 87.5%

23. No, the questionnaire allowed respondents to choose from only 6 reasons, and status was not one of them.

24. $\frac{1}{2} \times \frac{1}{2} \times \frac{1}{2} = \frac{1}{8}$

25. $\frac{1}{2}$ (The previous tosses do not affect the next toss.)

26. $\frac{3}{5} \times \frac{3}{5} = \frac{9}{25}$

Check Your Understanding

1. 100% − 54% = 46%

2. Answers will vary.

3. No, because the mean is not necessarily the middle number.

4. amount of increase = x% of original number

    10.5 = x% of 20

    $\frac{10.5}{20} \approx \frac{10}{20} = 50\%$

5. 100% − (24.2% + 16.2%) = 100% − 40.4% = 59.6%

6. 100% − (60% + 20%) = 100% − 80% = 20%

7. 100% − (12% + 42%) = 100% − 54% = 46%

8. $\frac{42}{20} \approx \frac{40}{20} = 2$ times

9. **(5)** $\frac{1}{5}$

    $\frac{200}{1,000} = \frac{1}{5}$

Lesson 28

GED Practice Test

Pages 231–245

1. **(4)** $\frac{5}{8}$

    $\frac{5}{8} = 62\frac{1}{2}\%$. If you did not remember this, you could have decided which fraction was between $\frac{1}{2}$ and $\frac{3}{4}$: $\frac{3}{8}$, $\frac{5}{8}$, or $\frac{7}{8}$?

    $\frac{5}{8}$ is more than 50% but less than 75%.

2. **(3)** −1

    Each tick mark represents 2. Point p is halfway between 0 and −2.

3. **(4)** 52

    16(2) + 5(4) = 32 + 20 = 52

4. **(4)** $6.92

    Estimate the price of gas as $1 per gallon: $20 − $12 = $8

    Since he paid more than $12, the exact answer must be less than $8: $20 − 12($1.09) = $6.92

5. **(2)** between 10 and 11 feet

    $10^2 = 100$, $11^2 = 121$

6. **(4)** 6,000

    $3 \times 20 \times 100 = 60 \times 100 = 6{,}000$

7. **(3)** 80 cm

    $\frac{20}{25} = \frac{x}{100}$

    $25x = 20 \times 100$

    $x = \frac{20 \times \overset{4}{\cancel{100}}}{\underset{1}{25}}$ OR   Looking across:

    $x = 80$ Since $25 \times 4 = 100$

                          Multiply $20 \times 4 = 80$

8. **(5)** Not enough information is given.

    To find the answer, you would need to know how many grams of milk are in the glass.

9. **(4)** 500 − (169 + 283)

    Order is important when writing subtraction problems. The amount to be taken away must be written second.

10. **(2)** 240

    $\frac{310 + 150 + 260}{3} = \frac{720}{3} = 240$

11. (4) $3.25

$$\frac{\text{cents}}{\text{cans}}: \frac{5}{2} = \frac{x}{130}$$

$$2x = 5 \times 130$$

$$x = \frac{5 \times 130}{2}$$

$$x = \frac{650}{2} = 325 \text{ cents} = \$3.25$$

12. (3) 40%

The entire circle represents 100%.

$$100\% - (30\% + 5\% + 25\%) =$$

$$100\% - 60\% = 40\%$$

13. (3) $125

10% of $2,500 = $250

$\frac{1}{2}$ of 10% of $2,500 = $125

14. (5) 150

$$\frac{3}{5} = \frac{x}{250}$$ OR   Looking across:

$3 \times 250 = 5x$ Since $5 \times 50 = 250$

$750 = 5x$ Multiply $3 \times 50 = 150$

$\frac{750}{5} = x$

$150 = x$

15. (1) $d - 85 = 308$

In time order, the original balance (d) minus the check (85) equals the remainder (308).

16. (5) b and c only

25% of $200 is $50. Both prices over $200 will qualify.

17. (3) Duluth

You can find this on the graph and the chart.

18. (5) Detroit

The range is the difference between the high and the low.

Detroit's range is the largest—from −15° to 15°, or 30°.

19. (1) 18°

By thinking of the two numbers, −3° and 15°, on a number line, you can visualize the difference between them as 18°.

20. (2) 3

First you can figure that it is 5 miles from José's house to the ballpark. Then, by subtracting (8 − 5), you can find that it is 3 miles from the ballpark to the restaurant.

21. (2) 232.8

Estimate that Vivian walks 10 miles each day:

$(31 - 7) \times 10 = 24 \times 10 = 240$ miles.

The closest answer is choice **(2)** 232.8 miles.

22. (5) $3(12) + 2(24) + 7$

This expression represents the cost of the 3 T-shirts plus the cost of the 2 pairs of shorts plus the shipping charge.

23. (3) 135

The relationship is $x = 2\frac{1}{4} \times$ number of seconds, so $x = 2\frac{1}{4} \times 60$.

$$x = 2(60) + \frac{1}{4}(60)$$

$$x = 120 + 15 = 135$$

Or, by using the graph, start at 60 on the horizontal axis, move straight up to the line, and go over to the left to approximately 135 on the vertical axis.

24. (1) 22

Estimate: $50 \div 2\frac{1}{4} \approx$

$50 \div 2 = 25$ seconds

25 seconds is closest to choice **(1)** 22.

Or you can look on the vertical axis to where 50 falls, go across to the line, and go down to the horizontal axis.

25. (2) the total number of hours you parked in the lot

You need to know the number of 24-hour periods plus the number of extra hours.

26. (5) $3\frac{1}{2}$ cups

You need to double the recipe:

$$2 \times 1\frac{3}{4} = (2 \times 1) + (2 \times \frac{3}{4}) =$$

$$2 + 1\frac{1}{2} = 3\frac{1}{2} \text{ cups}$$

27. (3) $\frac{64 \times 3}{24}$

This expression represents the total number of cans divided by the number of cans per case.

28. (3) 135°

$\angle ACB$ and the 45° angle make a straight angle that totals 180°, so $180° - 45° = 135°$.

29. (2) $10^2\pi$

$A = \pi r^2$ If $d = 20$, then $r = 10$.

$A = \pi10^2$ is the same as $A = 10^2\pi$.

30. (3) *AD*

The diameter extends from one side of the circle to the other, passing through the center.

31. (1) 3.02 in.

The acceptable range is $3 + 0.1 = 3.1$ to $3 - 0.1 = 2.9$. You know that $3.1 = 3.10$ and $2.9 = 2.90$. The only choice that falls within that range is **(1)** 3.02.

32. (3) 15

You may not have seen this type of problem. Think of it this way, and it becomes easy: *For each* skirt, Dorene can choose from 5 different tops. The number of combinations is $3 \times 5 = 15$.

33. (2) 9,000

$\underline{3}00 \times \underline{3}0 = 9,\underline{000}$

The number of people in the household is not needed to solve the problem.

34. (2) 81

Estimate: $2.7 \times 30 \approx 3 \times 30 = 90$

The exact answer will be a little less.

35. (4) $180° - (90° + 35°)$

Remember that the measure of a right angle is $90°$, and that the sum of the angles in a triangle is $180°$.

36. (3) 150 cm^2

$A = \frac{1}{2}bh$

$A = (\frac{1}{2} \cdot 20)\,15 = 10 \cdot 15 = 150$ cm^2

37. (1) *A*

$(-3, -1)$ is found by starting at the origin, moving 3 to the left, then down 1.

38. (2) 8 mph

$r = \dfrac{d}{t}$

$r = 2$ mi. $\div \frac{1}{4}$ hr.

$r = 2 \times 4 = 8$ mph

39. (3) $\dfrac{500}{x}$

This expression represents the total cost (in cents) divided by the cost per unit.

40. (4) $\frac{1}{2}$

$\dfrac{\text{rise}}{\text{run}} = \dfrac{4}{8} = \dfrac{1}{2}$

41. (4) $0.25\,(55,900 - 55,433)$

This solution shows the total miles traveled times 25¢ per mile.

42. (3) $20,150

Total income: $6,000 \times \$5 = \$30,000$

Estimated net profit: $\$30,000 - \$9,850 \approx$

$\$30,000 - \$10,000 = \$20,000$

Choice **(3)** $20,150 is a little more than $20,000.

43. (5) $\dfrac{1}{600}$

$\dfrac{10}{6,000} = \dfrac{1}{600}$

44. (2) 64

$2(12) + 2(20)$ or $2(12 + 20) = 64$

$\qquad \uparrow\ 25 - 13$

45. (4) 630

$(20 \times 12) + (30 \times 13) = 240 + 390 = 630$

OR $(30 \times 25) - (10 \times 12) =$

$750 - 120 = 630$

46. (4) 32

How many $\frac{5}{8}$s are there in 20?

$20 \div \frac{5}{8} = 20 \times \frac{8}{5} = 32$

You could also estimate that since $\frac{5}{8}$ is bigger than $\frac{1}{2}$, there would be fewer than 40 but more than 20.

47. (2) 21

$5^2 - 4 = 25 - 4 = 21$

48. (4) $w^2 = 16^2 + 12^2$

This requires the Pythagorean theorem, which was introduced in Lesson 11.

Since w is the longest side, use it for c (the longest side).

$c^2 = a^2 + b^2$

$w^2 = 16^2 + 12^2$

49. (5) $198

The Powers will *pay* $(100 - 56)\%$, or 44%, of $450. Estimate: this is less than $\frac{1}{2}$ of 450, or 198.

50. (1) $5,000 \times .12 \times 3$

Use the interest formula:

$i = prt$

$i = \$5,000 \times .12 \times 3$

51. (1) $\dfrac{6}{m} = \dfrac{9}{30}$

This proportion compares:

$\dfrac{\text{side}}{\text{side}} = \dfrac{\text{length}}{\text{length}}$

52. (4) $300

sale price = 80% of original price

$240 = 80\% \text{ of } x$

$240 = .80x$

$\dfrac{240}{.80} = x$

$300 = x$

53. (2) 9.6%

$\dfrac{1}{4}\% = 0.25\%$

$9.85\% - 0.25\% = 9.60\% = 9.6\%$

54. (4) $2 \times 1.5 \times 2$

$V = l \times w \times h$

$V = 2 \times 1.5 \times 2$

55. (3) $6n$

For four days, the bakery gets n dozen each day. On the fifth day, it gets $2n$ dozen:

$4n + 2n = 6n$

56. (1) 4

Phil earns $480 (40 • 12) for the first 40 hours. The extra money he was paid ($576 − $480) was earned at the rate of $24 per hour:

$\dfrac{576 - 480}{24} = \dfrac{96}{24} = 4 \text{ hours of overtime}$